Contents

Introduction to the Chrysler Alpine

Introduced in 1976 the Alpine received great acclaim from both the motoring press and the public alike and that same year won the Car of the Year Award.

The reason for the Alpine's success in both sales figures and proven performance is fairly straightforward; when planning the construction of the vehicle, Chrysler took all the best motor engineering design features and incorporated them into one car.

The four cylinder overhead valve engine is mounted transversely in the engine compartment and inclined rearwards to provide a low bonnet profile. This gives a smooth airflow over the body and reduces wind noise.

Power from the engine is transmitted through a four speed all-synchromesh gearbox and differential unit attached to the left-hand side of the engine, and then via short driveshafts to the front wheels.

Torsion bars and wishbone radius arms are used for the front suspension, while the independent rear suspension has trailing arms supported on coil springs. Telescopic dampers are fitted to both front and rear suspension systems.

The front wheel drive layout dispenses with the conventional propeller shaft, rear axle and associated floor bulges. This provides additional foot room in the passenger compartment and considerably increases the luggage area.

Although the Alpine is a fairly large car in terms of roominess, the performance, even with the smaller 1294 cc engine is very lively. For the customer who requires increased performance with a minimal loss in fuel economy the larger 1442 cc engine is available.

Buying spare parts and vehicle identification numbers

Buying spare parts

Spare parts are available from many sources, for example: Chrysler garages, other garages and accessory shops, and motor factors. Our advice regarding spare part sources is as follows:

Officially appointed Chrysler garages - This is the best source of parts which are peculiar to your car and are otherwise not generally available (eg; complete cylinder heads, internal gearbox components, badges, interior trim, etc). It is also the only place at which you should buy parts if your car is still under warranty - non-Chrysler components may invalidate the warranty. To be sure of obtaining the correct parts it will always be necessary to give the storeman your car's engine and chassis number, and if possible, to take the 'old' part along for positive identification. Remember that many parts are available on a factory exchange scheme - any parts returned should always be clean! It obviously makes good sense to go straight to the specialist on your car for this type of part for they are best equipped to supply you.

Other garages and accessory shops - These are often very good places to buy materials and components needed for the maintenance of your car (eg, oil filters, spark plugs, bulbs, fan belts, oils and greases, touch-up paint, filler paste etc). They also sell general accessories, usually have convenient opening hours, charge lower prices and can often be found not far from home.

Motor factors - Good factors will stock all of the more important components which wear out relatively quickly (eg, clutch components, pistons, valves, exhaust systems, brake cylinders/pipes/hoses/seals/shoes and pads etc). Motor factors will often provide new or reconditioned components on a part exchange basis - this can save a considerable amount of money.

Chr
Alpi
Ow
Wo
Mar

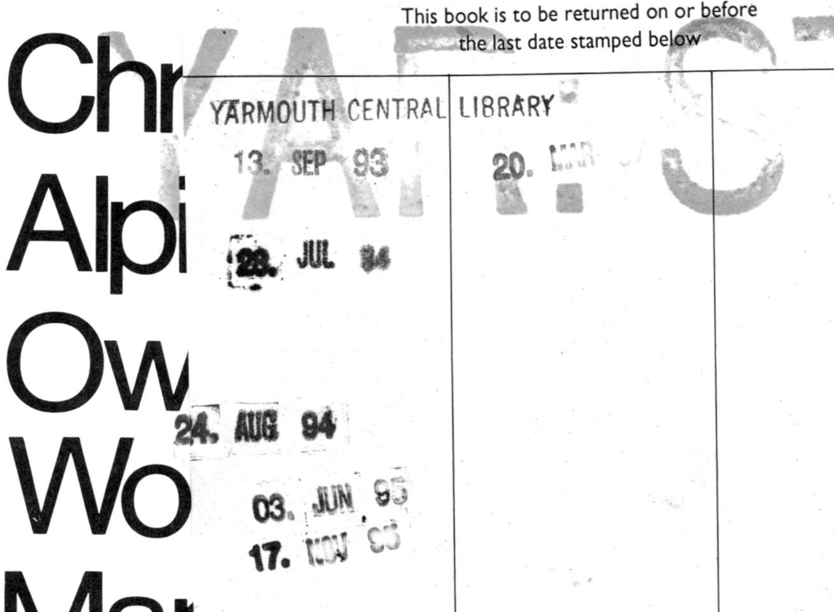

by J H H
Member of the Guild
and M S

Models covered

Alpine GL
Alpine S
Alpine GLS

ISBN 0 85696

Printed in England

HAYNES PUBLISHING GROUP
SPARKFORD YEOVIL SOMERSET ENGLAND
distributed in the USA by
HAYNES PUBLICATIONS INC
861 LAWRENCE DRIVE
NEWBURY PARK
CALIFORNIA 91320
USA

Acknowledgements

Our thanks are due to Chrysler UK Ltd for the supply of technical information and certain illustrations. Castrol Limited provided lubrication data, and the Champion Sparking Plug Company supplied the illustrations showing the various spark plug conditions. The bodywork repair photographs used in this manual were provided by Lloyds Industries Limited who supply 'Turtle Wax', 'Dupli-color Holts', and other Holts range products.

Lastly, thanks are due to all of those people at Sparkford who helped in the production of this manual. Particularly, Brian Horsfall and Leon Martindale who carried out the mechanical work and took the photographs respectively, Lee Saunders who planned the layout of each page, and John Rose the editor.

About this manual

Its aims

The aim of this book is to help you get the best value from your car. It can do so in two ways. First it can help you decide what work must be done (even should you choose to get it done by a garage) to make a repair, the routine maintenance and the diagnosis and course of action when random faults occur. However, it is hoped that you will also use the second, and fuller, purpose by tackling the work yourself. This can give you the satisfaction of doing the job personally. On the simpler jobs it may even be quicker than booking the car into a garage and going there twice, to leave and collect it. Perhaps more important, much money can be saved by avoiding the costs a garage must charge to cover labour and overheads.

The book has drawings and descriptions to show the function of the various components so that their layout can be understood. Then the tasks are described and photographed in a step-by-step sequence so that even a novice can cope with complicated work.

The jobs are described assuming only normal tools are available, and not special tools unless absolutely necessary. However, a reasonable outfit of tools will be a worthwhile investment. Many special workshop tools produced by the makers merely speed the work, and in these cases guidance is given as to how to do the job without them. On a very few occasions a special tool is essential to prevent damage to components, then its use is described. Though it might be possible to borrow the tool, such work may have to be entrusted to the official agent.

For further information on tools and equipment refer to the Section entitled 'Tools and working facilities'.

To avoid labour costs a garage will often give a cheaper repair by fitting a reconditioned assembly. The home mechanic can be helped by this book to diagnose the fault and make a repair using only minor spare parts.

Using the manual

The manual is divided into twelve Chapters. Each Chapter is divided into numbered Sections which are headed in **bold type** between horizontal lines. Each Section consists of serially numbered paragraphs.

There are two types of illustration: (1) Figures which are numbered according to Chapter and sequence of occurrence in that Chapter. (2) Photographs which have a reference number in their caption. All photographs apply to the Chapter in which they occur so that the reference figure pinpoints the pertinent Section and paragraph number.

Procedures, once described in the text, are not normally repeated. If it is necessary to refer to another Chapter the reference will be given by Chapter number and Section number. Cross-references given without use of the word 'Chapter' apply to a Section and/or paragraphs in the same Chapter.

When the left or right side of the car is mentioned it is as if one is seated in the driver's seat looking forward.

Three quarter front view of a Chrysler Alpine

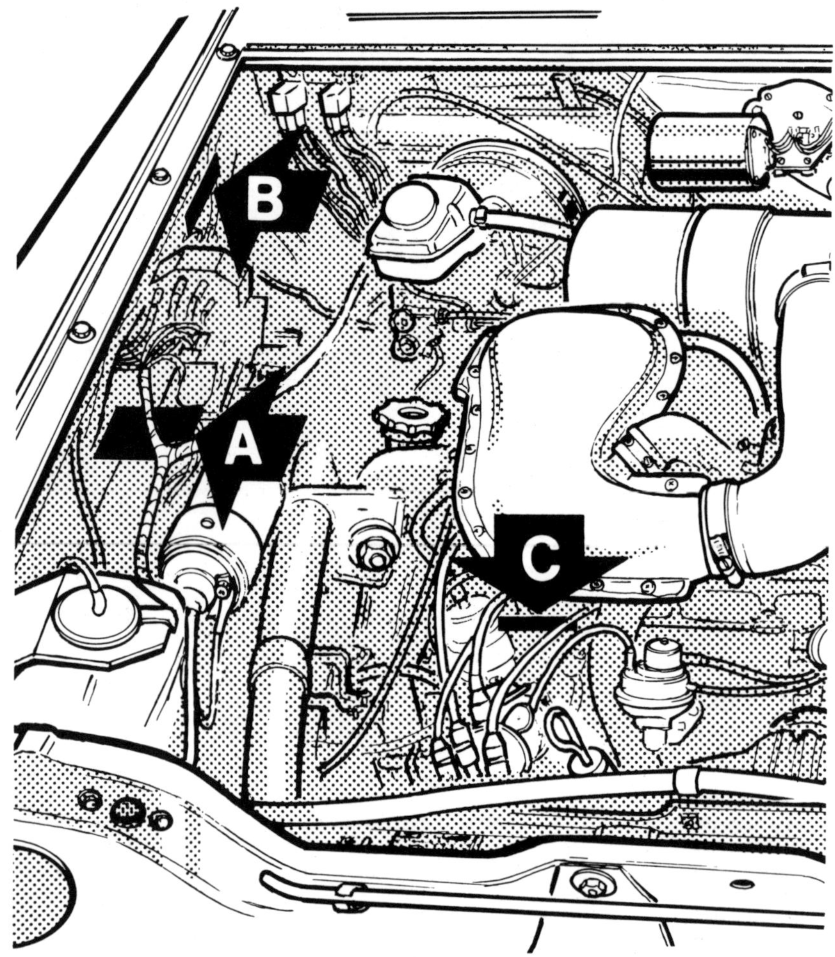

Location of vehicle identification numbers

A Vehicle identification plate B Body serial number C Engine number

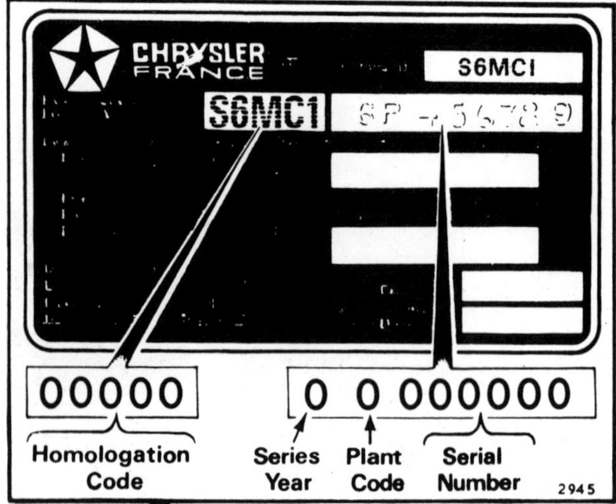

Example of vehicle identification plate

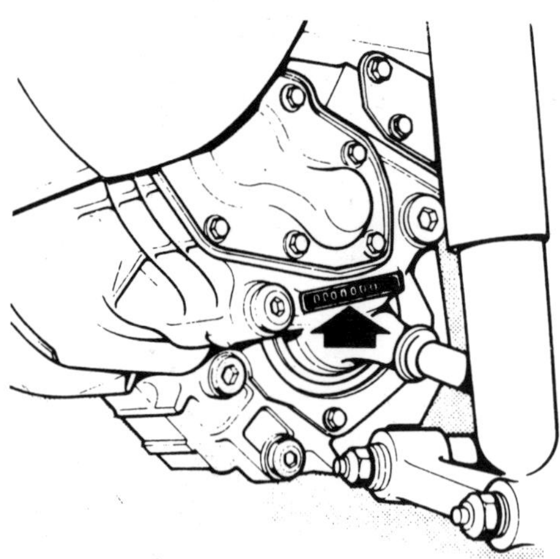

Location of gearbox number

Vehicle identification numbers

Always have details of the car, its serial and engine numbers available when ordering parts. If you can take along the part to be renewed, it is helpful. Modifications were and are being continually made and often are not generally publicised. A storeman in a parts department is quite justified in saying that he cannot guarantee the correctness of a part unless these relevant numbers are available.

The vehicle identification plate is attached to the right-hand wing valance in the engine compartment. The body serial number is located on the rear section of the wing valance (see illustration).

The engine number is stamped on a plate secured to the cylinder block adjacent to the distributor. In addition to the engine this number should also be quoted when ordering parts for the final drive assembly.

The gearbox number is located on the end of the casing as illustrated.

Jacking up the car

The jack and wheel brace are clipped to the wing valance inside the engine compartment. The spare wheel is secured beneath the rear end of the car. To remove it, lift up the luggage compartment carpet and slacken the carrier bolt using the wheelbrace until the wheel can be withdrawn from beneath the vehicle.

Before jacking-up the car, ensure it is standing on level ground and set the handbrake on firmly. Chock the wheel diagonally opposite the one being raised.

Insert the jack arm into the square socket nearest to the wheel being removed. Ensure the jack is upright and standing on firm ground before raising the car.

If work is to be carried out beneath the vehicle while it is jacked up, axle stands or suitable wooden blocks **must** be placed beneath the car to take its weight in the eventuality of jack failure.

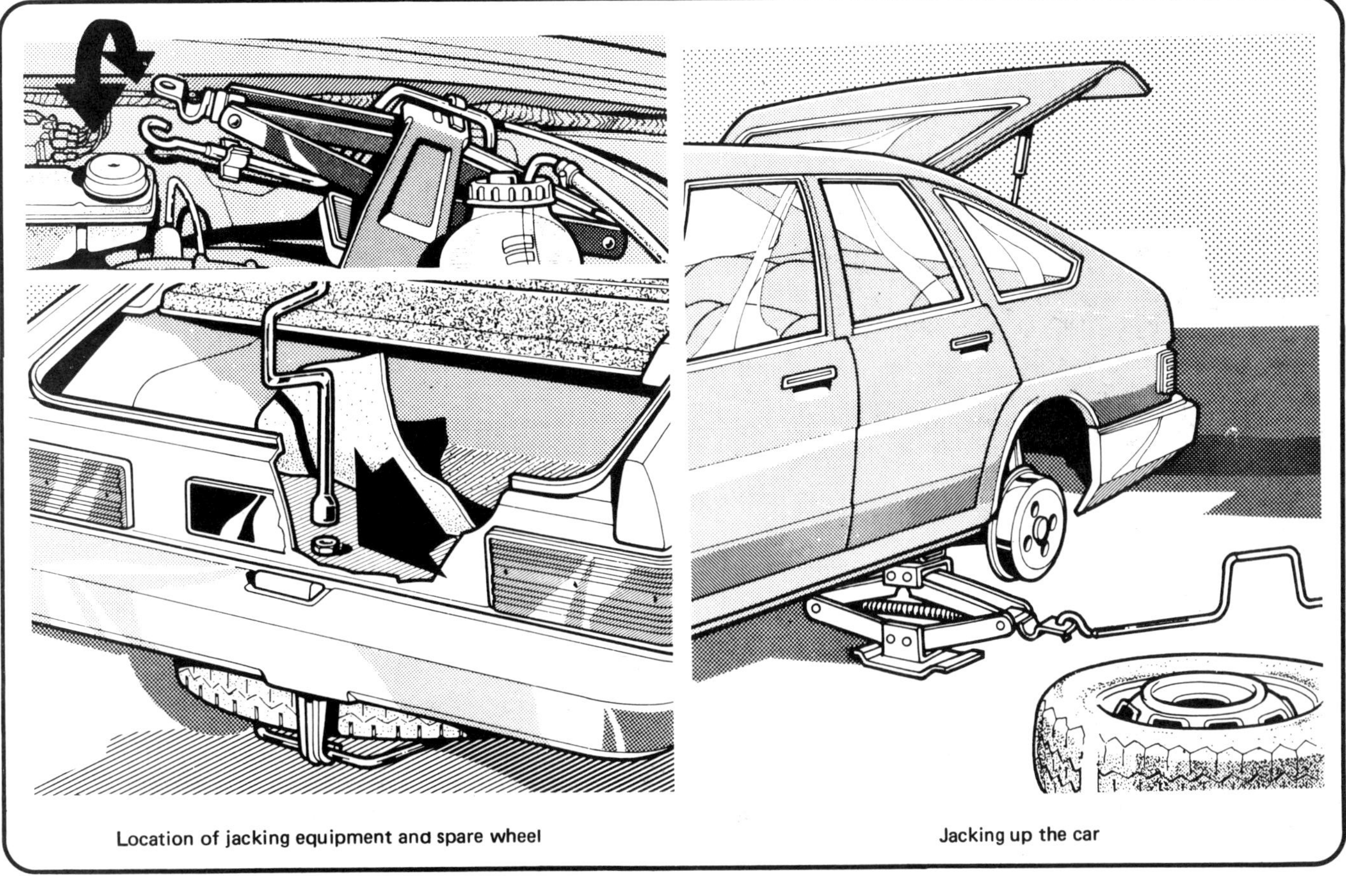

Location of jacking equipment and spare wheel

Jacking up the car

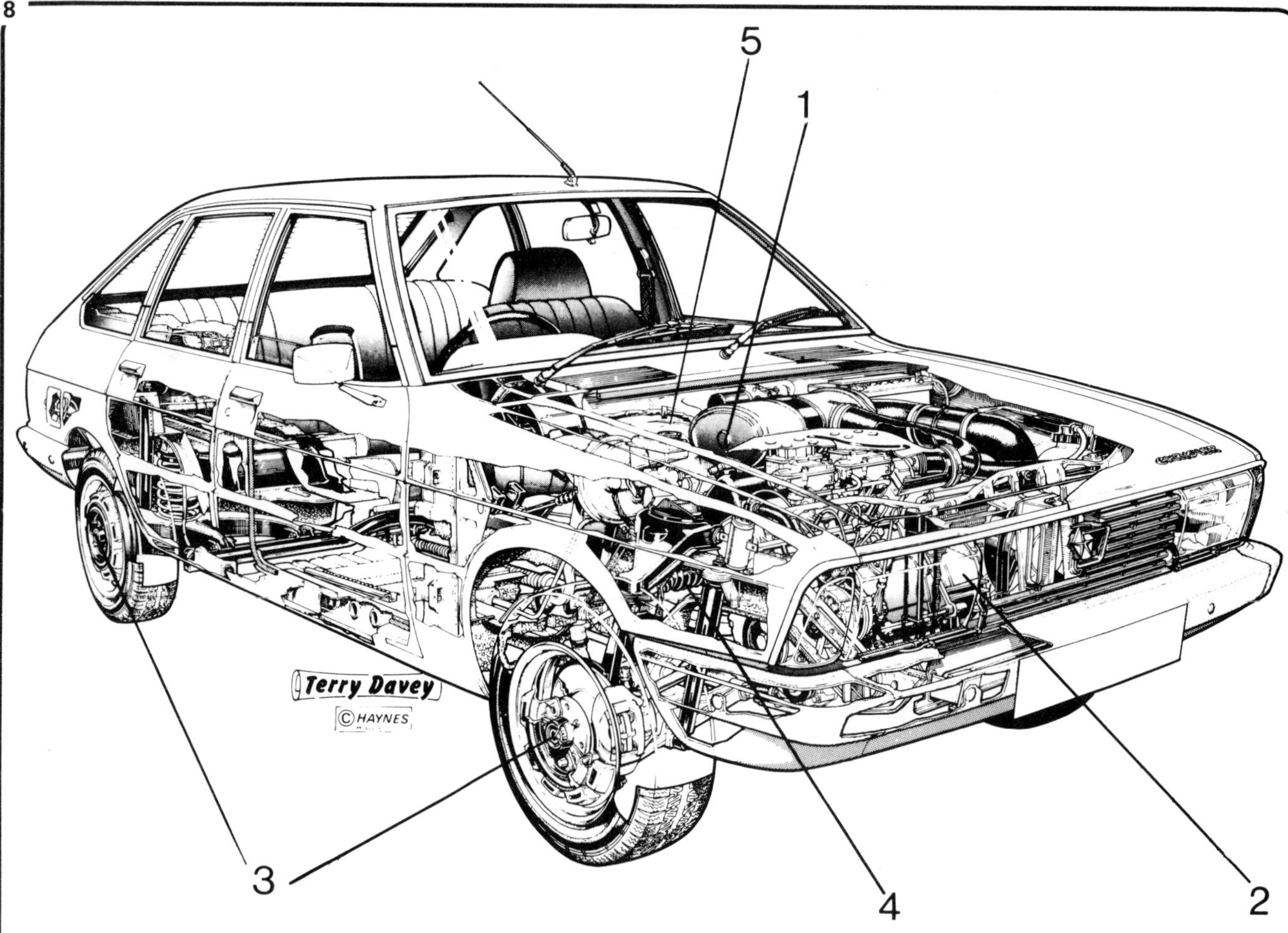

Recommended lubricants and fluids

Component	Correct Castrol Product	Nominal Refill Capacities
1 ENGINE	Castrol GTX	5.75 pints (3.3 litres)
2 GEARBOX AND FINAL DRIVE ...	Castrol Hypoy - Gearbox ... ... Final drive	0.9 pint (0.6 litre) 0.8 pint (0.5 litre)
3 FRONT AND REAR WHEEL BEARINGS	Castrol LM Grease	
4 STEERING RACK	Castrol MS3 Grease	
DISTRIBUTOR & GENERATOR BEARINGS	Castrol GTX or 'Everyman'	
5 BRAKE AND CLUTCH MASTER CYLINDERS	Castrol/Girling Universal Brake and Clutch Fluid	
ANTI-FREEZE	Castrol Anti-freeze	11.4 pints (6.5 litres)
BATTERY TERMINALS	Petroleum jelly (Vaseline)	

The above are general recommendations only. Different operating territories require different lubricants and if in doubt consult your nearest Agent.

Routine maintenance

Maintenance is essential for ensuring safety and desirable for the purpose of getting the best in terms of performance and economy from the car. Over the years the need for periodic lubrication - oiling, greasing and so on - has been drastically reduced if not totally eliminated. This has unfortunately tended to lead some owners to think that because no such action is required the items either no longer exist or will last for ever. This is a serious delusion. It follows therefore that the largest initial element of maintenance is visual examination. This may lead to repairs or renewals.

In the summary given here the 'essential for safety' items are shown in **bold type.** These **must** be attended to at the regular frequencies shown in order to avoid the possibility of accidents and loss of life. Other neglect results in unreliability, increased running costs, more rapid wear and more rapid depreciation of the vehicle in general.

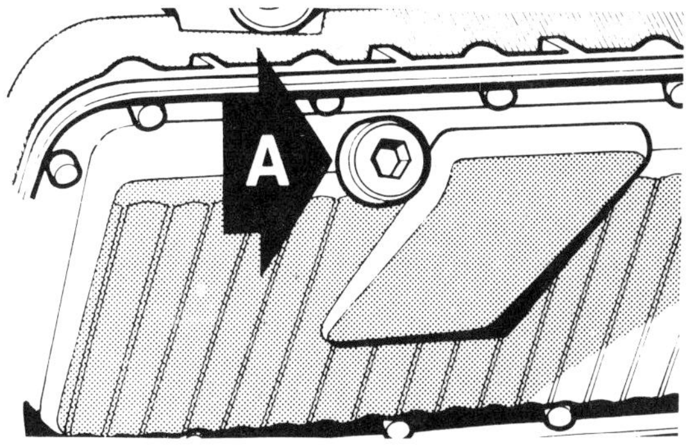

Engine oil drain plug 'A'

Every 250 miles (400 km) travelled or weekly

Steering

Check the tyre pressures, including the spare wheel.
Examine tyres for wear or damage.
Is steering smooth and accurate?

Brakes

Check reservoir fluid level.
Is there any fall off in braking efficiency?
Try an emergency stop. Is adjustment necessary?

Lights, wipers and horns

Do all bulbs work at the front and rear?
Are the headlamp beams aligned properly?
Do the wipers and horns work?
Check windscreen washer fluid level.

Engine

Check the sump oil level and top-up if required (photo).
Check the radiator coolant level and top-up if required.

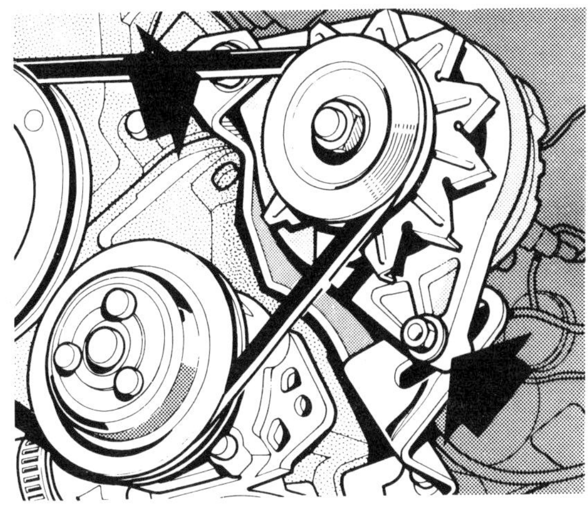

Alternator drive belt and tensioner bolt

Check the battery electrolyte level and top-up to the level of the plates with distilled water as needed.
Check the drivebelt tension.

First 1000 miles (1600 km)

With new cars, or cars fitted with new engines the following checks should be carried out:
Change engine oil.
Check tension of alternator drivebelt.
Check distributor points.
Check tightness of bolts on engine and manifolds.
Check valve clearances.
Check engine idle speed and fuel mixture.
Check cooling system hoses and fuel pipe connections for leaks and damage.
Check brake system pipes and hoses for leaks and damage.
Make a general check of all chassis and body components.

Service 'A'

Every 5000 miles (8000 km) or 5 months, whichever occurs first

Check electric cooling fan for correct operation.
Check strength of anti-freeze and top up if necessary.
Change engine oil and fit a new oil filter element.
Check alternator belt tension and adjust if necessary.
Clean air filter element using compressed air if available.
Inspect the disc brake pads for wear and examine calipers for any signs of fluid leakage.
Check the brake and clutch hydraulic fluid levels (photo).
Check carburettor idling and mixture control settings and adjust if necessary.
Check and if necessary, top-up gearbox oil level.
Check and if necessary, top-up final drive oil level.
Check brake hydraulic system for leaks, damaged pipes etc.
Examine thickness of tyre treads.
Check and adjust, if necessary, front wheel alignment.
Examine exhaust system for corrosion and leakage.
Lubricate all controls and linkages.
Check for wear in steering gear and balljoints and condition of rubber bellows, dust excluders and flexible coupling.
Clean and adjust spark plugs.
Clean the ignition HT cables and examine for signs of chafing.
Lubricate all door locks and hinges and ensure door drain holes are clear.

Topping up engine oil

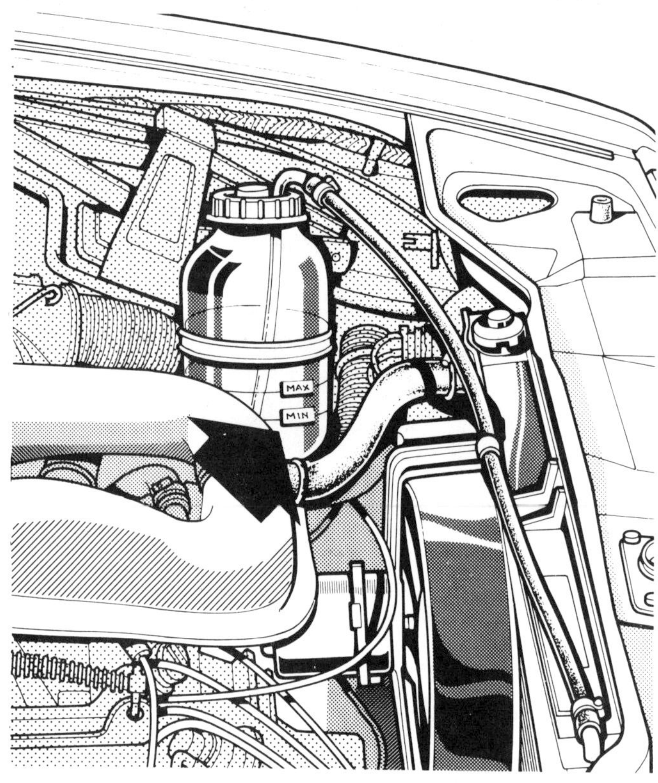

Cooling system expansion bottle

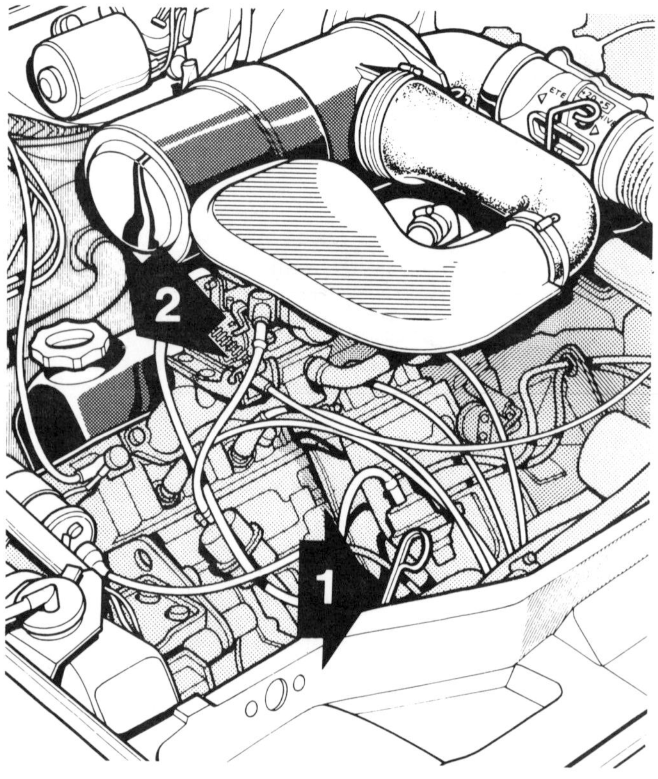

Engine oil checking points

1 Dipstick 2 Oil filler cap

Brake and clutch fluid reservoir

Refilling transmission with EP 90 gear oil

Service 'B'

Every 10000 miles (16000 km) or 10 months, whichever occurs first

Carry out the maintenance tasks listed under Service 'A', plus the following:

Blow out any dirt from the engine side of the radiator using a compressed air line.
Check valve clearances and adjust if necessary.
Renew air filter element.
Clean fuel pump filter and renew the in-line carburettor filter.
Remove rear brake drums and check linings for wear. Renew if necessary.
Check rear wheel brake cylinder for fluid leakage.
Adjust handbrake cable.
Examine shock absorbers for leakage and renew if necessary.
Check front driveshaft gaiters for damage or deterioration and renew if necessary.
Clean battery terminals and coat with petroleum jelly (Vaseline).
Drain and refill gearbox and final drive oil (photo).
Check fuel filler hose for leaks and tighten clips if necessary.
Fit a new set of spark plugs.

Service 'C'

Every 15000 miles (24000 km) or 15 months, whichever occurs first

Carry out the maintenance tasks listed under Service 'A', plus the following:

Examine the handbrake ratchet for excessive wear and renew if necessary.
Check the handbrake cable for corrosion or fraying and renew if necessary.
Check the handbrake linkage pivots and pins for wear.
Clean and re-pack the rear wheel hubs with grease and reset the end float as described in Chapter 8.

Service 'D'

Every 30000 miles (48000 km) or 30 months, whichever occurs first

Carry out the maintenance tasks listed under Services 'B' and 'C', plus the following:

Renew the brake servo unit filter element (refer to Chapter 9).
Examine all the metal brake pipes for signs of corrosion and renew if necessary.
Check the shock absorber mountings for security and renew the rubber bushes if worn or perished.
Renew the air cleaner element.
Drain and refill the gearbox and final drive units with SAE 90 gear oil.

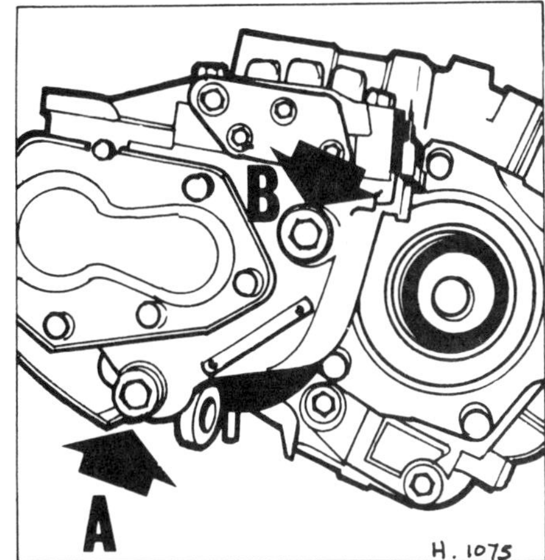

Gearbox - 'A' drain plug, 'B' filler plug

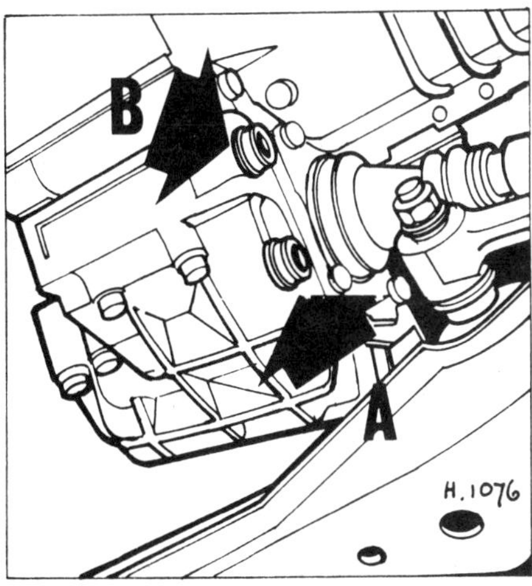

Final drive unit - 'A' drain plug, 'B' filler plug

Tools and working facilities

Introduction

A selection of good tools is a fundamental requirement for anyone contemplating the maintenance and repair of a motor vehicle. For the owner who does not possess any, their purchase will prove a considerable expense, offsetting some of the savings made by doing-it-yourself. However, provided that the tools purchased are of good quality, they will last for many years and prove an extremely worthwhile investment.

To help the average owner to decide which tools are needed to carry out the various tasks detailed in this manual, we have compiled three lists of tools under the following headings: Maintenance and minor repair, Repair and overhaul, and Special. The newcomer to practical mechanics should start off with the 'Maintenance and minor repair' tool kit and confine himself to the simpler jobs around the vehicle. Then, as his confidence and experience grows, he can undertake more difficult tasks, buying extra tools as, and when, they are needed. In this way, a 'Maintenance and minor repair' tool kit can be built-up into a 'Repair and overhaul' tool kit over a considerable period of time without any major cash outlays. The experienced do-it-yourselfer will have a tool kit good enough for most repair and overhaul procedures and will add tools from the 'Special' category when he feels the expense is justified by the amount of use these tools will be put to.

It is obviously not possible to cover the subject of tools fully here. For those who wish to learn more about tools and their use there is a book entitled 'How to Choose and Use Car Tools' available from the publishers of this manual.

Maintenance and minor repair tool kit

The tools given in this list should be considered as a minimum requirement if routine maintenance, servicing and minor repair operations are to be undertaken. We recommend the purchase of combination spanners (ring one end, open-ended the other); although more expensive than open-ended ones, they do give the advantages of both types of spanner.

Combination spanners - 10, 11, 13, 14, 17 mm
Adjustable spanner - 9 inch
Engine sump/gearbox/rear axle drain plug key (where applicable)
Spark plug spanner (with rubber insert)
Spark plug gap adjustment tool
Set of feeler gauges
Brake adjuster spanner (where applicable)
Brake bleed nipple spanner
Screwdriver - 4 in. long x 1/4 in. dia. (plain)
Screwdriver - 4 in. long x 1/4 in. dia. (crosshead)
Combination pliers - 6 inch
Hacksaw, junior
Tyre pump
Tyre pressure gauge
Grease gun (where applicable)
Oil can
Fine emery cloth (1 sheet)
Wire brush (small)
Funnel (medium size)

Repair and overhaul tool kit

These tools are virtually essential for anyone undertaking any major repairs to a motor vehicle, and are additional to those given in the Basic list. Included in this list is a comprehensive set of sockets. Although these are expensive they will be found invaluable as they are so versatile - particularly if various drives are included in the set. We recommend the 1/2 in. square-drive type, as this can be used with most proprietary torque wrenches. If you cannot afford a socket set, even bought piecemeal, then inexpensive tubular box spanners are a useful alternative.

The tools in this list will occasionally need to be supplemented by tools from the Special list.

Sockets (or box spanners) to cover range 6 to 27 mm
Reversible ratchet drive (for use with sockets)
Extension piece, 10 inch (for use with sockets)
Universal joint (for use with sockets)
Torque wrench (for use with sockets)
'Mole' wrench - 8 inch
Ball pein hammer
Soft-faced hammer, plastic or rubber
Screwdriver - 6 in. long x 5/16 in. dia. (plain)
Screwdriver - 2 in. long x 5/16 in. square (plain)
Screwdriver - 1 1/2 in. long x 1/4 in. dia. (crosshead)
Screwdriver - 3 in. long x 1/8 in. dia. (electricians)
Pliers - electricians side cutters

Pliers - needle nosed
Cold chisel - 1/2 inch
Pliers - circlip (internal and external)
Scriber (this can be made by grinding the end of a broken hacksaw blade)
Scraper (this can be made by flattening and sharpening one end of a piece of copper pipe)
Centre punch
Pin punch
Hacksaw
Valve grinding tool
Steel rule/straight edge
Allen keys
Selection of files
Wire brush (large)
Axle stands
Jack (strong scissor or hydraulic type)

Special tools

The tools in this list are those which are not used regularly, are expensive to buy, or which need to be used in accordance with their manufacturers instructions. Unless relatively difficult mechanical jobs are undertaken frequently, it will not be economic to buy many of these tools. Where this is the case, you could consider clubbing together with friends (or a motorists club) to make a joint purchase, or borrowing the tools against a deposit from a local garage or tool hire specialist.

The following list contains only those tools and instruments freely available to the public, and not those special tools produced by the vehicle manufacturer specifically for its dealer network. You will find occasional references to these manufacturers special tools in the text of this manual. Generally, an alternative method of doing the job without the vehicle manufacturers special tool is given. However, sometimes, there is no alternative to using them. Where this is the case and the relevant tool cannot be bought or borrowed you will have to entrust the work to a franchised garage.

Valve spring compressor
Piston ring compressor
Ball joint separator
Universal hub/bearing puller
Impact screwdriver
Micrometer and/or vernier gauge
Carburettor flow balancing device (where applicable)
Dial gauge
Stroboscopic timing light
Dwell angle meter/tachometer
Universal electrical multi-meter
Cylinder compression gauge
Lifting tackle
Trolley jack
Light with extension lead

Buying tools

For practically all tools, a tool factor is the best source since he will have a very comprehensive range compared with the average garage or accessory shop. Having said that, accessory shops often offer excellent quality tools at discount prices, so it pays to shop around.

Remember you don't have to buy the most expensive items on the shelf, but it is always advisable to steer clear of the very cheap tools. There are plenty of good tools around, at reasonable prices, so ask the proprietor or manager of the shop for advice before making a purchase.

Care and maintenance of tools

Having purchased a reasonable tool kit, it is necessary to keep the tools in a clean and serviceable condition. After use, always wipe off any dirt, grease and metal particles using a clean, dry cloth, before putting the tools away. Never leave them lying around after they have been used. A simple tool rack on the garage or workshop wall, for items such as screwdrivers and pliers is a good idea. Store all normal spanners and sockets in a metal box. Any measuring instruments, gauges, meters, etc., must be carefully stored where they cannot be damaged or become rusty.

Take a little care when the tools are used. Hammer heads inevitably become marked and screwdrivers lose the keen edge on their blades from time-to-time. A little timely attention with emery cloth or a file will soon restore items like this to a good serviceable finish.

Working facilities

Not to be forgotten when discussing tools, is the workshop itself. If anything more than routine maintenance is to be carried out, some form of suitable working area becomes essential.

It is appreciated that many an owner mechanic is forced by circumstance to remove an engine or similar item, without the benefit of a garage or workshop. Having done this, any repairs should always be done under the cover of a roof.

Wherever possible, any dismantling should be done on a clean flat workbench or table at a suitable working height.

Any workbench needs a vice: one with a jaw opening of 4 in. (100 mm) is suitable for most jobs. As mentioned previously, some clean dry storage space is also required for tools, as well as the lubricants, cleaning fluids, touch-up paints and so on which soon become necessary.

Another item which may be required, and which has a much more general usage, is an electric drill with a chuck capacity of at least 5/16 in. (8 mm). This, together with a good range of twist drills, is virtually essential for fitting accessories such as wing mirrors and reversing lights.

Last, but not least, always keep a supply of old newspapers and clean, lint-free rags available, and try to keep any working area as clean as possible.

Spanner jaw gap comparison table

Jaw gap (in.)	Spanner size
0.250	1/4 in. AF
0.275	7 mm AF
0.312	5/16 in. AF
0.315	8 mm AF
0.340	11/32 in. AF/1/8 in. Whitworth
0.354	9 mm AF
0.375	3/8 in. AF
0.393	10 mm AF
0.433	11 mm AF
0.437	7/16 in. AF
0.445	3/16 in. Whitworth/1/4 in. BSF
0.472	12 mm AF
0.500	1/2 in. AF
0.512	13 mm AF
0.525	1/4 in. Whitworth/5/16 in. BSF
0.551	14 mm AF
0.562	9/16 in. AF
0.590	15 mm AF
0.600	5/16 in. Whitworth/3/8 in. BSF
0.625	5/8 in. AF
0.629	16 mm AF
0.669	17 mm AF
0.687	11/16 in. AF
0.708	18 mm AF
0.710	3/8 in. Whitworth/7/16 in. BSF
0.748	19 mm AF
0.750	3/4 in. AF
0.812	13/16 in. AF
0.820	7/16 in. Whitworth/1/2 in. BSF
0.866	22 mm AF
0.875	7/8 in. AF
0.920	1/2 in. Whitworth/9/16 in. BSF
0.937	15/16 in. AF
0.944	24 mm AF
1.000	1 in. AF
1.010	9/16 in. Whitworth/5/8 in. BSF
1.023	26 mm AF
1.062	1 1/16 in. AF/27 mm AF
1.100	5/8 in. Whitworth/11/16 in. BSF
1.125	1 1/8 in. AF
1.181	30 mm AF
1.200	11/16 in. Whitworth/3/4 in. BSF
1.250	1 1/4 in. AF
1.259	32 mm AF
1.300	3/4 in. Whitworth/7/8 in. BSF
1.312	1 5/16 in. AF
1.390	13/16 in. Whitworth/15/16 in. BSF
1.417	36 mm AF
1.437	1 7/16 in. AF
1.480	7/8 in. Whitworth/1 in. BSF

Jaw gap (in.)	Spanner size
1.500	*1 1/2 in. AF*
1.574	*40 mm AF/15/16 in. Whitworth*
1.614	*41 mm AF*
1.625	*1 5/8 in. AF*
1.670	*1 in. Whitworth/1 1/8 in. BSF*
1.687	*1 11/16 in. AF*
1.811	*46 mm AF*
1.812	*1 13/16 in. AF*
1.860	*1 1/8 in. Whitworth/1 1/4 in. BSF*
1.875	*1 7/8 in. AF*
1.968	*50 mm AF*
2.000	*2 in. AF*
2.050	*1 1/4 in. Whitworth/1 3/8 in. BSF*
2.165	*55 mm AF*
2.362	*60 mm AF*

Chapter 1 Engine

Contents

Specifications

General

Engine type	ohv, four cylinder in-line, crossflow head
Location	Transverse, inclined to rear 41°
Material	Crankcase - cast iron
	Cylinder head - aluminium alloy
Firing order	1 - 3 - 4 - 2
Direction of crankshaft location	Anticlockwise viewed from flywheel end

Engine data (1294 cc type)

Bore	3.02 in (76.7 mm)
Stroke	2.75 in (70 mm)
Compression ratio	9.5 : 1
Maximum rpm	5,700 in 4th gear
Idling	850

Engine data (1442 cc type)

Bore	3.02 in (76.7 mm)
Stroke	3.07 in (78 mm)
Compression ratio	9.5 : 1
Maximum rpm	6,100 in 4th gear
Idling rpm	900

Crankshaft and connecting rods

Main bearing, journal diameter (red)	2.0463 - 2.0467 in (51.975 - 51.985 mm)
Main bearing, journal diameter (blue)	2.0459 - 2.0463 in (51.966 - 51.976 mm)
Shell thickness (red)	0.075 - 0.076 in (1.915 - 1.924 mm)
Shell thickness (blue)	0.076 - 0.077 in (1.924 - 1.933 mm)
Running clearance	0.00158 - 0.00307 in (0.040 - 0.078 mm)
Big end crankpin diameter (red)	1.6125 - 1.6128 in (40.957 - 40.965 mm)
Big end crankpin diameter (blue)	1.6122 - 1.6125 in (40.949 - 40.958 mm)
Shell thickness (red)	0.059 - 0.060 in (1.492 - 1.501 mm)
Shell thickness (blue)	0.060 - 0.061 in (1.500 - 1.509 mm)
Running clearance	0.00118 - 0.00252 in (0.030 - 0.064 mm)
Endfloat of crankshaft	0.0016 - 0.0031 in (0.040 - 0.078 mm)
Connecting rod side play	0.0012 - 0.0025 in (0.030 - 0.065 mm)
Crankshaft undersizes	0.004 - 0.008 - 0.020 in (0.1 - 0.2 - 0.5 mm)
Width of centre main bearing journal	1.237 - 1.239 in (31.43 - 31.47 mm)
Small end bore diameter	0.8648 - 0.8652 in (21.965 - 21.976 mm)
Crankshaft thrust washer thickness	0.091 - 0.093 in (2.31 - 2.36 mm)

Pistons

Material	Aluminium alloy
Rings	2 compression, 1 oil control
Maximum weight difference allowable between any two pistons	3 grammes

Piston diameters

Class A	3.0180 - 3.0183 in (76.6575 - 76.6650 mm)
Class B	3.0183 - 3.0186 in (76.6650 - 76.6725 mm)
Class C	3.0186 - 3.0188 in (76.6725 - 76.6800 mm)
Class D	3.0188 - 3.0191 in (76.6800 - 76.6875 mm)
Oversize pistons available	+ 0.0039 - 0.0157 in (+ 0.1 – 0.4 mm)
Piston clearance in bore	0.0008 - 0.0015 in (0.022 - 0.037 mm)

Piston ring gaps

Top ring	0.010 - 0.018 in (0.25 - 0.45 mm)
Second ring	0.010 - 0.018 in (0.25 - 0.45 mm)
Oil control ring	0.008 - 0.016 in (0.20 - 0.40 mm)

Gudgeon pins

Material	Steel
Length	2.5197 in (64 mm)
Outside diameter	0.8658 - 0.8659 in (21.991 - 21.995 mm)
Clearance in piston	0.0004 - 0,0007 in (0.010 - 0.019 mm)
Interference fit in con rod small end	0.0006 - 0.0012 in (0.016 - 0.030 mm)

Camshaft

Bearing journal diameter (numbered from flywheel end):	
No.1	1.39495 - 1.39595 in (35.444 - 35.459 mm)
No. 2	1.61195 - 1.61255 in (40.944 - 40.959 mm)
No. 3	1.63165 - 1.63224 in (41.444 - 41.459 mm)
Bearing clearance	0.00098 - 0.00299 in (0.025 - 0.076 mm)
Endfloat	0.004 - 0.008 in (0.10 - 0.20 mm)

Tappets (cam followers)

Outside diameter	0.9044 - 0.0955 in (22.974 - 23.000 mm)
Clearance in bore	Zero - 0.018 in (zero - 0.047 mm)
Length	1.554 - 1.594 in (39.5 - 40.5 mm)

Pushrod lengths

1294 cc engine	7.9133 in (201 mm)
1442 cc engine	8.523 in (216.5 mm)

Valves

Inlet valves	
Head diameter	1.33858 in (34 mm)
Stem diameter	0.31005 - 0.31456 in (7.875 - 7.990 mm)
Stem to guide clearance	0.0013 - 0.0022 in (0.032 - 0.056 mm)
Face angle	46°
Exhaust valves	
Head diameter	1.10 in (28 mm)
Stem diameter	0.313 - 0.314 in (7.950 - 7.965 mm)
Stem to guide clearance	0.0022 - 0.0035 in (0.057 - 0.090 mm)
Face angle	46°

Valve guides

Inside diameter	0.31583 - 0.31653 in (8.022 - 8.040 mm)
Outside diameter	0.55071 - 0.55130 in (13.988 - 14.033 mm)
Length	2.04725 in (52 mm)
Seat angle	44° - 44° 30′
Seat width	0.059 in (1.5 mm)

Valve springs

Free length	1.905 in (48.4 mm)

Valve clearances

Inlet (cold)	0.010 in (0.25 mm)
Inlet (hot)	0.012 in (0.30 mm)
Exhaust (cold)	0.012 in (0.30 mm)
Exhaust (hot)	0.014 in (0.35 mm)

Lubrication system

Oil pump	Externally mounted, camshaft driven
Oil filter	Full flow, disposable cartridge type
Oil pump shaft side play	0.002 - 0.020 in (0.05 - 0.50 mm)
Sump capacity	5.28 Imp. pints (3.0 litres)

Torque wrench settings

	lb f ft	kg f m
Cylinder head bolts	45	6.22
Main bearing cap bolts	47	6.50
Connecting rod cap bolts	26	3.59
Oil relief valve cap	20	2.77
Flywheel to crankshaft bolts	40	5.53
Drive plate to crankshaft (auto. gearbox)	40	5.53
Drive plate to torque converter (Auto. gearbox)	26	3.59
Crankshaft pulley bolt	96	13.28
Oil pressure switch	22	3.04
Inlet manifold nuts	10	1.38
Exhaust manifold nuts	14.5	2.01
Spark plugs	20	2.77
Crankshaft oil seal housing to cylinder block	8.5	1.18
Camshaft retaining plate	10.5	1.45
Camshaft sprocket bolts	10.5	1.45
Timing gear cover bolts	14.5	2.01
Sump to block bolts	8.5	1.18
Sump pan bolts	6.5	0.89
Oil pump retaining bolts	8.5	1.18

1 General description

The models covered in this manual are available with either the 1294 cc or 1442 cc engine. Both engines have the same bore, but the larger capacity is achieved by fitting longer connecting rods in conjunction with a taller block, increasing the piston stroke.

The engines are identical in design comprising a four cylinder in-line overhead valve unit, with a cast iron block and aluminium cylinder head. The engine is located in a transverse position, (east-west) within the engine compartment and is inclined to the rear to provide clearance for the low profile bonnet.

The power unit transmits motion to the front road wheels through a unitary gearbox/differential (mounted ahead of and below left of the engine) and open drive shafts.

A forged steel crankshaft is fitted, supported on five bearings with renewable shells.

The valves are operated by push rods and the pistons are of aluminium alloy with two compression and one oil control ring. Piston assemblies are removed through the top of the block.

Lubrication is by means of an externally mounted, camshaft driven pump. A full flow oil filter is incorporated in the system and closed circuit type of crankcase breathing is employed.

Cooling is by sealed system and the radiator is cooled by an electrically driven, thermostatically controlled fan.

An electronic ignition system is fitted and in addition to being extremely reliable, requires no adjustment, unlike the earlier contact breaker type.

2 Major operations with engine in position in vehicle

The following operations may be carried out with the power unit in position in the vehicle.

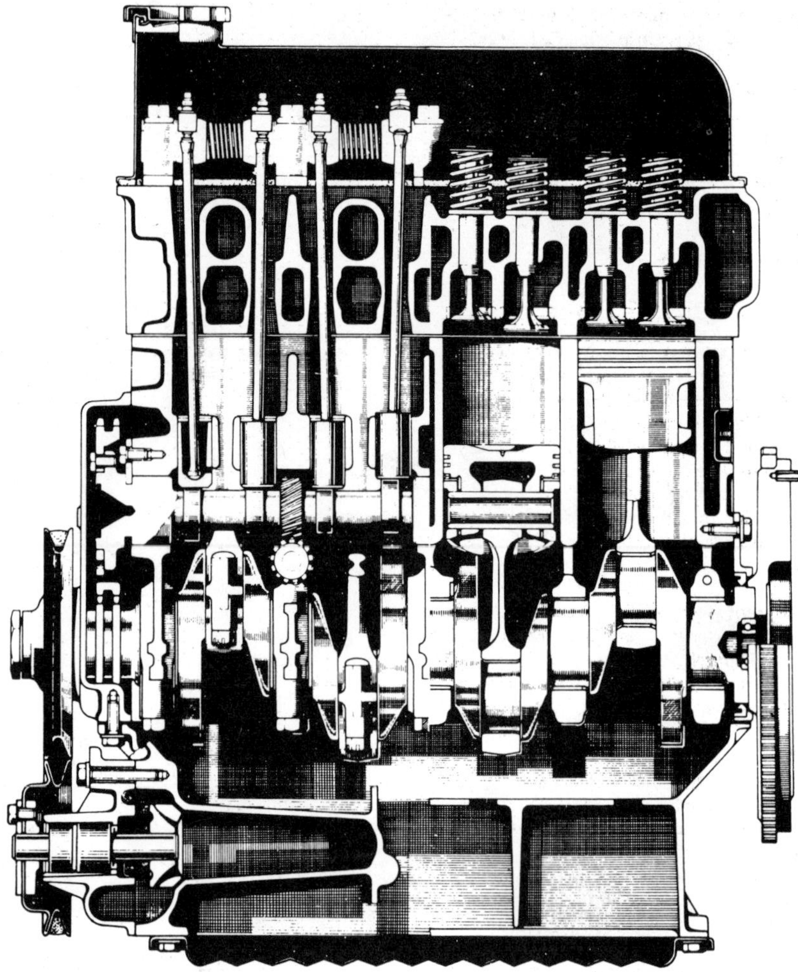

Fig. 1.1. Cross-sectional view of engine

a) Removal and refitting of the cylinder head assembly.
b) Removal and refitting of the oil pump.
c) Removal and refitting of sump.
d) Removal and refitting of pistons and connecting rods. (After removal of sump and cylinder head).
e) Removal and refitting of the engine and gearbox mountings.
f) Removal of the gearbox/differential for access to clutch and flywheel.
g) Removal and renewal of the major ancillaries, starter motor, water pump, distributor, alternator, oil filter.

3 Major operations with engine/gearbox removed from vehicle

a) Renewal of engine main bearings.
b) Removal of crankshaft.
c) Removal of camshaft.

4 Engine/gearbox/differential (single unit) removal

1 There is no point in removing the gearbox/differential unit separately from the engine when major servicing operations are to be carried out on the engine but the combined engine/gearbox/differential should be removed as a single unit for later separation.
2 Before commencing operations, hire or borrow a hoist or lifting tackle and a trolley onto which the engine unit can be lowered after removal from **below** the vehicle.
3 Jack up the car securely. A sufficient height is essential to enable the power unit to be withdrawn forwards from the engine compartment. Suitable jacks, stands and chocks should therefore be acquired. Alternatively, an inspection pit may be used but this method will present difficulties in moving the car after engine removal and hoisting from the pit floor.
4 Engine lifting eyes are provided in the front engine mountings and to ensure the engine is supported at the correct angle, a wire or terylene rope sling 44.5 in (1130 mm) in length and terminating in 'S' hooks should be used.
5 Begin by disconnecting both battery terminals.
6 Mark the position of the bonnet hinges using a soft-leaded pencil or chalk. Get an assistant to support the weight of the bonnet, remove the two bolts from each hinge and lift away the bonnet assembly.
7 Remove the filler cap from the coolant expansion bottle, unscrew the drain plug from the bottom of the water pump housing (Fig. 1.3) and drain the coolant into a suitable container.
8 Apply the handbrake firmly, place chocks behind the rear wheels and slacken the front wheel securing bolts.
9 Using a trolley jack placed beneath the front suspension cross-member, raise the car as high as possible and support it on axle stands placed under the roll bar support brackets or front jacking pads. Use wooden packing pieces if necessary.
10 Remove both front road wheels.
11 Referring to Fig. 1.4 unscrew the alternator drive belt guard bolts and remove the guard.
12 Disconnect the electrical leads from the rear of the alternator.
13 Disconnect the cable and leads from the starter motor solenoid.
14 Remove the clutch slave cylinder from the bellhousing and tie it out of the way. Do not disconnect the hydraulic feed pipe from the cylinder otherwise it will be necessary to bleed the system.
15 Detach the gearchange linkage balljoints and brackets where necessary and lower it away from the engine.
16 Remove the front exhaust pipe from the engine manifold flange.
17 Drain the gearbox and final drive units into a suitable container.

18 Remove both front telescopic dampers and in their place fit the special retaining rods. These are obtainable from your Chrysler dealer. (Tool No. CF 0004). These should be fitted as shown in Fig. 1.5.
19 The purpose of these rods is to prevent the suspension arms springing apart when at a later stage the bottom balljoint is removed.
20 An alternative method is to place a jack beneath the outer end of the suspension arm and raise it sufficiently to counteract the downward thrust of the suspension torque rod. However, extreme care must be taken to ensure there is no possibility of the jack slipping off the end of the suspension arm. If the latter method is used it is not necessary to remove the telescopic dampers.
21 Remove the balljoint securing nuts from the lower suspension arms and using a suitable extractor disconnect the joints from the suspension arms (photo).
22 Remove the large nut from the centre of each wheel hub and carefully pivot the complete hub and brake assembly outwards and upward until the outer splined end of the drive shaft can be withdrawn from the centre of the hub (see Fig. 1.6 and photo).
23 The inner end of each drive shaft is retained in the differential unit by a spring ring and the shaft should be pulled firmly outwards to disengage it from the final drive unit. If possible try and avoid pulling the inner universal joint apart during this operation. If difficulty is experienced in extracting the drive shafts, try prising them out using a large screwdriver placed between the inner end of the drive shaft and the final drive casing.
24 When both shafts have been removed, lower the hub and brake assembly back into position and temporarily refit the balljoints to the suspension arms and refit the securing nuts.
25 Remove the complete engine rear mounting rubber and bracket assembly from the engine and crossmember (see Fig. 1.7).
26 Remove the air cleaner, intake hoses and carburettor intake adaptor.
27 Detach the brake servo hose from the servo unit.
28 Disconnect all the cooling system and heater hoses from the engine.
29 Disconnect the choke and throttle controls from the carburettor referring to Chapter 3 if necessary.
30 Disconnect the fuel feed hose from the fuel pump. Plug the hose and tie it back out of the way.
31 Disconnect the earthing leads from the engine block.
32 Disconnect all electrical leads from the engine. Tie them back out of the way and mark them for ease of reconnection.
33 Remove the distributor cover and rotor arm.
34 Fit the prepared lifting sling to the engine.
35 Take the weight of the engine on a hoist and then unscrew and remove the engine side mounting bolts to leave the bonded rubber blocks still secured to the vehicle frame.
36 Lower the engine carefully onto a trolley jack taking care not to damage the oil filter assembly.
37 Remove the lifting sling and withdraw the engine/gearbox/transmission unit forward from beneath the car. Adjust the height of the supporting jacks if necessary to accomplish this.

4.21 Removing the lower arm balljoint

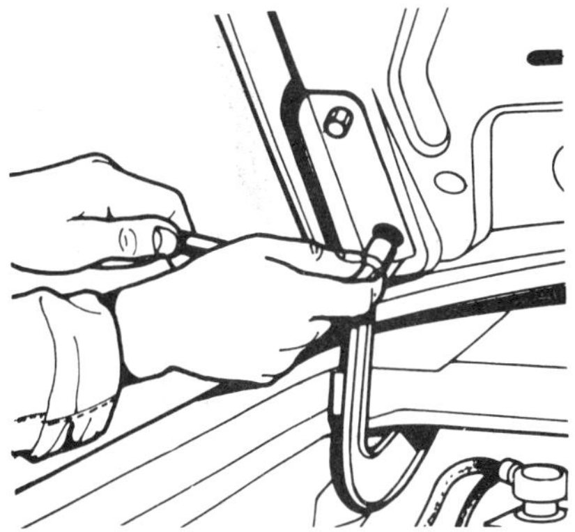

Fig. 1.2. Removing the bonnet hinge bolts

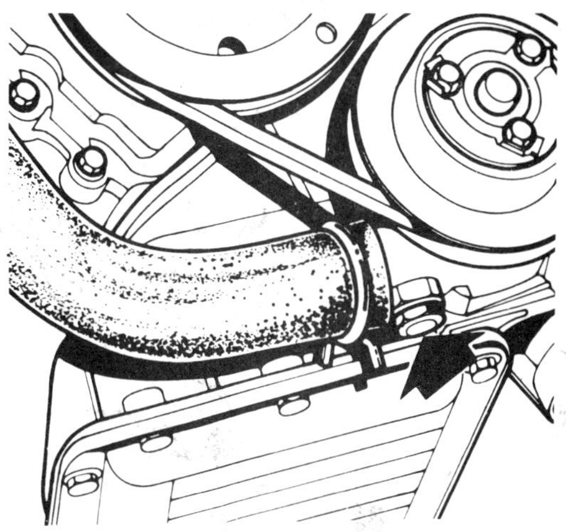

Fig. 1.3. Location of coolant drain plug

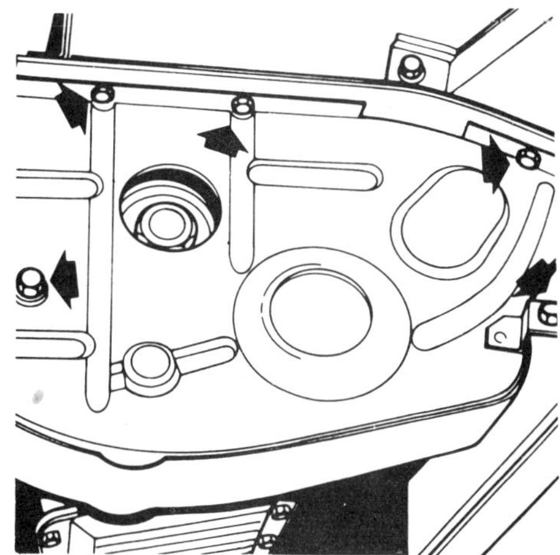

Fig. 1.4. Alternator drive belt cover securing bolts

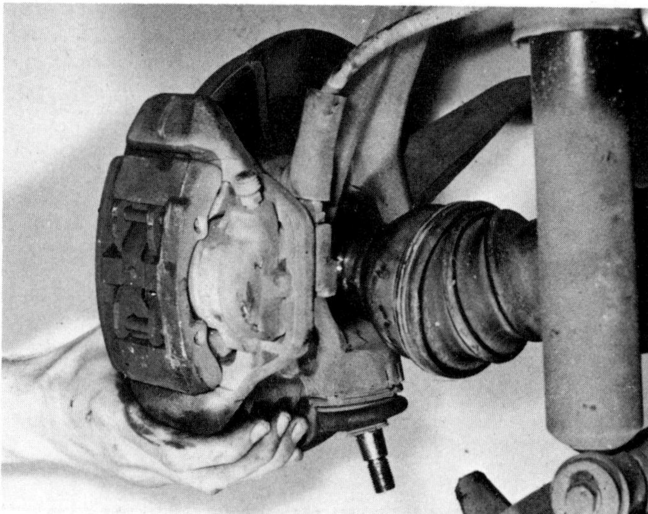

4.22 Lifting the brake and hub assembly clear of the suspension arm

Fig. 1.5. Suspension tool No. CF0004 correctly positioned

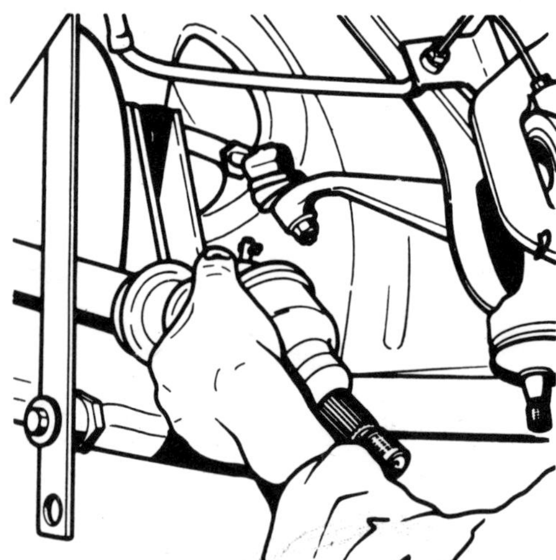

Fig. 1.6. Removing a drive shaft

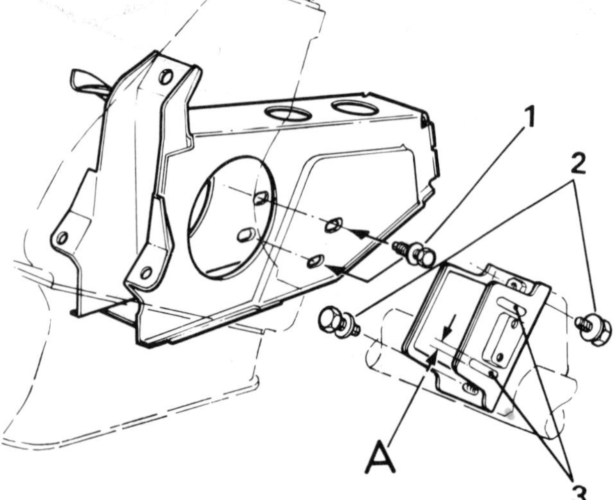

Fig. 1.7. Engine rear mounting bracket assembly

A Engine mounting rubber
1 Bolts securing mounting rubber to support bracket
2 Bolts securing mounting to crossmember
3 Slots in rubber mounting

5 Engine dismantling - general

1 It is best to mount the engine on a dismantling stand but if one is not available, then stand the engine on a strong bench so as to be at a comfortable working height. Failing this, the engine can be stripped down on the floor.

2 During the dismantling process the greatest care should be taken to keep the exposed parts free from dirt. As an aid to achieving this, it is a sound scheme to clean down the outside of the engine, removing all traces of oil and congealed dirt.

3 Use paraffin or a good grease solvent such as 'Gunk'. The latter compound will make the job much easier, as, after the solvent has been applied and allowed to stand for a time, a vigorous jet of water will wash off the solvent and all the grease and filth. If the dirt is thick and deeply embedded, work the solvent into it with a stiff paint brush.

4 Finally, wipe down the exterior of the engine with a rag and only then, when it is quite clean should the dismantling process begin. As the engine is stripped, clean each part in a bath of paraffin or petrol.

5 Never immerse parts with oilways in paraffin, ie, the crankshaft, but, to clean, wipe down with a petrol dampened rag. Oilways can be cleaned out with wire. If an air line is present all parts can be blown dry and the oilways blown through as an added precaution.

6 Re-use of oil engine gaskets is a false economy and can give rise to oil and water leaks, if nothing worse. To avoid the possibility of trouble after the engine has been reassembled **ALWAYS** use new gaskets throughout.

7 Do not throw the old gaskets away as it sometimes happens that an immediate replacement cannot be found and the old gasket is then very useful as a template. Hang up the old gaskets as they are removed on a suitable hook or nail.

8 To strip the engine it is best to work from the top down. The sump provides a firm base on which the engine can be supported in an upright position. When the stage where the sump must be removed is reached, the engine can be turned on its side and all other work carried out with it in this position.

9 Wherever possible, refit nuts, bolts and washers finger-tight from wherever they were removed. This helps avoid later loss and muddle. If they cannot be refitted then lay them out in such a fashion that it is clear from where they came.

6 Engine/gearbox/differential - separation

1 The gearbox/differential unit should now be removed from the engine. First remove the starter motor.

2 Unscrew the securing bolts and remove the flywheel cover plates. There are two of these, one adjacent to the starter motor and the other near the differential.

3 Remove the bolts which secure the differential unit to the clutch

housing, noting their differing lengths.
4 Remove the bolts which secure the clutch housing to the cylinder block and withdraw the gearbox. During this operation do **NOT** allow the weight of the gearbox to hang upon the primary shaft while it is still engaged with the splined hub of the clutch friction disc or damage to the clutch components may result.

7 Ancillary engine components - removal

1 Before basic engine dismantling begins the engine should be stripped of all its ancillary components. These items should also be removed if a factory exchange reconditioned unit is being purchased. The items comprise:

Warm air intake
Rocker cover
Spark plugs
Distributor and attachment plate, vacuum pipe and HT cables
Fuel pump (retain the thick insulating washer)
Carburettor
Inlet and exhaust manifolds
Sump breather plug and pipe
Thermostat housing on cylinder head
Temperature sender unit
Water inlet pipe on the crankcase
Water manifold
Oil dipstick and bracket
Alternator
Water pump and pulley
Oil filter element
Oil pump and housing assembly

2 Remove the sump plug and drain the oil into a suitable container.
3 The ancillary components have now been removed and the engine can now be dismantled as described in the following Sections.

8 Cylinder head - removal

1 This operation may be carried out with the engine still in position in the car but of course the cooling system must first be drained.
2 Unscrew each cylinder head bolt, a turn at a time, starting at number 10 and following in reverse to the order shown in Fig. 1.9.
3 When all the bolts have been withdrawn, lift off the rocker assembly.
4 Withdraw the pushrods from the tappet blocks (cam followers) by using a twisting motion to break the sealing effect of the oil and prevent displacement of the tappet blocks. Keep the pushrods in exact order for refitting.
5 Remove the cylinder head. Should it be stuck to the block, strike it in several places with a wooden or plastic faced mallet or refit the spark plugs and turn the engine over to enable compression to assist its removal. Never insert a chisel in the gasket joint or attempt to prise the head from the block.
6 Withdraw the tappet blocks and keep them in strict order for exact refitting.

9 Valves and rocker gear - dismantling

1 The valves should be removed from the cylinder head with the aid of a conventional valve spring compressor. Take great care to protect the alloy surfaces of the head from damage during these operations.
2 Compress the valve springs and remove the split cotters, cups and valve springs, seals and washers.
3 Place each valve and its components in strict order so that they may be refitted in their original positions.
4 Where necessary, the rocker shaft assembly may be dismantled by drifting the pins from their locations in the support brackets (Fig. 1.12).

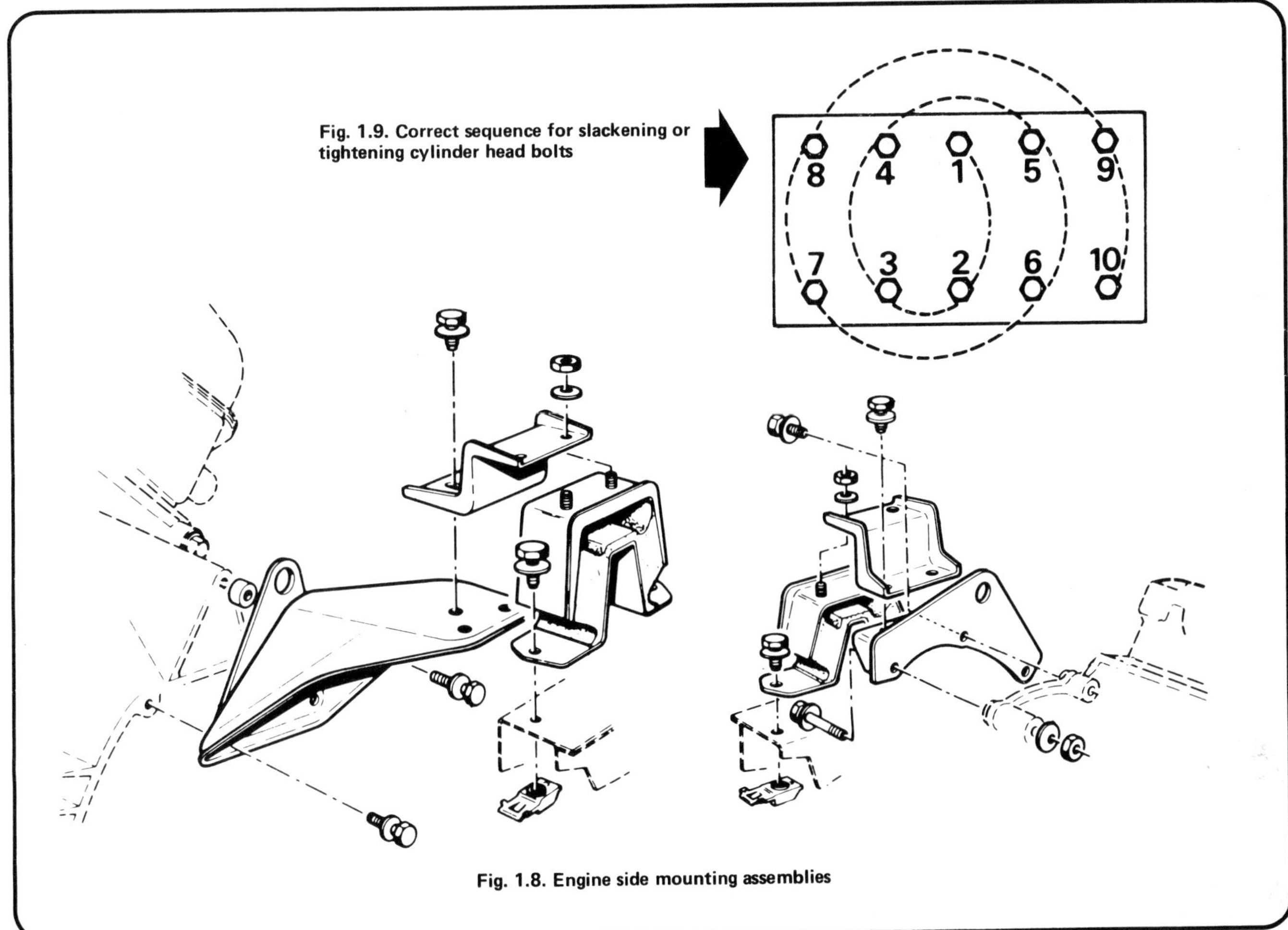

Fig. 1.9. Correct sequence for slackening or tightening cylinder head bolts

Fig. 1.8. Engine side mounting assemblies

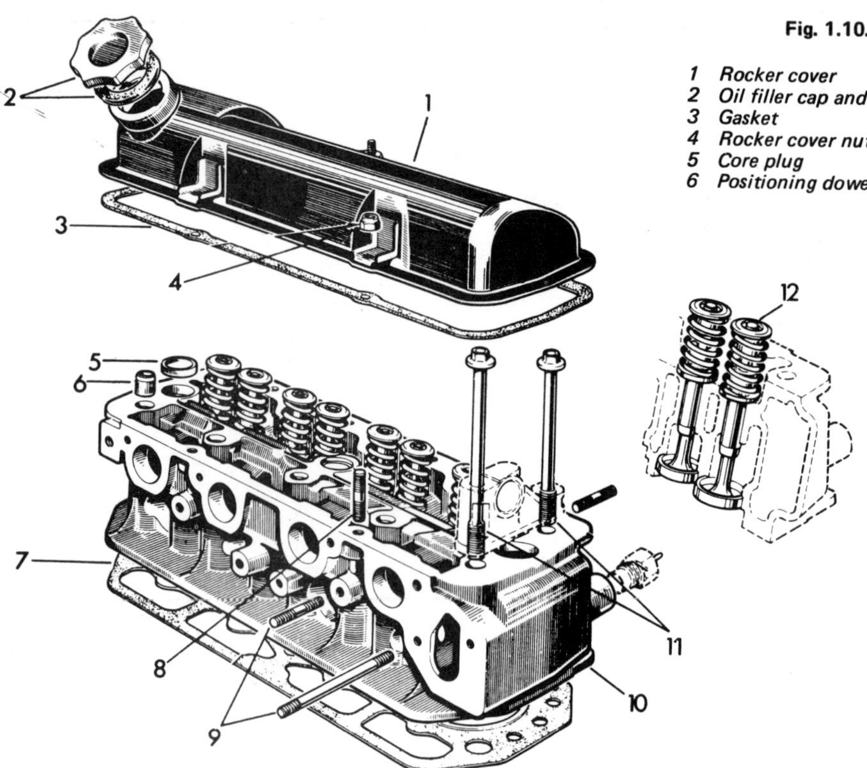

Fig. 1.10. Cylinder head assembly

1 *Rocker cover*
2 *Oil filler cap and washer*
3 *Gasket*
4 *Rocker cover nut*
5 *Core plug*
6 *Positioning dowel*
7 *Cylinder head gasket*
8 *Stud*
9 *Manifold stud*
10 *Cylinder head*
11 *Cylinder head bolts*
12 *Valve assemblies*

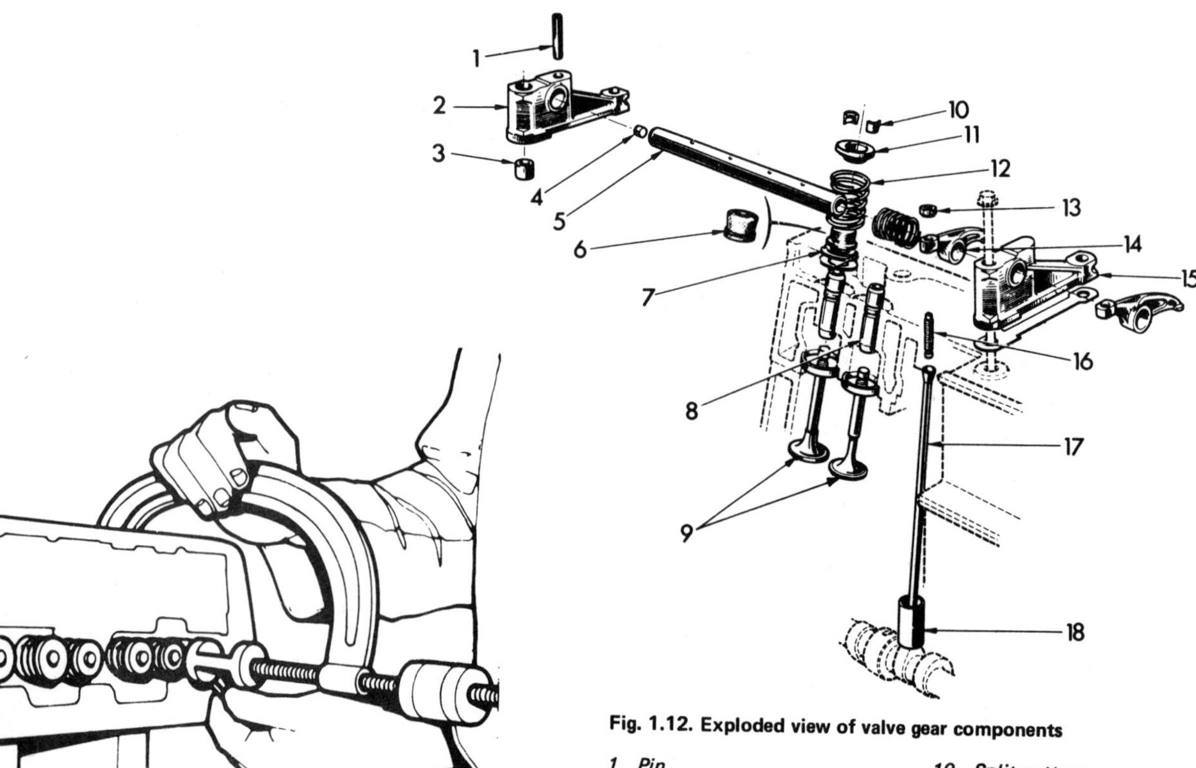

Fig. 1.11. Removing a valve

Fig. 1.12. Exploded view of valve gear components

1 *Pin*
2 *Rocker shaft pillar*
3 *Positioning dowel*
4 *Plug*
5 *Rocker shaft*
6 *Seal*
7 *Washers*
8 *Valve guide*
9 *Valve*
10 *Split cotters*
11 *Cup*
12 *Spring*
13 *Locknut*
14 *Rocker arm*
15 *Rocker shaft pillar*
16 *Adjuster screw*
17 *Pushrod*
18 *Tappet (cam follower)*

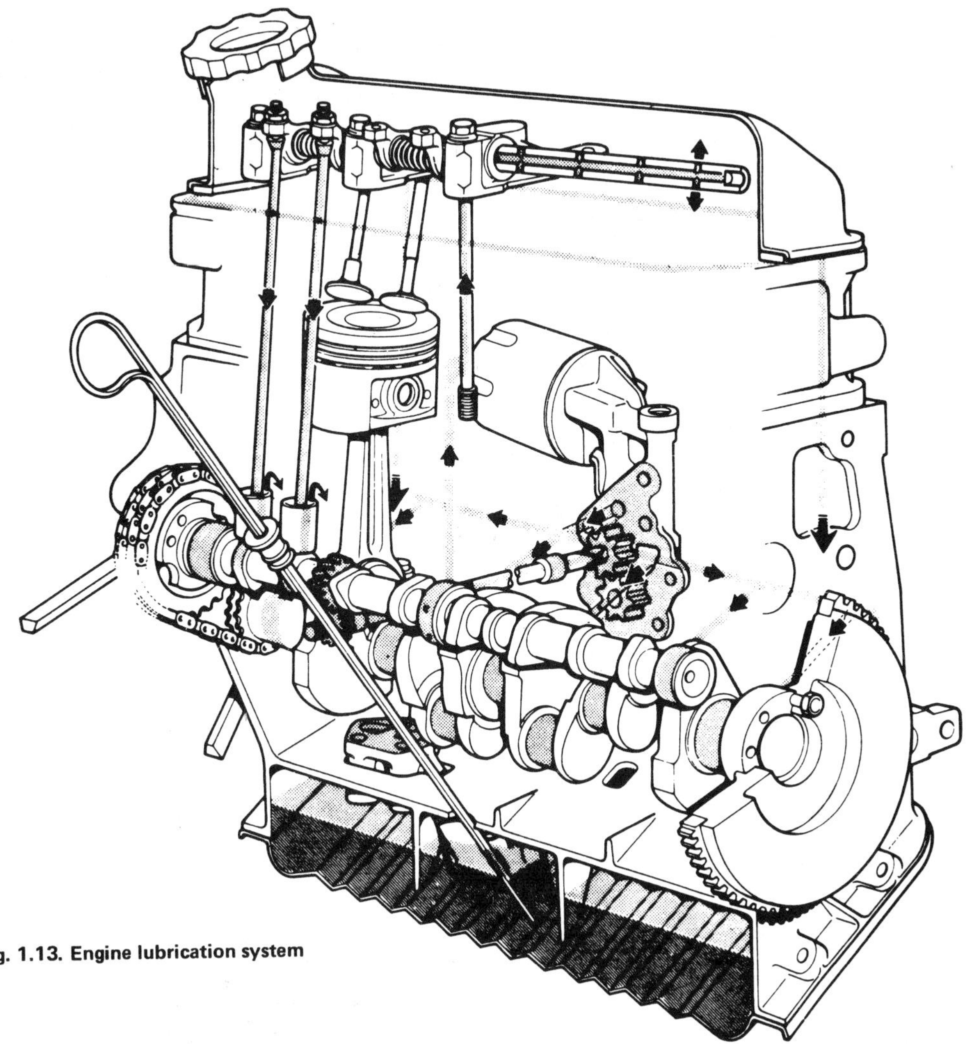

Fig. 1.13. Engine lubrication system

10 Lubrication system and oil sump - removal

1 The engine lubrication system is shown in diagrammatic form in Fig. 1.13.
2 Oil contained in the sump is drawn through a strainer and delivered under pressure by the action of a camshaft-driven pump mounted on the rear of the cylinder block.
3 The oil passes through a full-flow type filter and is fed to the connecting rod, camshaft and crankshaft bearings, the rocker assembly and the distributor and oil pump drive shafts. The cylinder bores, gudgeon pins and valve stems are splash lubricated.
4 To remove the sump assembly, turn the engine upside down, undo the securing screws and lift off the sump base plate and gasket.
5 Remove the oil pump strainer assembly.
6 Remove all the bolts securing the sump to the cylinder block not forgetting the bolts inside the sump casting. Carefully lift the sump assembly away from the cylinder block and remove the paper gasket.
7 If required, the sump can be removed with the engine still in the car by draining the cooling system and engine oil and then removing the starter motor and water pump assembly.

11 Clutch assembly - removal

1 Unscrew and remove the securing bolts which retain the clutch pressure plate cover to the flywheel. Unscrew them a few turns at a time in alternate sequence and mark the position of the cover relative to the flywheel for exact refitting.
2 Lift the cover away and catch the driven plate. Do not let it fall to the ground or it may fracture. Damage could also occur to the friction linings.

12 Crankshaft pulley and timing gear - removal

1 Lock the engine to prevent rotation by inserting a lever or large screwdriver blade in the flywheel ring gear.
2 Unscrew the crankshaft pulley. Several sharp blows on the arm of the spanner will loosen the retaining bolt where leverage will fail.
3 Remove the securing bolts from the timing cover.
4 Unscrew and remove the three bolts which secure the camshaft sprocket flange.
5 Remove the camshaft sprocket with chain which should be detached from the crankshaft sprocket.
6 Remove the crankshaft sprocket which may require the use of a puller or two levers placed behind it. Withdraw the key.

13 Camshaft and oil pump drive shaft - removal

1 From the distributor location hole in the side of the cylinder block, withdraw the distributor dog from the splined end of the drive shaft.
2 Using a small screwdriver, extract the circlip retaining the drive gear to the shaft, remove the gear and withdraw the shaft from the oil pump side of the cylinder block (see Fig. 1.15).
3 Unbolt and remove the camshaft thrust plate.
4 Withdraw the camshaft carefully from the cylinder block so that the bearings are not knocked or damaged by the passage of the cams through them.

14 Piston/connecting rod assemblies - removal

1 Rotate the crankshaft by turning the flywheel so that each piston

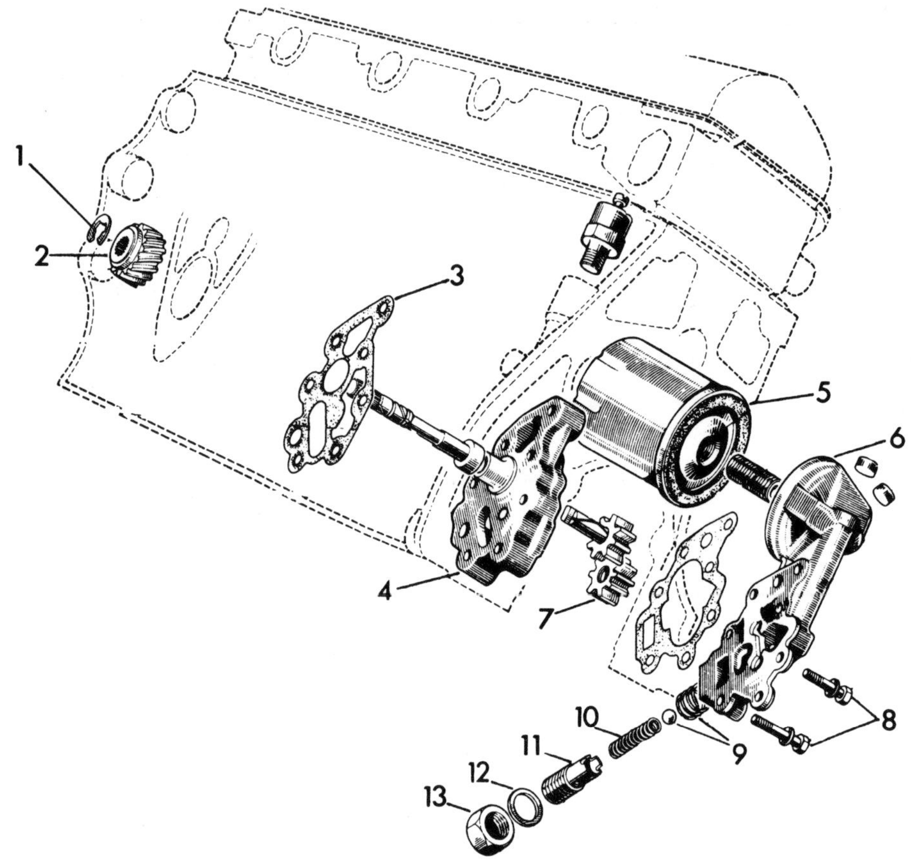

Fig. 1.14. Oil pump and driveshaft components

1 *Circlip*
2 *Drive gear*
3 *Gasket*
4 *Body*
5 *Filter*
6 *Pump cover*
7 *Pump gears*
8 *Securing bolts*
9 *Relief valve ball*
10 *Relief valve spring*
11 *Relief valve body*
12 *Washer*
13 *Locknut*

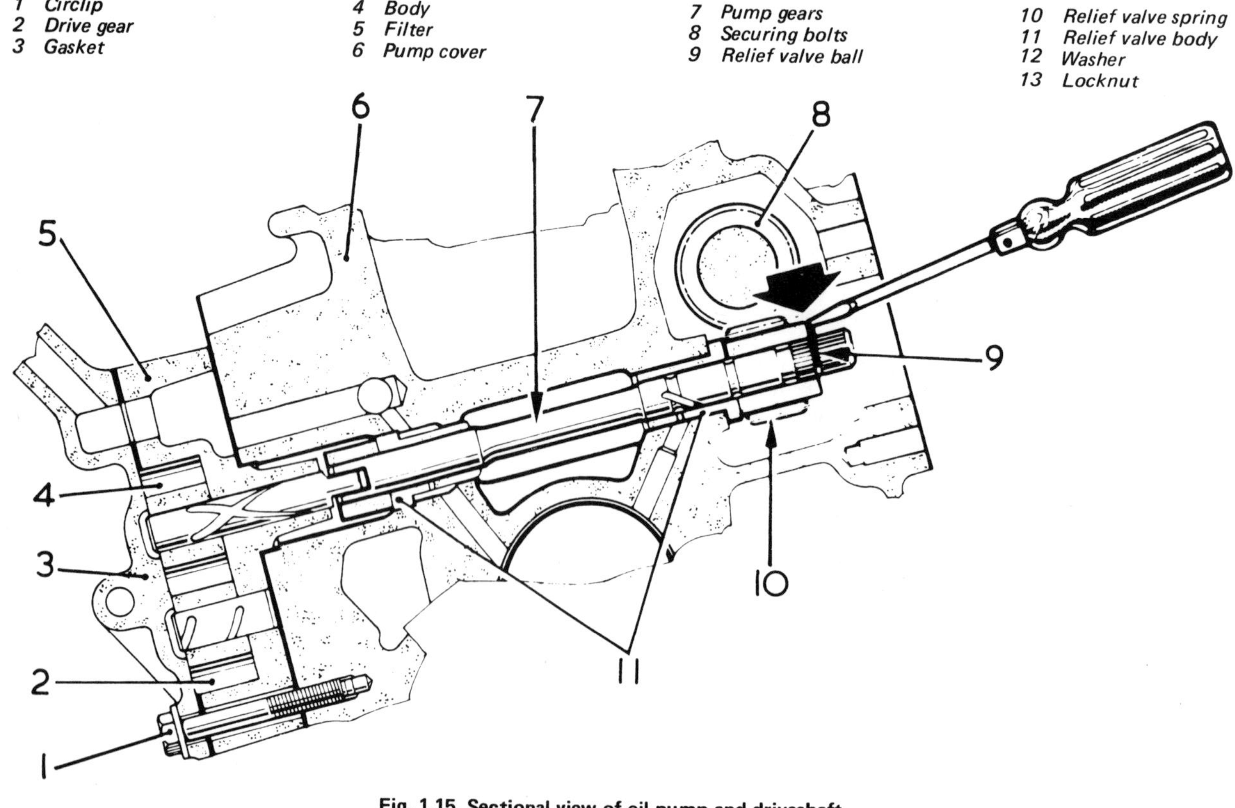

Fig. 1.15. Sectional view of oil pump and driveshaft

1 *Fixing bolt*
2 *Idler gear*
3 *Cover*
4 *Driven gear*
5 *Body*
6 *Crankcase*
7 *Driveshaft*
8 *Camshaft*
9 *Circlip*
10 *Drive gear*
11 *Driveshaft bushes*

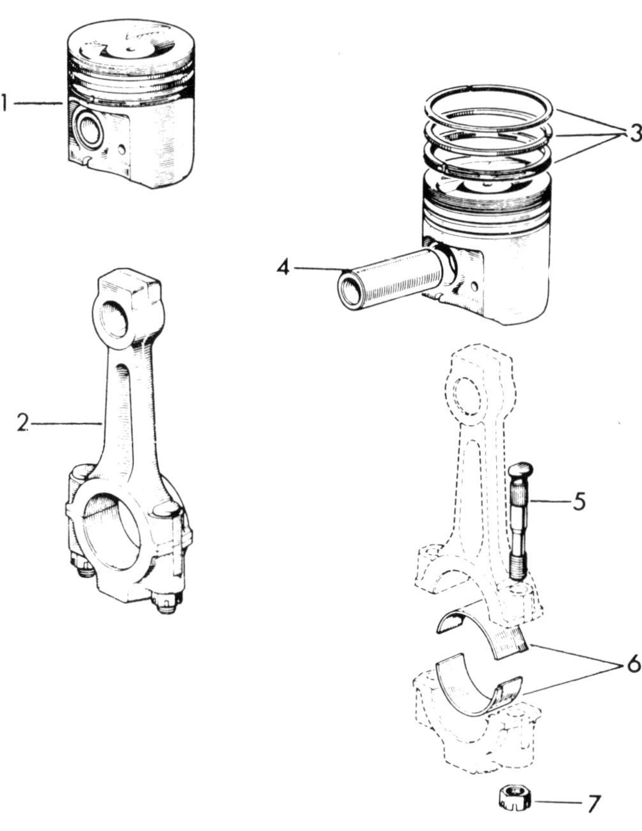

Fig. 1.16. Piston and connecting rod assembly

1 Piston
2 Connecting rod
3 Piston rings
4 Gudgeon pin
5 Big-end bolt
6 Big-end shell bearings
7 Big-end bolt nut

is (approximately) positioned half way down each bore.

2 Taking extreme care, scrape off the carbon ring which will be found to have formed at the top of each cylinder bore. Where the engine has seen considerable service, a 'wear' ring will also have been formed due to the lower portion of the cylinder bore having worn away. It is essential not to score the lower surfaces of the cylinder bore during the scraping operation. Removal of the carbon and 'wear' rings is necessary to permit the pistons and rings to pass out through the top of the block during withdrawal without fracturing the rings.

3 Invert the cylinder block and turn the flywheel until number one piston is either at TDC or alternatively the big-end is at its lowest point.

4 Unscrew and remove the big-end bearing cap nuts.

5 Remove the big-end bearing cap and extract the shells.

6 Push the piston/rod assembly out through the top of the cylinder block but restraining the outward expansion of the piston rings as they emerge from the bore to prevent them breaking.

7 Ensure that the big-end bolt threads do not score the inside of the bore as they travel upwards.

8 Refit the bearing cap to the connecting rod by screwing on the securing nuts a few turns. Mark the bearing cap with the bore location number and note particularly the correct orientation of the connecting rod for refitting.

9 Repeat the operations on the remaining three piston/connecting rod assemblies.

15 Flywheel, crankshaft and main bearings - removal

1 Unscrew and remove the securing bolts from the flywheel.

2 Pull off the flywheel and inset plate.

3 Unscrew and remove the cover plate and gasket and extract the oil seal.

4 Unbolt the five main bearing caps and remove them, noting carefully their numbered sequence.

5 Lift the crankshaft from the crankcase bearings.

6 Remove the shells from the crankshaft main bearing caps and from the crankcase locations. Temporarily refit the main bearing caps.

7 Retain the thrust washers (two) noting their location.

8 The engine is now completely dismantled and checking, examination and renovation of the components should commence as described in the following Sections.

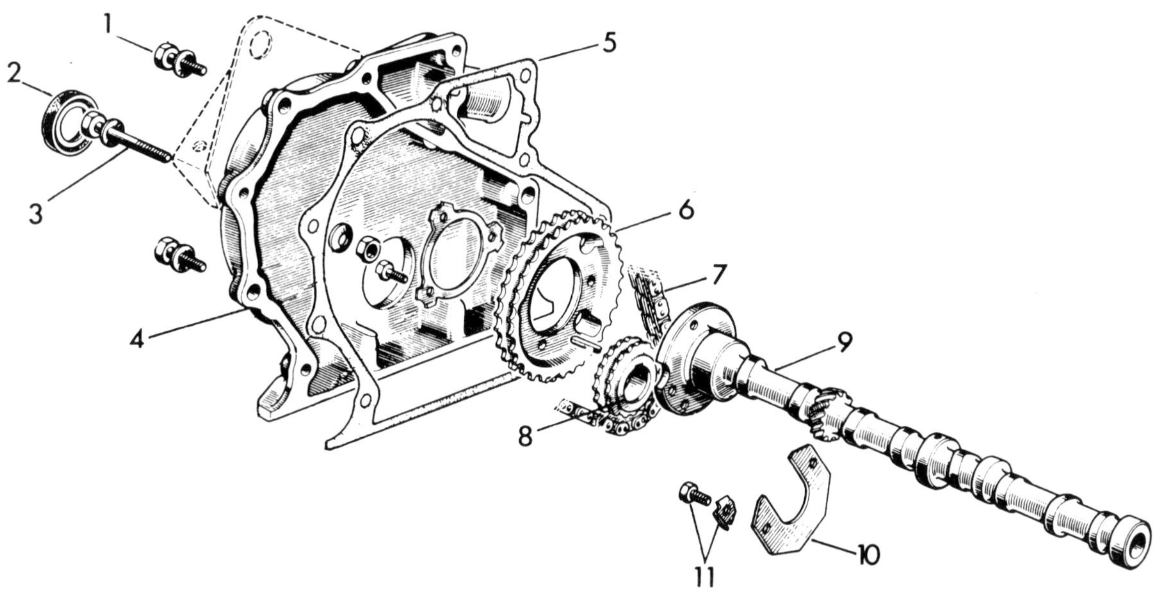

Fig. 1.17. Camshaft and front timing cover

1 Bolt
2 Crankshaft pulley oil seal
3 Timing cover bolt
4 Timing cover
5 Gasket
6 Camshaft sprocket
7 Timing chain
8 Crankshaft sprocket
9 Camshaft
10 Camshaft thrust plate
11 Thrust plate bolt

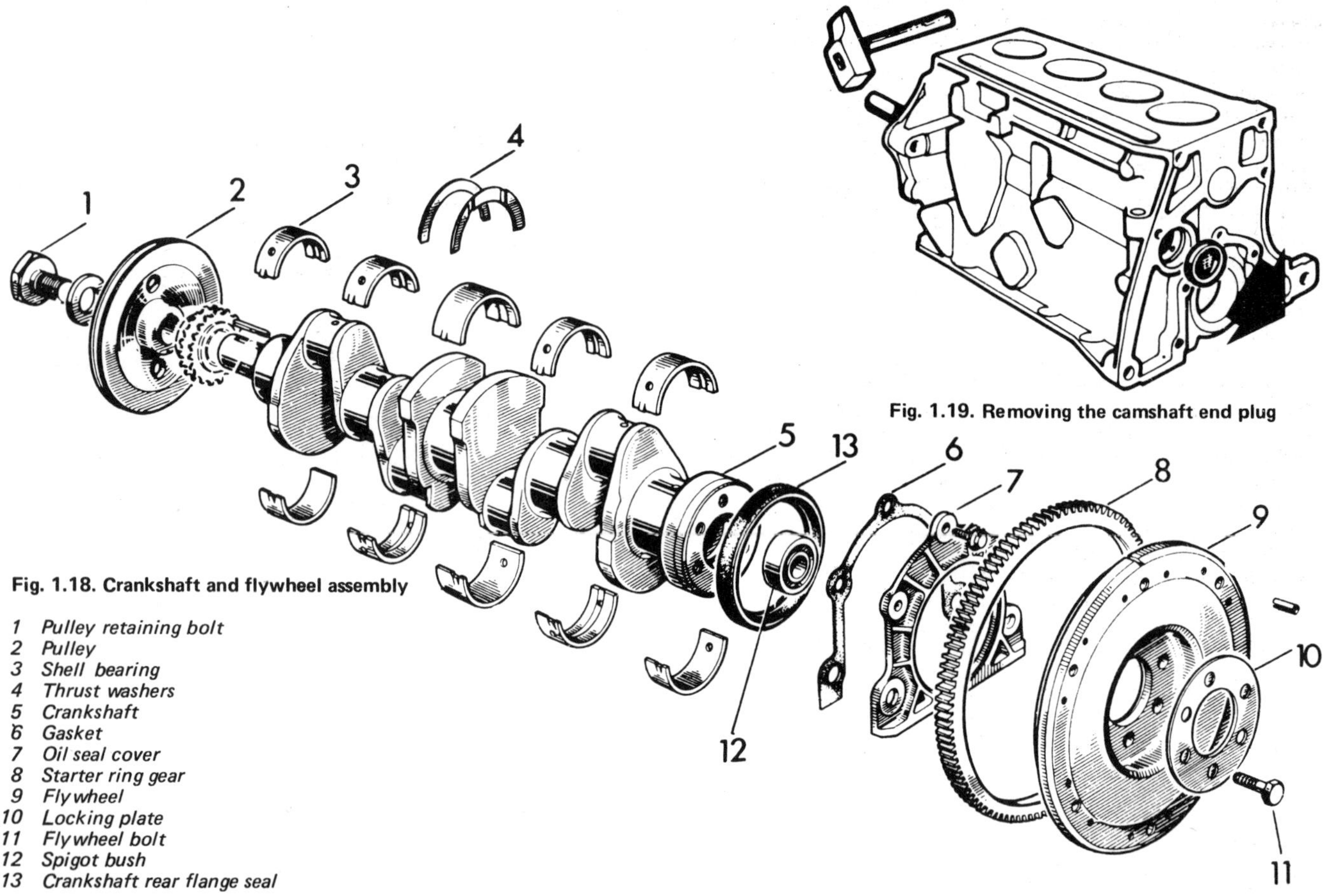

Fig. 1.19. Removing the camshaft end plug

Fig. 1.18. Crankshaft and flywheel assembly

1 *Pulley retaining bolt*
2 *Pulley*
3 *Shell bearing*
4 *Thrust washers*
5 *Crankshaft*
6 *Gasket*
7 *Oil seal cover*
8 *Starter ring gear*
9 *Flywheel*
10 *Locking plate*
11 *Flywheel bolt*
12 *Spigot bush*
13 *Crankshaft rear flange seal*

16 Engine components - examination for wear

Before any detailed examination of the dismantled components can be carried out, they must be thoroughly cleaned. A paraffin bath and stiff brush is an ideal method for the removal of grease, oil and grit. Where heavy deposits of grease and dirt have to be cleaned from the exterior of the engine casting, the use of a high pressure air hose is recommended, but this should have been done before dismantling the engine.

17 Crankcase and cylinder block - examination and renovation

1 Thoroughly clean the interior and exterior surfaces of the casting and inspect for cracks. Should any be apparent then the cost of repairing by a specialist welder must be compared with the purchase of a new or secondhand unit.
2 Check the security of studs and for stripped threads in all tapped holes. If necessary have thread inserts fitted such as 'Helicoil' or examine the possibility of fitting oversize bolts and studs.
3 Where there is evidence of water or oil leakage from the various core plugs these should be renewed. Remove the cap or plug by either drilling a central hole and levering out or tapping a thread and using a bolt and bridge piece as an extractor. With the smaller plugs or caps, they may be tapped inwards on one side and levered out. Protect the edge of the hole with a piece of wood as shown in Fig. 1.20. When driving a new plug or cap, do not knock it harder than is required to effect a good seating.
4 Examine the camshaft and if the bearing bushes are worn, scored or chipped, renew them as described in Section 21.
5 Examine the oil pump drive shaft bearings and renew them if necessary as described in Section 26.
6 Examine the cylinder bores for scoring and wear. This operation is undertaken in conjunction with the examination of the pistons and by consideration of the previous history of oil consumption and smoke emission. Reference should be made to Section 24.

Fig. 1.20. Removing a core plug

18 Crankshaft - examination and renovation

1 A rough visual check for wear in the crankshaft main bearings and big-end bearings may be carried out before removal of the crankshaft from the crankcase. If movement can be felt by pushing and pulling it and also slackness observed in the big-ends, then almost certainly the crankshaft will have to be reground.
2 With the crankshaft removed, all journals should be measured at two or three different points for ovality with a micrometer. If the measurements taken at one journal differ by more than 0.011 inch (0.03 mm) then the crankshaft must be reground.
3 Regrinding must be undertaken by a specialist firm who will regrind to the permitted tolerances and supply matching oversize shell bearings (see Specifications).

19 Main and big-end shell bearings - examination and renewal

1 When connecting rods are removed from the crankshaft the bearing shells will be released and even though the crankshaft journals are in good condition the bearings may need renewal. Certainly if their bearing surfaces are anything other than an even, matt grey colour they should be renewed. Any scores, pitting or discolouration is an indication of damage by metal particles or the top bearing surface wearing away. If there are any doubts it is always a good idea to renew them anyway, unless there is a definite record that they have only been fitted for a small mileage. The backs of the shells are marked with serial numbers and an indication of whether or not they are undersized due to the crankshaft having been reground previously. If in doubt take them to your supplier who will be able to ensure that you are sold new ones of the correct type. If the crankshaft is being reground new bearings will be required anyhow and these are always available from the firm which does the regrinding.

20 Tappets - examination and renovation

1 The tappets should be checked in their respective bores in the crankcase and no excessive side-play should be apparent. The faces of the tappets which bear against the camshaft lobes should also have a clear, smooth shiny surface. If they show signs of pitting or serious wear they should be renewed. Re-facing is possible with proper grinding facilities but the economics of this need investigating first.

21 Camshaft and bearings - examination and renovation

1 The lobes of the camshaft should be examined for any indications of flat spots, pitting or extreme wear on the bearing surfaces. If in

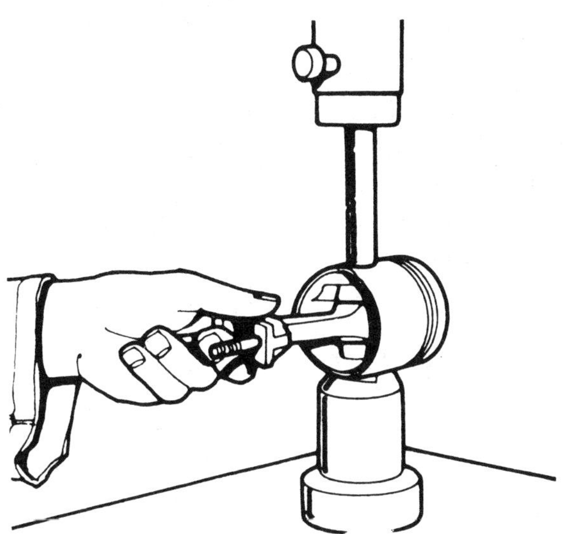

Fig. 1.22. Removing a gudgeon pin using a press

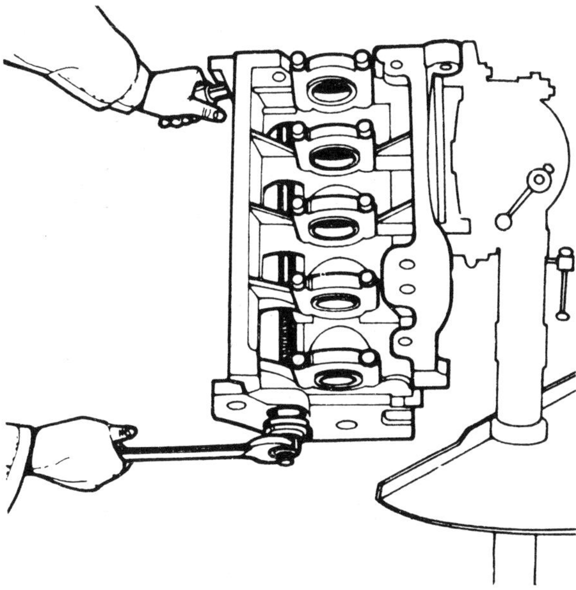

Fig. 1.21. Method of fitting new camshaft bearings

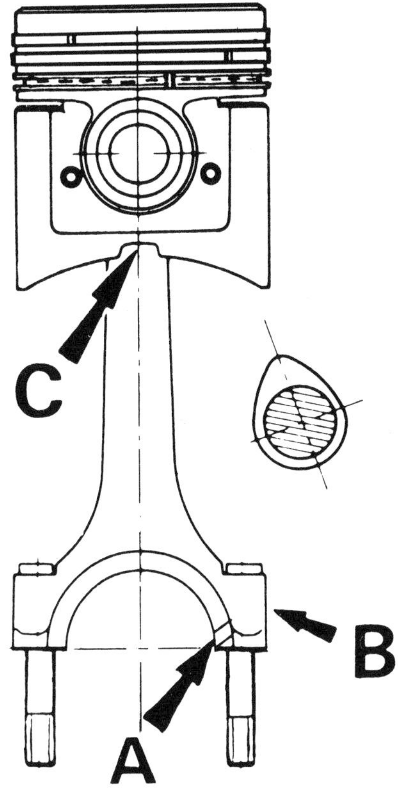

Fig. 1.23. Correct position of piston and connecting rod in engine

A Lubrication groove
B Production marking
C Notch in piston skirt face towards timing cover

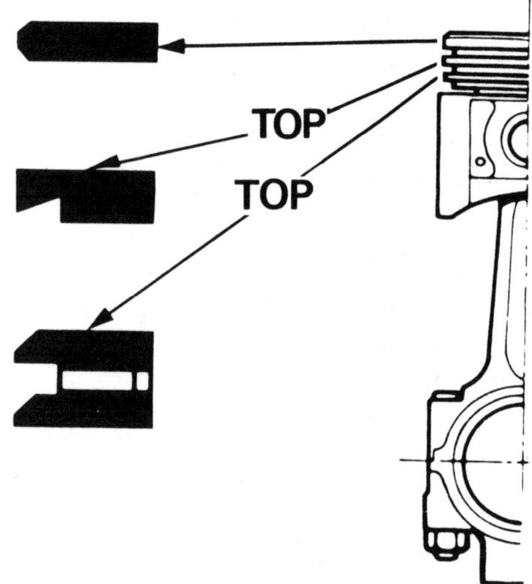

Fig. 1.24. Identification of piston rings

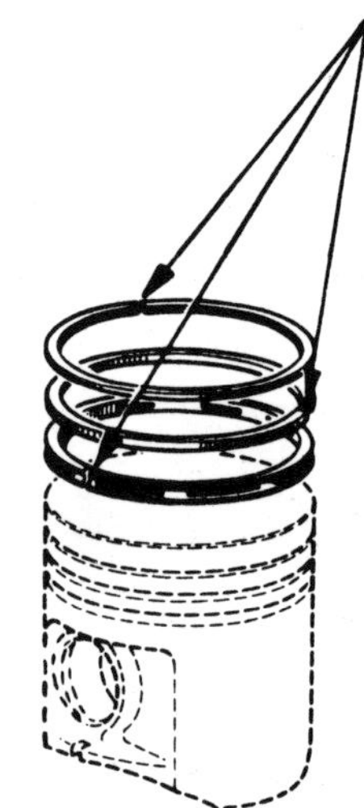

Fig. 1.25. Correct positioning of piston ring gaps

Fig. 1.26. Checking the piston ring gaps in cylinder bore

doubt get the profiles checked against the specification dimensions with a micrometer. Minor blemishes may be smoothed down with a 120 grain oil stone and polished with one of 300 grain. The bearing journals also should be checked in the same way as those on the crankshaft. The camshaft bearings are renewable.

2 Drive out the camshaft front bearing (flywheel end) sealing cap. To do this, insert a rod or tube from the other end of the crankcase (Fig. 1.19).

3 Removal of the front, rear and centre camshaft bushes is best accomplished by the use of a length of threaded rod and nuts with suitable tubular distance pieces (see Fig. 1.21).

4 Note the precise positioning of each bearing bush before removal and ensure that the bearing seats are not damaged during the removal operation.

5 Fit the new bearing bushes using the same method as for removal, starting with the centre one. It is essential that the bearing oil hole is in exact alignment with the one drilled in the bearing seat and marks should be made on the edge of the bearing bush and seat before pulling into position.

6 Fit a new camshaft front bearing sealing cap.

22 Connecting rods and small end bushes - examination and renovation

1 It is unlikely that a connecting rod will be bent except in cases of severe piston damage and seizure. It is not normally within the scope of the owner to check the alignment of a connecting rod with the necessary accuracy, so if in doubt have it checked by someone with the proper facilities. It is in order to have slightly bent connecting rods straightened - the manufacturers provide special jigs for the purpose.

2 If a connecting rod is bent or damaged beyond repair all four rods must be renewed as they are only supplied in weight matched sets of four.

3 The connecting rod small end is a shrink fit on the gudgeon pin and therefore is not subject to wear. The gudgeon pin pivots within the piston, and excessive wear in the piston bores will necessitate the renewal of the piston and gudgeon pin assembly as described in the following Section.

23 Pistons and piston rings - removal and refitting

1 A piston ring should be removed by prising the open ends of the ring just sufficiently far to enable three feeler blades or strips of tin to be slid round behind it. Position the strips at equidistant points to provide guides so that the piston ring may be slid over the hands and other grooves and removed.

2 The gudgeon pin is a press fit in the connecting rod small end bearing and it must be removed on a press using suitable distance pieces to prevent damage to the soft alloy of the piston body. (It is too difficult to do at home).

3 Refitting of the gudgeon pin is carried out on a press but the small end bearing must be expanded by placing the connecting rod in an oven (220 - 250°C) or immersing it in hot oil.

4 When assembling the piston to the connecting rod ensure that the notch in the bottom of the piston skirt faces towards the front, (timing cover end) of the engine, and the oil groove in the face of the big-end is towards the camshaft (see Fig. 1.23).

5 Check that when the small end is located centrally between the bosses inside the piston, the ends of the gudgeon pin are inset an equal distance from the outside of the piston bosses. If necessary adjust the position of the gudgeon pin by pressing it in the appropriate direction.

6 Refit the piston rings using the reverse of the removal procedure, but first check the ring gap in the cylinder bore as described in the next Section. Three rings are fitted; the top compression ring can be fitted either way up but the second scraper ring and bottom oil control ring must be fitted with the word 'TOP' uppermost (see Fig. 1.24).

7 Set the ring gaps at an angle of 120° to each other around the perimeter of the piston to reduce gas blow-by, (see Fig. 1.25).

24 Piston, ring and cylinder bore wear - examination and renovation

1 Piston and cylinder bore wear are contributory factors to excessive

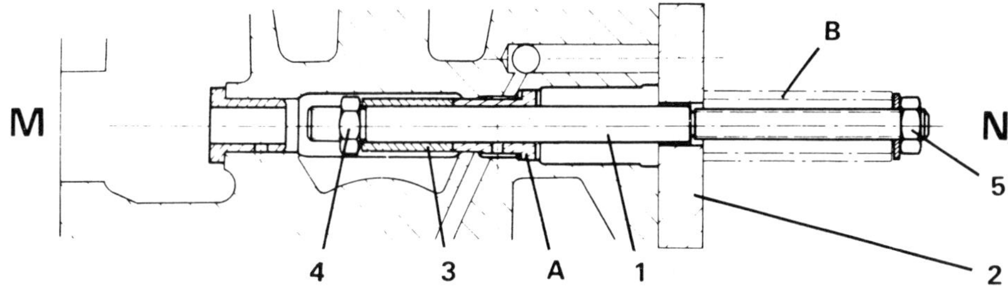

Fig. 1.27. Extracting the oil pump/distributor driveshaft bushes

1 Rod
2 Plate
3 Sleeve
4 Nut
5 Nut
A Shaft bush
B Old gudgeon pin
M Side towards distributor
N Side towards oil pump

oil consumption (over 1 pint to 300 miles) and general engine noise. They also affect engine power output due to loss of compression. If you have been able to check the individual pressures before dismantling so much the better. They will indicate whether one or more is losing compression which may be due to cylinders and pistons if the valves are satisfactory.

2 Determining the degree of wear on pistons and cylinders is complementary. In some circumstances the pistons alone may need renewal, the cylinders not needing reboring. If the cylinders need reboring then new pistons must be fitted. First check the cylinders. A preliminary check can be done simply by feeling the walls about ½ inch down from the top edge. If a ridge can be felt at any point then the bores should be measured with an inside micrometer or calipers to see how far they vary from standard. The measurement should be taken across the bore of the cylinder about 15 mm (0.6 in) down from the top edge at right angles to the axis of the gudgeon pin. Then measure the piston, also at right angles to the gudgeon pin across the skirt at the bottom. The two measurements should not differ by more than 0.008 to 0.0015 in (0.022 to 0.037 mm).

3 Further measurement of the cylinder across the bore will indicate whether or not the wear is mostly on the piston. If the cylinder bore is uniform in size fitting new pistons in the original bore size is possible. However, it is a very short sighted policy. If new pistons are needed anyway the cost of reboring will add 20 - 25% to the cost of the pistons so it would be as well to get it done whilst the engine is out of the vehicle.

4 Another feature of the pistons to check is the piston ring side clearance in the grooves. This should not exceed 0.12 mm (0.0047 in) for the top ring and 0.10 mm (0.004 in) for the other two. Usually however, this wear is proportionate to the rest of the piston which is otherwise apparently little worn. If you think that only a new set of rings is required it would be a good idea to take your pistons to the supplier of the new rings and check the new rings in the gaps. You may change your mind about how worn the pistons really are! Once a cylinder has been rebores twice (to + 0.0157 in (0.4 mm) diameter) it must not be rebored again.

5 Remove the piston rings from each piston in turn and keep them identified for their respective bore. Similarly, if new rings are being fitted, keep them identified in respect of piston location and bore.

6 Press each ring squarely an inch or two (25 to 50 mm) down the cylinder bore and check the ring gap with feeler gauges. The gaps should be 0.010 to 0.018 in (0.25 to 0.45 mm) for the compression rings and 0.008 to 0.016 in (0.20 to 0.40 mm) for the oil control rings.

25 Flywheel - examination and renovation

1 The clutch friction disc mating surface of the flywheel should be examined for scoring. If this is apparent then it should either be exchanged for a new unit or if the scoring is very light it may be skimmed.

2 The starter ring gear should be examined and if the teeth are worn or chipped it must be renewed.

3 To remove the ring, support the flywheel and drive off the ring gear using a bronze or steel bar.

4 Take care not to damage the flywheel locating dowels during this operation or they will have to be renewed.

5 Place the new ring gear in position on the flywheel ensuring that the teeth have their lead-ins (chamfer) facing the correct way as originally fitted.

6 Using a blow lamp or torch, heat the ring gear evenly all round until it just starts to drop into position.

7 Drive the ring gear squarely onto the flywheel shoulder using a drift.

26 Oil pump and drive shaft bushes - examination and renovation

1 The oil pump gears and drive shaft should be checked for wear and play compared with the tolerances given in Specifications. Renew components as required or exchange the complete unit.

2 Check the pressure relief valve components and renew as appropriate if the ball or body are scored or seats appear pitted.

3 Check the wear of the oil pump/distributor drive shaft bushes. Where these have to be renewed, either extract them using a threaded rod and nuts and distance pieces similar to the method used in Fig. 1.27.

4 Alternatively, tap a thread in each bush and use a bolt as an extractor.

5 Fit the shorter bush to the distributor side (M) pulling it in tight to the machined surface of the cylinder block. It is vital that the oil hole in the bush aligns with the crankshaft bearing oil passage.

6 Fit the bush to the oil pump side (N) again using the threaded rod and nut method and avoiding damage to the bush just fitted. There is no need to align the oil hole on this bush as it opens into a circular oil chamber in the cylinder block.

7 Test the drive shaft in the bushes for ease or rotation. A hard spot will indicate mis-alignment or distortion.

27 Cylinder head, rocker gear, valves - examination and renovation

1 As previously described, the alloy cylinder head must be handled very carefully to avoid scoring or damage. Do not stand it on a bench which is covered with filings or they may become embedded in the surface of the head.

2 Remove carbon using a blunt scraper taking great care not to damage the machined surfaces.

3 If there are any visible cracks the head should be scrapped. Cracks are most likely to occur round the valve seats or spark plug holes. Bearing in mind that a head will cost (new) nearly 20% of the cost of a complete, new engine, economies should be considered as well as the likelihood of obtaining a used head from a breaker's yard. If the latter, make sure that the head you get is the same type as the old one - and in better condition!

4 The valve seats should be examined for signs of pitting or ridging. Slight pitting can be ground away using carborundum paste and an **old** valve. New valves are specially plated and must not be used to grind in the seats. If the valve faces are burnt or cracked, new valves must be obtained. If the valve seats require re-cutting, ensure that the width is maintained at 0.060 in (1.5 mm) and at an angle of 46°

5 The rocker gear should be dismantled and thoroughly cleaned of the sludge deposits which normally tend to accumulate on it. The

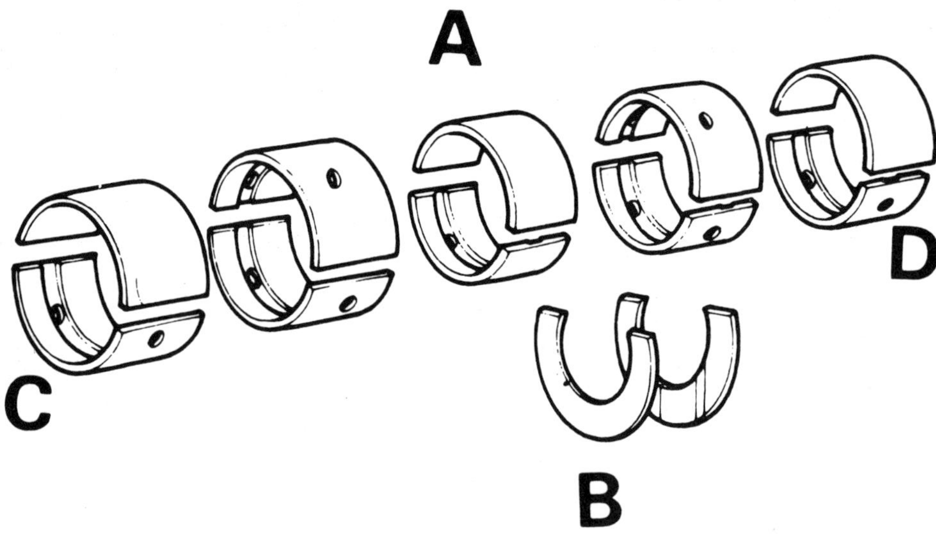

Fig. 1.28. Identification of main bearing shells and thrust bearings

A Lower (cap) half-shells *B Upper (cyl. block) thrust bearings* *C Timing cover end* *D Flywheel end*

29.1 Fitting the main bearings in the crankcase

29.3 Correct locations of crankshaft thrust washers

29.5 Lowering the crankshaft into position

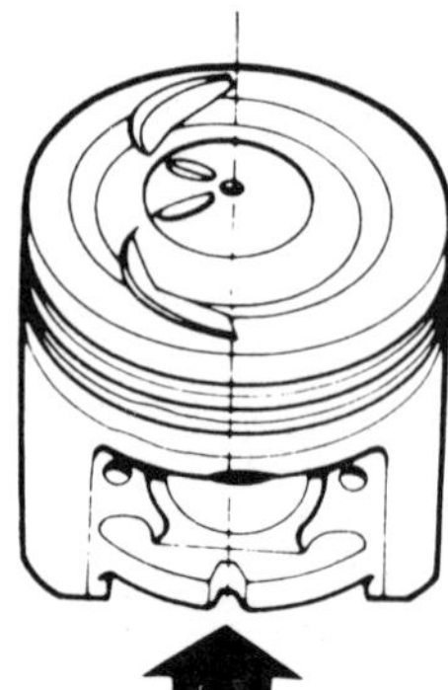

Fig. 1.29. Correct position of valve cut-outs in piston as viewed from timing cover end of engine

rocker arms should be a smooth fit on the shaft with no play. If there is any play it is up to the owner to decide whether it is worth the cost of renewal. The effects on engine performance and noise may not be serious although wear tends to accelerate once it is started. The valve clearance adjusting screws should also be examined. The domed ends that bear on the valve stems tend to get hammered out of shape. If bad, renewal is relatively cheap and easy.

6 The valves themselves must be thoroughly cleaned of carbon. The head should be completely free of cracks or pitting and must be perfectly circular. The edge which seats into the cylinder head should also be unpitted and unridged and if any are evident, the valve must be renewed.

7 Refit the valve into its guide in the head and note if there is any sideways movement which denotes wear between the stem and guide. Here again the degree of wear can vary. If excessive, the performance of the engine can be noticeably affected and oil consumption increased. The maximum tolerable sideways rock, measured at the valve head with the end of the valve stem flush with the end of the guide, is 0.8 mm (0.031 in). Wear is normally in the guide rather than on the valve stem but check a new valve in the guide if possible first. Valve guide renewal is a tricky operation and should be left to a Chrysler Dealer.

8 Check that the end face of the valve stem is not 'hammered' or ridged by the action of the rocker arm. If it is, dress it square and smooth with an oilstone.

9 The cylinder head surface can be ground to a maximum of 0.024 in (0.6 mm) providing a cylinder head gasket of 0.070 in (1.8 mm) is used on reiftting to maintain the correct compression ratio. The correct type of gasket is obtainable from a Chrysler Dealer.

28 Engine reassembly - general

Ensure absolute cleanliness during assembly operations and lubricate each component with clean engine oil before fitting.

Renew all lockwashers, gaskets and seals as a matter of course.

Take care to tighten nuts and bolts to the torque specified in Specifications and watch out for any differences in bolt lengths which might mean attempting to screw a long bolt into a short hole with subsequent fracturing of a casting.

Follow the sequence of reassembly given in the following Sections and do not skip any adjustment procedure essential at each fitting stage.

29 Crankshaft and main bearings - reassembly

1 Fit the new main bearing shells to the crankcase locations (photo).
2 Fit the two semi-circular thrust washers.
3 The thrust washers should be retained in position with grease at each side of the main bearing centre web of the crankcase and must have their oil grooves facing outwards (photo).
4 Oil the crankcase bearing shells liberally.
5 Lower the crankshaft carefully into position in the crankcase (photo).
6 Fit the shell bearings to the main bearing caps (photo).
7 Place the main bearing caps in order, ready for fitting. The caps are numbered 1 to 5, number 1 being positioned nearest the flywheel. The shells in caps 2 and 4 have oil grooves, 1, 3 and 5 do not. Fit the main bearing caps in their correct order (photo).
8 Fit the main bearing cap bolts and tighten them to the correct torque of 47 lb f ft (6.4 kg f m) (photo).
9 The crankshaft endfloat must now be checked. To do this, lever the crankshaft in one direction and then the other and, using feeler gauges, measure the gap between the thrust washers and the face of each side of the centre main bearing web. The total endfloat should be between 0.0035 and 0.011 in (0.09 and 0.27 mm), photo. Where the clearance is outside the permitted tolerance then the thrust washers must be changed for ones of different thickness. These are available in a variety of thicknesses.

30 Flywheel, spigot bearing and oil seal - refitting

1 It is an advantage to fit the flywheel at this stage as it will provide a means of rotating the crankshaft when installing the connecting rod/piston assemblies.
2 Check the condition of the spigot bearing which is located in the centre of the flywheel mounting flange. If it is worn, extract it and drift in a new one (photo).
3 Stick a new paper gasket in position on the cylinder block.
4 Fit a new oil seal to the inner rim of the crankshaft/flywheel flange oil seal cover.
5 Locate the oil seal cover so that the lip of the oil seal is not damaged and then fit and tighten the five securing bolts, each fitted with a lockwasher (photo).
6 If the paper gasket stands proud of the lower joint face, trim it.
7 Locate the flywheel on the crankshaft mounting flange (photo).
8 Locate the circular plate and insert the securing bolts and tighten them to 40 lb f ft (5.4 kg f m).
9 The flywheel can only be fitted one way as the bolt holes are not equidistant.

Note: Loctite should be smeared on the threads of the flywheel bolts.

31 Connecting rod/piston assemblies - refitting to crankshaft

1 Fit the piston rings to the piston as described in Section 23. Oil them liberally and ensure that the gaps are staggered.
2 Fit a piston ring clamp and then locate the shell bearings in the connecting rod big-end.
3 Oil the cylinder bores and insert the piston/connecting rod assembly into its cylinder. Take care not to damage the bore surfaces with the big-end bolts (photo).
4 Note that with the piston correctly positioned in the cylinder bore the valve recesses in the top of the piston must be nearest the left-hand side of the cylinder block when viewing the engine from the timing cover end (see Fig. 1.29). Gently tap the pistons into the bore using a piece of wood or hammer handle.

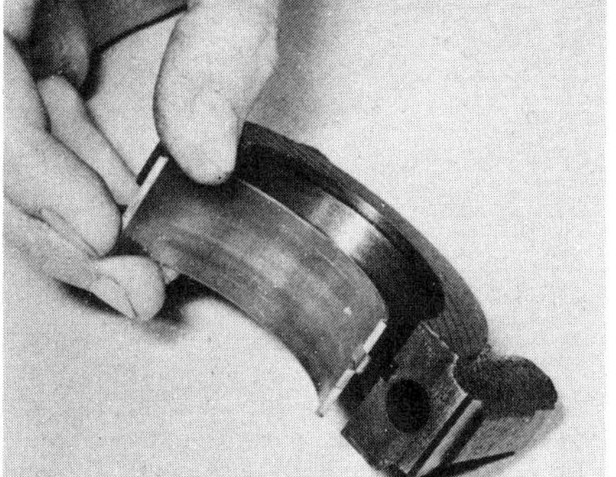
29.6 Fitting the shell into the main bearing cap

29.7 Installing the main bearing caps

29.8 Tightening the main bearing cap bolts

29.9 Checking the crankshaft end-float

30.2 Spigot bearing in crankshaft flange

30.5 Crankshaft oil seal cover in position

30.7 Flywheel in position

30.8 Tightening the flywheel bolts

31.3 Inserting a piston into the block

31.6 Fitting a big-end bearing cap

31.7 Tightening the big-end cap nuts

31.9 Crankshaft sprocket in position

32.1 Installing the camshaft

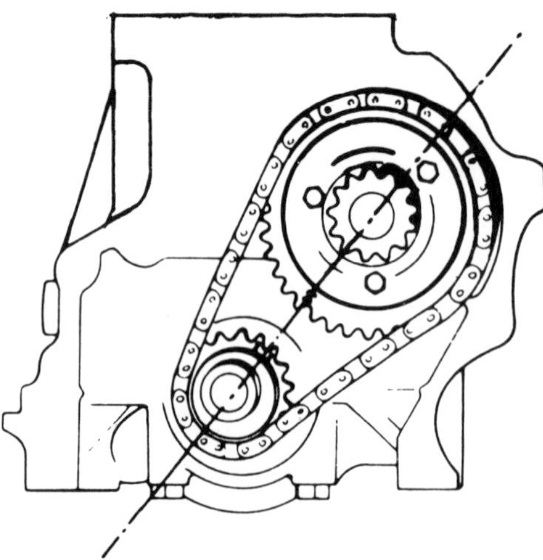
Fig. 1.30. Correct alignment of timing sprockets (No. 1 piston at TDC)

32.3 Camshaft thrust plate correctly fitted

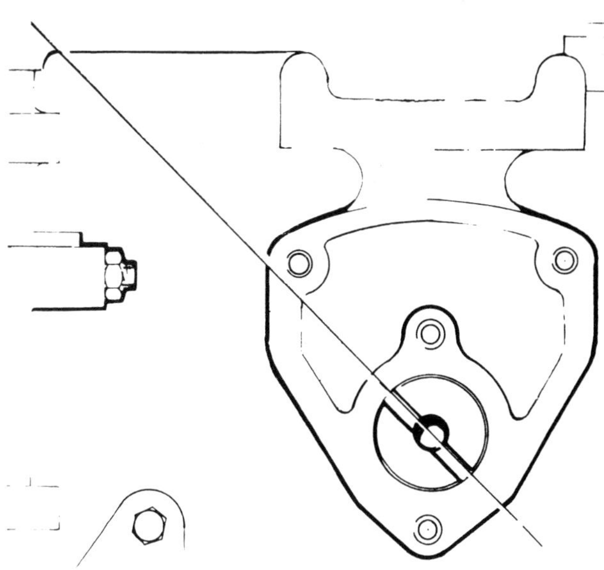

Fig. 1.31. Correct position of distributor drive dog with No. 1 piston 10° BTDC (Note smaller segment is towards the bottom of cylinder block)

32.8 Fitting the camshaft sprocket and timing chain (Note position of timing marks)

32.10 Inserting the oil pump driveshaft

5 Fit the shells to the big-end caps, ensuring that when the caps are correctly located, the notches of both halves of the shells will coincide.
6 Fit the big-end caps by hand pressure (photo), rotating the crankshaft by means of the flywheel to tdc or bdc to facilitate fitting.
7 Fit the big-end nuts and tighten them to a torque of 26 lb f ft (3.5 kg f m) (photo).
8 Fit the Woodruff key to the crankshaft.
9 Fit the crankshaft sprocket, using a tubular drift if necessary and ensuring that the countersunk side of the sprocket faces the engine (photo).

32 Camshaft, timing gear, distributor/oil pump drive - reassembly

1 Oil the camshaft bearings liberally and insert the camshaft into the cylinder block taking care not to damage the bearings as the cam lobes pass through them (photo).
2 Fit the camshaft thrust plate so that it engages in the groove of the journal.
3 Fit and tighten the thrust plate retaining screws using new locking tabs (photo).
4 At this stage check the camshaft endfloat, using either a dial gauge or feelers. The tolerance is between 0.005 and 0.008 in (0.10 and 0.20 mm) and endfloat outside these recommendations should be rectified by the substitution of a new thrust plate.
5 Bend over the thrust plate bolt locking tabs.
6 Turn the crankshaft by means of the flywheel until the No. 1 piston (nearest the flywheel) is in the tdc position.
7 Temporarily fit the sprocket onto the camshaft ensuring the bolt holes are aligned and then rotate the camshaft until the single mark on the sprocket is in line with the two marks on the crankshaft sprocket as shown in Fig. 1.30.
8 Remove the camshaft sprocket without rotating the camshaft and lift the timing chain over both sprockets. Refit the sprocket onto the camshaft (photo), and check that the timing marks are in alignment using a straight edge, if necessary, and refit the three camshaft sprocket securing bolts.
9 Tighten the bolts to the specified torque wrench setting and bend over the locking tabs.

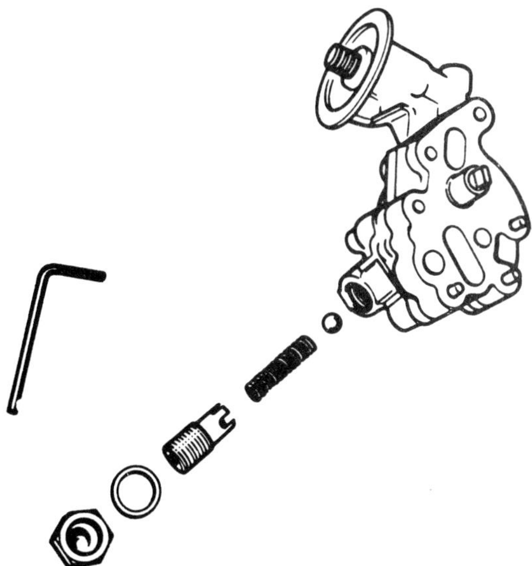

Fig. 1.32. Oil pump relief valve assembly

10 Smear the oil pump drive shaft with engine oil and insert it in position (photo).
11 Insert the shaft drive gear, engaging it with the camshaft worm. The gear must be fitted the correct way round so that the splined part of the bore is to the outside. Secure the gear with the circlip (photo).
12 From the opposite side to the oil pump insert the distributor drive so that the large and small segments are in the position shown in Fig. 1.31.
13 It is imperative that during the foregoing operations No. 1 piston is on the compression stroke and the flywheel timing mark is aligned with the 10° btdc mark in the clutch housing 'window' (photo).
14 Locate the distributor base plate so that its boss is towards the timing cover and tighten the securing bolts (photo).

32.11A Inserting the drive shaft gear ...

32.11B ... and securing it with the circlip

32.13 Flywheel timing marks

32.14 Fitting the distributor base plate

33.3 Fitting the oil pump

34.3 Correct location of timing cover oil seal

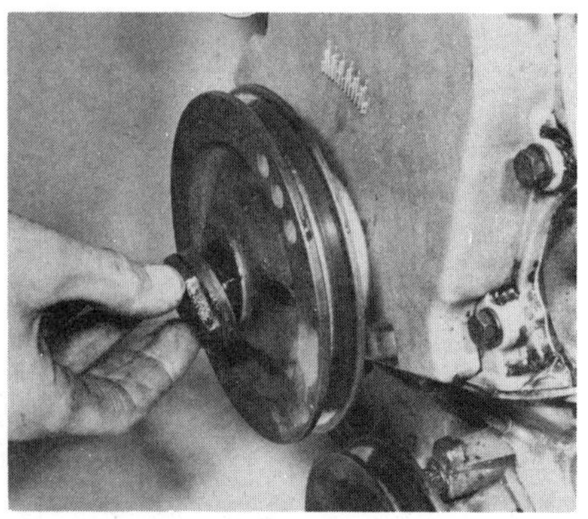
34.6 Fitting the crankshaft pulley

35.2 Installing the sump case

35.3 Fitting the oil pump strainer

35.5 Fitting the sump pan

36.2 Fitting the water pump

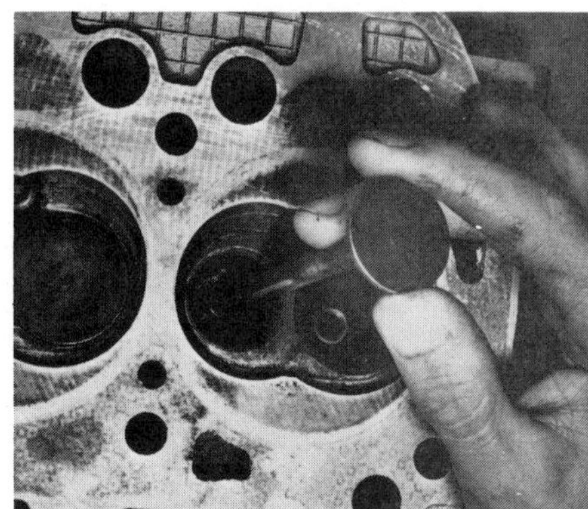
37.2 Inserting a valve

33 Oil pump - refitting

1 Locate the oil pump body and a new gasket on the cylinder block.
2 Insert the oil pump gears.
3 Locate the oil pump cover and fit the securing bolts (photo).
4 Tighten the bolts evenly to the specified torque wrench setting.
5 If the relief valve has been dismantled, reassemble it and screw it securely into position (see Fig. 1.32).

34 Timing cover and seal and crankshaft pulley - refitting

1 Examine the timing cover oil seal for wear or damage and renew it, also if there has been previous evidence of oil leakage.
2 Extract the old seal and drive in the new one squarely using a suitable drift.
3 Before fitting the seal, check that the directional arrow on the seal follows the direction of rotation of the engine and that the seal spring faces inwards (photo).
4 Using a new gasket, fit the timing cover to the cylinder block.
5 Tighten the retaining bolts noting that two different sizes of setscrews and one nut and bolt are used.
6 Fit the crankshaft pulley and retaining bolt (photo).

35 Sump and oil strainer - refitting

1 Locate a new sump case gasket to the cylinder block, using grease to hold it in position.
2 Lower the sump case into position on the block and secure with the internal and external bolts (photo).
3 Fit the oil pump strainer into position (photo).
4 Locate the cork sump pan gasket in position.
5 Locate the sump pan (photo) and tighten the bolts evenly.

36 Water pump - refitting

1 Locate the water pump gasket to the sump case using grease to hold it in position.
2 Fit the water pump and tighten the securing bolts to the correct torque (photo).
3 Connect the water hose between the water pump and the crankcase outlet.
4 Re-fit the water pump drain plug and sealing washer.

37 Cylinder head, valves and rocker gear - reassembly and refitting

1 The components of the cylinder head should have been examined for wear, carbon removed and the valves renewed, if necessary, as described in Section 27.
2 Insert the first valve into its guide in the cylinder head, and, if they have been kept in strict order, the valve will be fitted to its original location (photo).
3 Place the lower valve spring seat in position (photo).
4 Place a new oil seal in position (photo).
5 Place the valve spring and collar in position on the valve stem (photo). If the original valve springs have been in service for 15000 miles (24000 km) or more they should be renewed.
6 Using a suitable compressor, compress the valve spring and insert the split collets (photo).
7 Release the valve spring compressor and check that the components of the valve are correctly fitted. Place a small block of wood on the end face of the valve stem and give it a blow with a hammer in order to settle the collets and to ensure that later valve clearance adjustment is precise. Repeat the fitting operations on the other seven valves.
8 Insert the tappet blocks (cam followers) into their original sequence in the cylinder block (photo).
9 Clean both mating surfaces of block and head, ensuring that no

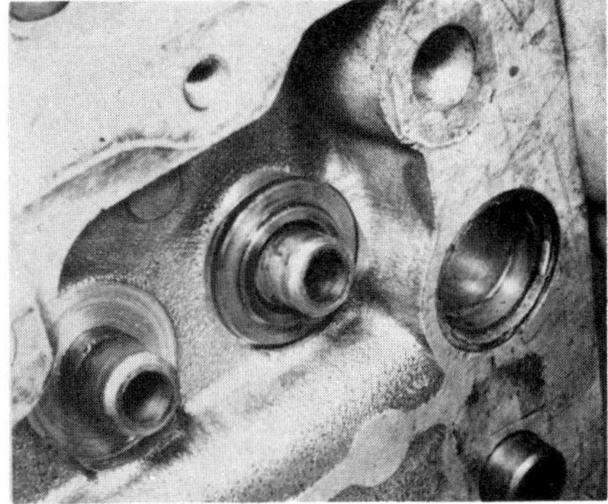
37.3 Valve spring seat in position

37.4 Fitting the valve oil seal

37.5 Fitting the valve spring and collar

37.6 Compressing a valve spring

37.8 Inserting a cam follower into the block

37.10 Cylinder head gasket in position

trace of carbon, scale or grit remains.

10 Locate a new cylinder head gasket in position on the block, ensuring that the word **'DESSUS'** is visible on the upper surface (photo)

11 Check that the two alignment dowels are correctly positioned through the gasket. The gasket should normally be fitted dry but if there has been evidence of oil or water leaks from the head gasket or if the surfaces of the block or head are scratched, then a thin film of non-setting compound should be applied to both sides of the gasket. This compound also provides a protection against corrosion of the alloy head.

12 Lower the cylinder head gently into position on the cylinder block (photo).

13 At this stage, check that the rocker pillar alignment dowels are securely in position on the top face of the cylinder head.

14 Fit the pushrods, carefully engaging their lower ends in the tappet blocks.

15 If the rocker shaft assembly has been dismantled for the renewal of worn components, it should be reassembled with the parts fitted in the sequence in Fig. 1.33.

16 Fit a new pin to the centre rocker shaft pillar, ensuring that the plugged ends of the hollow shafts face outwards.

17 Lower the assembled rocker shaft onto the locating dowels on the cylinder head.

18 Drop the cylinder head bolts into their holes, noting that the longer bolts locate in the thicker side of the rocker pillars (photo).

19 Check that the pushrods locate correctly with each rocker arm. It will be essential to have slackened the rocker arm adjuster screws right off to ensure that there is no valve spring pressure applied when tightening down the cylinder head bolts.

20 Using a torque wrench, tighten the cylinder head bolts to 45 lb f ft (6.22 kg f m) in the sequence shown in Fig. 1.9 (photo).

21 Adjustment of the valve clearances may be carried out now or at a later stage when the engine has been fitted but if the operation is undertaken now, it will permit the rocker cover and other ancillaries to be fitted and obviate their removal again later.

22 The valve clearances must be adjusted when the engine is cold. The inlet valves should be set to 0.010 in (0.25 mm) and the exhaust valves to 0.012 in (0.30 mm). Counting from the flywheel end of the engine, the inlet valves are numbers 1, 3, 6 and 8 and exhaust valves are 2, 4, 5 and 7.

23 Turn the engine by means of the flywheel and refer to the following table, adjusting each valve clearance in the sequence given. Counting from flywheel end of block.

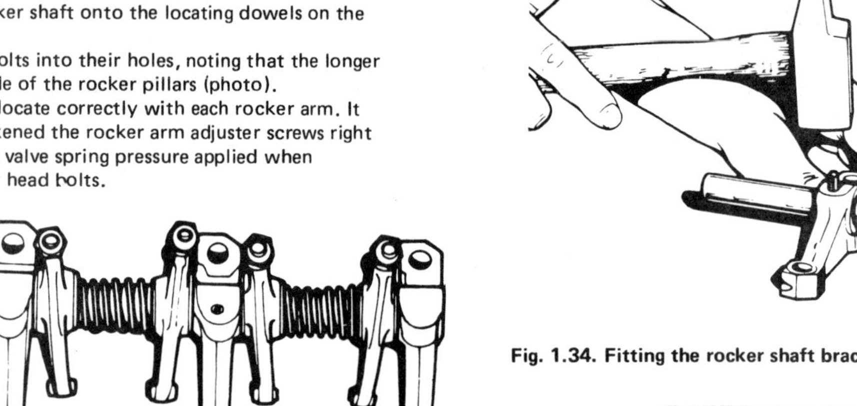

Fig. 1.34. Fitting the rocker shaft bracket retaining pin

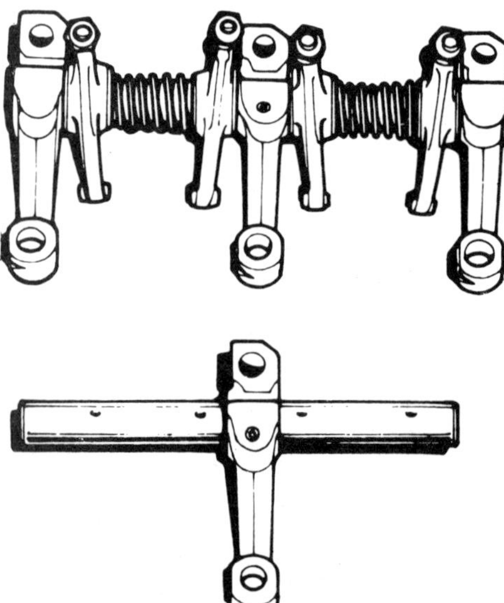

Fig. 1.33. Correct assembly of rocker shaft

37.12 Lowering the cylinder head into position

37.18 Correct installation of rocker shaft assembly

37.19 Tightening the cylinder head bolts

37.24 Setting the valve clearances

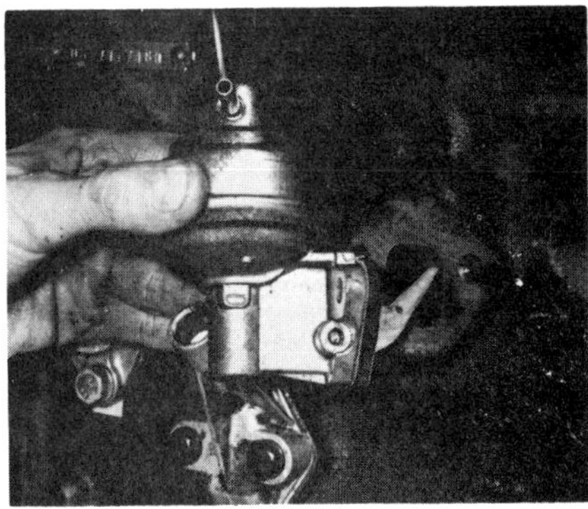
38.2 Fitting the fuel pump

38.3 Dipstick retainer installed

38.8 Fitting the inlet manifold

38.19 Correct position of carburettor heater box

39.2 Refitting the gearbox to engine

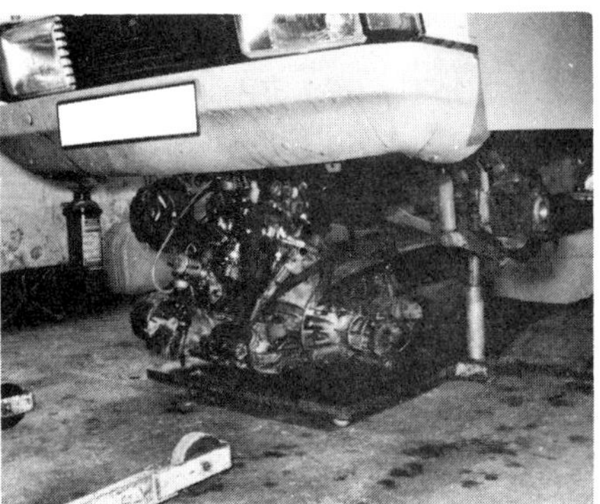
40.1 Positioning the engine beneath the car

Valve clearances to adjust	*Valves in balance*
1 and 2	7 and 8
3 and 4	5 and 6
5 and 6	3 and 4
7 and 8	1 and 2

24 Insert the feeler blade between the heel of the rocker arm and the valve stem end face. Turn the adjuster screw until the feeler is a stiff sliding fit and then tighten the locknut (photo).
25 Repeat the adjustment on the other valves, then recheck all clearances and fit the rocker cover.

38 Engine ancillaries - refitting

1 Place a new gasket either side of the insulating washer which locates between the fuel pump and the crankcase.
2 Fit the fuel pump to the crankcase ensuring that the pump actuating arm fits between the crankcase wall and the camshaft (photo).
3 Fit the dipstick retainer to the crankcase, using a new gasket (photo).
4 Rotate the crankshaft until the segments on the distributor drive are in the position shown in Fig. 1.31 and insert the distributor into the crankcase aperture, ensuring that the drive dogs are correctly engaged.
5 Check that the distributor rotor is in line with the timing mark on the distributor body as described in Chapter 4.
6 Fit the distributor retaining plate by sliding it behind the distributor mounting bolt head.
7 Fit the thermostat housing to the cylinder head (two bolts).
8 Fit the inlet manifold to the cylinder head using a new gasket (photo). Before completing this operation, fit the pre-heat pipe from the thermostat elbow, pull the inlet manifold downwards and slide the pre-heat pipe under the manifold securing studs.
9 Connect the crankcase breather tube to the carburettor.
10 Fit the fuel pipe to the carburettor.
11 Fit the pre-heat pipe which runs between the water pump and the inlet manifold noting carefully its correct positioning against the crankcase.
12 Fit a new exhaust manifold gasket and bolt the manifold to the cylinder head, using only the specified brass nuts.
13 Fit the clutch assembly to the flywheel. Full details of the fitting procedure and centralising the driven plate are given in Chapter 5.
14 Position the thermostat in its housing, noting the tab for correct location.
15 Fit the thermostat housing cover, using a new gasket.
16 Fit the water pump pulley.
17 Fit the water pump pulley spacer and locking tab ring. Tighten the securing bolts and bend up the tabs.
18 Fit the alternator and drive belt. Adjust the belt tension as described in Chapter 2 and tighten the alternator securing bolts.
19 Lower the heater box (which provides warmed air to the carburettor) onto the rocker cover. Ensure that the nut underneath the heater box is tight before fitting it (photo).

39 Gearbox to engine - reconnection

1 If previously removed, reassemble the clutch operating mechanism, release bearing and fork as described in Chapter 5.
2 Position the engine and gearbox units as shown (photo).
3 Having aligned the driven plate (Chapter 5) the gearbox should slide easily as the gearbox primary shaft passes through the splined hub of the driven plate and engages with the spigot bearing which is located in the centre of the flywheel to crankshaft mounting flange.
4 Insert the gearbox to engine securing bolts and tighten to a torque of 32 lb f ft (4.4 kg f m).
5 Fit the cover plate on the exhaust side of the engine and secure with the three retaining bolts.
6 Fit the starter motor in position and secure it with the three retaining bolts.

40 Combined engine/gearbox/differential unit - refitting to vehicle

1 Check that the vehicle is raised sufficiently high at the front to

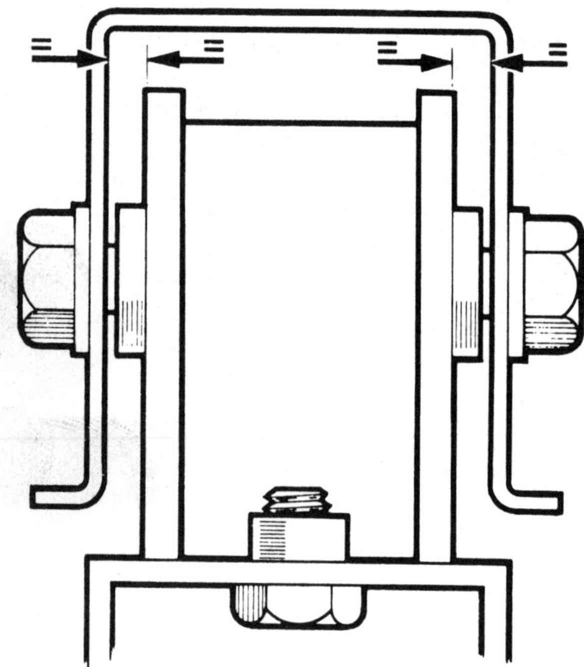

Fig. 1.35. Positioning the engine rear mounting bracket

permit the engine/gearbox unit to pass beneath it (photo).
2 Attach suitable lifting chains or slings.
3 Slide the power unit under the vehicle and then lift it upwards into the engine compartment using a suitable hoist.
4 Enter the three engine mounting bolts into the left-hand mounting (photo).
5 Enter the two engine mounting bolts on the right-hand side (photo).
6 Fit the engine rear mounting bracket to the crankcase but do not tighten the rubber mounting bolts at this stage.
7 Refit the drive shafts into the final drive unit and if necessary tap the outer end of the shafts with a soft faced mallet to ensure the inner splines are fully engaged in the differential.
8 Engage the outer splined end of each shaft through the front wheel hub assemblies, fit the lower balljoints in each bottom suspension arm and secure with the retaining nuts. Tighten both nuts to the specified torque wrench setting.
9 Now rock the engine from side to side to centralize it and then position the engine rear rubber mounting in the slotted holes, so that there is equal clearance on each side of the bracket as shown in Fig. 1.35. Check that the slots are parallel and tighten the securing bolts.
10 Remove the clamping rods that were fitted to retain the front suspension in position and refit the dampers.
11 Refit the driveshaft securing nuts, get an assistant to apply the footbrake and tighten the nuts. The nuts can be finally tightened to the specified torque wrench setting after the wheels have been fitted and the vehicle is lowered to the ground.
12 Attach the exhaust pipe flange to the manifold and secure the clamping bracket.
13 Refit the accelerator brackets and balljoints and adjust the brackets to obtain a clearance of 1/8 to 3/16 in (3 to 5 mm) between the peg and the slot in the gearbox selector shaft (see Chapter 3).
14 Refit the alternator drivebelt cover beneath the front right-hand wheel arch.
15 Jack-up the front of the car, remove the axle stands and lower the vehicle to the ground. Tighten the wheel nuts and check that the driveshaft securing nuts are tightened to the specified torque wrench setting (photo). Lock the nuts by peening the flange of each nut into the driveshaft groove.

40.4 LH side engine mounting bolts

40.5 RH side engine mounting bolts

40.14 Tightening the drive shaft nuts

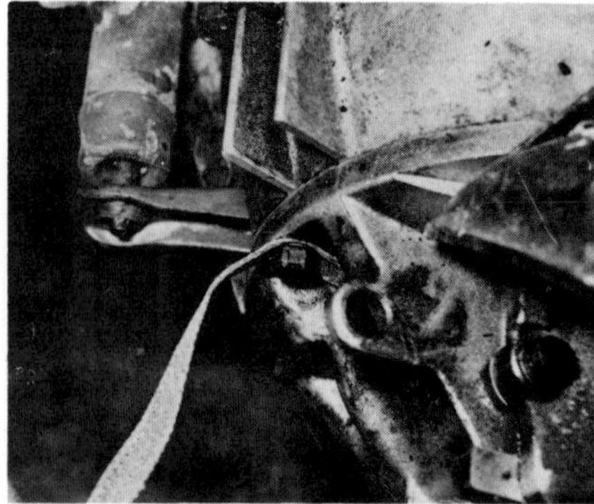

41.7 One of the two engine earthing leads

41.8A Water temperature transmitter unit

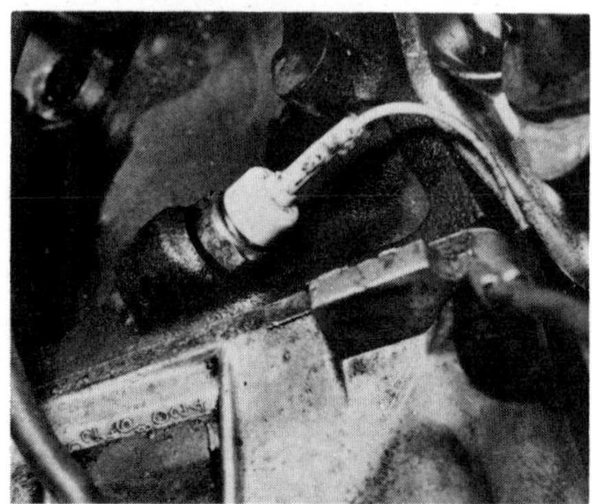

41.8B Oil pressure transmitter unit

41 Engine - final reassembly, connections and replenishment of lubricants

1 Refit the clutch slave cylinder ensuring that the pushrod is correctly engaged in the operating lever.
2 Fit the rotor arm and distributor cap. Refit the spark plugs and HT leads and connect the LT leads to the coil.
3 Reconnect the fuel pipe to the pump and the pipe from the pump to the carburettor.
4 Refit the heater hoses and top and bottom radiator hoses.
5 Refit the coolant expansion bottle and attach the hoses to the radiator.
6 Refit the throttle cable and choke cable on the carburettor, referring to Chapter 3 if necessary.
7 Refit the two earth leads to the engine block (photo).
8 Reconnect the leads to the water temperature and oil pressure transmitter units (photo).
9 Fit the air cleaner assembly, referring to Chapter 3 if necessary.
10 Reconnect the leads to the rear of the alternator and the starter motor solenoid.
11 Fit a new oil filter, check that the sump drain plug is tight and fill the engine with the correct grade and quantity of oil.
12 Fill the radiator with coolant and top the expansion bottle up to the level mark on the side.
13 Fill the gearbox and final drive unit with the correct grade and quantity of oil.
14 With the help of an assistant, refit the bonnet ensuring the hinges line up with the marks made before removal.
15 Carry out a careful check to make sure all hoses, electrical leads and controls have been correctly refitted and then connect the battery terminals.

42 Engine - initial start up after overhaul or major repair

Make sure that the battery is fully charged and that all lubricants, coolant and fuel are replenished.

If the fuel system has been dismantled, it will require several revolutions of the engine on the starter motor to pump petrol to the carburettor. It will help to remove the spark plugs, which will enable the engine to turn over much easier, and enable oil to be pumped around the engine before starting it.

Refit the spark plugs and as soon as the engine fires and runs, keep it going at a fast tickover only (no faster) and bring it up to normal working temperature.

As the engine warms up, there will be odd smells and some smoke from parts getting hot and burning off oil deposits. Look for water or oil leaks which will be obvious if serious. Check also the clamp connection of the exhaust pipe to the manifold as these do not always 'find' their exact gas tight position until the warmth and vibration have acted on them, and it is almost certain that they will need tightening further. This should be done, of course, with the engine stationary.

When the engine running temperature has been reached, adjust the idling speed as described in Chapter 3.

Stop the engine and wait a few minutes to see if any lubricant or coolant leaks.

Road test the car to check that the timing is correct and giving the necessary smoothness and power. Do not race the engine. If new bearings and or pistons and rings have been fitted, it should be treated as a new engine and run in at reduced revolutions for 500 miles (800 km).

43 Modifications

The operations described in this Chapter apply to both engine types but it is essential when ordering spare parts that exact particulars of the vehicle (model, engine number, etc), are quoted. See 'Ordering spare Parts'.

44 Fault finding

Symptom	Reason/s	Remedy
Engine will not turn over when starter switch is operated	Flat battery Bad battery connections Bad connections at solenoid switch and/or starter motor	Check that battery is fully charged and that all connections are clean and tight.
	Starter motor jammed	Rock car back and forth with a gear engaged. If ineffective remove starter.
	Defective solenoid	Remove starter and check solenoid.
	Starter motor defective	Remove starter and overhaul.
Engine turns over normally but fails to fire and run	No spark at plugs	Check ignition system according to procedures given in Chapter 4.
	No fuel reaching engine	Check fuel system according to procedures given in Chapter 3.
	Too much fuel reaching the engine (flooding)	Slowly depress accelerator pedal to floor and keep it there while operating starter motor until engine fires. Check fuel system if necessary as described in Chapter 3.
Engine starts but runs unevenly and misfires	Ignition and/or fuel system faults	Check the ignition and fuel system as though the engine had failed to start.
	Incorrect valve clearances	Check and reset clearances.
	Burnt out valves	Remove cylinder heads and examine the overhaul as necessary.
Lack of power	Ignition and/or fuel system faults	Check the ignition and fuel system for correct ignition timing and carburettor settings.
	Incorrect valve clearances	Check and reset the clearances.
	Burnt out valves	Remove cylinder head and examine and overhaul as necessary.
	Worn out piston or cylinder bores	Remove cylinder head and examine pistons and cylinder bores. Overhaul as necessary.

Symptom	Reason/s	Remedy
Excessive oil consumption	Oil leaks from crankshft oil seal, rocker cover gasket, oil pump, drain plug gasket, sump plug washer, oil cooler	Identify source of leak and repair as appropriate.
	Worn piston rings or cylinder bores resulting in oil being burnt by engine Smoky exhaust is an indication	Fit new rings or rebore cylinders and fit new pistons depending on degree of wear.
	Worn valve guides and/or defective valve stem seals	Remove cylinder heads and recondition valve stem bores and valves and seals as necessary.
Excessive mechanical noise from engine	Wrong valve to rocker clearances	Adjust valve clearances.
	Worn crankshaft bearings Worn cylinders (piston slap)	Inspect and overhaul where necessary.
Unusual vibration	Misfiring on one or more cylinders	Check ignition system.
	Loose mounting bolts	Check tightness of bolts and condition of flexible mountings.

Note: *When investigating starting and uneven running faults do not be tempted into snap diagnosis. Start from the beginning of the check procedure and follow it through. It will take less time in the long run. Poor performance from an engine in terms of power and economy is not normally diagnosed quickly. In any event the ignition and fuel systems must be checked first before assuming any further investigation needs to be made.*

Chapter 2 Cooling system

Contents

Specifications

System type	Semi-sealed, thermo-syphon, water pump assisted with electric cooling fan	
Radiator material	Steel	
Cooling area	194 in^2 (1250 cm^2)	
Thermostat fully open	96°C (205°F) begins to open 83°C (181°F)	
Electric fan operation		
Actuates at water temperature of	95°C (± 1.5°C) 203°F (± 2.7°F)	
Switches off at water temperature of	86°C (± 2°C) 187°F (± 3.6°F)	
Capacities		
System including vehicle heater	1.3 gals (6 litres)	
Difference between 'MAX' and 'MIN' marks on expansion bottle	4/5 pint (0.45 litre)	
Water pump belt tension	½ in (12 mm) maximum free movement of longest run between pulleys.	
Torque wrench settings	**lb f ft**	**kg f m**
Thermoswitch to radiator	25	3.46
Radiator mounting bolts	12	1.68
Thermostat housing to cylinder head	8.5	1.18

Thermostat housing cover	8.5	1.18
Water temperature transmitter to cylinder head	10.5	1.45
Water pump to sump casing	8.5	1.18
Water pump inlet housing to sump casing	8.5	1.18
Water pump drain plug	11.5	1.59
Water pump pulley bolt	10.5	1.45
Water inlet housing to cylinder block	14.5	2.01
Water return manifold to cylinder block	12.0	1.66

1 General description

The cooling system is of conventional type and operates by means of thermo-syphon action with the assistance of a belt driven water pump. A diagrammatic presentation of the circulation pattern and the location of the major components is shown in Fig. 2.1.

The coolant in the radiator flows from right to left instead of in the more common downward direction and the 'header' tanks are situated on either side of the radiator matrix.

Coolant heated in the cylinder jackets is cooled by the ram effect of air passing through the radiator matrix when the car is in motion and assisted by a thermostatically, electrically operated fan which operates within a pre-determined temperature range.

Coolant from the system also circulates through the vehicle heater and is used to pre-heat the inlet manifold.

The system is semi-pressurised and incorporates an expansion bottle to accept coolant displaced when the engine is hot and to act as a reservoir when the system cools down or in the event of minor leakage.

A thermostat is fitted in the system to restrict coolant circulation until the normal engine operating temperature has been reached.

The original coolant is effective indefinitely but where a loss has occurred or the strength of the coolant (antifreeze mixture) is suspect, then the system should be drained, flushed and refilled as described in later Sections of this Chapter.

All flexible hose joints are secured by Corbin type clips and they should only be prised open sufficiently far to enable them to slide over the hose. Ordinary pliers may be used for their removal but special types are more satisfactory. However, the cost of these need not be incurred if the Corbin type are replaced by reliable worm drive clips.

2 Cooling system - draining

1 If it is wished to retain the coolant for further use, place a clean receptacle beneath the engine and then set the car interior heater to the full on position.

2 Unscrew and remove the plug and sealing washer from the base of the water pump and remove the lid of the expansion bottle.

3 To expedite the draining operation, the radiator filler cap may be removed.

4 Do not allow the coolant to come into contact with the paintwork of the car as its antifreeze content will damage the surface of the finish.

5 The coolant should be retained in a covered vessel pending return to the system and any sediment which precipitates should be discarded.

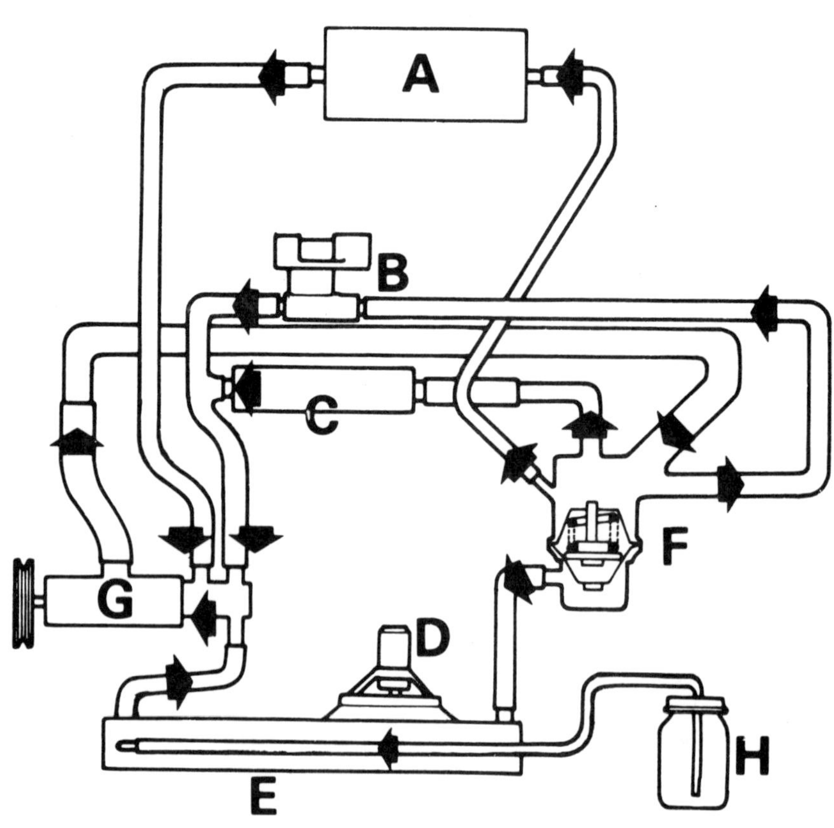

Fig. 2.1. Layout of cooling and interior heating system

A Car heater matrix
B Heated carburettor flange (1294 cc single carb)
C Heated inlet manifold
D Electric cooling fan
E Radiator
F Thermostat
G Water pump
H Expansion bottle

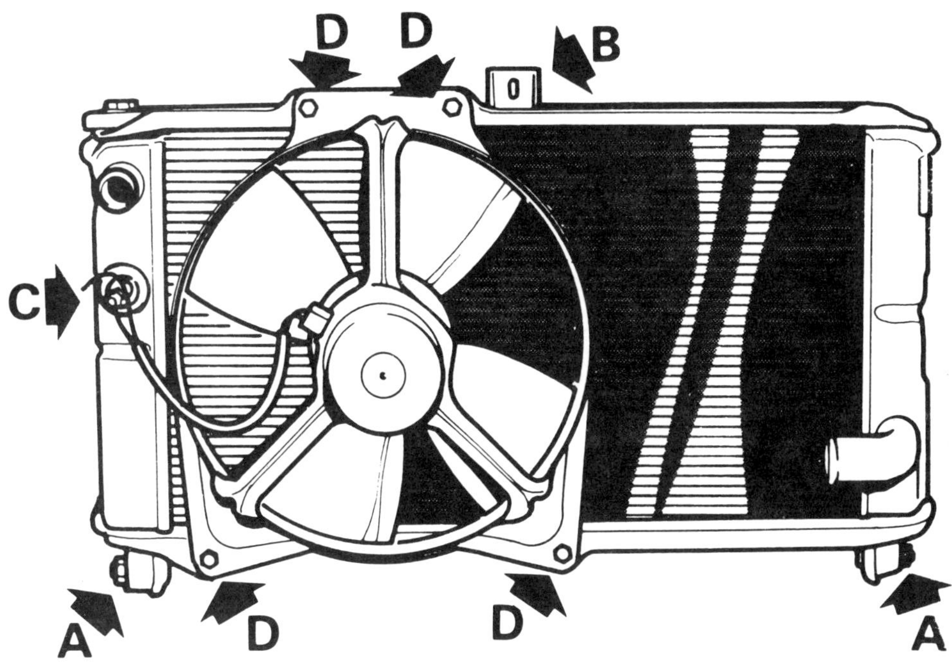

Fig. 2.2. Radiator and cooling fan assembly

A Lower radiator attachment points *B Top radiator attachment point* *C Temperature sensing unit* *D Cooling fan securing bolts*

3 Cooling system - flushing

1 Provided the cooling system is maintained in good order then periodic flushing should not be necessary. Where the coolant has discoloured or become contaminated with oil due to gasket failure, then the system should be thoroughly cleansed.
2 To do this, remove the radiator filler cap and insert a hose in the filler neck, then, with the water pump drain plug removed and the heater control full on, allow the water to flow until it is quite clear when emerging from the water pump drain plug.
3 If the radiator appears blocked then it should be removed as described in Section 6 and reverse flushed. This is carried out by placing the hose in the right-hand radiator outlet so that the water flow is in the opposite direction to normal.
4 The removal of scale from the system should not normally be a problem as, with a semi-sealed circuit, only initial scaling occurs unless, due to leaks, continual topping up is required.
5 The use of chemical de-scalers and cleansers is not recommended as, unless specifically formulated, damage to the aluminium cylinder head, water pump and thermostat housings may occur.
6 Never flush a hot engine cooling system with cold water or cracks or distortion of the block or head may be caused.
7 In the event of blockages in the heater matrix then this should be removed as described in Chapter 12 and serviced as previously described for the radiator.

4 Cooling system - filling

1 Place the heater control to the full on position.
2 Remove the expansion bottle cap.
3 Remove the radiator cap.
4 Fill the radiator slowly right to the top of the filler neck with coolant of the correct antifreeze mixture strength (see next Section). If a new solution is being made up it is preferable to use soft or de-mineralised water.
5 Fill the expansion bottle to the 'maximum' mark.
6 Refit the radiator cap but do not overtighten it.
7 Refit the expansion bottle cap.
8 Start the engine and run it at an even speed until bubbles cease to be visible in the coolant contained in the expansion bottle.
9 Top up the level of the coolant in the expansion bottle until it reaches the 'maximum' mark.
10 Do not allow coolant solution to contaminate the valve in the expansion bottle cap due to overfilling or gas pressure which could be caused by a blown gasket. The valve should be renewed in either event.

5 Antifreeze mixture

1 The use of antifreeze mixture in the cooling system fulfills two purposes. To protect the engine and heater components against fracture during periods of low ambient temperature and to utilise the effects of the rust and corrosion inhibitors incorporated in the anti-freeze product.
2 A 'long-life' type of antifreeze mixture may be used but where a normal commercial type is used it is wise to renew it or at least check its strength with a hydrometer every year.
3 Ensure that the mixture is of a type compatible with aluminium components and refer to the following table for strength recommendations.

Quantity of antifreeze	Gives protection to
1.7 pints (1 litre)	*−17.8°C (0°F)*
2.0 pints (1.3 litres)	*−28.9°C (−20°F)*
2.3 pints (1.43 litres)	*−34.5°C (−30°F)*
3.0 pints (1.7 litres)	*−40°C (−40°F)*

4 Due to the searching action of antifreeze mixture, always check the security of hose clips and gasket joints before filling.

6 Radiator - removal, inspection, cleaning and refitting

1 Drain the cooling system as described in Section 2 of this Chapter.
2 Disconnect the battery earth terminal.
Note: It is possible to remove the radiator and fan unit as one assembly, however, the task is easier if the fan unit is removed first.

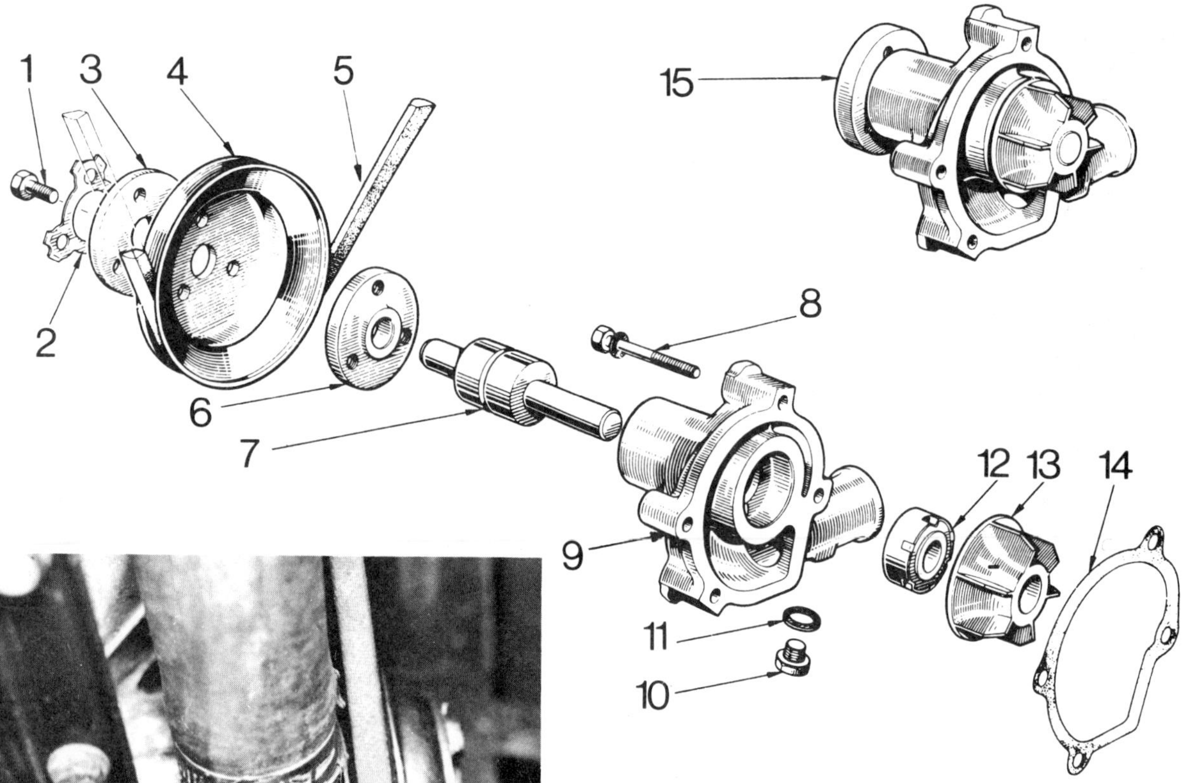

Fig. 2.3. Exploded view of water pump

1 Pulley retaining bolt
2 Lockplate
3 Plate
4 Pulley
5 Drive belt
6 Hub
7 Shaft/bearing assembly
8 Bolt
10 Drain plug
11 Drain plug seal
12 Seal
13 Impeller
14 Gasket
15 Assembled water pump

8.5 Water pump to engine hose (note the drain plug)

Fig. 2.4. Fitting the water pump seal

3 Disconnect the two wires from the temperature sensing unit located at the rear left-hand side of the radiator.
4 Referring to Fig. 2.2, remove the bolts securing the fan unit to the radiator and lift away the fan and cowl.
5 Disconnect the top and bottom radiator hoses.
6 Disconnect the expansion bottle hose from the top of the radiator and slide it out of the retaining clip.
7 Remove the nuts and washers from both the lower radiator mountings and the top mounting.
8 Tilt the radiator assembly towards the engine and then lift it clear of the lower mounting plates.
9 The radiator matrix should be cleaned internally as described in Section 3. Any accumulation of flies on the radiator fins should be removed by lightly brushing or blowing out with compressed air.
10 If the radiator is leaking, do not attempt to repair it yourself as the heat used for soldering must be carefully localised if further leaks are not to be created. Take the unit to a specialist repairer or exchange the unit for a factory reconditioned one. The use of any type of leak sealant is at best, a temporary cure and its use may clog the fine tubes of the heater matrix and damage the water pump seals.
11 Refitting the radiator is a reversal of removal. Refill the system as described in Section 4.

7 Thermostat - removal, testing and refitting

1 Drain the cooling system as previously described.
2 Unscrew and remove the two bolts which secure the thermostat housing cover in position.
3 Remove the cover and gasket and withdraw the thermostat. If it is stuck in its seat do not try to lever it out but cut round its seat joint with a pointed blade to break the seal.

Fig. 2.5. Fitting the water pump shaft/bearing assembly

4 To test whether the thermostat is serviceable, suspend it in a pan of water into which a thermometer has been placed. Heat the water and check that the thermostat begins to open when the water temperature reaches that at which the thermostat is rated (see Specifications).
5 Similarly, when the thermostat is fully open, place it into cooler water and observe its closure. Any failure in the opening or closing actions of the unit will necessitate renewal. Fit one with the specified temperature marked on it, nothing is to be gained by fitting one having a different operating temperature range and could cause cool running or overheating of the engine and heater inefficiency.
6 Refitting is a reversal of removal but ensure that the locating tab on the thermostat is correctly aligned and use a new cover gasket. Do not overtighten the cover securing bolts.
7 Refill the system as described in Section 4.

8 Water pump - removal and refitting

1 Disconnect the battery negative terminal.
2 Set heater control to full on, remove the expansion bottle cap and unscrew the drain plug at the base of the water pump. Retain the coolant if required.
3 From under the wing remove the pulley driving belt cover as described in Chapter 1.
4 Slacken the adjuster bracket bolt on the alternator and having pushed the alternator in towards the engine, slip off the driving belt.
5 Disconnect the water pump to crankcase hose (photo).
6 Unscrew and remove the four water pump cover retaining bolts and lift the pump from its crankcase location.
7 Peel off the old gasket and clean the mating faces of both the pump and crankcase.
8 Refitting is a reversal of removal but always use a new gasket.
9 Refill the cooling system and reconnect the battery.

9 Water pump - dismantling and reassembly

1 The water pump is designed for long trouble-free service and if it has been in operation for a considerable mileage then it will probably be more realistic to exchange the complete unit for one which has been factory reconditioned, rather than attempt to repair a pump without the necessary experience and tools.
2 Check the condition of the impeller for corrosion. Other than this, any fault will lie with a worn shaft seal (Fig. 2.3).
3 Press off the hub from the shaft. To achieve this, support the rear face of the hub and exert pressure on the end of the shaft. (If only the seal is to be renewed, do not remove the hub).
4 Turn the pump over and again, adequately supporting the rear face of the impeller, press the end of the shaft to expel it from the impeller bore.
5 Now immerse the pump body in boiling water for two or three minutes. Remove the pump quickly and drive out the shaft/bearing assembly by driving it out from the seal end with a copper or plastic faced hammer.
6 Drive the seal from the water pump body by means of a drift inserted from the front end of the pump.
7 The shaft/bearing assembly cannot be separated, and if necessary,

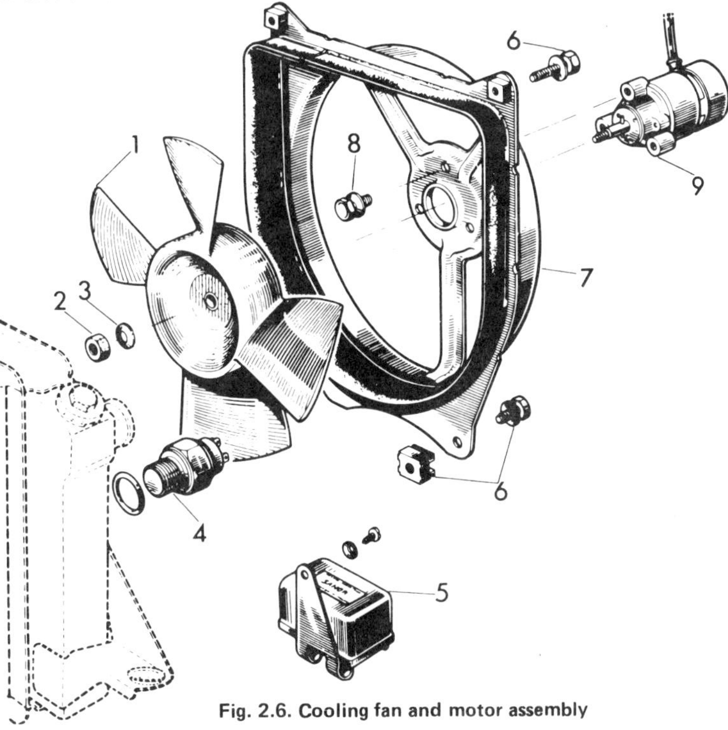

Fig. 2.6. Cooling fan and motor assembly

1 *Fan*
2 *Securing nut*
3 *Lockwasher*
4 *Thermostatic contactor*
5 *Relay*
6 *Mounting bolt*
7 *Frame*
8 *Motor securing bolt*
9 *Electric motor*

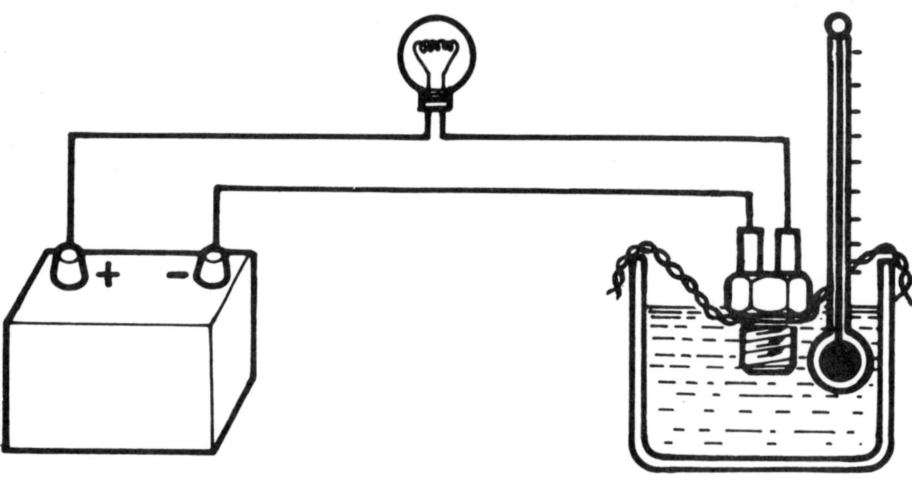

Fig. 2.7. Method of testing the temperature sensor unit

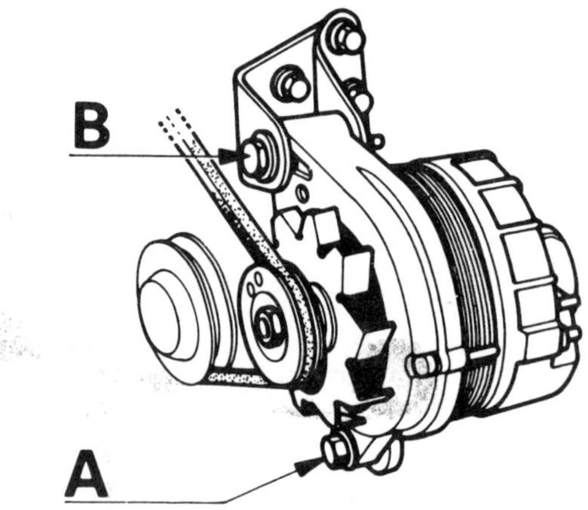

Fig. 2.8. Drive belt adjusting bolts

A Locking bolt *B Pivot bolt*

must be renewed as a single component.
8 Check the condition of the seal and shaft bearing mating surfaces of the pump body. Where necessary, these may be improved with grade '600' paper.
9 Press the water pump seal into its seating in the body (Fig. 2.4).
10 Again heat the pump body in boiling water and then press the shaft bearing assembly into the body ensuring that the bearing seats securely against the bore inner shoulder. Note that the longer end of the shaft is at the seal end (Fig. 2.5).
11 Supporting the end face of the shaft at the seal end, press on the flanged hub so that its boss is towards the shaft bearing. The hub is correctly positioned on the shaft when there is a clearance of 0.050 in (1.270 mm) between the pump and hub faces measured with feeler gauges.
12 Support the front end face of the shaft and press on the impeller (vanes outwards) until there is again a clearance of 0.050 in (1.270 mm) between the pump and impeller faces.
13 Check for free rotation by turning the vanes of the impeller.

10 Radiator cooling fan - description and servicing

1 The radiator cooling fan is shown in exploded form in Fig. 2.6.
2 The assembly comprises a four bladed fan attached to the driving spindle of an electric motor.
3 The fan motor is controlled by a temperature sensing unit that is screwed into the rear left-hand side of the radiator.
4 When the coolant temperature reaches 95°C (203°F) the temperature sensor contacts close and energise the fan. When the water temperature falls to between 86 and 88°C (187 and 191°F) the contacts open and the fan is de-energised.
Warning: *It must be realised that during adjustments within the engine compartment, with the engine at operating temperature, the fan blades may turn unexpectedly if the ignition is switched on. From the point of view of safety, disconnect the fan motor leads before carrying out adjustments in close proximity to the radiator, but watch the coolant temperature if the engine is running!*
5 If the operation of the temperature sensing unit is suspect it should be removed for testing.
6 Disconnect the battery earth terminal, drain the cooling system as described in Section 2 and unscrew the sensor unit from the radiator.
7 Suspend the sensor unit in a water filled container with a thermometer of a suitable temperature range and connect up a 12V battery and test lamp as shown in Fig. 2.7.
8 Heat the water on a stove and check that the lamp lights at a temperature of 95°C (203°C) and extinguishes when the water is allowed to cool to 86°C (187°C).
9 If the lamp does not light, or lights and extinguishes at a different temperature than specified, the sensor unit is faulty and must be renewed.
10 Should the sensor unit function correctly then the fault must be in the fan motor itself.
11 Remove the fan motor and blade assembly after disconnecting the electrical leads and withdrawing the four securing bolts.
12 Unscrew and remove the nut and spring washer which secures the

fan blades to the motor shaft. This has a left-hand thread and the nut must therefore be unscrewed in a clockwise direction.
13 Unscrew and remove the three bolts which secure the motor to the fan assembly outer frame. Renew the motor on an exchange basis.
14 Reassembly and refitting of the fan cooling unit is a reversal of removal and dismantling.

11 Drivebelt - adjustment, removal and refitting

1 To adjust the alternator drivebelt, slacken the pivot bolt and locking bolt shown in Fig. 2.8 and move the alternator in the necessary direction.
2 The correct tension for the belt is ½ in (12 mm) of free movement on the longest run of the belt. When correctly adjusted tighten the pivot and locking bolts.
3 To remove the belt, slacken the bolts and push the alternator in towards the engine as far as possible. Ease the belt off the pulleys rotating the alternator if necessary.
4 Fit the new belt using the reverse procedure to removal and adjust the tension as described previously.

12 Water temperature gauge - fault finding

1 Correct operation of the water temperature gauge is important as the engine could attain a considerable degree of overheating, unnoticed, if giving false readings.
2 To check the correct operation of the gauge, first disconnect the 'Lucar' connector from the sender unit plug screwed into the side of the inlet manifold. With the ignition 'on' the gauge should be at the cold mark. Then earth the lead to the engine block when the needle should indicate hot, at the opposite end of the scale. This test shows that the gauge on the dash is functioning properly. If it is not then it will need renewal. If there is still a fault in the system with this check completed satisfactorily, there will be a fault in the sender unit or the wire leading from it to the gauge. Renew these as necessary.

13 Fault finding - cooling system

Symptom	Reason/s	Remedy
Overheating		
Heat generated in cylinder not being successfully disposed of by radiator	Drivebelt slipping	Check tension.
	Insufficient water in cooling system	Top up radiator.
	Cooling fan inoperative	Overhaul or renew fan.
	Radiator core blocked or radiator grille restricted	Reverse flush radiator, remove obstruction.
	Bottom water hose collapsed, impeding flow	Remove and fit new hose.
	Thermostat not opening properly	Remove and fit new thermostat.
	Ignition advance and retard incorrectly set (accompanied by loss of power, and perhaps, misfiring)	Check and reset ignition timing.
	Carburettor(s) incorrectly adjusted (mixture too weak)	Tune carburettor(s).
	Exhaust system partially blocked	Check exhaust pipe for constrictive dents and blockages.
	Oil level in sump too low	Top up sump to full mark on dipstick.
	Blown cylinder head gasket (water/steam being forced down the radiator overflow pipe under pressure)	Remove cylinder head, fit new gasket.
	Engine not yet run-in	Run-in slowly and carefully.
	Brakes binding	Check and adjust brakes if necessary.
Underheating		
Too much heat being dispersed by radiator	Thermostat jammed open	Remove and renew thermostat.
	Incorrect grade of thermostat fitted allowing premature opening of valve	Remove and replace with new thermostat which opens at a higher temperature.
	Thermostat missing	Check and fit correct thermostat.
Loss of cooling water		
Leaks in system	Loose clips on water hoses	Check and tighten clips if necessary.
	Top, bottom, or by-pass water hoses perished or leaking	Check and renew any faulty hoses.
	Radiator core leaking	Remove radiator and repair.
	Thermostat gasket leaking	Inspect and renew gasket.
	Radiator cap seal ineffective	Renew radiator pressure cap seal.
	Blown cylinder head gasket (pressure in system forcing water/steam into expansion bottle)	Remove cylinder head and fit new gasket.
	Cylinder wall or head cracked	Dismantle engine, despatch to engineering works for repair.

Chapter 3 Carburation; fuel and exhaust systems

Contents

Specifications

Fuel pump

Type ...	Mechanical, driven from camshaft
Make ...	SEV
Pressure at zero output ...	200-300 m/bars (2.9-4.4 lb in^2)
Mean operating pressure ...	133 m/bars (1.9 lb in^2)

Carburettor type and data (Solex)

Engine type	**1294 cc single carb. (except Germany)**	**1294 cc single carb. (Germany only)**
Engine code ...	6 G 1	6 G 1D
From engine no. ...	67 400 021	67 530 021
Compression ratio ...	9.5 : 1	8.2 : 1
Carburettor make ...	Solex	Solex
Type ...	32 BISA 5	32 BISA 5
Ref no. ...	81	87
Choke tube ...	27	23
Main jet ...	140 ± 2.5	112 ± 2.5
Air correction jet ...	165 ± 5	185 ± 5
Emulsion tube ...	E7	E7

Econostat fuel jet	45	40
Idling fuel jet	39 to 45	39 to 45 with damper
Idling air jet	180	180
Progression holes	4 x 0.6	4 x 0.6
Pump injector	—	45
Pump stroke	3 mm	3 mm
Float needle	1.5	1.5
Float weight	5.7 g	5.7 g
Starting system	Strangler	Strangler
Fast idle gap (at throttle plate)	1.00 mm ± 0.05	1.05 mm ± 0.05
Constant CO circuit:		
Air intake aperture	500	500
Fuel calibration	30	30
Air calibration	100	100
CO content at idling	1 to 1.5%	1 to 1.5%

Carburettor type and data (Weber)

Engine type	**1294 cc 2 double choke carbs**		**1442 cc 1 double choke carb**	
Engine code	6 G 4		6 Y 2	
From engine no.	67 600 021		68 000 021	
Compression ratio	9.5 : 1		9.5 : 1	
Carburettor make	Weber		Weber	
Type	36 DCNF		36 DCNV	
Ref no.	49 - 50		2	
Choke tube	29	29	28	28
Secondary venturi	3.5 long	3.5 long	4.5 short	4.5 short
Main jet	125	125	132 ± 2.5	132 ± 2.5
Air correction jet	200 ± 15	200 ± 5	175 ± 5	175 ± 5
Emulsion tube	F 36	F 36	F 36	F 36
Idling fuel jet	45	45	40 - 42	40 - 42
Idling air jet	135 ± 15	135 ± 15	145 ± 5	145 ± 5
Progression holes	80-90-90-105	80-90-90-105	—	—
Pump injector	40	40	50	50
Pump bypass	40		—	
Float needle	1.75		1.75	
Float weight	20 g		20 g	
Float level	52 ± 0.25 mm		52 ± 0.25 mm	
Starting system	Manual		Strangler	
Air jet	250	250	—	—
Fuel jet	70	70	—	—
Emulsion tube	F 5	F 5	—	—
Fast idle gap	—	—	0.35 - 0.40 mm	
Vacuum kick opening	—	—	6.0 - 6.5 mm	
Mechanical opening	—	—	8.0 - 8.5 mm	
CO content at idling	1 to 1.5%		1 to 1.5%	

Idling speeds

1294 cc engine (single carb)	850 rpm
1294 cc engine (twin carbs)	900 rpm
1442 cc engine (single carb)	900 rpm

Torque wrench settings

	lb f ft	**kg f m**
Inlet manifold	10.0	1.38
Exhaust manifold nuts	14.5	2.01
Carburettor mounting flange nuts	14.5	2.01
Air cleaner securing bolts	9.5	1.31
Fuel pump to crankcase	10.5	1.45

1 General description

The basic components of the fuel system comprise, a rear mounted fuel tank, a mechanically driven fuel pump, and either a single or twin downdraught type carburettor with all the associated fuel pipes and controls.

Several types of fuel pumps have been fitted but they are all similar in operation and the removal and servicing procedure is basically the same.

The 1294 cc engine is fitted with either the single Solex carburettor or two twin choke Weber types. The 1442 cc engine is equipped with one twin choke Weber.

Each carburettor is carefully tested during production and the most suitable sized jets are selected for that carburettor and, in the case of the Weber type, the jets fitted to one barrel may differ in size to those of the other. Therefore when removing the jets a careful note must be made of which barrel they belong to.

The inlet manifold is water heated on all models and the Solex carburettors have a water heated flange to improve fuel atomization.

2 Air cleaner - description and servicing

1 All models are fitted with a renewable paper element air filter housed in a plastic casing on top of the engine which is retained by a quick-release strap.

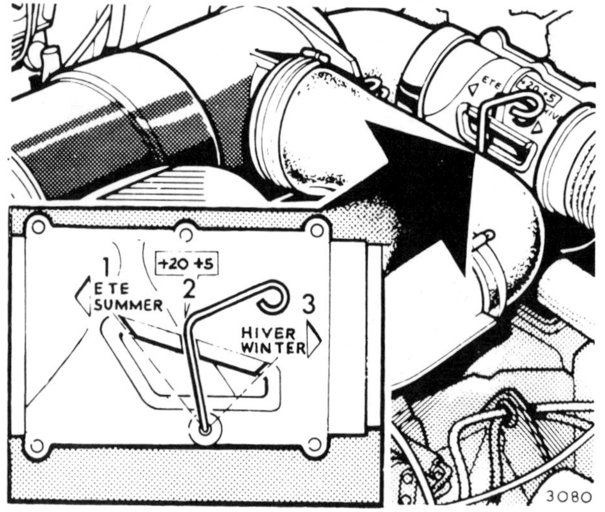

Fig. 3.1. Air inlet temperature control lever

1 Summer position
2 Mid position
3 Winter position

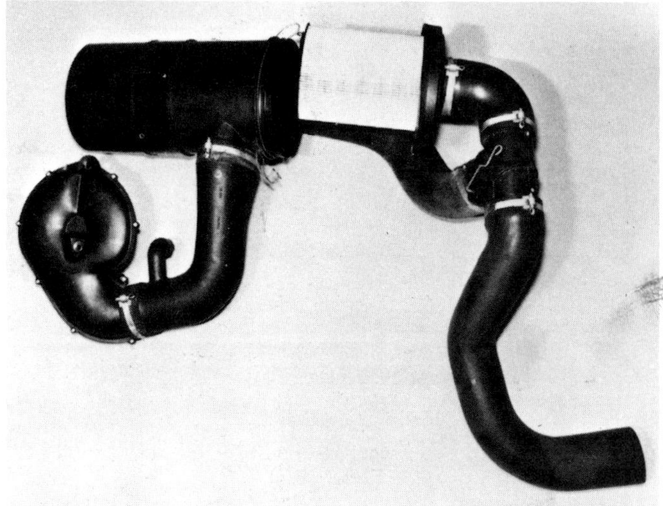

2.6 Air cleaner assembly complete with Solex adaptor

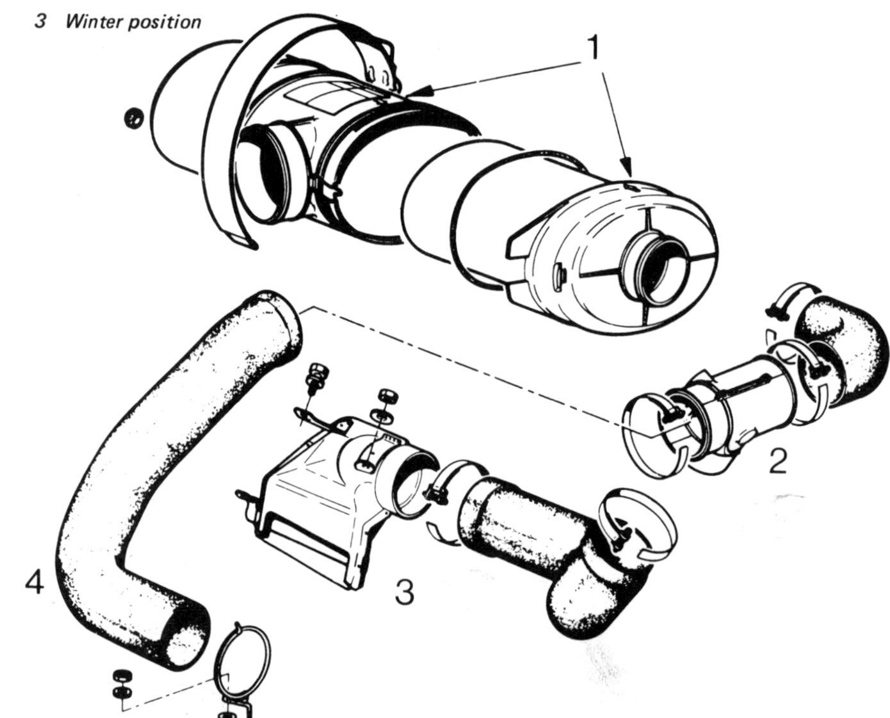

Fig. 3.2. Air cleaner components

1 Alignment marks *2 Temperature control duct* *3 Hot air pick-up duct* *4 Cool air hose*

2 The temperature of the air entering the air cleaner can be controlled by means of a SUMMER(ETE)/WINTER(HIVER) selector lever on the intake duct (see Fig. 3.1). In the 'summer' position cold air is drawn into the air cleaner assembly via a hose leading in from the front wing, while the 'winter' position allows air to be drawn in through a hot air duct fitted over the exhaust manifold.

3 To renew the filter element, disconnect the inlet hose from the end cover, release the spring clips and withdraw the end cover complete with filter element (See Fig. 3.2).

4 The end cover is integral with the filter element and the complete assembly must be discarded.

5 When fitting the new filter and end cover, ensure that the arrows on top of the cover and filter housing are in alignment before fastening the clips and refitting the intake hose.

6 To remove the complete filter housing assembly, remove the intake and outlet hoses, release the large retaining strap and lift the filter assembly away from the engine (photo).

7 Three different carburettor-to-air cleaner adaptors are used depending on the carburettor(s) fitted.

8 To remove the adaptor on all models, first remove the complete air cleaner as previously described. Disconnect the inlet hose from the adaptor and remove the fume extractor hose if fitted.

9 On the 1294 cc engine remove the nuts securing the adaptor to the carburettor(s), lift the adaptor off the studs and retrieve the sealing ring (single carburettor) or two gaskets (twin carburettors).

10 In the case of the 1442 engines, release the seven clips securing the two halves of the adaptor together and prise off the top half. Remove the retaining nuts, lift off the bottom half and retrieve the gasket and stiffener plate (Fig. 3.3).).

11 Refit the adaptor assemblies using the reverse procedure to that of removal. On the 1442 cc engine ensure that the seal is correctly fitted between the two halves of the adaptor.

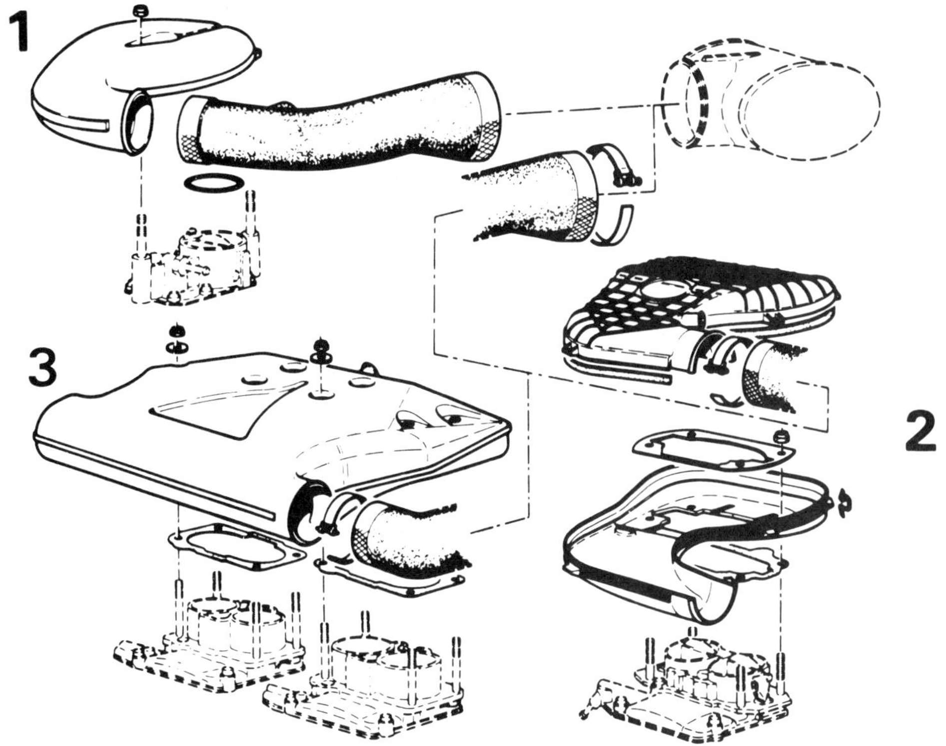

Fig. 3.3. Carburettor adaptor assemblies

1 Solex *2 Single Weber* *3 Twin Weber*

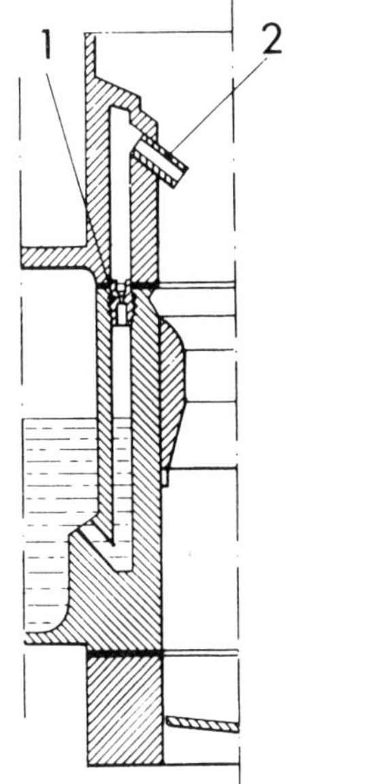

Fig. 3.4. Sectional view of Solex carburettor

1 Econostat jet
2 Econostat discharge nozzle
3 Fuel filter
4 Fuel needle valve
5 Fuel float
6 Idling jet
7 Idling air bleed (calibrated drilling)
8 Choke plate
9 Choke plate by-pass valve
10 Emulsion tube and air correction jet
11 Accelerator pump discharge nozzle
12 Venturi (choke tube)
13 Accelerator pump diaphragm
14 Accelerator pump lever
15 Pre-heater water connections
16 Throttle plate
17 Idling mixture adjustment screw
18 Main jet
19 Accelerator pump non-return valve

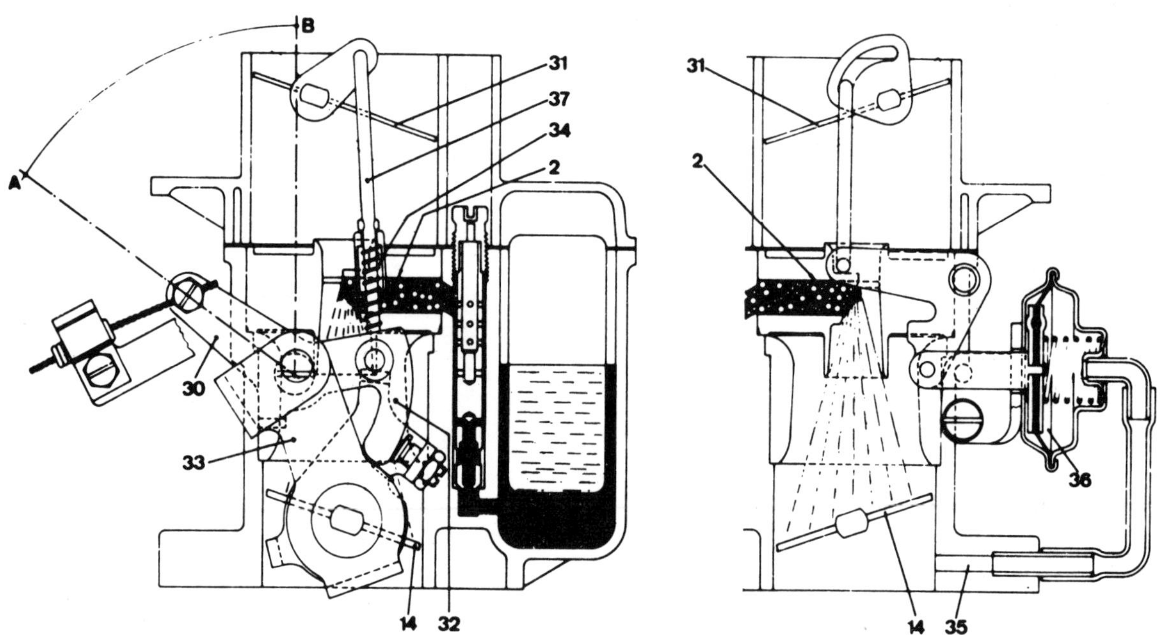

Fig. 3.5. Choke operation of Weber single carburettor (type 36DCNV). Refer to Section 3 for key details.

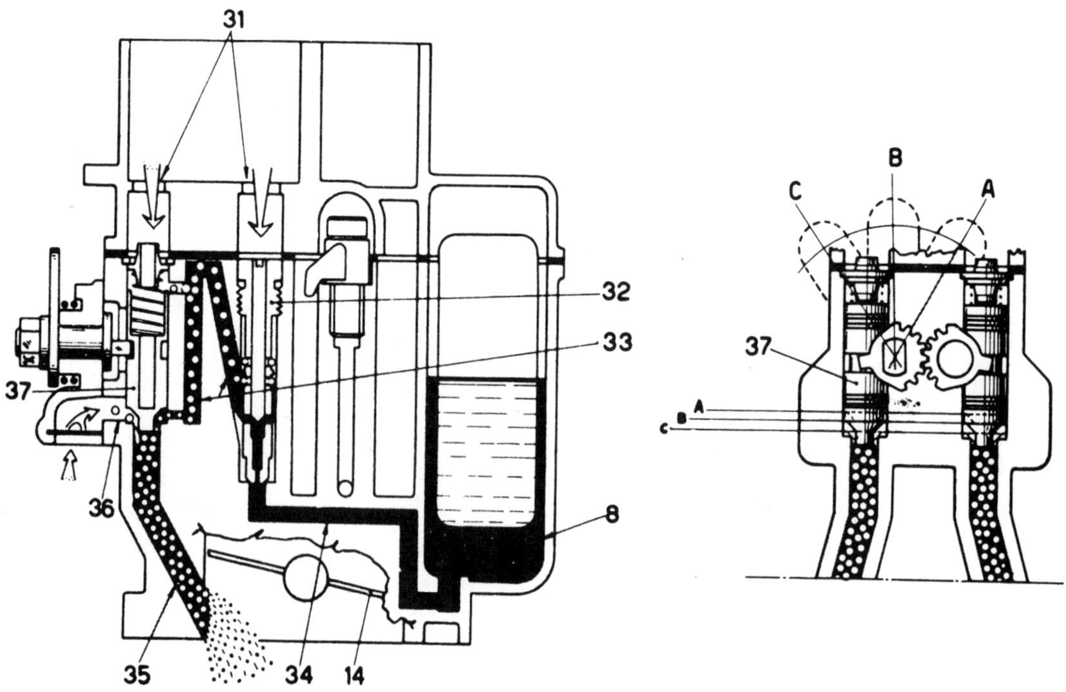

Fig. 3.6. Choke operation of Weber twin carburettor (type 36DCNF). Refer to Section 3 for key details.

3 Carburettors - description and operation

1 Three types of carburettor are used with the engines covered by this manual (see Specifications for engine/carburettor type). These comprise, the Solex 32 BISA 5, the Weber 36 DCNV and the Weber 36 DCNF. The 36 DCNV type is used on single carburettor models and the 36 DCNF is used on the twin carburettor versions. Both the Weber types are very similar in construction, the main difference being in the type of choke mechanism used.
2 The Solex carburettor is shown in sectional form in Fig. 3.4.
3 It comprises three main units, the throttle block, the main body and the top cover. The throttle block embodies the throttle plate and control assembly and incorporates a water heated jacket connected to the engine cooling system to provide pre-heating of the carburettor.
4 The main body incorporates the choke tube, float chamber, accelerator pump and the jets, also the distributor vacuum and crankcase breather connections.
5 The top cover comprises the starting plate assembly, needle valve, inlet connection and filter and the econostat discharge nozzle.
6 The starting device comprises a choke plate fitted with a bypass valve and a fast idle connecting link to the throttle control arm.
7 The accelerator pedal is connected to the throttle spindle which in turn actuates the accelerator pump to discharge neat fuel into the choke tube when accelerating hard.
8 The econostat device operates from the air intake flow and comes into action at high engine speeds only, to provide a rich mixture at full load conditions.
9 The twin type carburettors (Weber DCNF) fitted to the 1294 cc engine are of twin choke downdraught design with manually operated choke. Each choke tube supplies one engine cylinder and the twin carburettors therefore provide the effect of four individual units.
10 The carburettors are identical in construction but the throttle control layout varies between left- and right-hand units.
11 The throttle and cold start controls are both connected to one carburettor but the design of the control arms permits synchronising of the two carburettors and the individual cold-start devices are interconnected.
12 As stated previously the single Weber carburettor is virtually identical to the type used on the twin carburettor installation with the exception of the choke mechanism. The following paragraphs describe the various operating cycles of the Weber type carburettors.
13 *Choke in operation (single carburettor Fig. 3.5).* The choke valves (31) are offset on the spindle. A lever on one end of the spindle is connected to another lever (30) operated by the choke control knob and a lever on the other end of the spindle is connected to the vacuum kick diaphragm (36). When the choke valves are closed by the spring loaded rod (37), the cam (32) on the operating lever opens the throttle valves (14) a pre-set amount. When the starter motor is operated a rich mixture is drawn from the main discharge passage (2) in the secondary venturi. When the manifold depression increases as the engine starts, the vacuum kick valve assists the operation of the choke valves via the passage (35) and control linkage.
14 *Choke in operation (twin carburettors Fig. 3.6).* Fuel from the bowl (8) passes through channels (34) and jets (32) and is emulsified by air from the holes (31). The fuel reaches the valve seat (37) through the channels (33) and again emulsified by air from the holes (36). It flows through channels (35) into the area below the butterfly valve (14).
15 *Idling and progression (Fig. 3.7).* The fuel flows to the idling jets (19) through the channels (18) and emulsified with air supplied through the jets (15). The volume of air admitted is regulated by adjustment of the idling screws (20). The fuel then passes through channels (17) and holes (16) to the tubes located below the butterfly valve (14). From idling, as the butterfly valves (14) are opened progressively, the mixture reaches the tubes and flows through the progression holes (13) so enabling the engine speed to be increased progressively.
16 *Normal running at constant throttle opening (Fig. 3.8).* The fuel flows through the needle valve (12) towards the bowl (8) where the float (9) pivoted on the spindle (10) regulates the position of the inlet needle valve (11) and so maintains a pre-determined level of fuel in the bowl. The fuel then passes through jets (7) to the wells (6). It then mixes with air from the emulsion tubes (5) and correction jets (1) and as a vapour passes through holes (2) to reach the carburation area formed by the venturi components (3) and (4).
17 *Accelerator pump (Fig. 3.9).* The action of the pump is twofold.

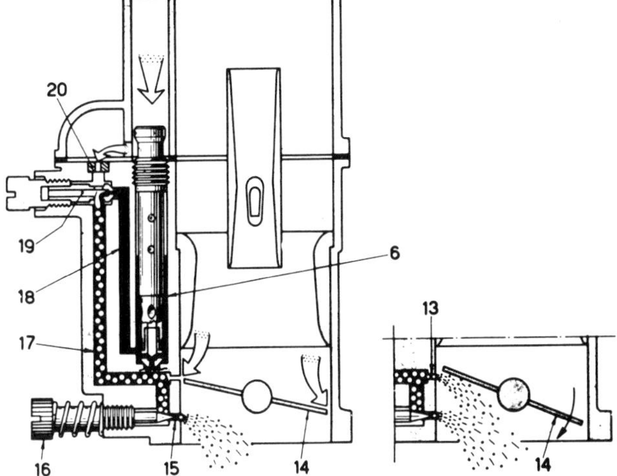

Fig. 3.7. Idling and progression cycle of Weber carburettors (see Section 3 for key details)

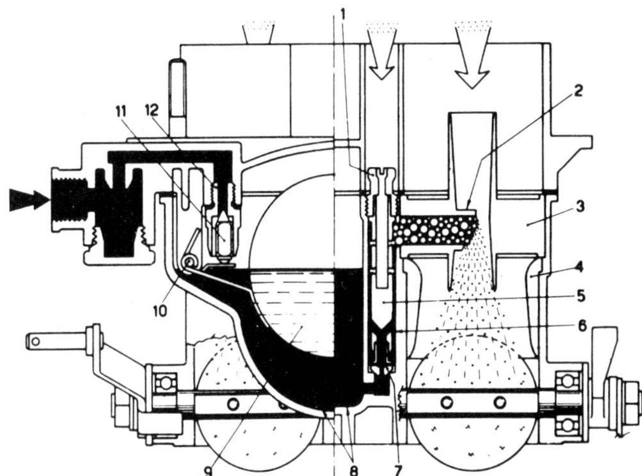

Fig. 3.8. Normal running cycle of Weber carburettors (see Section 3 for key details)

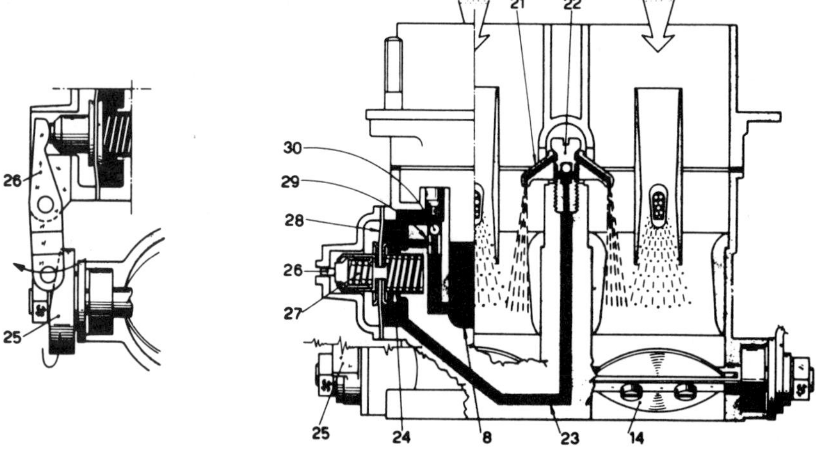

Fig. 3.9. Function of accelerator pump in Weber carburettors (See Section 3 for key details)

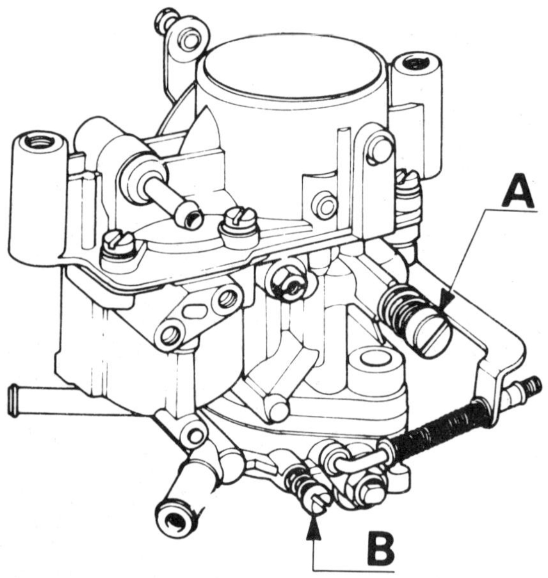

Fig. 3.10. Solex carburettor adjustment screws

A Volume screw *B Mixture screw*

5.2 Accelerator and choke cable connections on the Solex carburettor

When the butterfly valve (14) is being closed, the lever (26) releases the diaphragm (28) which, due to the effect of the spring (24) draws fuel by suction from the bowl (8) through the ball valve (30). As the butterfly valve is being opened by means of the cam (25) and lever (26) the diaphragm (28) ejects fuel into the carburettor tubes (23) through the valve (22) and the jets (21). The spring (27) dampens the action of the butterfly valve and so extends the period of fuel injection. Excess fuel from the accelerator pump is returned to the carburettor bowl together with the fumes from the pump chamber through the calibrated hole (29).

4 Solex carburettor - idling adjustment

1 The carburettor is carefully adjusted at the factory using precision tuning equipment and the settings will not normally require any adjustment.
2 The only adjustment that may be necessary is setting the idling speed by means of the volume screw and mixture screw (see Fig. 3.10).
3 Before setting the idling adjustment, check the following for condition and adjustment. The ignition timing, valve clearances, sparking plugs, air cleaner, fuel pump screen and the ease of operation of the accelerator control mechanism.
4 The most satisfactory method of adjusting the idling speed of the engine is by connecting a vacuum gauge to the inlet manifold. With the engine running at normal operating temperature, adjust the mixture and speed screws until the gauge needle indicates maximum depression.
5 If a vacuum gauge is not available, first run the engine until it reaches normal operating temperature.
6 Connect a tachometer to the engine and turn the volume control screw in or out as necessary to achieve the idling speed given in the Specifications.
7 Next turn the mixture control screw in or out to obtain the highest possible engine idling speed.
8 Finally, reset the idling speed to the correct speed by readjusting the volume control screw.

5 Solex carburettors - removal and refitting

1 Remove the air cleaner and adaptor assembly as described in Section 2 and retain the rubber sealing ring.
2 Disconnect the choke and accelerator cables (photo).
3 Disconnect the vacuum advance pipe and fuel supply pipe.
4 Remove the filler cap from the expansion bottle and partially drain the cooling system.
5 Disconnect the two water hoses from their throttle block connections and plug both hoses to prevent loss of coolant.
6 Unscrew and remove the two carburettor securing nuts and lockwashers, lift off the carburettor and peel off the gasket.
7 Refitting is a reversal of removal but use a new flange gasket and check the satisfactory operation of the choke and accelerator cables.
8 Top up the cooling system expansion bottle if required.

6 Solex carburettors - setting and adjustment of components

1 *Float level.* Incorrect setting will be indicated by flooding or fuel leakage at the carburettor or evidence of fuel starvation causing stalling or loss of power of the engine.
2 Remove the air cleaner and disconnect the fuel pipe and choke cable from the carburettor.
3 Disconnect the fast idle link from the throttle control arm.
4 Remove the retaining screws and lift off the carburettor top cover.
5 Invert the top cover so that the float arm rests against the fuel inlet needle valve.
6 Use a small rule and measure the distance between the cover mating face of the carburettor and the upper edge of the float collar (Fig. 3.11).
7 The correct distance is 0.5315 to 0.6496 in (13.5 to 16.5 mm) and should be adjusted, if necessary, by gently bending the float operating arm.
8 Flooding of fuel from the float chamber may sometimes be caused by the needle valve housing not being fully tightened in its seat or a damaged sealing washer. Fuel would, in these circumstances, enter the float chamber without passing through the needle valve orifice.
9 *Accelerator pump stroke.* This adjustment will necessitate removal of the carburettor from the manifold. Invert the carburettor and close the throttle butterfly valve. To ensure complete closure, the idling speed adjustment screw will have to be unscrewed.
10 Pull the accelerator pump operating lever fully back gently and, using twist drills, test the distance between the edge of the butterfly valve plate and the choke tube wall. A 4 mm twist drill should just slide between the throttle valve and body (Fig. 3.12).
11 If the clearance is found to be incorrect, adjust the accelerator pump control rod.
12 *Throttle butterfly valve plate, fast idle setting.* This adjustment will again require removal of the carburettor. Invert the carburettor and close the butterfly valve plate.
13 Pull the choke plate to the fully closed position and check the clearance between the edge of the plate and the choke tube wall.
14 Again using twist drills as gauges, a 1 mm diameter drill should pass through but a 1.1 mm drill should not.
15 Where the clearance is incorrect, adjust the fast idle screw as necessary (Fig. 3.13).

7 Solex carburettors - dismantling, servicing and reassembly

1 Disconnect the fast idle link (9) (Fig. 3.14).
2 Remove the top cover securing screws and remove the cover and gasket.
3 Remove the fuel filter retaining plug (15) and extract the filter (14).
4 Unscrew and remove the fuel inlet valve (5) and retain the sealing washer.
5 If absolutely necessary, the choke plate (3) and spindle (4) may be removed after removal of the two retaining screws and the spindle circlip.
6 Disconnect the accelerator pump operating rod (13).
7 Remove the two screws which secure the throttle block to the carburettor body.
8 Withdraw the throttle block and gasket, (and spacer if fitted).
9 If absolutely necessary, the throttle spindle (17) and throttle valve plate (10) may be removed after unscrewing the spindle nut and the two plate retaining screws.
10 Remove the float (6) and unscrew the various jets.
11 Remove the four securing screws from the accelerator pump cover assembly (12) and withdraw the diaphragm and return spring.
12 With the carburettor now dismantled, clean the components in clean fuel. Blow out the jets using air from a tyre pump; never probe with wire.
13 Examine the spindles and their housing bores for wear and slackness in operation. If this is evident then it will be realistic to exchange the complete unit for a reconditioned one on an exchange basis.
14 Check the jet sizes and other calibrated components against the

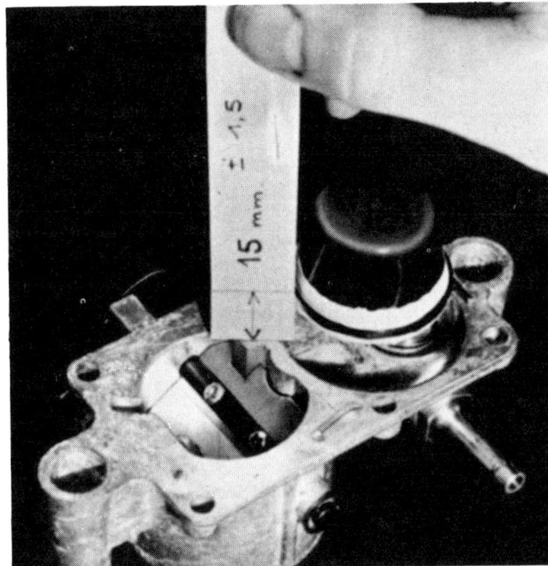

Fig. 3.11. Checking the float position on the Solex carburettor

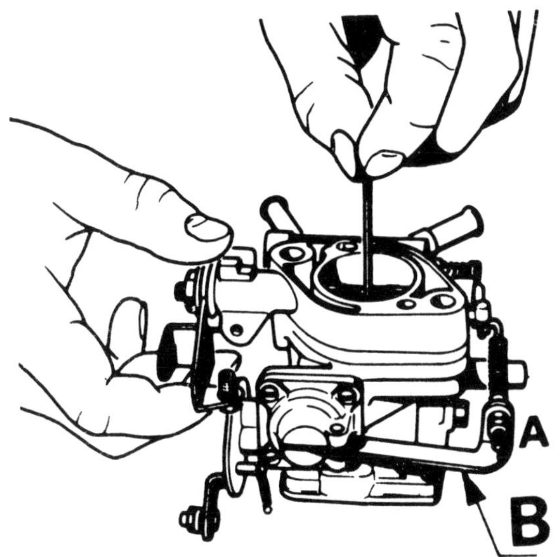

Fig. 3.12. Setting the accelerator pump stroke on the Solex carburettor

A Adjusting nut *B Pump lever*

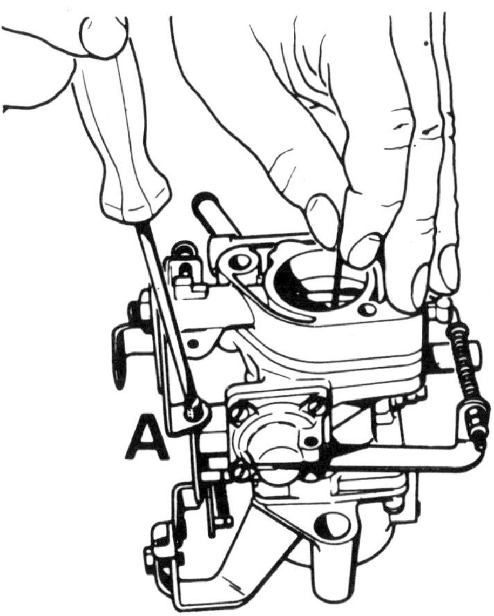

Fig. 3.13. Setting the fast idle adjusting screw 'A' (Solex)

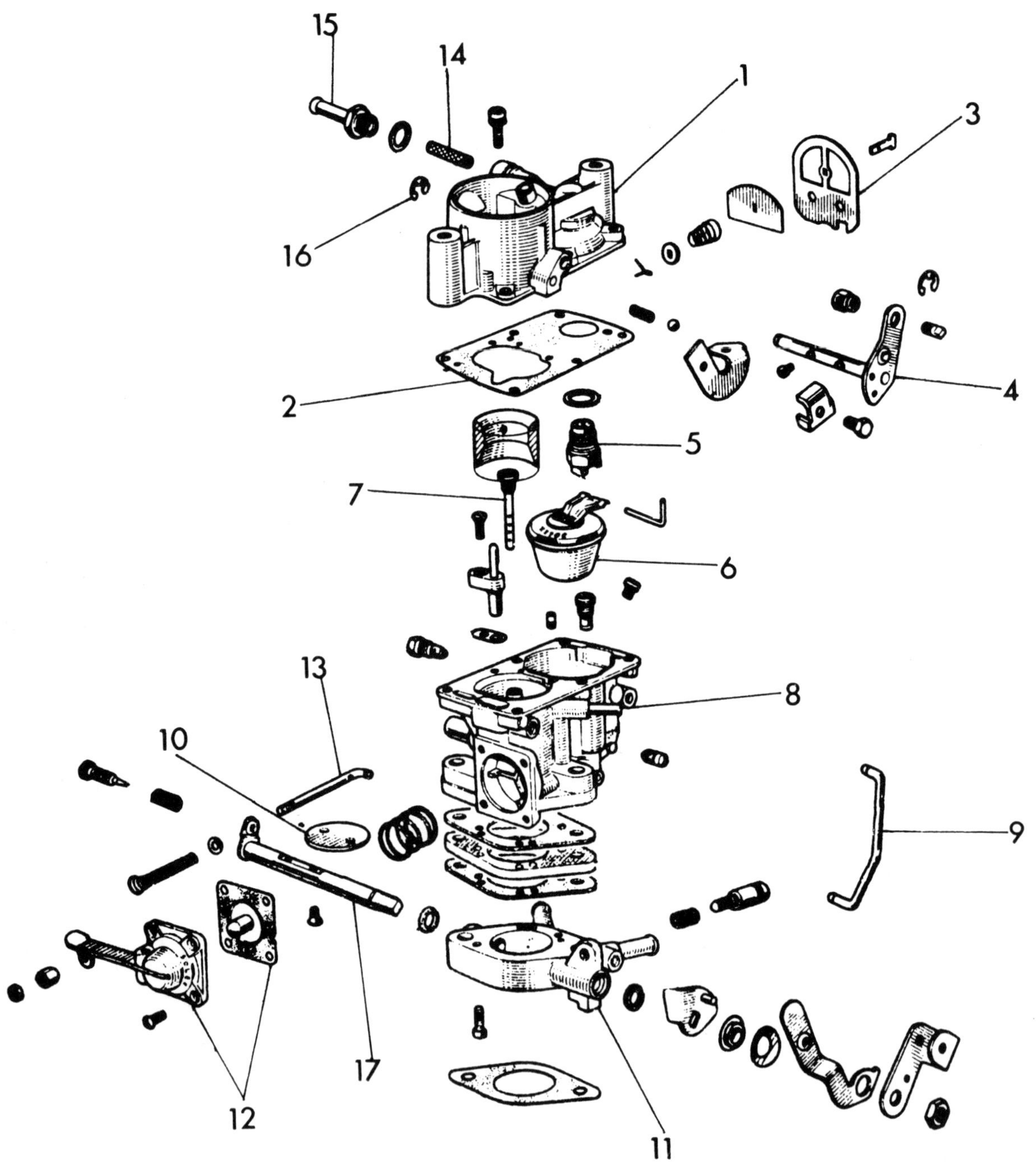

Fig. 3.14. Exploded view of Solex carburettor

1 Top cover
2 Cover gasket
3 Choke plate
4 Choke spindle
5 Inlet valve
6 Float
7 Air correction jet
8 Body
9 Fast idle link
10 Throttle plate
11 Water heated throttle block
12 Accelerator pump assembly
13 Accelerator pump operating rod
14 Filter
15 Inlet tube and filter retaining plug
16 Choke spindle circlip
17 Throttle spindle

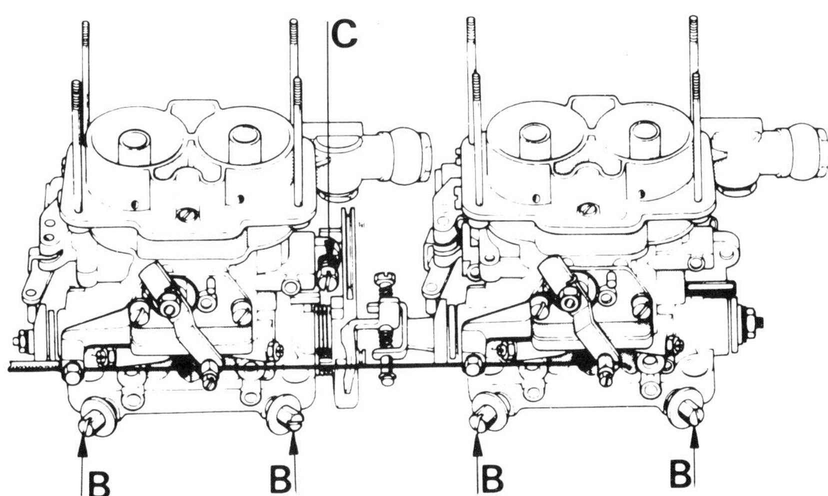

Fig. 3.15. Idling adjustment control screws (Twin Weber installation)

B Idling mixture screw
C Throttle stop screw

specification listed at the beginning of this Chapter and renew any that have previously been incorrectly substituted.

15 Obtain a repair kit which will contain a complete set of new gaskets and washers and other essential items.

16 Reassembly is a reversal of dismantling but remember to check the various settings and adjustments as described in the preceding Section. Use all the items found in the repair kit and refit the original sealing washer beneath the inlet valve housing. Any alteration in the washer will affect the fuel level in the carburettor bowl.

8 Weber (twin) carburettors - idling, adjustment and synchronisation

1 Before adjusting the carburettors, run through the check list given in Section 4.

2 The flow rates through the balancing channels are set in production and the screws 10, 11, 12 and 13 should not be altered, Fig. 3.16.

3 With the engine at normal operating temperature, set the idling speed adjustment screw (C) in Fig. 3.15, so that the engine idling speed is set to the figure given in the Specifications.

4 Screw the first mixture control screw (B) in Fig. 3.15 in or out until the engine speed is the highest obtainable. Adjust the idling speed screw so that the engine again runs at approximately 900 rpm.

5 Repeat the sequence of operations with each of the other mixture control screws (B) in turn.

6 Test check the four screws again to obtain the best balance at the required engine speed and note that screw number (9) will require unscrewing two turns more than the others to achieve the best idling adjustment as there is an additional air flow connection to its internal passage.

7 With the mixture control screws now correctly set, the units must be synchronised. To do this it is preferable to obtain one of the several proprietary balancing devices which indicate (visually) correct synchronisation of twin carburettor installations. This is achieved simply by balancing the intake suction of each carburettor by locating the device in the intake of each carburettor in rotation and turning the screw (5) (Fig. 3.16) until the correct readings are obtained. An alternative method of synchronising is to place a length of hose in each of the carburettor intakes in turn and attempt to match the 'hiss' from each carburettor. At best this is a temporary expedient until more precise tuning can be carried out.

9 Weber (single) carburettor - idling adjustment

1 Adjust the idling mixture control screws (two only) in a similar manner to that already described for the twin carburettor installation.

2 No synchronisation will of course, be required.

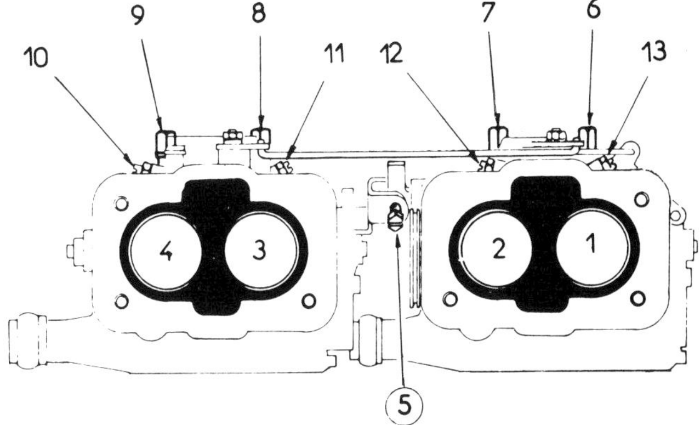

Fig. 3.16. Adjustments screws (Twin Weber installation)

1 to 4 Carburettor throats
5 Synchronising screw
6 to 9 Idling mixture adjustment screws
10 to 13 Fuel flow rate control screws (not to be altered

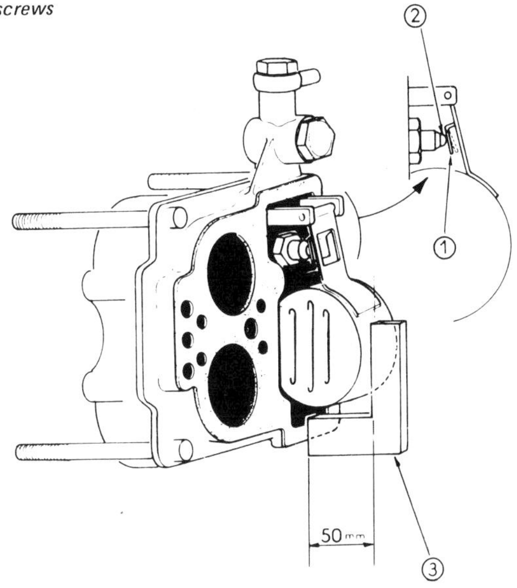

Fig. 3.17. Checking the float position (Weber carburettors)

1 Float arm tab
2 Needle valve
3 Measuring tool

10 Weber carburettors - removal and refitting

1 Remove the air cleaner and adaptor assembly as described in Section 2 and retain the gasket(s).
2 Disconnect the choke and accelerator control cables.
3 Disconnect the vacuum advance pipe and fuel supply pipe.
4 Remove the carburettor retaining nuts and lift the carburettor(s) away from the manifold studs. On the twin carburettor installation, disengage the throttle control linkage by pulling the two carburettors away from each other.
5 Remove the heat insulators and gaskets and place a piece of clean cloth in the manifold aperture(s) to prevent any dirt getting in.
6 Refitting is a reversal of removal but use new flange gaskets and check that the choke and accelerator controls operate correctly.

11 Weber carburettors - setting and adjustment of components

1 *Float level adjustment.* This may be required where there is evidence of flooding or fuel starvation.
2 Remove the carburettor and detach the cover. With the carburettor body in the altitude shown in Fig. 3.17 and the tab (1) in contact with the fuel inlet valve ball, the distance between the exposed surface of the gasket and the outside face of the float should be as specified.
3 Where this dimension varies from that specified, bend the tab to rectify.

12 Weber carburettors - dismantling, servicing and reassembling

1 Refer to Fig. 3.19.
2 Unscrew and remove the cover securing screws and withdraw the lid and gasket.
3 Remove the float arm pivot pin and withdraw the float (6).
4 Unscrew and remove the inlet needle valve and its housing retaining the sealing washer located beneath it.
5 Remove the filter plug (14) and withdraw the filter (15).
6 Remove the venturis (19) from the carburettor body.
7 Unscrew the jets and adjusting screws (not flow rate screws see Fig. 3.15).
8 Disconnect the link from the choke control arm (20) and the starting device operating lever. Remove the retaining screw and detach the choke control arm.
9 On the type 36 DCNF (twin carburettors), remove the retaining screws and the starting device cover (21).
10 The starting device piston assembly (13) may be dismantled after removal of the retaining circlip (22).
11 Remove the four retaining screws from the accelerator pump assembly cover (7).
12 Withdraw the diaphragm (23) and return spring (24).

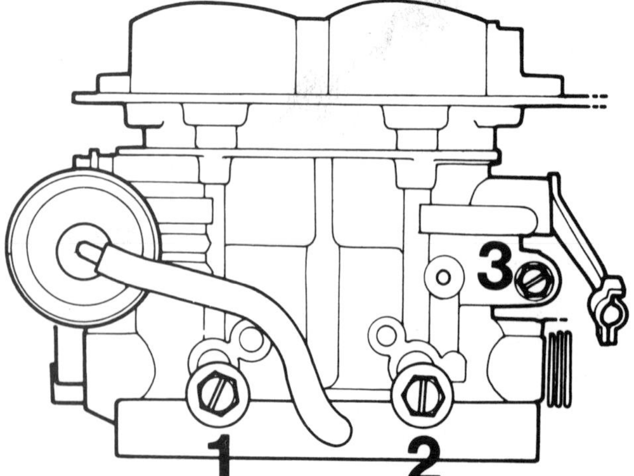

Fig. 3.18. Idling adjustment control screws (Single Weber carburettor)

1 Mixture screw, left-hand barrel
2 Mixture screw, right-hand barrel
3 Throttle stop screw

13 Dismantle the throttle plate and spindle only if essential. The throttle plate may be slid from its locating slot after the two retaining screws have been removed.
14 Having dismantled the carburettor into its components, carefully inspect them for wear, damage or distortion and renew as appropriate. If there are any cracks in the carburettor body exchange the complete unit for a reconditioned one.
15 Blow all jets clear with air from a tyre pump, never probe with wire.
16 Obtain a repair kit, specifying carefully the exact carburettor type number.
17 Reassembly is a reversal of dismantling, use the new components and gaskets supplied in the repair kit and carry out the settings and adjustments described in the preceding Section.
18 When the carburettor is refitted to the engine, carry out the idling (and synchronising if applicable) adjustments as described in Sections 8 and 9.
19 Do not screw the mixture control screws fully home or damage to their seating may result. Do not alter the thickness of the inlet needle valve seating washer and check that the chamfer on the throttle plate is fitted so that it seals against the choke tube when closed.

13 Fuel pump - routine maintenance

1 Detach the fuel supply hose from the fuel pump and plug the hose to prevent loss of fuel.
2 Unscrew the cover retaining screw and remove the cover from the pump.
3 Withdraw the filter screen and wash it in petrol.
4 Remove all traces of dirt and sediment from the interior of the pump chamber.
5 Refit the filter screen, check that the cover gasket is in good condition. If it is not, renew it. Fit the cover but do not use excessive force on the retaining screw.
6 Reconnect the fuel line, start the engine and check for leaks.

14 Fuel pump - removal and refitting

1 Disconnect the fuel supply line from the pump and plug the line to prevent loss of fuel.
2 Disconnect the fuel lines between the pump and carburettor.
3 Unscrew and remove the two pump securing bolts and remove the pump, noting the insulating and sealing washers, fitted between the pump flange and the cylinder block.
4 Withdraw the pump in a downward direction so that the pump actuating arm can be extracted from between the crankcase wall and the camshaft.
5 Refitting is a reversal of removal but check the location and condition of the flange washers.
Note: The fuel pump cannot be dismantled for repair, and if faulty must be renewed.

15 Fuel system - fault finding

There are three main types of fault to which the fuel system is prone. They may be summarised as follows:

a) Lack of fuel at engine
b) Weak mixture
c) Rich mixture.

16 Lack of fuel at engine

1 If it is not possible to start the engine, first check that there is fuel in the tank, and then check the ignition system as detailed in Chapter 4. If the fault is not in the ignition system then disconnect the fuel inlet pipe from the carburettor and turn the engine over by the starter relay switch.
2 If petrol squirts from the end of the inlet pipe, reconnect the pipe and check that the fuel is getting to the float chamber. This is done by unscrewing the bolts from the top of the float chamber, and lifting the

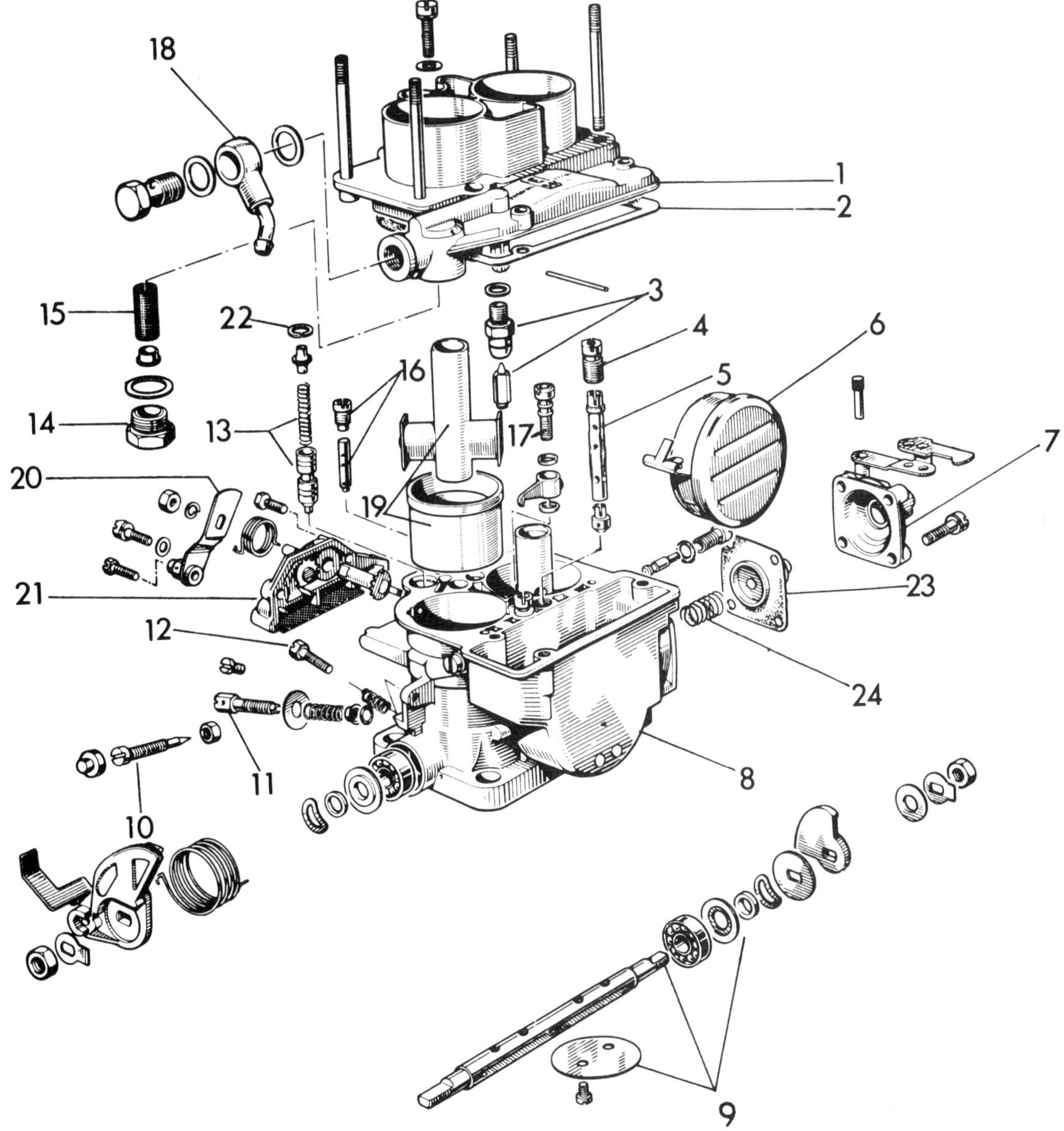

Fig. 3.19. Exploded view of Weber type 36DCNF carburettor. (Weber type 36DCNV is similar except for choke details)

1 *Cover*
2 *Gasket*
3 *Inlet needle valve*
4 *Main air correction jet*
5 *Emulsion tube*
6 *Float*
7 *Accelerator pump*
8 *Body*
9 *Throttle spindle butterfly*
10 *Flow rate screw*
11 *Idling mixture screw*
12 *Idling speed screw*
13 *Starting device piston*
14 *Filter plug*
15 *Filter*
16 *Starting fuel jet*
17 *Pump discharge valve*
18 *Fuel inlet coupling*
19 *Venturi*
20 *Choke control arm*
21 *Starting device cover*
22 *Circlip (starting device piston*
23 *Accelerator pump diaphragm*
24 *Accelerator pump return spring*

cover just enough to see inside.

3 If fuel is there then it is likely that there is a blockage in the starting jet, which should be removed and cleaned.

4 No fuel in the float chamber, is caused either by a blockage in the pipe between the pump and float chamber or a sticking float chamber valve. Alternatively on the Weber carburettor the gauze filter at the top of the float chamber may be blocked. Remove the securing nut and check that the filter is clean. Washing in petrol will clean it.

5 If it is decided that it is the float chamber valve that is sticking, remove the fuel inlet pipe, and undo the screws and lift the cover, complete with valve and floats, away.

6 Remove the valve needle and valve and thoroughly wash them in petrol. Petrol gum may be present on the valve or valve needle and this is usually the cause of a sticking valve. Refit the valve in the needle valve assembly, ensure that it is moving freely, and then reassemble the float chamber. It is important that the same washer be placed under the needle valve assembly as this determines the height of the floats and therefore the level of petrol in the chamber.

7 Reconnect the fuel pipe and refit the air cleaner.

8 If petrol does not squirt from the end of the pipe leading to the carburettor then disconnect the pipe leading to the inlet side of the fuel pump. If fuel runs out of the pipe then there is a fault in the fuel pump, and the pump should be checked as detailed in Section 14.

9 No fuel flowing from the tank when it is known that there is fuel in there indicates a blocked pipe line. The line to the tank should be blown out. It is unlikely that the fuel tank vent would become blocked, but this could be a reason for the reluctance of the fuel to flow. To test for this, blow into the tank down the filler orifice. There should be no build up of pressure in the fuel tank, as the excess pressure should be carried away down the vent pipe.

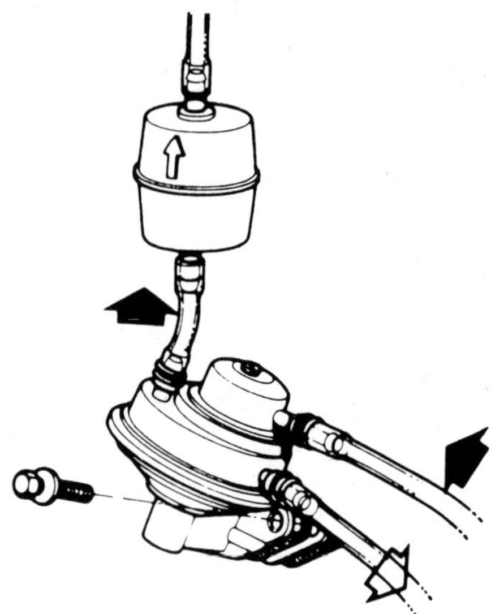
Fig. 3.20. Fuel pump assembly (arrows indicate fuel flow)

17 Weak mixture

1 If the fuel/air mixture is weak there are six main clues to this condition:

a) *The engine will be difficult to start and will need much use of the choke, stalling easily if the choke is pushed in.*
b) *The engine will overheat easily.*
c) *If the spark plugs are examined (as detailed in Chapter 4), they will have a light grey/white deposit on the insulator nose.*
d) *The fuel consumption may be light.*
e) *There will be a noticeable lack of power.*
f) *During acceleration and on the overrun there will be a certain amount of spitting back through the carburettor.*

2 As the carburettors are of the fixed jet type, these faults are invariably due to circumstances outside the carburettor. The only usual fault likely in the carburettor is that one or more of the jets may be partially blocked. If the car will not start easily but runs well at speed, then it is likely that the starting jet is blocked, whereas if the engine starts easily but will not rev, then it is likely that the main jets are blocked.
3 If the level of petrol in the float chamber is low this is usually due to a sticking valve or incorrectly set floats.
4 Air leaks either in the fuel lines, or in the induction system, should also be checked for. Also check the distributor vacuum pipe connection as a leak in this is directly felt in the inlet manifold.
5 The fuel pump may be at fault as has already been detailed.

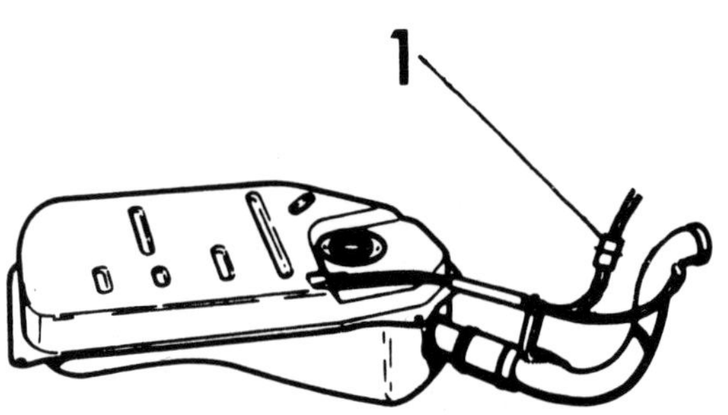

Fig. 3.21. Fuel tank and vent pipe (1)

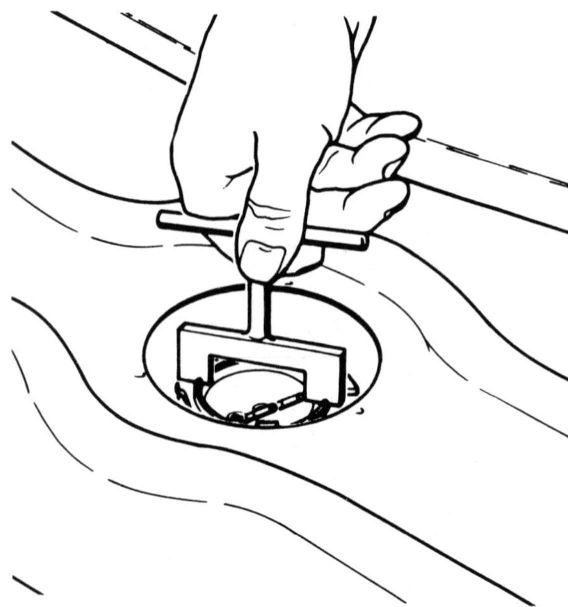
Fig. 3.22. Removing the fuel tank transmitter unit

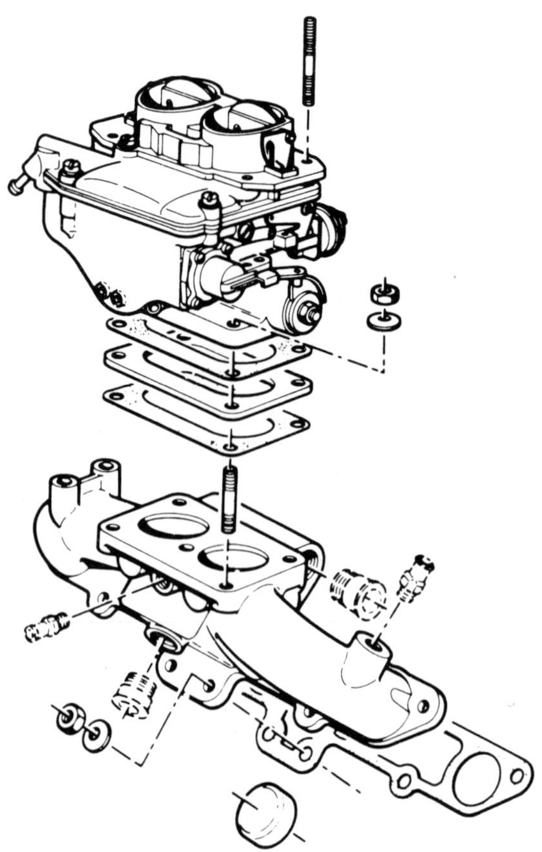
Fig. 3.23. Inlet manifold for single Weber carburettor

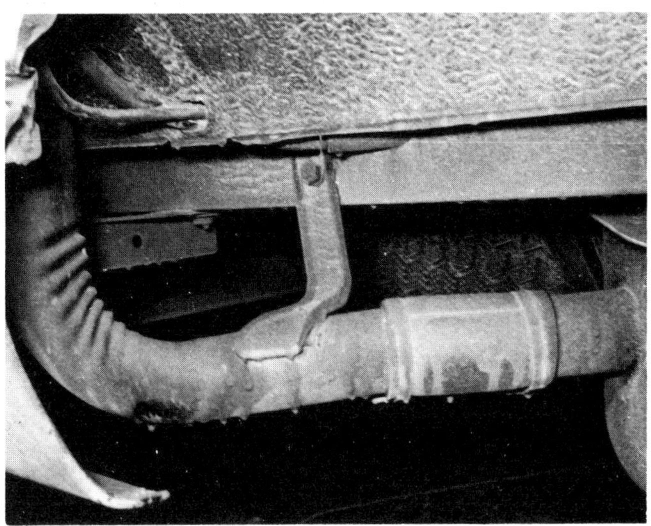

19.9 Fuel tank filler pipe

20.6 Rear flexible strap holding the centre pipe and tailpipe in position

18 Rich mixture

1 If the fuel/air mixture is rich there are also six main clues to this condition:

a) If the spark plugs are examined they will be found to have a black sooty deposit on the insulator nose.
b) The fuel consumption will be heavy.
c) The exhaust will give off black smoke, especially when accelerating.
d) The interior deposits on the exhaust pipe will be dry, black and sooty (if they are wet, black and sooty this indicates worn bores, and oil is being burnt).
e) There will be a noticeable lack of power.
f) There will be a certain amount of back-firing through the exhaust system.

2 The faults in this case are usually in the carburettor and most usual is that the level of petrol in the float chamber is too high. This is due either to dirt behind the needle valve, or a leaking float which will not close the valve properly, or a sticking needle.
3 With very high mileages (or because someone has tried to clean the jets out with wire), it may be that the jets have become enlarged.
4 If the air correction jets are restricted in any way the mixture will tend to become very rich.
5 Occasionally it is found that the choke control is sticking or has been maladjusted.
6 Again, occasionally, the fuel pump pressure may be excessive so forcing the needle valve open slightly until a higher level of petrol is reached in the float chamber.

19 Fuel tank and transmitter unit - removal, servicing and refitting

1 The pressed steel fuel tank is located beneath the rear floor section of the vehicle.
2 The air vent pipe is fitted with an expansion device to reduce the possibility of fuel blowback if the tank is filled too quickly.
3 The fuel gauge transmitter unit is fitted to the top of the tank and can be detached without having to remove the fuel tank from the car.
4 To remove the complete fuel tank assembly, first disconnect the battery earth terminal and remove the spare wheel from beneath the vehicle.
5 Pull back the luggage compartment mat, remove the fuel tank access cover securing screws and lift away the cover.
6 Make a note of the colour and position of the two wires and disconnect them from the transmitter unit.
7 From beneath the car remove the clip securing the wiring harness to the rear of the fuel tank.
8 Place a clean container beneath the fuel tank outlet pipe, disconnect the pipe and drain the tank. Note that on some models there is a fuel

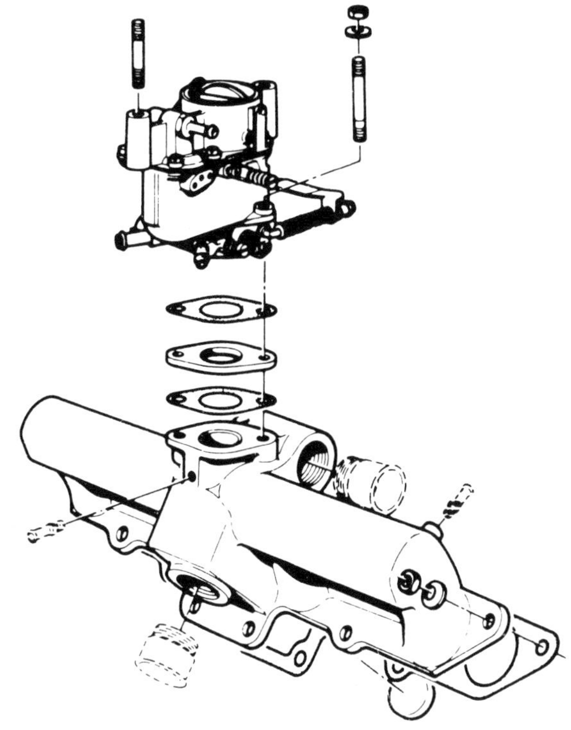

Fig. 3.24. Inlet manifold used for Solex carburettor

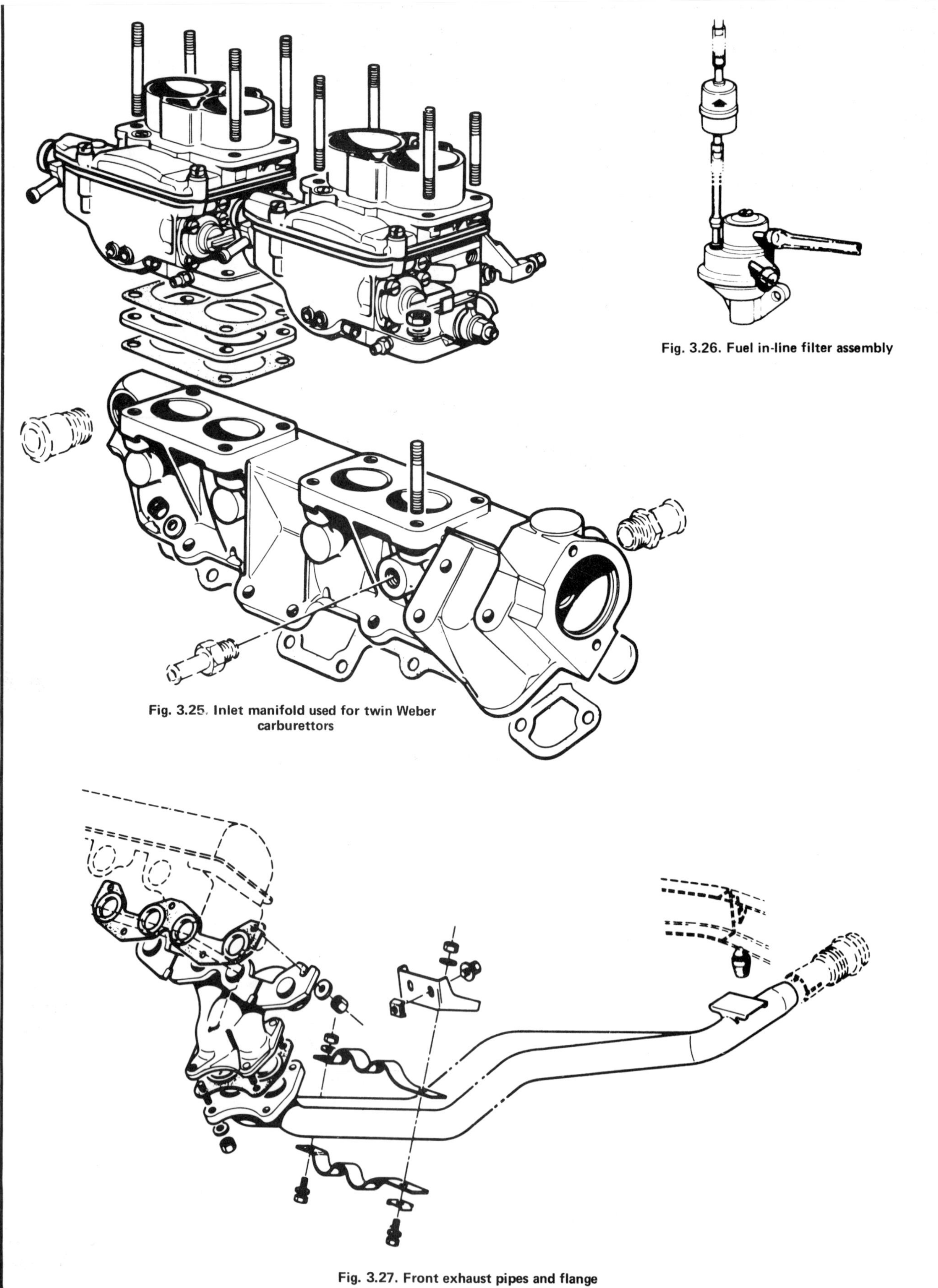

Fig. 3.25. Inlet manifold used for twin Weber carburettors

Fig. 3.26. Fuel in-line filter assembly

Fig. 3.27. Front exhaust pipes and flange

return pipe from the pump and this must also be disconnected.
9 Remove the clip and disconnect the tank filler hose from beneath the rear right-hand wing (photo).
10 Support the weight of the tank and remove the four securing bolts. Lower the tank sufficiently to disconnect the top vent pipe and then withdraw the tank from beneath the vehicle.
11 If the tank is dirty or contains sediment, use two or three lots of clean paraffin to wash it out and then let it drain thoroughly. Do not shake the tank too vigorously or use a stick to probe the interior or damage may be caused to the transmitter float and arm.
12 Do not try to solder a leak in a fuel tank. This is a specialists job. If the leak cannot be repaired with a cold setting compound then the tank should be renewed.
13 The fuel gauge transmitter unit can be unscrewed from the tank using a tool similar to that shown in Fig. 3.22. It is not necessary to remove the tank from the car. The unit is not repairable and if faulty must be renewed.
14 Refit the fuel tank and transmitter unit using the reverse procedure to that of removal. Ensure that the yellow wire is fitted to the outer terminal on the transmitter unit and the red wire to the inner (centre) terminal.

20 Inlet manifolds and exhaust system - general description

1 Three different types of inlet manifold are used on the models covered in this manual. One type is fitted to the 1442 cc engine in conjunction with the single Weber carburettor (see Fig. 3.23) and one of two types is fitted to the 1294 cc engine to cater for either the single Solex carburettor or the twin Weber installation (see Figs. 3.24 and .3.25).
2 All three types of manifold are water heated and it is therefore

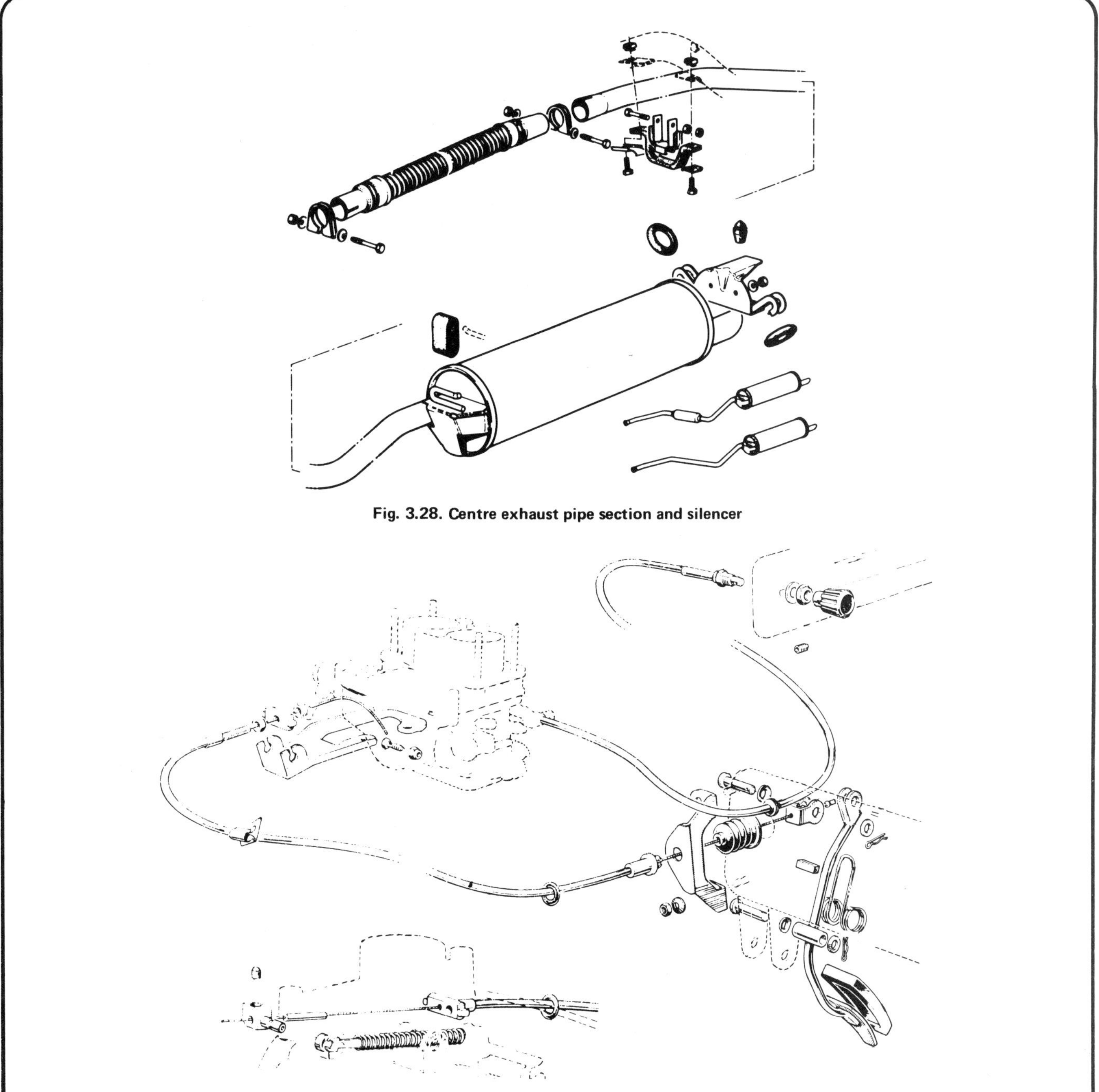

Fig. 3.28. Centre exhaust pipe section and silencer

Fig. 3.29. Typical layout of throttle and choke control cables

necessary to drain the cooling system before removal.
3 Always use new gaskets when refitting the manifold and carburettor.
4 The exhaust system comprises three main sections, twin pipes are connected to the engine manifold flange and converge into a single flexible pipe section. This in turn is attached to the rear silencer and tailpipe.
5 The front pipes are attached to the engine manifold by means of a flange and gasket, and secured by four bolts. Whenever the joint is dismantled a new gasket should always be used (Fig. 3.26).
6 The centre pipe and rear silencer/tailpipe assembly is secured to the underfloor by means of rubber rings hooked onto brackets (see Fig. 3.27) and a rear flexible strap (photo).
7 It is wise to use only properly made exhaust system parts and exhaust pipe shackles. Remember that the exhaust pipes and silencers corrode internally as well as externally and therefore when any one section of pipe or a silencer demands renewal, it often follows that the whole system is best renewed.
8 It is most important when fitting exhaust systems that the twists and contours are carefully followed and that each connecting joint overlaps the correct distance (1.5 in/32.5 mm). Any stresses and strains imparted in order to force the system to fit the vehicle will result in premature system failure.
Note: The front twin pipe assembly fitted to the 1442 cc engine is slightly longer than that used on the 1294 cc engine and is identified by a paint mark.

21 In-line fuel filter - general

On some models a filter is fitted in the pipeline between the fuel pump and carburettors (Fig. 3.28).

It cannot be cleaned and should be renewed at the recommended service intervals.

22 Accelerator and choke controls

1 The layout of the carburettor controls is shown in Fig. 3.29.
2 Ensure that the accelerator cable has enough slack in the idling position for correct closure of the butterfly valve to occur when the accelerator pedal is released.
3 On the Solex and single Weber carburettors check that the choke butterfly valve is fully open when the control knob is pushed in and closes completely when the knob is pulled right out. Adjust the cable if necessary.
4 Lightly oil the moving levers and swivels of the controls at regular intervals.

23 Fault finding chart - carburation; fuel and exhaust systems

Symptom	Reason/s	Remedy
Fuel consumption excessive		
Carburation and ignition faults	Air cleaner choked and dirty causing a rich mixture	Remove, clean and refit air cleaner.
	Fuel leaking from carburettor(s), fuel pumps or fuel lines	Check for and eliminate all fuel leaks. Tighten fuel line union nuts.
	Float chamber flooding	Check and adjust float level.
	Generally worn carburettor(s)	Remove, overhaul and refit.
	Distributor condenser faulty	Remove, and fit new unit.
	Balance weights or vacuum advance mechanism in distributor faulty	Remove, and overhaul distributor.
Incorrect adjustment	Carburettor(s) incorrectly adjusted, mixture too rich	Tune and adjust carburettor(s).
	Idling speed too high	Adjust idling speed.
	Contact breaker gap incorrect	Check and reset gap.
	Valve clearances incorrect	Check rocker arm to valve stem clearances and adjust as necessary.
	Incorrectly set sparking plugs	Remove, clean and regap.
	Tyres under-inflated	Check tyre pressures and inflate if necessary.
	Wrong sparking plugs fitted	Remove and fit correct units.
	Brakes dragging	Check and adjust brakes.
Insufficient fuel delivery or weak mixture due to air leaks		
Dirt in system	Petrol tank air vent restricted	Remove petrol cap and clean out air vent.
	Partially clogged filters in pump and carburettor(s)	Remove and clean filters.
	Dirt lodged in float chamber needle housing	Remove and clean out float chamber and needle valve assembly.
Fuel pump faults	Incorrectly seating valves in fuel pump	Renew fuel pump.
	Fuel pump diaphragm leaking or damaged	Renew fuel pump.
	Gasket in fuel pump damaged	Renew fuel pump.
	Fuel pump valves sticking due to petrol gumming	Renew fuel pump.
Air leaks	Too little fuel in fuel tank (prevalent when climbing steep hills)	Refill fuel tank.
	Union joints on pipe connections loose	Tighten joints and check for air leaks.
	Split in fuel pipe on suction side of fuel pump	Examine, locate, and repair.
	Inlet manifold to block or inlet manifold to carburettor(s) gasket leaking	Test by pouring oil along joints - bubbles indicate leak. Renew gasket as appropriate.

Chapter 4 Ignition system

Contents

Specifications

Type ... Electronic

Distributor

Make	SEV or Bosch
Direction of rotation	Clockwise
Firing order	1 - 3 - 4 - 2 (No. 1 piston at flywheel end of engine)

Ignition coil

Primary resistance	1.4 - 1.6 ohms
Secondary resistance	8000 - 10,000 ohms
Ballast resistor	0.50 to 0.60 ohms

Spark plugs

Type	
1294 with 2 twin choke carbs	Champion N6Y
1294 with single carb, except Sweden	Champion N7Y or Marchal GT 34-5HA
1294 with single carb, Sweden	Champion N9Y
1442 except Sweden	Champion N7Y or Marchal GT 34-5HA
1442 Sweden	Champion N7Y
Gap	0.024 - 0.028 in (0.6 - 0.7 mm)

Ignition timing (dynamic)

Engine	btdc	Idling speed
1294 cc (single carb)	10°	850
1294 cc (twin carb)	10°	950
1442 cc (all models)	10°	900

Torque wrench settings

	lb f ft	kg f m
Spark plugs	22	3.04
Distributor clamp bolt	7	0.97
Distributor mounting bolts	15	2.07

1 General description

In order that the engine can run correctly it is necessary for an electrical spark to ignite the fuel/air mixture in the combustion chamber and at exactly the right moment in relation to engine speed and load. The ignition system is based on feeding low tension voltage from the battery to the coil where it is converted to high tension voltage. The high tension voltage is powerful enough to jump the spark plug gap in the cylinders many times a second under high compression pressures providing that the system is in good condition and that all adjustments are correct.

The Alpine models are fitted with an electronic ignition system which provides a high degree of reliability with virtually no servicing requirements apart from periodically checking the HT (high tension) and LT (low tension) lead connections.

This new system retains the normal ignition coil, distributor advance mechanism and distributor cap, but replaces the conventional contact breaker points and condenser with a reluctor and pick-up unit operating in conjunction with a control unit.

The reluctor unit is a four-toothed wheel, (one for each cylinder) that is fitted to the distributor shaft in place of the conventional contact breaker operating cam.

The pick-up unit is also located in the distributor and comprises basically of a coil and permanent magnet.

The control unit is a transistorised amplifier that is used to boost the voltage induced by the pick-up coil.

A simplified circuit diagram is shown in Fig. 4.2 while the complete wiring diagram with colour coding is given in Fig. 4.1.

When the ignition switch is ON, the ignition primary circuit is energised. When the distributor reluctor 'teeth' or 'spokes' approach the magnetic coil assembly, a voltage is induced which signals the amplifier to turn off the coil primary current. A timing circuit in the amplifier module turns on the coil current after the coil field has collapsed.

When switched on, current flows from the battery through the ignition switch, through the coil primary winding, through the amplifier module and then to ground. When the current is off, the magnetic field in the ignition coil collapses, inducing a high voltage in the coil secondary winding. This is conducted to the distributor cap where the rotor directs it to the appropriate spark plug. This process is repeated for each power stroke of the car engine.

The distributor is fitted with devices to control the actual point of ignition according to the engine speed and load. As the engine speed increases two centrifugal weights move outwards and alter the position of the armature in relation to the distributor shaft to advance the spark slightly. As engine load increases (for example when climbing hills or accelerating), a reduction in intake manifold depression causes the base plate assembly to move slightly in the opposite direction (clockwise) under the action of the spring in the vacuum unit, thus retarding the spark slightly and tending to counteract the centrifugal advance. Under light loading conditions (for example at moderate steady speeds) the comparatively high intake manifold depression on the vacuum advance diaphragm causes the baseplate assembly to move in a counterclockwise direction to give a larger amount of spark advance.

2 Distributor - servicing

1 Periodically the condition of the distributor cap and rotor should be checked.

2 Remove the protective boot from around the distributor cap, release the two spring clips and lift off the cap.

3 Clean the inside and outside of the distributor cap with a clean cloth and check the centre contact and four segments on the inside of the cap for excessive wear or burning. If evident the cap should be renewed.

4 Remove the rotor and check the end of the brass segment for burning. Renew if necessary.

5 The air gap between the reluctor rotor tips and the magnetic pick-up point is pre-set. It cannot be adjusted and requires no servicing.

6 Refit the rotor and cap and secure with the spring clips. Refit the protective boot.

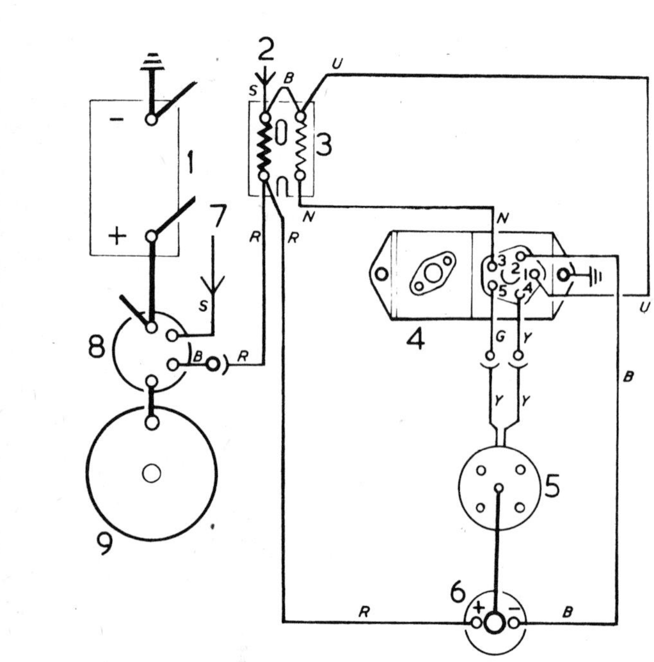

Fig. 4.1. Ignition system wiring circuit and colour code

1 Battery
2 Supply from Ign. sw.
3 Resistor block
4 Control unit
5 Distributor
6 Ignition coil
7 Supply from key start
8 Starter solenoid
9 Starter motor

Colour code
B = Black
G = Green
N = Brown
R = Red
S = Slate
U = Blue
Y = Yellow

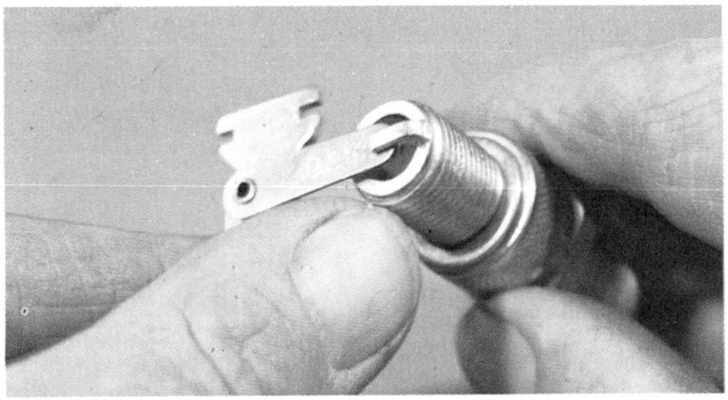

Measuring plug gap. A feeler gauge of the correct size (see ignition system specifications) should have a slight 'drag' when slid between the electrodes. Adjust gap if necessary

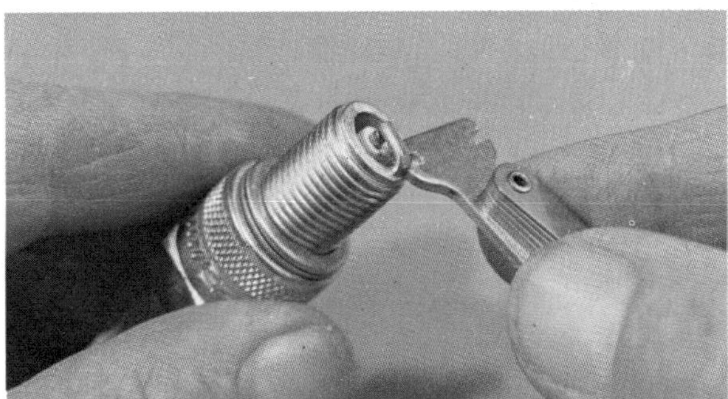

Adjusting plug gap. The plug gap is adjusted by bending the earth electrode inwards, or outwards, as necessary until the correct clearance is obtained. Note the use of the correct tool

Normal. Grey-brown deposits lightly coated core nose. Gap increasing by around 0.001 in (0.025 mm) per 1000 miles (1600 km). Plugs ideally suited to engine and engine in good condition

Carbon fouling. Dry, black, sooty deposits. Will cause weak spark and eventually misfire. Fault: over-rich fuel mixture. Check: carburettor mixture settings, float level and jet sizes; choke operation and cleanliness of air filter. Plugs can be re-used after cleaning

Oil fouling. Wet, oily deposits. Will cause weak spark and eventually misfire. Fault: worn bores/piston rings or valve guides; sometimes occurs (temporarily) during running-in period. Plugs can be re-used after thorough cleaning

Overheating. Electrodes have glazed appearance, core nose very white - few deposits. Fault: plug overheating. Check: plug value, ignition timing, fuel octane rating (too low) and fuel mixture (too weak). Discard plugs and cure fault immediately

Electrode damage. Electrodes burned away; core nose has burned, glazed appearance. Fault: initial pre-ignition. Check: as for 'Overheating' but may be more severe. Discard plugs and remedy fault before piston or valve damage occurs

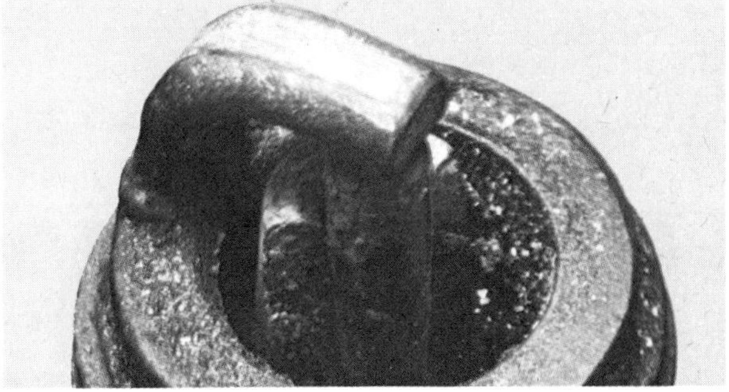

Split core nose (may appear initially as a crack). Damage is self-evident, but cracks will only show after cleaning. Fault: pre-ignition or wrong gap-setting technique. Check: ignition timing, cooling system, fuel octane rating (too low) and fuel mixture (too weak). Discard plugs, rectify fault immediately

3.6A Distributor aperture and drive shaft

3.6B Fitting the distributor into the engine

3.7 Distributor correctly fitted

3 Distributor - removal and refitting

1 Remove the distributor cap as described in the previous Section and disconnect the vacuum pipe.
2 Disconnect the wires from the distributor to the control unit at the twin plug.
3 Using a small sharp screwdriver or similar instrument carefully scribe an alignment mark between the distributor body and the crankcase mounting bracket.
4 Undo the distributor clamp bolt, remove the clamp and lift out the distributor from the engine. Do **not** rotate the engine after the distributor has been removed unless absolutely necessary.
5 The distributor is not repairable and if it is known to be faulty (see Section 8) it must be renewed.
6 To refit the distributor, enter it into the crankcase aperture and ensure the tongue on the end of the distributor drive shaft engages with the offset slot in the engine drive shaft (photo).
7 Rotate the distributor body to line up the scribe marks, refit the clamp and tighten the securing bolt (photo).
8 Refit the remaining distributor components using the reverse procedure to that of removal.
9 Providing the engine was not rotated while the distributor was removed and the scribe marks are correctly aligned it should not be necessary to re-time the ignition. However, if any doubt exists, time the ignition using the procedure described in Section 5.
10 If the engine was rotated while the distributor was removed it will be necessary to re-time it to the engine as described in the following Section.

4 Distributor - timing to the engine

1 To time the distributor to the engine, first remove No. 1 spark plug (nearest the flywheel end of the engine).
2 Place a finger over the spark plug hole and rotate the engine until pressure is felt, this indicates the piston is on the compression stroke.
3 Continue turning the engine until the mark on the flywheel (seen through the clutch housing aperture) is opposite the degree mark given in the 'Specifications' (see Fig. 4.3).
4 With the distributor removed from the engine, turn the rotor until it is aligned with the groove in the body on Bosch type distributors (see Fig. 4.4) or, in the case of the SEV distributor, the mark on the base of the rotor is between the two lines scribed on the arch shield (see Fig. 4.5).
5 Refit the distributor to the engine as described in Section 3, ensuring that the driveshaft is correctly engaged. Check that the timing marks are still in alignment (rotate the distributor body if necessary) and lightly tighten the clamp bolt.
6 Finally, check the ignition timing using a strobe lamp as described in the following Section.

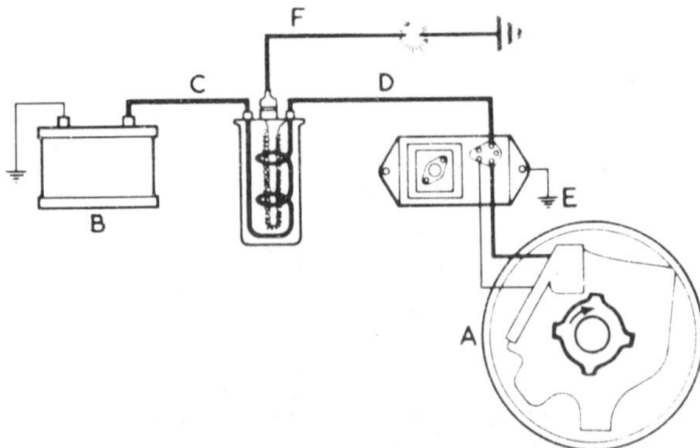

Fig. 4.2. Simplified diagram of ignition system

A Pick-up coil inducing negative voltage
B Battery
C Supply to ignition coil
D Coil L.T. to control unit
E L.T. open circuit in control unit
F H.T. induced in coil secondary

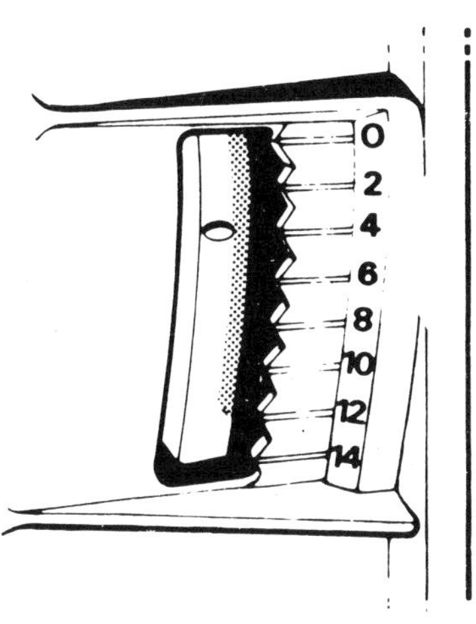

Fig. 4.3. Timing aperture in clutch housing

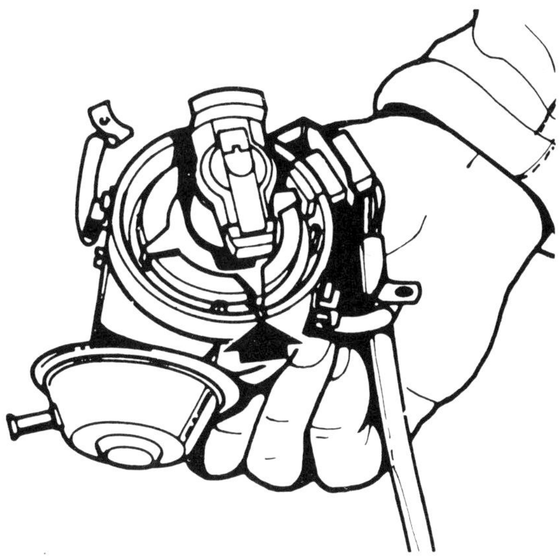

Fig. 4.4. Timing marks on Bosch distributor

5 Ignition timing

1 Because the distributor only gives a timing signal when the shaft is rotating, a strobe lamp must be used with the engine running at idling speed.

2 First disconnect the vacuum advance pipe from the distributor and connect the strobe lamp between No. 1 spark plug and its associated HT lead.

3 Remove the rubber plug from the clutch housing aperture. Clean the flywheel and housing timing marks with a piece of rag and mark them with a spot of white paint. For the correct degree mark, refer to the Specifications at the beginning of this Chapter.

4 Start the engine and set the idling speed using a tachometer to the correct idling speed given in the Specifications.

5 Aim the strobe light at the clutch housing aperture and check that the timing marks line up as the light flashes.

6 Rotate the distributor body clockwise to retard the ignition and anticlockwise to advance it. When the timing marks are in perfect alignment, tighten the distributor clamp.

7 Re-check the timing and then disconnect the strobe light and reconnect the vacuum advance pipe.

8 The centrifugal advance mechanism can also be adjusted, but it requires specialised bench testing equipment and the task is best left to your Chrysler Dealer.

6 Coil - general

The two LT wire connections on top of the coil should be periodically checked for security. Remove the rubber sleeve from the centre HT lead and make sure that the end of the wire is clean and making good contact with the coil.

A possible source of arcing is between the top of the coil or sleeve and the LT terminals (See Fig. 4.6). To avoid this, keep the top of the coil clean and renew the rubber sleeve if cracked or perished.

The coil cannot be repaired and if it is thought to be faulty, it should be either taken to an electrical dealer for testing or renewal.

As the coil operates in conjunction with two ballast resistors it **must** be replaced with one of the same specifications.

7 Spark plugs and leads

1 The correct functioning of the spark plugs is vital for the correct running and efficiency of the engine.

2 At intervals of 6,000 miles (9,500 km) the plugs should be removed, examined, cleaned, and if worn excessively, renewed. The condition of the spark plugs will also tell much about the overall condition of the engine.

3 If the insulator nose of the spark plug is clean and white, with no deposits, this is indicative of a weak mixture, or too hot a plug. (a hot plug transfers heat away from the electrode slowly - a cold plug transfers it away quickly).

4 The plugs fitted as standard are listed in the Specifications at the beginning of this Chapter. If the tip and insulator nose is covered with hard, black looking deposits, then this is indicative that the mixture is too rich. Should the plug be black and oily, then it is likely that the engine is fairly worn, as well as the mixture being too rich.

5 If the insulator nose is covered with light tan to greyish brown deposits, then the mixture is correct and it is likely that the engine is in good condition.

6 If there are any traces of long brown tapering stains on the outside of the white portion of the plug, then the plug will have to be renewed, as this shows that there is a faulty joint between the plug body and the insulator, and compression is being allowed to leak away.

7 Plugs should be cleaned by a sand blasting machine, which will free them from carbon more thoroughly than cleaning by hand. The machine will also test the condition of the plugs under compression. Any plug that fails to spark at the recommended pressure should be renewed.

8 The spark plug gap is of considerable importance, as, if it is too large or too small, the size of the spark and its efficiency will be seriously impaired. The spark plug gap should be set to the figure given in the Specifications at the beginning of this Chapter.

9 To set it, measure the gap with a feeler gauge, and then bend open, or close, the outer plug electrode until the correct gap is achieved. The centre electrode should never be bent as this may crack the insulation and cause plug failure if nothing worse.

10 When refitting the plugs, remember to use new plug washers, and refit the leads from the distributor in the correct firing order, which is 1 - 3 - 4 - 2, No. 1 cylinder being the one nearest the flywheel.

11 The plug leads require no routine attention other than being wiped over regularly and kept clean. At intervals of 6,000 miles (9,500 km) however, pull the leads off the plugs and distributor one at a time and make sure no water has found its way onto the connections. Remove any corrosion from the brass ends, wipe the collars on top of the distributor, and refit the leads.

8 Fault diagnosis - ignition system

By far the majority of breakdown and running troubles are caused by faults in the ignition system either in the low tension or high tension circuits.

There are two main symptoms indicating faults. Either the engine will not start or fire, or the engine is difficult to start and misfires. If it is a regular misfire (ie, the engine is running on only two or three cylinders), the fault is almost sure to be in the secondary or high tension circuit. If the misfiring is intermittent the fault could be in either the high or low tension circuits. If the car stops suddenly, or will not start at all, it is likely that the fault is in the low tension circuit. Loss of power and overheating, apart from faulty carburation settings, are normally due to faults in the distributor or to incorrect ignition timing.

By eliminating the conventional (and troublesome) contact breaker points and condenser the electronic ignition system fitted to the Alpine is extremely reliable.

If a fault does develop in the system it will usually result in complete engine stoppage or failure to start. Misfiring is unlikely to be caused by the electronic side of the ignition system.

Specialised electrical equipment is required to test the electronic ignition components and this task should be entrusted with your nearest Chrysler Dealer.

Before assuming however, that the electronic side of the ignition system has failed, the following basic ignition system checks should be carried out.

Engine fails to start

1 If the engine fails to start and the car was running normally when it was last used, first check there is fuel in the petrol tank. If the engine turns over normally on the starter motor and the battery is evidently well charged, then the fault may be in either the high or low tension circuits. First check the HT circuit. **Note:** If the battery is known to be fully charged, the ignition light comes on, and the starter motor fails to turn the engine **check the tightness of the leads on the battery terminals and also the secureness of the earth lead to its connection to the body.** It is quite common for the leads to have worked loose, even if they look and feel secure. If one of the battery terminal posts gets very hot when trying to work the starter motor this is a sure indication of a faulty connection to that terminal.

2 One of the commonest reasons for bad starting is wet or damp spark plug leads and distributor. Remove the distributor cap. If condensation is visible internally dry the cap with a rag and also wipe over the leads. Refit the cap.

3 If the engine still fails to start, check that voltage is reaching the plugs by disconnecting each plug lead in turn at the spark plug end, and holding the end of the cable about ¼ in (6 mm) away from the cylinder block. Spin the engine on the starter motor.

4 Sparking between the end of the cable and the block should be fairly strong with a strong regular blue spark. (Hold the lead with rubber to avoid electric shocks). If voltage is reaching the plugs, then remove them and clean and regap them. The engine should now start.

5 If there is no spark at the plug leads, take off the HT lead from the centre of the distributor cap and hold it to the block as before. Spin the engine on the starter once more. A rapid succession of blue sparks between the end of the lead and the block indicates that the coil is in order and that the distributor cap is cracked, and the rotor arm is faulty, or the carbon brush in the top of the distributor cap is not making good contact with the spring on the rotor arm.

6 If there are no sparks from the end of the lead from the coil, check the connection at the coil end of the lead. If it is in order start checking the low tension circuit.

7 Before checking the low tension circuit reference should be made to Fig. 4.2 which shows the ignition wiring diagram and the colour coding of each wire.

8 Using a voltmeter or test bulb, first check that current is reaching the coil. Switch on the ignition and connect the test wires between the (+) terminal on the coil and earth. No reading indicates either a break in the supply from the ignition switch or a fault in the ballast resistor. Check the ignition switch connections and test the input wire (coloured slate) on the resistor block located on the wing valance.

9 With the ignition switch still on check that a voltage reading can be obtained at the (—) terminal on the coil and the No. 2 terminal on the electronic control box.

10 If no voltage reading can be obtained, check the wires for breaks and the terminal connections for security. If a positive voltage reading is obtained but the engine still refuses to start it is possible that some part of the electronic circuitry is at fault and the assistance of a Chrysler Dealer will be required to check it out.

Engine misfires

1 If the engine misfires regularly run it at a fast idling speed. Pull off each of the plug caps in turn and listen to the note of the engine. Hold the plug cap in a dry cloth or with a rubber glove as additional

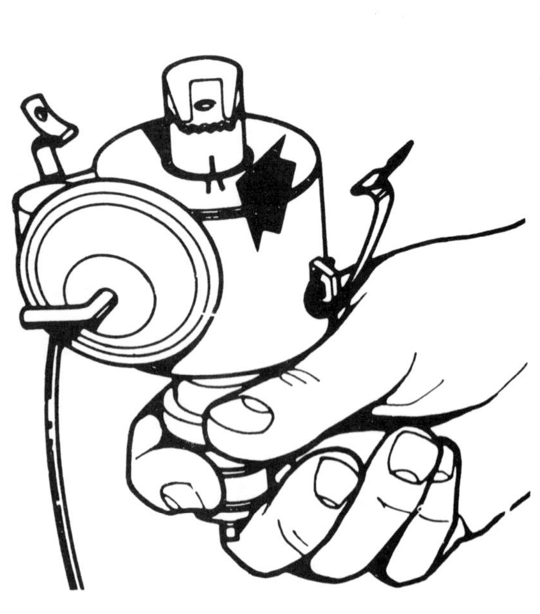

Fig. 4.5. Timing marks on SEV distributor

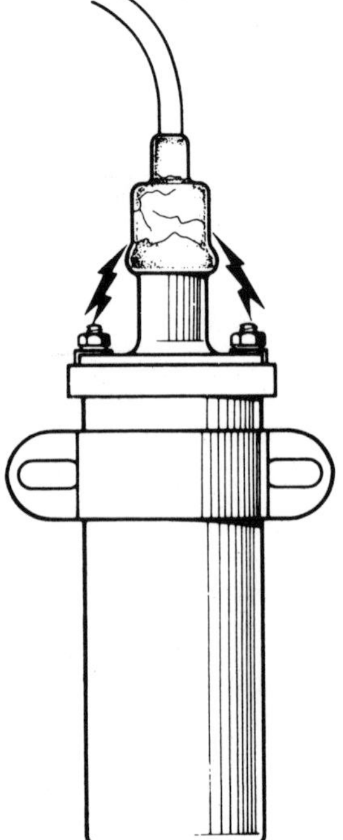

Fig. 4.6. Possible source of arcing on coil

protection against a shock from the HT supply.
2 No difference in engine running will be noticed when the lead from the defective circuit is removed. Removing the lead from one of the good cylinders will accentuate the misfire.
3 Remove the plug lead from the end of the defective plug and hold it about 3/16th in (5 mm) away from the block. Restart the engine. If the sparking is fairly strong and regular the fault must lie in the spark plug.
4 The plug may be loose, the insulation may be cracked, or the points may have burnt away giving too wide a gap for the spark to jump. Worse still, one of the points may have broken off. Either renew the plug, or clean it, reset the gap, and then test it.
5 If there is no spark at the end of the plug lead, or, if it is weak and intermittent, check the ignition lead from the distributor to the plug. If the insulation is cracked or perished, renew the lead. Check the connections at the distributor cap.
6 If there is still no spark, examine the distributor cap carefully for tracking. This can be recognised by a very thin black line running between two or more electrodes, or between an electrode and some other part of the distributor. These lines are paths which now conduct electricity across the cap thus letting it run to earth. The only answer is a new distributor cap.
7 Apart from the ignition timing being incorrect, other causes of misfiring have already been dealt with under the section dealing with the failure of the engine to start. To recap - these are that:

a) The coil may be faulty giving an intermittent misfire.
b) There may be a damaged wire or loose connection in the low tension circuit.
c) There may be a mechanical fault in the distributor (broken driving spindle)

8 If the ignition timing is too far retarded, it should be noted that the engine will tend to overheat, and there will be a quite noticeable drop in power. If the engine is overheating and the power is down, and the ignition timing is correct then the carburettor should be checked, as it is likely that this is where the fault lies.

Chapter 5 Clutch

Contents

Specifications

Type	Ferodo 180DBR or 190DBR, single dry plate	
Pressure plate		
Type	Diaphragm spring	
Outer diameter	9.17 in (233 mm)	
Total depth of assembly	1.77 in (45 mm)	
Driven plate (friction disc)		
Friction lining:		
Outer diameter	7.15 in (181.5 mm)	
Inner diameter	4.88 in (124 mm)	
Thickness (under load)	0.31 to 0.33 in (7.8 to 8.4 mm)	
Master cylinder		
Type	Lockheed	
Bore	0.75 in (19 mm)	
Stroke	0.875 in (22.5 mm)	
Slave cylinder		
Type	Lockheed, self-adjusting	
Bore	1.0 in (25.4 mm)	
Stroke	0.625 in (16.2 mm)	
Torque wrench settings	**lb f ft**	**kg f m**
Clutch assembly to flywheel	10.5	1.45
Slave cylinder to clutch housing	16.0	2.21
Release fork pivot pin to gearbox face	32.0	4.42
Release bearing support tube to gearbox	10.5	1.45

1 General description

The clutch assembly comprises a single (dry) driven plate, a pressure plate, release bearing and mechanism. The driven plate (friction disc) is free to slide along the gearbox primary shaft and is held in position between the flywheel and pressure plate faces by the pressure exerted by the diaphragm spring of the pressure plate. The friction linings are riveted to the driven plate which incorporates a spring cushioned hub to absorb transmission shocks and to assist smooth take up of the drive.

The diaphragm spring is mounted on shouldered pins and is held in place in the cover by fulcrum rings. The clutch is actuated by a pendant type foot pedal which operates a hydraulic master and slave cylinder. Depressing the clutch pedal pushes the release bearing, mounted on its hub, forward to bear against the spring fingers of the diaphragm. This action causes the diaphragm spring outer edge to deflect and move the pressure plate rearwards to disengage the pressure plate face from the driven plate linings. When the clutch pedal is released, the diaphragm spring forces the pressure plate into contact with the friction linings and sandwiches the driven plate between it and the flywheel so taking up the drive.

As the friction linings wear, the pressure plate automatically moves closer to the driven plate to compensate.

The release bearing is a ball race type, grease packed and sealed for life. The slave cylinder is the hydrostatic type that automatically compensates for clutch lining wear. No clutch adjustment is required or provided.

2 Clutch hydraulic system - bleeding

1 Gather together a clean jam jar, a length of rubber tubing which fits tightly over the bleed nipple in the slave cylinder, a tin of hydraulic brake fluid, and the help of an assistant.

2 Check that the master cylinder is full and if not, fill it, and cover the bottom inch of the jar with hydraulic fluid.

3 Remove the rubber dust cap from the bleed nipple on the slave cylinder and, with a suitable spanner, open the bleed nipple one turn.

4 Place one end of the tube securely over the nipple and insert the other end in the jam jar so that the tube orifice is below the level of the fluid.

5 The assistant should now pump the clutch pedal up and down slowly until air bubbles cease to emerge from the end of the tubing. He should also check the reservoir frequently to ensure that the hydraulic fluid does not get so low as to let air into the system.

6 When no more air bubbles appear, tighten the bleed nipple on the downstroke.

7 Refit the rubber dust cap over the bleed nipple. Allow the hydraulic fluid in the tin to stand for at least 24 hours before using it, to allow all the minute air bubbles to escape.

8 Never re-use old hydraulic fluid.

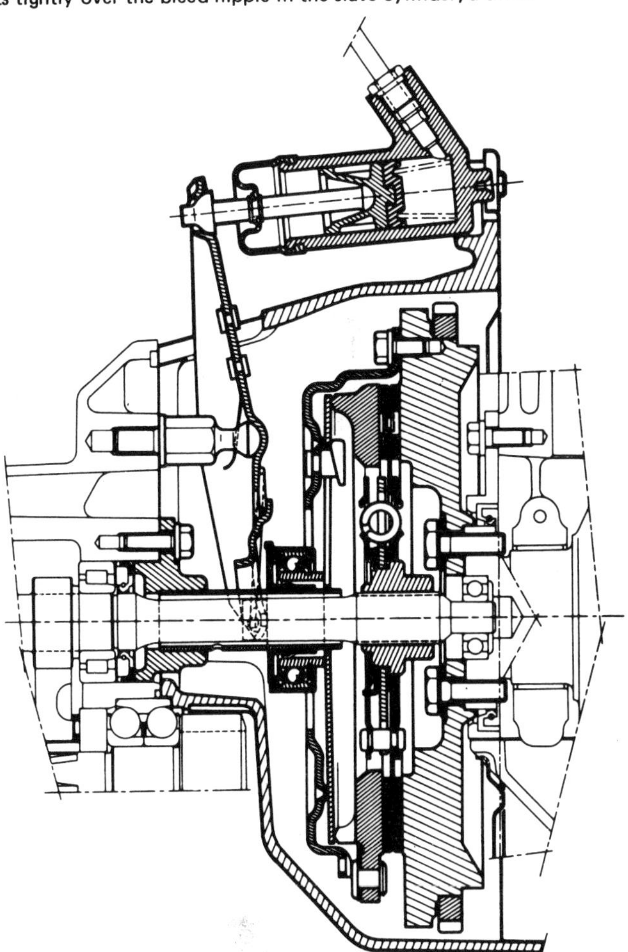

Fig. 5.1. Cross-sectional view of clutch assembly

3 Clutch pedal - removal and refitting

1 Disconnect the clutch master cylinder pushrod from the clutch pedal by removing the pin and cotter.

2 Remove the pin from the pedal cross shaft (Fig. 5.2).

3 Detach the pedal return spring (if fitted).

4 Withdraw the cross shaft sufficiently far to enable the clutch pedal to be removed downwards. Take care to note the sequence of the various cross shaft washers, spacers and springs.

5 Refitting is a reversal of removal but grease the cross shaft and use new pins.

4 Clutch - removal and refitting

1 Access to the clutch may be gained in one of two ways. Either the complete engine/transmission unit should be removed as described in Chapter 1 and the gearbox/transmission separated from the engine or the engine left in the car and the gearbox/transmission unit removed independently. The latter procedure is fully described in the next Chapter.

2 Note the alignment of the paint spots on both the flywheel and the pressure plate assembly for exact refitting.

3 Unscrew the six pressure plate retaining bolts from the flywheel, working in a diametrically opposite removal sequence and slackening the bolts only a few turns at a time (Fig. 5.3).

4 Withdraw the pressure plate assembly and driven plate.

5 It is important that no oil or grease gets on the clutch disc friction linings, or the pressure plate and flywheel faces. It is advisable to refit the clutch with clean hands and to wipe down the pressure plate and flywheel faces with a clean dry rag before assembly begins.

6 Place the clutch disc against the flywheel with the longer end of the hub, which is the end with the chamfered splines, facing the flywheel. On no account should the clutch disc be refitted with the shorter end of the centre hub facing the flywheel as on reassembly it will be found quite impossible to operate the clutch in this position.

7 To clarify the position some disc's are marked 'flywheel side' on the centre and it should be noted that the grooves in the friction lining must face towards the pressure plate (photo).

8 Refit the clutch cover assembly loosely on the two dowels. Refit the six bolts and spring washers and tighten them finger-tight so that the clutch disc is gripped but can still be moved.

9 The clutch disc must now be centralised so that when the engine and gearbox are mated the gearbox input shaft splines will pass through the splines in the centre of the driven plate hub.

10 Centralisation can be carried out quite easily by inserting a round bar or long screwdriver through the hole in the centre of the clutch, so that the end of the bar rests in the small hole in the end of the crankshaft containing the input shaft bearing bush.

11 Using the input shaft bearing bush as a fulcrum, moving the bar sideways or up and down will move the clutch disc in whichever direction is necessary to achieve centralisation.

12 Centralisation is easily judged by removing the bar and viewing the driven plate hub in relation to the hole in the release bearing. When the hub appears exactly in the centre of the release bearing hole all is correct.

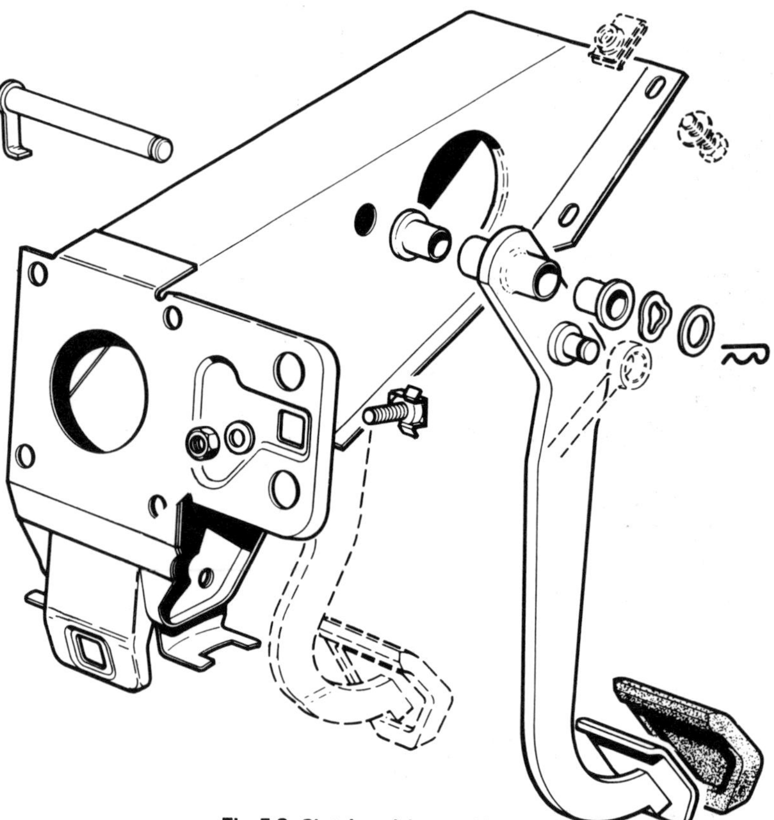

Fig. 5.2. Clutch pedal assembly

4.7 Refitting the clutch disc and cover assembly

4.13 Centralising the clutch disc using the gearbox primary shaft

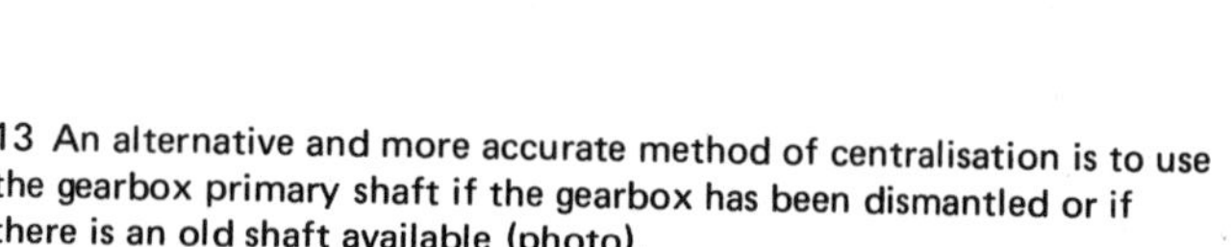

13 An alternative and more accurate method of centralisation is to use the gearbox primary shaft if the gearbox has been dismantled or if there is an old shaft available (photo).
14 Tighten the clutch bolts in a diagonal sequence to ensure that the cover plate is pulled down evenly and without distortion of the flange.
15 Grease the splines of the gearbox primary shaft sparingly with molybdenum type grease.
16 Refit the gearbox as described in the next Chapter.

5 Clutch assembly - inspection

1 In the normal course of events, clutch dismantling and reassembly, is the term used for simply fitting a new clutch pressure plate and friction disc. Under no circumstances should the diaphragm spring clutch unit be dismantled. If a fault develops in the pressure plate assembly, an exchange unit must be fitted.
2 If a new clutch disc is being fitted it is false economy not to renew the release bearing at the same time. This will preclude having to renew it at a later date when wear on the clutch linings is very small.
3 Examine the clutch disc friction linings for wear or loose rivets, the disc for rim distortion, cracks and worn splines. If any of these faults are evident the disc must be renewed.
4 Check the machined faces of the flywheel and the pressure plate. If either is badly grooved it should be machined until smooth, or renewed. If the pressure plate is cracked or split it must be renewed.
5 Examine the hub splines for wear and also make sure that the centre hub is not loose.

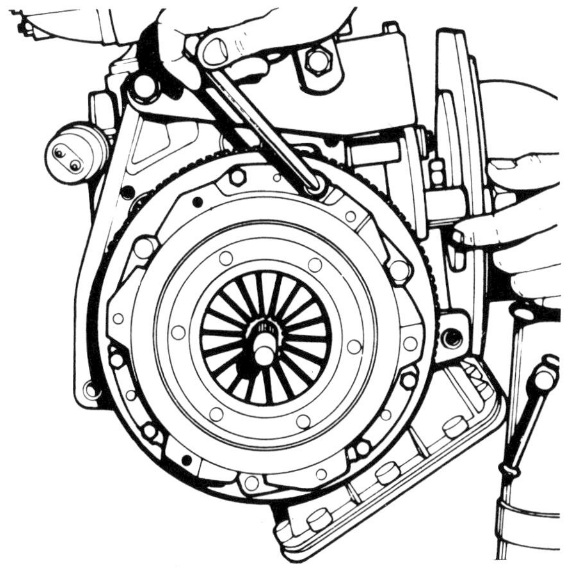
Fig. 5.3. Removing the clutch cover securing bolts

6.1 Clutch release bearing

6 Clutch release bearing - removal and refitting

1 With the gearbox and engine separated to provide access to the clutch, attention can be given to the release bearing located in the bell-housing, over the input shaft (photo).
2 The release bearing is a relatively inexpensive but important component and unless it is nearly new it is a mistake not to renew it during an overhaul of the clutch.
3 To remove the release bearing, first pull off the release arm rubber gaiter.
4 The release arm and bearing assembly can then be withdrawn from the clutch housing.
5 To free the bearing from the release arm simply unhook it, and then with the aid of two blocks of wood and a vice press off the release bearing from its hub.
6 Refit the release arm and bearing using the reverse procedure to that of removal. Make sure the spring clip on the release arm (photo) is correctly engaged on the pivot ball. Note that the small lug on the release bearing must be positioned between the bosses on the housing as shown in Fig. 5.4.
7 Refit the retaining spring on the release arm and engage the ends in the release bearing (see Fig. 5.4).

7 Clutch master cylinder - removal, servicing and refitting

1 Remove the brake and clutch fluid reservoir cap, place a clean piece of polythene sheet over the aperture and refit the cap. This will reduce the loss of fluid when the hydraulic pipes are disconnected.
2 From the rear engine compartment bulkhead, disconnect the clutch master cylinder outlet pipe (Fig. 5.5).
3 From inside the car, place a container below the master cylinder to catch any fluid and disconnect the hydraulic supply pipe from the master cylinder.
4 Disconnect the master cylinder operating pushrod from the top of the clutch pedal.

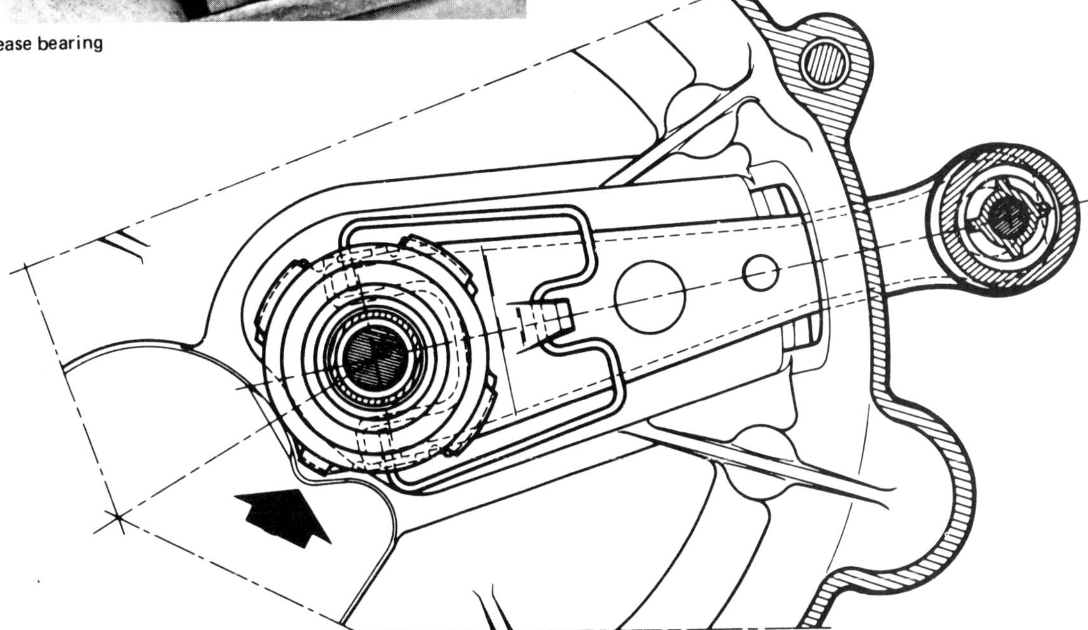
Fig. 5.4. Correct location of release bearing and retaining spring

5 Unscrew and remove the master cylinder retaining nuts and lift the unit from the bulkhead.
6 Expel the fluid from the master cylinder by depressing the pushrod two or three times.
7 Obtain a master cylinder repair kit which will contain the essential seals and components most likely to require renewing.
8 Pull off the rubber dust excluder.
9 Withdraw the pushrod.
10 Referring to Fig. 5.6, push the piston in slightly and remove the circlip and washer from the end of the cylinder.
11 Withdraw the piston complete with seals and return spring. If the piston sticks in the bore, gently tap the body of the master cylinder on the bench to release it.
12 With the master cylinder now completely dismantled, wash all components and the interior of the cylinder body with methylated spirit or clean hydraulic fluid.
13 Discard the old seals, first noting (and sketching if necessary) the way they are fitted to the piston in respect of chamfers and lips.
14 Examine the master cylinder bore and the piston surfaces for scoring and 'bright' spots. If these are evident, then the complete unit should be reassembled and exchanged for a factory reconditioned one.
15 Commence reassembly by dipping the new seals, supplied in the repair kit, in clean brake fluid and fitting them to the piston assembly, using the fingers only to manipulate them into position. Take particular care that the lips and chamfered edges have not been deformed or cut during storage in the repair kit packet.
16 Locate the return spring in the cylinder bore and then lubricate the bore liberally with clean hydraulic fluid. Insert the piston assembly using a twisting motion and ensuring that the lips of the seals are not trapped or pinched during the operation.
17 Refitting of the remaining components is a reversal of dismantling.
18 Refit the master cylinder to the bulkhead and reconnect the inlet and outlet hydraulic pipes and operating pushrod.
19 Remove the polythene sheeting from the fluid reservoir and top up the reservoir with the correct grade of clutch fluid.
20 Refit the cap and bleed the system as described in Section 2.

8 Clutch slave cylinder - removal, servicing and refitting

1 Remove the fluid reservoir cap, place a thin sheet of polythene over the aperture and screw the cap back on. This will seal the system and reduce the loss of fluid.
2 Disconnect the supply pipe from the slave cylinder and plug the

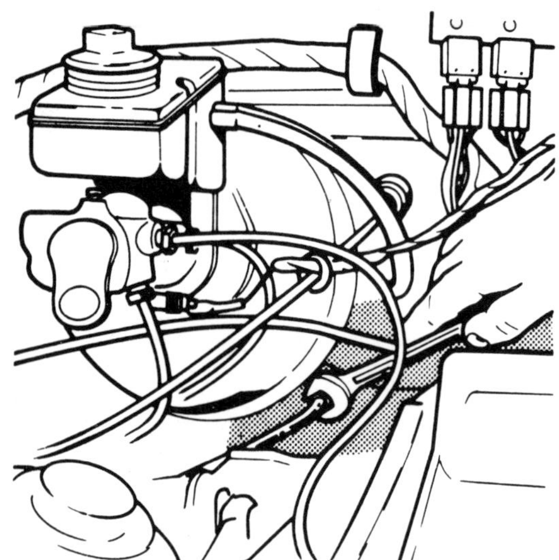

Fig. 5.5. Disconnecting the clutch master cylinder outlet pipe

6.6 Spring retaining clip on the release arm

Fig. 5.6. Clutch master cylinder components

1 *Circlip*
2 *Stop washer*
3 *Secondary cup*
4 *Piston*
5 *Primary cup*
6 *Spring*

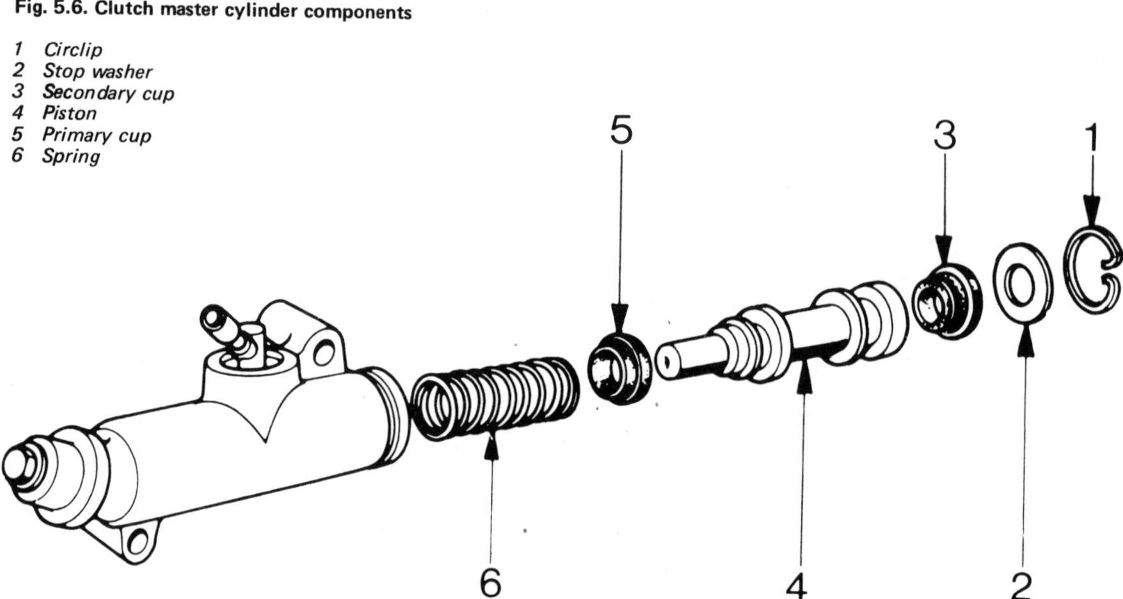

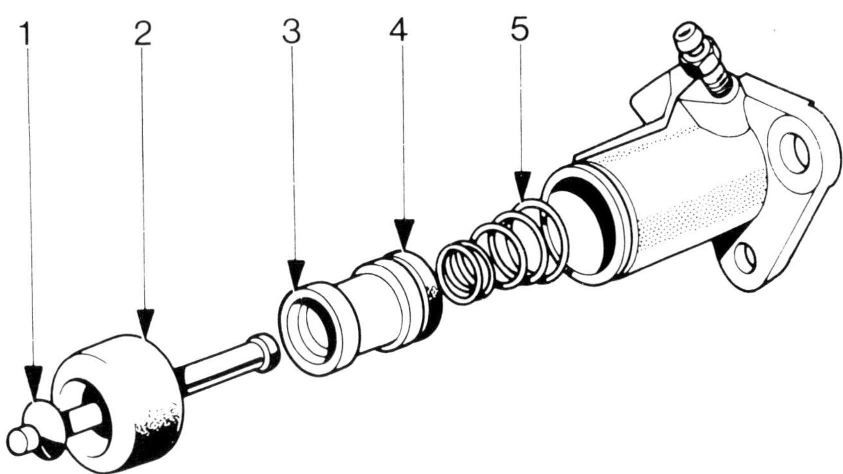

Fig. 5.7. Clutch slave cylinder components

1 *Pushrod*
2 *Rubber boot*
3 *Piston*
4 *Seal*
5 *Spring*

end of the pipe to prevent dirt ingress.
3 Remove the bolts securing the slave cylinder to the clutch housing, push the outer end of the clutch release fork towards the front (timing cover) of the engine and withdraw the complete slave cylinder assembly.
4 Obtain a slave cylinder repair kit of the correct type.
5 Referring to Fig. 5.7, remove the pushrod and rubber dust excluder.
6 Withdraw the piston complete with seal followed by the return spring.
7 Inspect the components for wear and fit a new piston seal using the procedures described for the master cylinder in the preceding Section.
8 Reassemble the slave cylinder and refit it to the engine using the reverse procedure to that of removal.
9 Remove the polythene sheet from the reservoir, top up the system with fluid and bleed it as described in Section 2.
10 The slave cylinder is the hydrostatic type and no adjustment is necessary.

9 Fualt diagnosis - clutch

There are four main faults to which the clutch and release mechanism are prone. They may occur by themselves or in conjunction with any of the other faults. They are squeal, slip, spin and judder.

Clutch squeal - diagnosis and cure
1 If on taking up the drive or when changing gear, the clutch squeals, this is a sure indication of a badly worn clutch release bearing.
2 As well as regular wear due to normal use, wear of the clutch release bearing is much accentuated if the clutch is ridden, or held down for long periods in gear, with the engine running. To minimise wear of this component the car should always be taken out of gear at traffic lights and for similar holdups.

Clutch slip - diagnosis and cure
3 Clutch slip is a self evident condition which occurs when the clutch friction plate is badly worn, when oil or grease have got onto the flywheel or pressure plate faces, or when the pressure plate itself is faulty.
4 The reason for clutch slip is that, due to one of the faults listed above, there is either insufficient pressure from the pressure plate, or insufficient friction from the friction plate to ensure solid drive.
5 If small amounts of oil get into the clutch, they will be burnt off under the heat of clutch engagement, and in the process, gradually darken the linings. Excessive oil on the clutch will burn off leaving a carbon deposit which can cause quite bad slip, or fierceness, spin and judder.
6 If clutch slip is suspected, and confirmation of this condition is required, there are several tests which can be made.
7 With the engine in top gear and pulling lightly up a moderate incline sudden depression of the accelerator pedal may cause the engine to increase its speed without any increase in road speed.
8 In extreme cases of clutch slip the engine will race under normal acceleration conditions.
9 If slip is due to oil or grease on the linings a temporary cure can sometimes be effected by squirting carbon tetrachloride into the clutch. The permanent cure is, of course, to renew the clutch driven plate and trace and rectify the oil leak.

Clutch spin - diagnosis and cure
10 Clutch spin is a condition which occurs when the release arm travel is excessive, there is an obstruction in the clutch either on the primary gear splines or in the operating lever itself, or the oil may have partially burnt off the clutch linings and have left a resinuous deposit which is causing the clutch to stick to the pressure plate or flywheel.
11 The reason for clutch spin is that due to any, or a combination of the faults just listed, the clutch pressure plate is not completely freeing from the centre plate even with the clutch pedal fully depressed.
12 If clutch spin is suspected, the condition can be confirmed by extreme difficulty in engaging first gear from rest, difficulty in changing gear, and very sudden take up of the clutch drive at the fully depressed end of the clutch pedal travel as the clutch is released.
13 Check that the clutch cable is correctly adjusted and, if in order, the fault lies internally in the clutch. It will then be necessary to remove the clutch for examination, and to check the gearbox input shaft.

Clutch judder - diagnosis
14 Clutch judder is a self evident condition which occurs when the gearbox or engine mountings are loose or too flexible, when there is oil on the faces of the clutch friction plate, or when the clutch pressure plate has been incorrectly adjusted during assembly.
15 The reason for clutch judder is that due to one of the faults just listed, the clutch pressure plate is not freeing smoothly from the friction disc, and is snatching.
16 Clutch judder normally occurs when the clutch pedal is released in first or reverse gears, and the whole car shudders as it moves backwards or forwards.

Chapter 6 Gearbox and final drive

Contents

Specifications

Gearbox

Type	Four forward speeds (all with synchromesh) and reverse
Gear ratios	
1st	3.9 : 1
2nd	2.31 : 1
3rd	1.52 : 1
4th	1.08 : 1
Reverse	3.77 : 1

Final drive

Type	Helical gears
Gear ratios	
1294 cc (Germany only)	3.937 : 1
1294 cc (except Germany)	3.706 : 1
1442 cc (Germany only)	3.706 : 1
1442 cc (except Germany)	3.588 : 1

Lubricants and oil capacities

Gearbox	1 pint (0.60 litre)
Final drive	0.90 pint (0.50 litre)
Gearbox and final drive	SAE 90 gear oil

Torque wrench settings

	lb f ft	kg fm
Clutch bellhousing to cylinder block bolts	32.0	4.43
Gearbox to clutch bellhousing bolts	16.0	2.21
Gearbox selector fork cover to gearbox bolts	8.5	1.18
Gearbox and final drive drain and filler plugs	25.0	3.46
Clutch release fork pivot pin to gearbox	10.5	1.45
Clutch thrust bearing support tube to gearbox bolts	10.5	1.45
Output shaft locknut (LH thread)	107	14.79
Differential half housing bolts	16.0	2.21
Large bearing thrust plate bolts	16.0	2.21

1 General description

The integrated manual gearbox and final drive unit is located on the right-hand end of the engine when viewed from the front of the car.

The front roadwheels are driven through driveshafts of unequal lengths.

The clutch bellhousing incorporates the final drive unit and the gearbox is mounted on the outer face of the clutch housing (Fig. 6.1).

The differential assembly is of conventional design having the inner ends of the driveshafts splines to the differential gears.

2 Gearbox - removal and refitting

1 The removal of the gearbox with the engine is described in Chapter 1. The gearbox may be removed without removing the engine using the following method.

2 Disconnect the leads from the battery terminals.

3 Raise the front of the vehicle and support it on stands.

4 Disconnect the gearshift rod assembly from the gearbox, see Section 10.

5 Unbolt the clutch slave cylinder from the clutch bellhousing and release the pushrod from the clutch release arm. The slave cylinder may now be tied up out of the way without disconnecting the hydraulic fluid line.

6 Make up an engine support which will take the weight of the unit when the gearbox mounting is removed.

7 Remove the left-hand front roadwheel.

8 Remove the left-hand damper and then drain the oil from the gearbox.

9 Disconnect the left-hand front engine mounting as described in Chapter 1.

10 Obtain two guide studs each 2.17 inch (55 mm) in length and threaded (8 x 125) over 0.6 inch (15 mm) of their length. Insert them

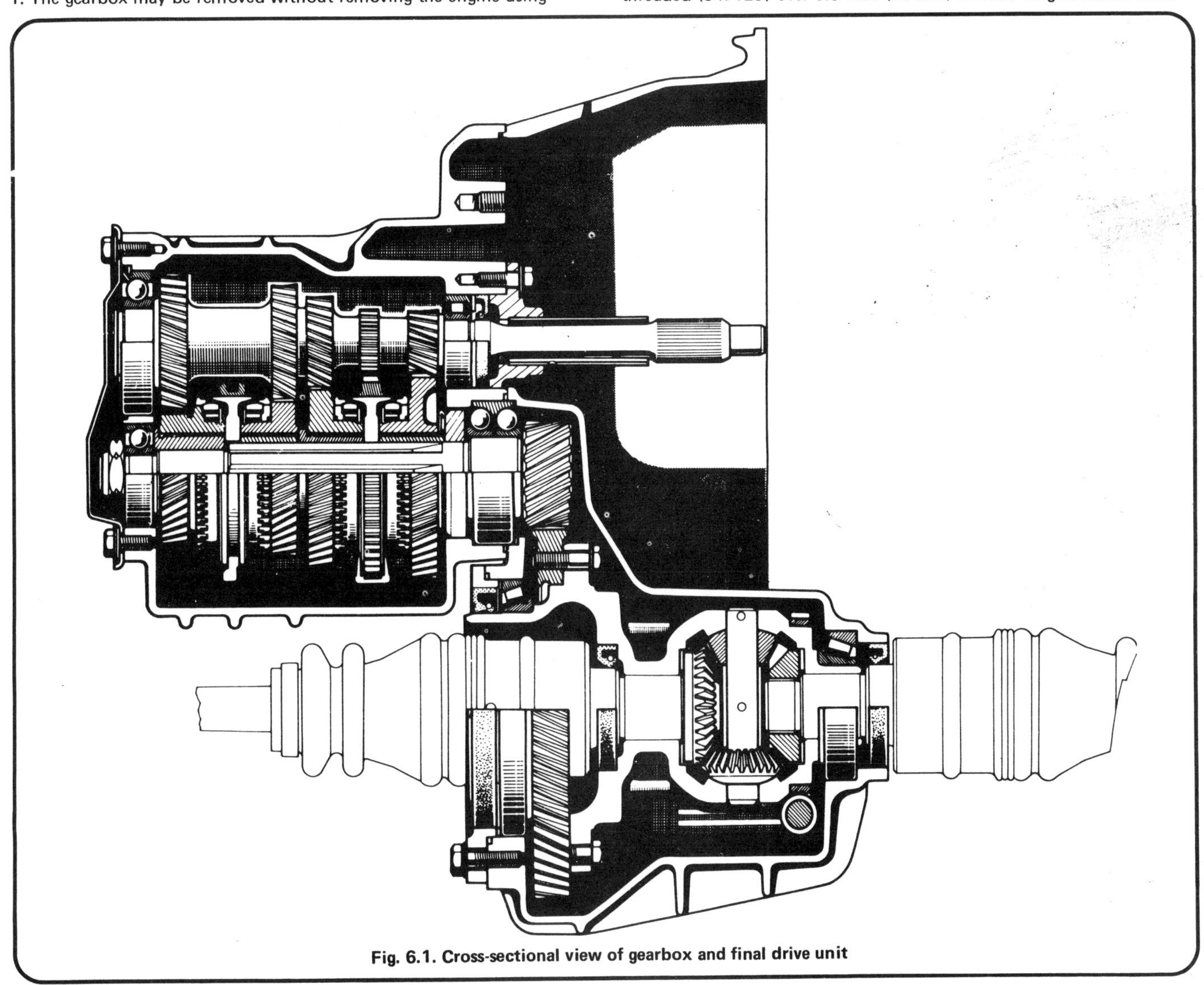

Fig. 6.1. Cross-sectional view of gearbox and final drive unit

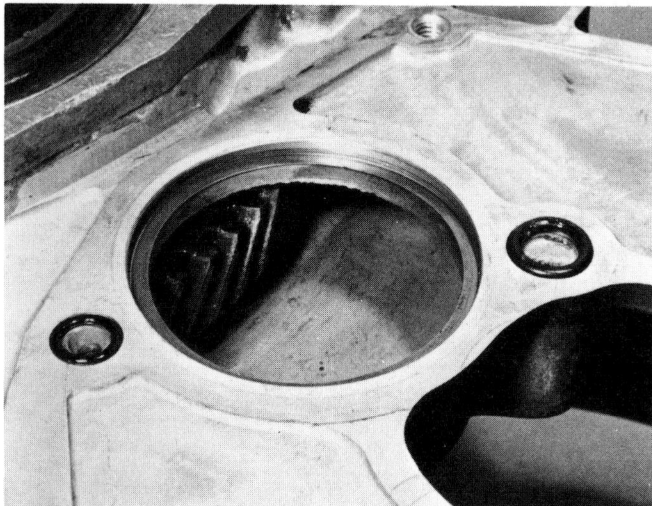

2.15 Location of 'O' ring seals in transmission casing

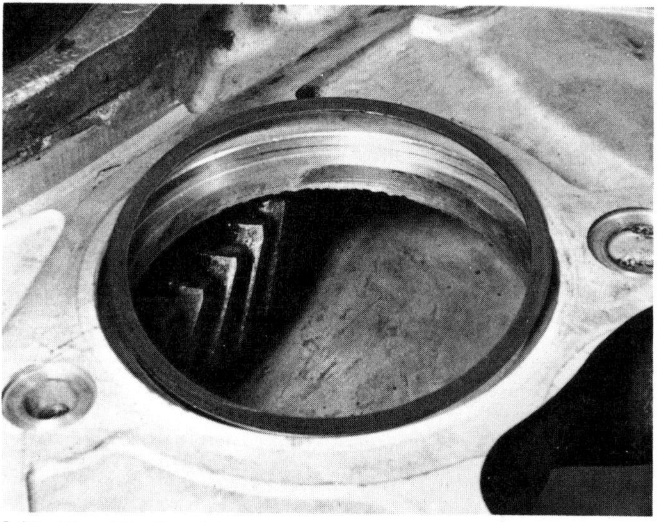

2.17 Shims fitted in pinion aperture

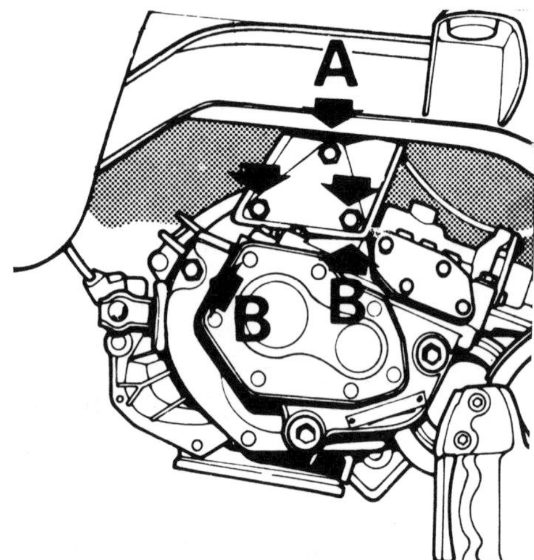

Fig. 6.2. Gearbox securing bolts

A Gearbox mounting bolts *B Guide bolt holes*

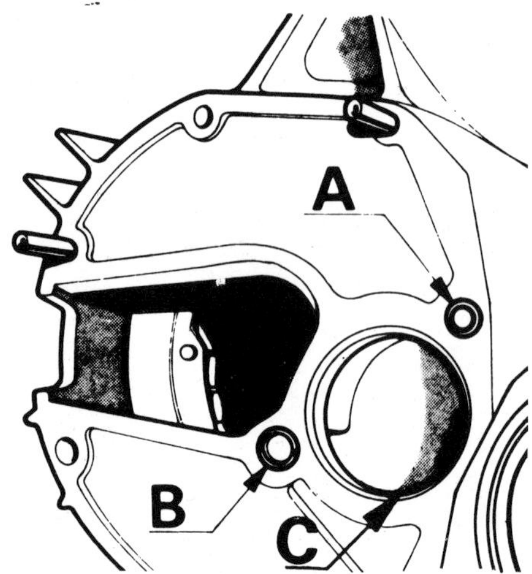

Fig. 6.3. Rear face of clutch/final drive housing

A 'O' ring seal
B 'O' ring seal
C Gearbox pinion aperture

in the holes, (B) (Fig. 6.2).

11 Take out the bolts which secure the gearbox to the clutch bell-housing.

12 Withdraw the gearbox, carefully retaining the shims fitted at the gearbox pinion aperture (Fig. 6.3).

13 Before refitting the gearbox, secure the clutch release arm in position using a piece of wire or string to ensure it does not become dislodged during refitting.

14 Select a gear and then refit the shims removed at (C) Fig. 6.3, using grease to retain the shims in position.

15 Check that the two small sealing 'O' rings are correctly located round the gearbox to differential connecting oil passages (photo).

16 Where major overhaul or renewal of internal components has been carried out, then the correct sealing of the gearbox to the clutch bellhousing/final drive unit must be checked. To do this, first drive the pinion fully home using a soft faced mallet.

17 Fit the original shims into the recess in the clutch/final drive housing (photo).

18 Place four lengths of 1 mm diameter soft soldering wire at equi-distant points on the bearing mating surface of the clutch/final drive recess.

19 Remove the 'O' ring seal from the gearbox pinion bearing recess (photo).

20 Carefully locate the gearbox onto the clutch/final drive housing. To facilitate this, remove the clutch assembly.

21 Tighten the securing bolts to 16 lb f ft (2.21 kg fm).

22 Remove the bolts and gearbox and measure the thickness of the crushed wire and then add shims to the equivalent thickness.

23 Refit the 'O' ring seal into the groove surrounding the output shaft pinion.

24 Pass the clutch release bearing through the aperture in the clutch bellhousing and insert the gearbox input shaft into the splined hub of the driven plate. The driving gear may require moving slightly to facilitate meshing of the splines and to engage the gearbox housing on the two guide studs.

25 Screw in and tighten the gearbox retaining bolts evenly to a torque of 16 lb f ft (2.21 kg fm).

26 Remove the guide bolts and fit the engine mounting assembly and spacer.

27 Remove the temporary engine support bar.

28 Refit the clutch slave cylinder.

29 Reconnect the gearshift control mechanism, and adjust if necessary, see Section 10.

30 Refit the damper and roadwheel.

31 Fill the gearbox and check the oil level in the final drive unit.

32 Reconnect the battery leads and remove the jacks from the front of the vehicle.

3 Gearbox - dismantling

1 Clean the external surfaces of the gearbox and dry thoroughly.

Place the unit in a servicing frame or secure it to a bench. Remove the mounting assemblies from the outside of the gearbox housing.
2 Remove the gearshift selector cover, using a swivelling action to clear the forks (photo).
3 Remove the rear cover (Fig. 6.4) and the clutch release bearing guide tube.
4 Slide two gears into engagement to lock the gearbox.
5 Remove the nut (20) which locks the rear bearing (19) to the output shaft, Fig. 6.5. Note that it has a left-hand thread.
6 Make up a plate to the dimensions shown in Fig. 6.6.
7 Fit this between the face of the first gear wheel and the inside face of the gearbox housing. Using a strengthening plate on the outside of the gearbox and a bridge piece and bolt, press the shaft through the gears and rear bearing until it can be withdrawn completely from the gear case.
8 Withdraw the spacer and special roller thrust washer from the front of the gearbox.
9 Lift out the 1st/2nd gear cluster complete with synchromesh unit (Fig. 6.7).
10 Lift out the 3rd/4th gear cluster complete with synchromesh unit.
11 Remove the circlip locating pin from the reverse gear shaft (Fig. 6.8).
12 Using a suitable sized drift, carefully tap the shaft out through the front of the casing. If difficulty is experienced a special tool (No. 39963) is available from your Chrysler dealer.
13 Remove the single securing screw and withdraw the clutch release bearing guide tube from the front of the casing.
14 Using a suitable sized piece of tubing or Chrysler tool No. 20888V, drive out the input shaft complete with bearings from the front to rear of the casing (Fig. 6.10).
15 Discard the oil seal from the front of the shaft and retrieve the shim(s).
16 Do not attempt to remove the primary shaft bearings or the output shaft bearings unless you have a press and extractors suitable for the job. It is better to take them to a Chrysler agent.
17 If necessary, the gearshift control and selector fork assembly may be dismantled. Commence by setting the selector shafts and forks in neutral and removing the end cover (Fig. 6.11).
18 Unscrew and remove the 3rd/4th selector fork securing screw, withdraw the selector shaft slowly and retain the detent ball as it is removed.
19 Remove the 3rd/4th selector fork.
20 Remove the 1st/2nd selector fork screw, withdraw the shaft just sufficiently far to permit removal of the 1st/2nd selector fork.
21 Rotate the 1st/2nd selector shaft through 90° to facilitate removal of the detent ball.
22 Withdraw the 1st/2nd selector shaft completely but retaining the detent balls and springs during the operation.
23 Remove the reverse selector fork securing screw, drift out the reverse shaft sufficiently far to enable the fork to be removed. Withdraw the reverse shaft completely and retain the detent and interlocking balls and springs.
24 Remove the securing screw from the fork control lever.
25 Withdraw the spindle and fork control lever and the three springs which impinge upon the detent balls.
26 The gearbox is now completely dismantled and both the inside of the gearbox case and all components should be thoroughly washed in paraffin so that examination may be carried out as described in the following Section.

4 Gearbox - examination

1 Examine each component for wear, distortion, chipping or scoring and renew if apparent.
2 Examine the gear wheels, particularly for wear and chipping of teeth and renew as necessary.
3 Check all ball and roller bearings for play. If even the slightest wear is evident then they must be withdrawn from their shafts and renewed.
4 The condition of the synchromesh units will be known from previous driving experience. The units can be dismantled for inspection and renewal of components using the following method.

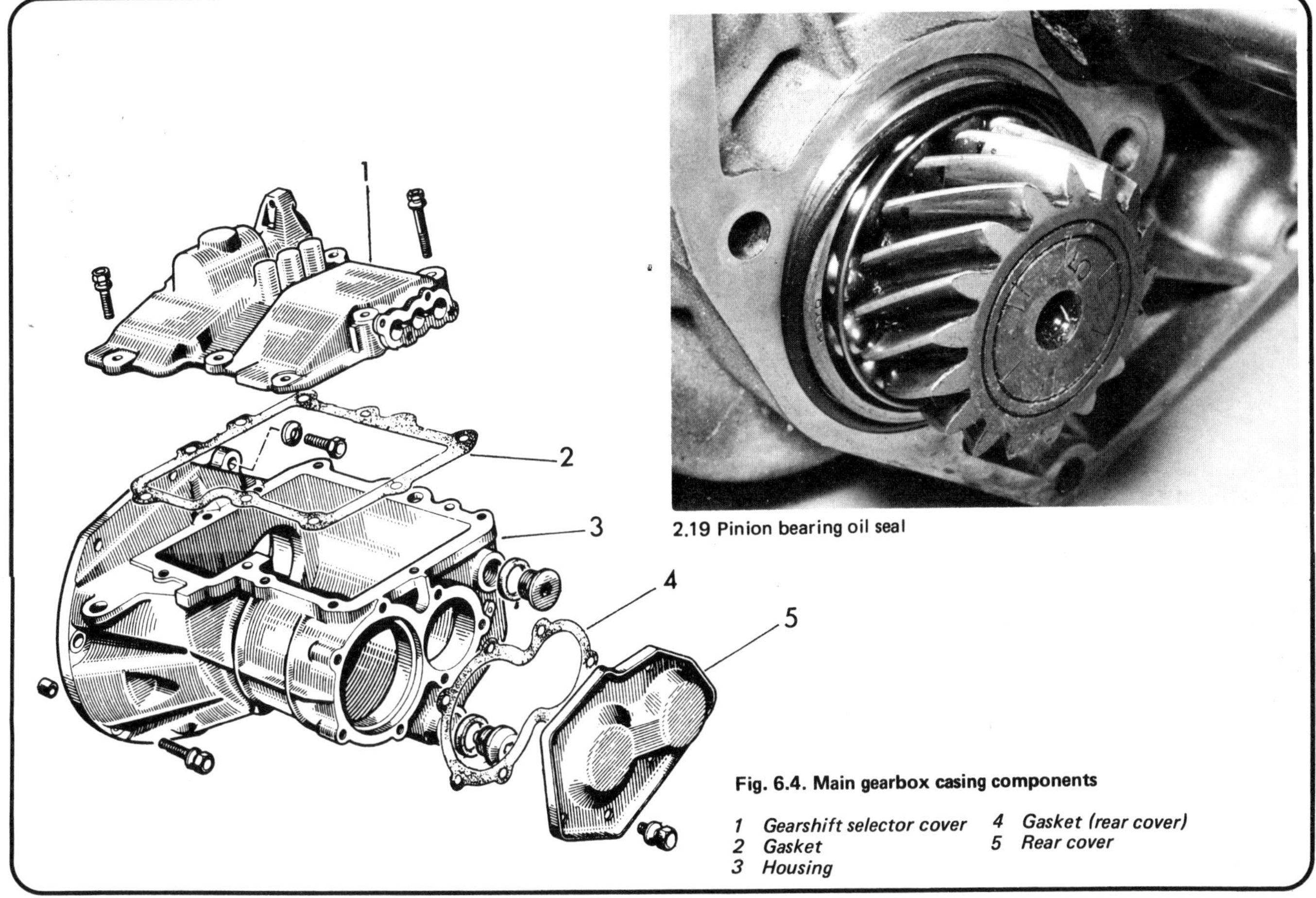

2.19 Pinion bearing oil seal

Fig. 6.4. Main gearbox casing components

1 Gearshift selector cover
2 Gasket
3 Housing
4 Gasket (rear cover)
5 Rear cover

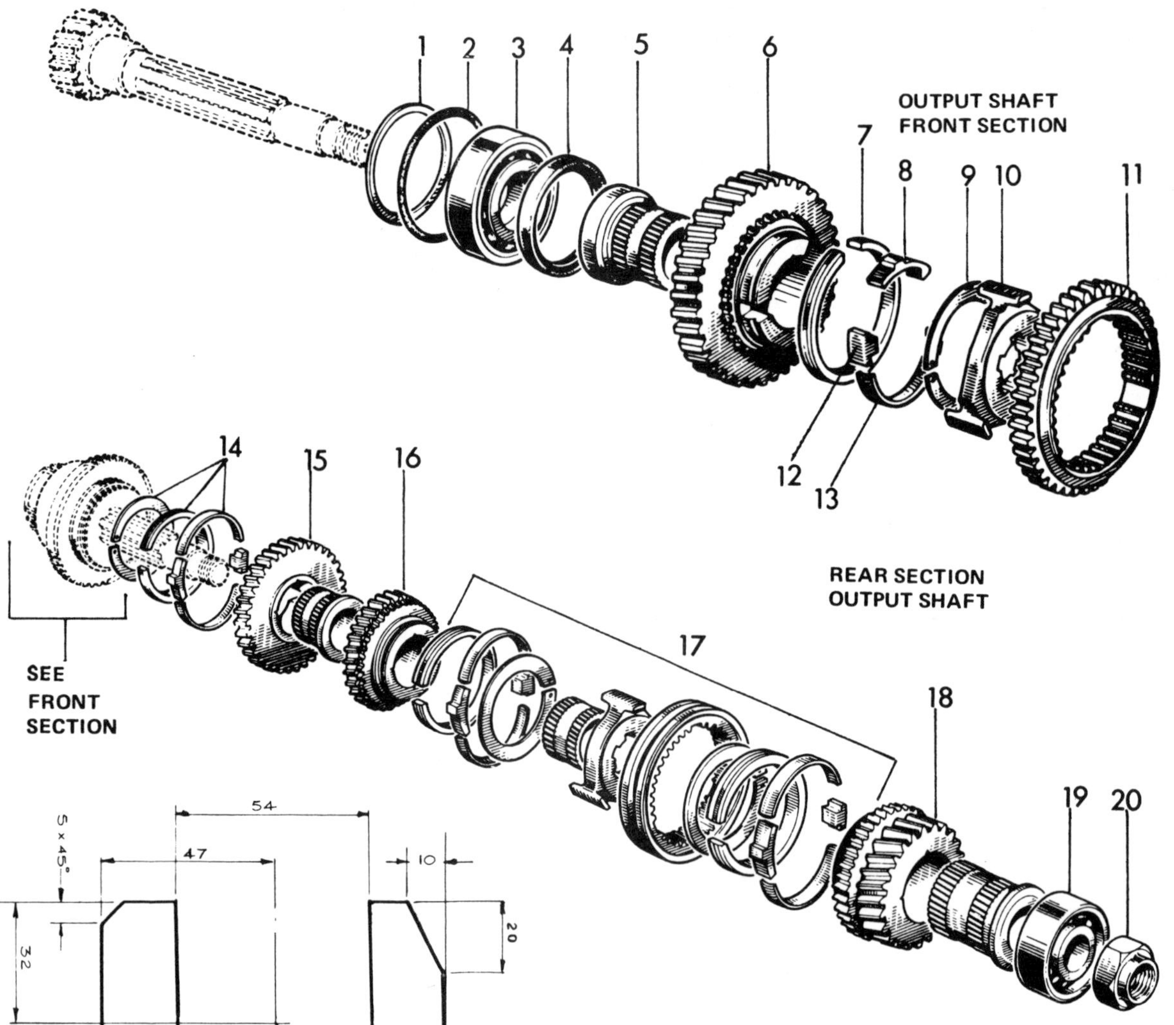

OUTPUT SHAFT FRONT SECTION

REAR SECTION OUTPUT SHAFT

SEE FRONT SECTION

1 2 3 4 5 6 7 8 9 10 11 12 13 14 15 16 17 18 19 20

Fig. 6.5. Exploded view of gearbox output shaft (mainshaft)

1 Spacer
2 O-ring seal
3 Double ball race
4 Oil seal
5 Bush
6 1st gear
7 Synchroniser ring
8 Synchro locking piece
9 Synchro circlip
10 Synchro hub
11 1st/2nd synchro sleeve (reverse on periphery)
12 Retainer stop
13 Spring
14 1st/2nd synchro assembly (part)
15 2nd gear
16 3rd gear
17 3rd/4th synchro unit
18 4th gear
19 Bearing
20 Locking nut

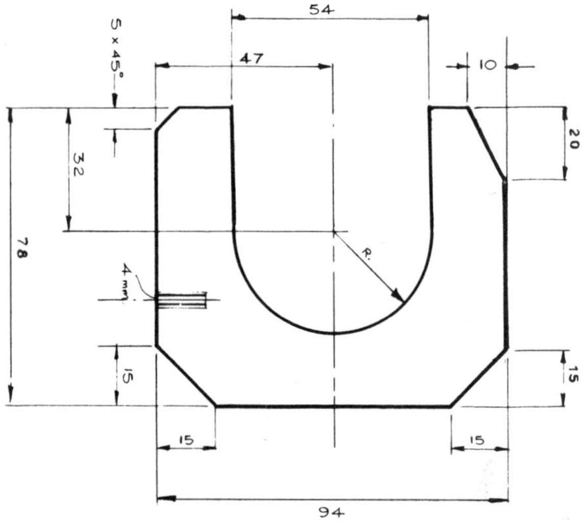

54
47
10
5 x 45°
20
32
78
R
4 mm
15
15
15
15
94

Fig. 6.6. Mainshaft packing plate (dimensions in mm)

3.2 Removing the gearbox top cover

4.6 Synchro unit with circlip removed

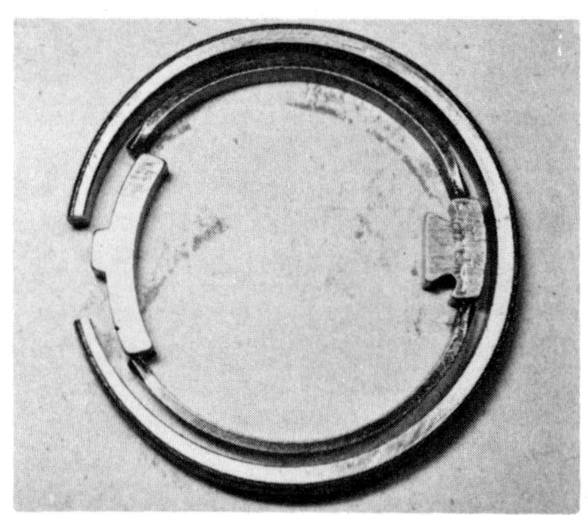

4.10A Correct positioning of synchro unit components prior to assembly

5 Using a strong pair of circlip pliers, carefully remove the large circlip from the synchro unit (Fig. 6.13).
6 With the circlip removed, make a careful note of the position of the baulk ring, the two curved springs and pawls (see photo).
7 Lift out the components and check the ends of the springs for burrs and ensure the edges of the spring stop and locking pawl are smooth and square.
8 Check the small internal teeth for wear or breakage. The sliding sleeve and hub are meant to be a fairly loose fit, and this should not be mistaken for wear.
9 If difficult gearchanging has been experienced or any doubts exist about the synchro units, the best policy is to obtain complete new units.
10 If fitting new components, reassemble them on the bench first (photo) before fitting them into the gear. Carefully secure them with the circlip and refit the sleeve and hub (photo).
11 Examine the ends of the selector forks at their points of contact. Comparison of their profiles with new components will give a guide to renewal requirements.
12 Check the gearbox casing for cracks, particularly around the shaft bearing and bolt holes.

5 Gearbox - reassembly

1 From the rear end of the gearbox casing, carefully drive in the primary shaft complete with bearings using a soft faced hammer.
2 Continue to drive the shaft in until the rear bearing circlip is firmly seated against the casing (photo).
3 Assemble the 1st/2nd and 3rd/4th gears and synchro assemblies (photos).
4 Fit the front mainshaft ball bearing into its outer race in the casing (photo).
5 Insert the thick spacer into the front bearing aperture (photo). **Note:** If there is a groove in the spacer it must face towards the outside of the gear casing.
6 Fit the roller bearing thrust washer onto the front face of the 1st gear assembly (photo). Use grease to hold it in place if necessary.
7 Lower the 3rd/4th gear assembly into the casing (photo), followed by the 1st/2nd gear assembly and thrust washer.
8 Holding the gear assemblies in place, carefully insert the mainshaft through the front of the casing. Rotate the gears as necessary to align them with the shaft (photo).
9 Fit the mainshaft rear bearing (photo) and gently tap it into the casing.
10 Fit the mainshaft rear nut but do not attempt to tighten it fully at this stage.

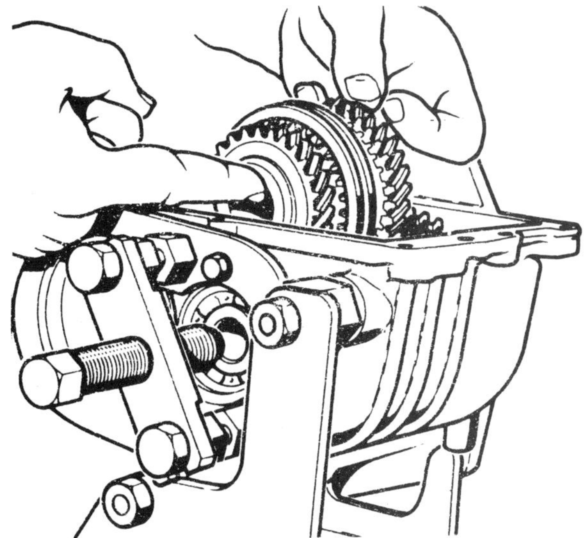

Fig. 6.7. Lifting out the 1st/2nd gear cluster

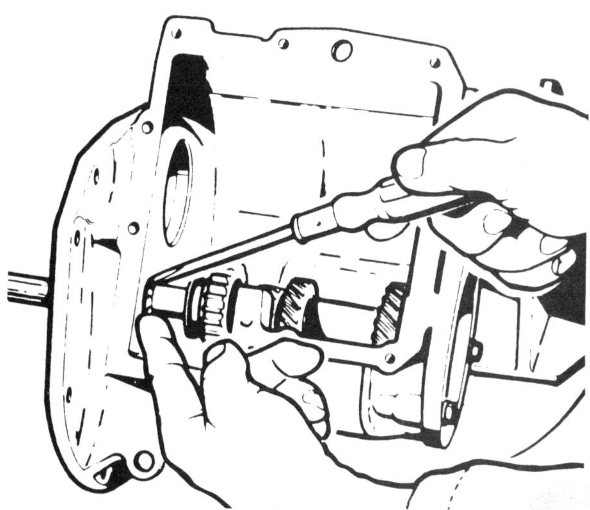

Fig. 6.8. Removing the reverse gear shaft circlips

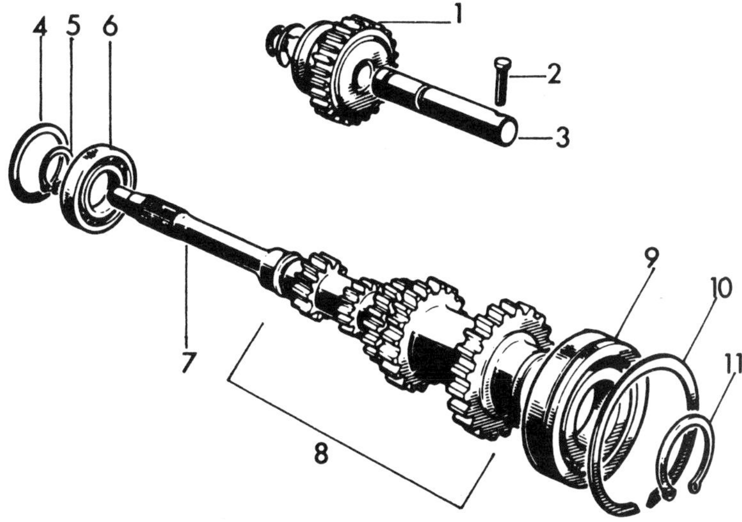

Fig. 6.9. Exploded view of reverse gear assembly and input shaft

1 Reverse gear
2 Pin
3 Reverse idler shaft
4 Spacer
5 Circlip
6 Bearing
7 Primary shaft
8 Gear assembly
9 Bearing
10 Bearing snap ring
11 Circlip

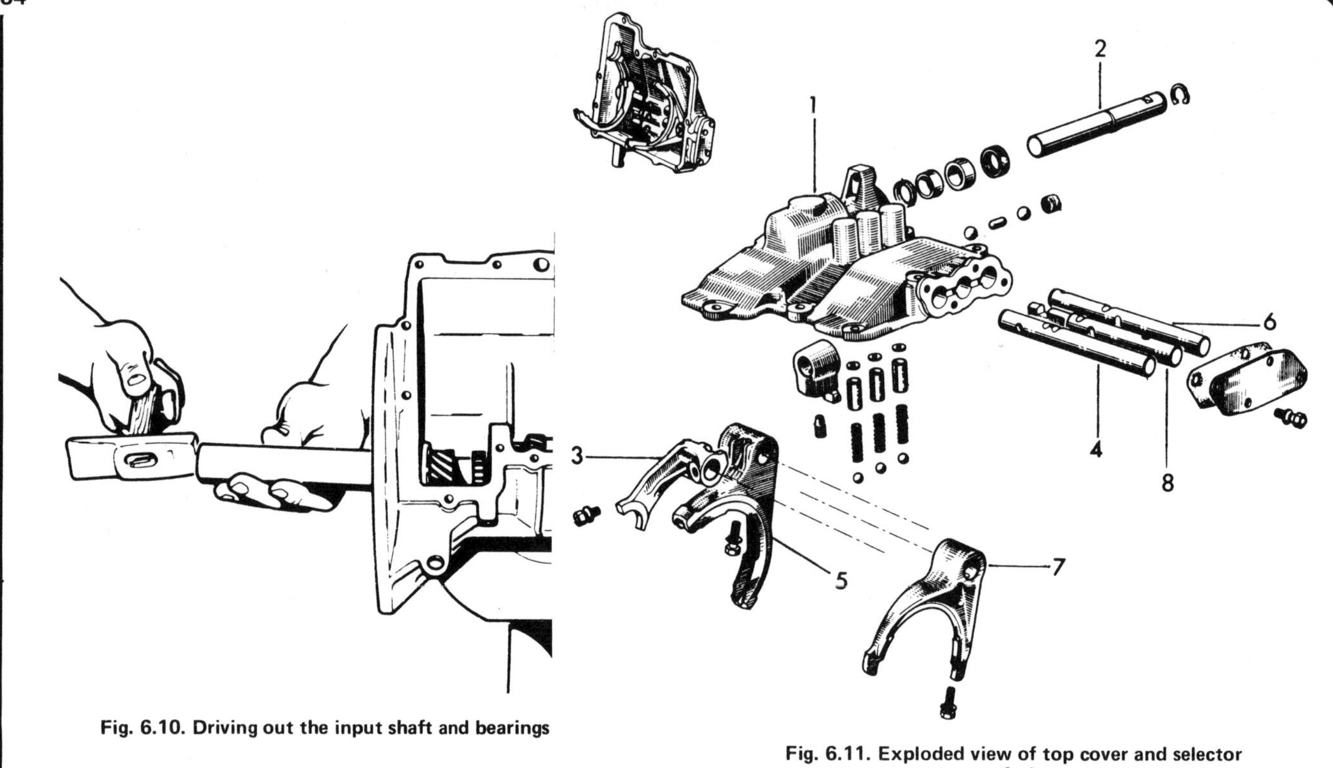

Fig. 6.10. Driving out the input shaft and bearings

Fig. 6.11. Exploded view of top cover and selector forks

1	*Cover*	*5*	*3rd/4th selector fork*
2	*Fork control lever*	*6*	*3rd/4th selector shaft*
3	*Reverse selector fork*	*7*	*1st/2nd selector fork*
4	*Reverse selector shaft*	*8*	*1st/2nd selector shaft*

4.10B Assembling the synchro sleeve and hub

5.2 Fitting the primary (input) shaft complete with bearings

5.3A 1st/2nd gear cluster assembly

5.3B 3rd/4th gear cluster assembly

5.4 Inserting the front mainshaft bearing ...

5.5 ... followed by the spacer

5.6 Fitting the mainshaft thrust washer

5.7 Positioning the 3rd/4th gear cluster in the casing

5.8 Sliding the mainshaft through the gears

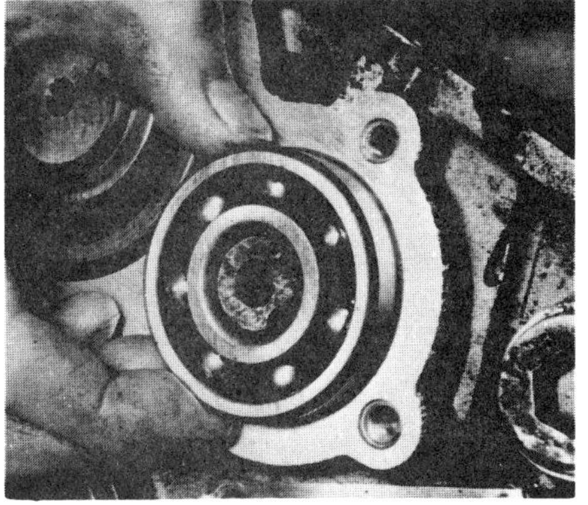
5.9 Fitting the mainshaft rear bearing

5.11 Fitting the reverse roller gear and shaft

5.12 Inserting the reverse gear shaft pin

5.14 Mainshaft rear retaining nut peened over

5.16 Fitting the primary shaft shims ...

5.17 ... followed by the oil seal

5.18 Location of clutch release bearing guide

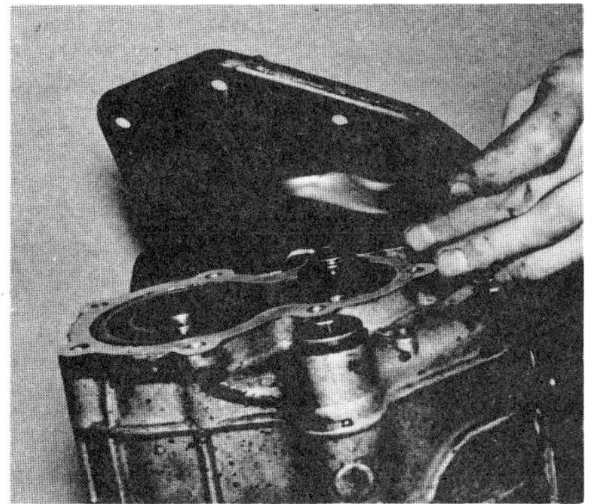
5.22 Fitting the gearbox rear cover

5.23 Clutch release arm in position

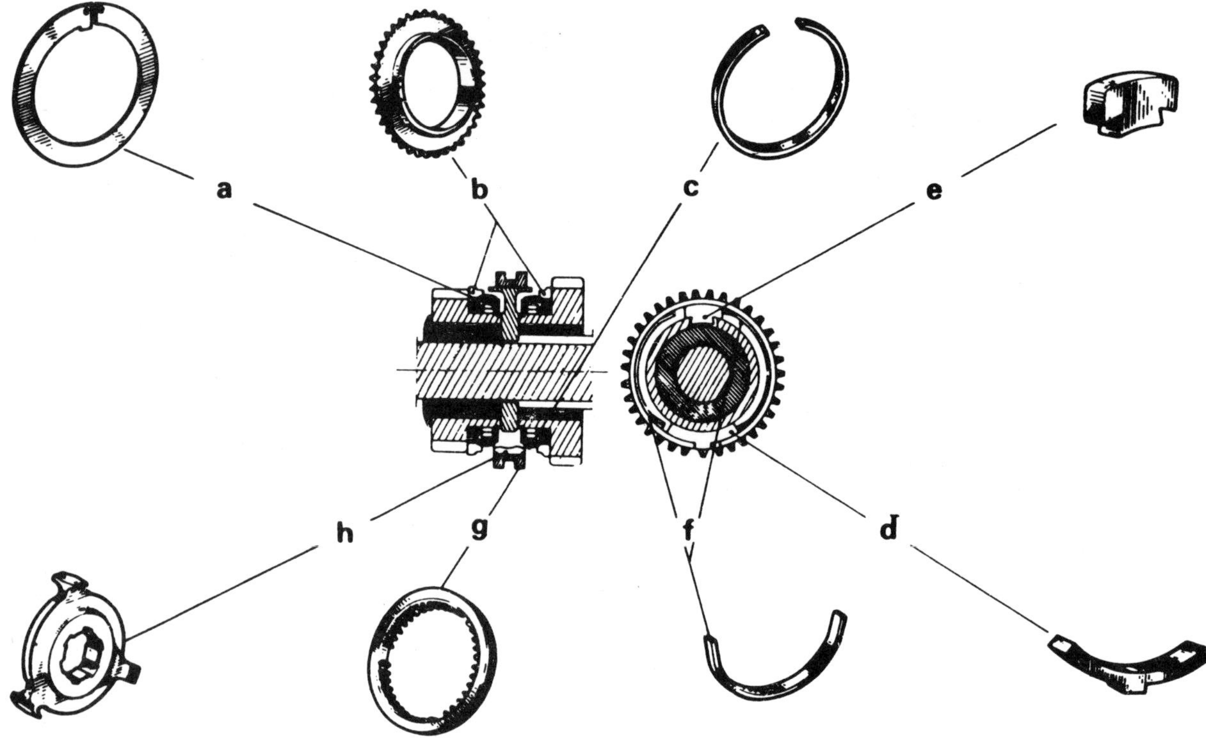

Fig. 6.12. Exploded view of synchromesh assembly

A Circlip
B Dog tooth ring, driven gear
C Baulk ring
D Locking pawl
E Spring stop
F Drive springs
G Sliding sleeve
H Driving hub

11 Fit a new 'O' ring on the reverse idler gear shaft, hold the reverse gear in position and slide the shaft through the casing and gear (photo).
12 Fit the circlip on the front of the reverse gear shaft and insert the retaining pin into the top of the casing (photo).
13 Engage the reverse gear and one forward gear to lock the shafts, and tighten the mainshaft rear nut to the specified torque wrench setting. Do not forget that the nut has a left-hand thread.
14 Lock the nut bv peening it into the groove in the mainshaft (photo).
15 Disengage the gears and check that both shafts rotate freely and the gears mesh correctly.
16 Fit the original shim(s) into the primary shaft front bearing recess (photo).
17 Coat the outer diameter of a new oil seal with oil and fit it into the front bearing recess, ensuring the internal lip faces towards the bearing (photo).
18 Slide the clutch release bearing guide tube over the primary shaft and tighten the single securing bolt (photo).
19 Fit a new gasket to the gearshift fork cover (photo).
20 Engage the selector forks and locate and bolt the cover into position.
21 Fit a new rear cover gasket.
22 Fit the cover and gasket to the gearbox (photo).
23 If the clutch release arm pivot has been removed then it should be refitted (photo).
24 Refit the mounting plates.

6 Final drive (differential) unit - removal and refitting

1 Remove the gearbox as described in Section 2 of this Chapter.
2 Drain the oil from the differential unit by removing the drain plug.
3 Unbolt the speedometer cable from the lower differential unit.
4 Remove the left-hand driveshaft/stub axle assembly as described for engine removal (Chapter 1).
5 Unscrew and remove the gearbox guide bolts which were fitted to facilitate removal of the gearbox.
6 Remove the starter motor.
7 Remove the bolts securing the gearchange relay bracket to the final drive unit.

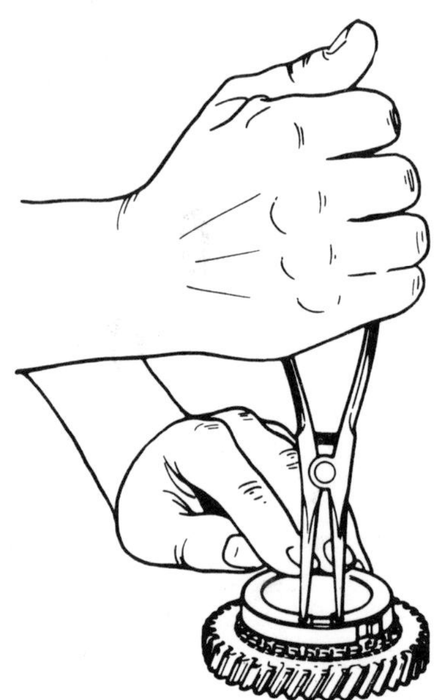

Fig. 6.13. Removing a synchromesh unit circlip

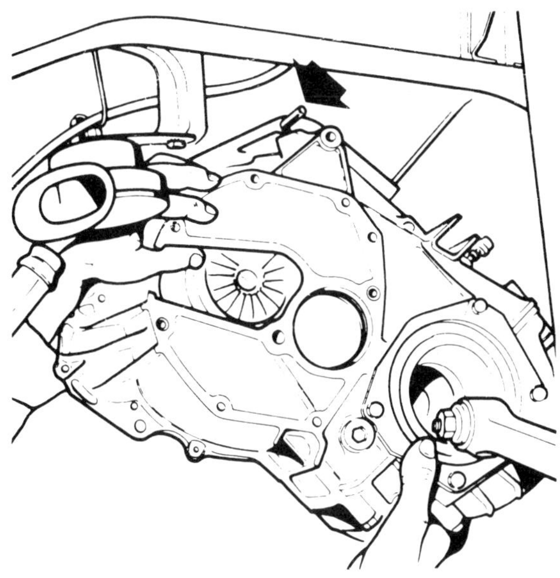

Fig. 6.14. Location of guide stud used when replacing transmission

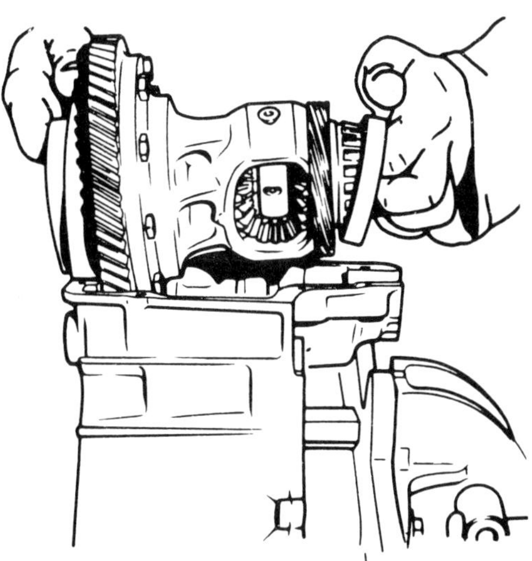

Fig. 6.15. Lifting out the differential assembly

Fig. 6.16. Removing the crownwheel securing bolts

8 Remove the dirt shield from the clutch housing.

9 Remove the bolts which secure the clutch bellhousing to the engine block.

10 Pull the combined clutch bellhousing, final drive unit outwards sufficiently far to disengage the right-hand driveshaft. Do not allow the driveshaft to drop but have an assistant support it and lower it gently.

11 To refit the clutch bellhousing/final drive unit, first screw in a guide stud as shown in Fig. 6.14.

12 Offer up the transmission unit and engage it on the guide stud.

13 Engage the right-hand driveshaft in the differential.

14 Slowly push the clutch bellhousing/final drive unit into its correct position, turning the driveshaft at the same time.

15 Fit the securing bolts and tighten them to a torque of 32 lb f ft (4.43 kg fm). Remove the guide stud.

16 Refit the left-hand driveshaft, stub axle and brake disc as described in Chapter 1.

17 Reconnect the speedometer drive cable to the final drive unit.

18 The gearbox may now be refitted as described in Section 2 of this Chapter.

7 Final drive (differential) unit - dismantling

1 Place the clutch bellhousing face downwards on the bench and remove the securing bolts from the bearing thrust plate.

2 Remove the thrust plate, retain the shims fitted below it and remove the 'O' ring seal.

3 Remove the securing bolts from the differential half housing and then remove the half housing complete with the seal located on the smaller bearing side.

4 Lift the differential assembly from the casing (Fig. 6.15).

5 Wash all components and the interior of the differential housing in paraffin.

8 Final drive (differential) unit - inspection and servicing

1 Inspect each component for wear, scoring or damage. Examine the teeth of the crownwheel for chipping and also the gear wheels in the differential cage.

2 Examine the roller bearings for wear and cracks in the inner and outer tracks.

3 To remove the crownwheel, (if this component is renewed, the gearbox output shaft with matched pinion will also have to be renewed) support the unit in a vice and unscrew the securing bolts (Fig. 6.16).

4 The differential bearings may be renewed if a suitable extractor is available (Fig. 6.17).

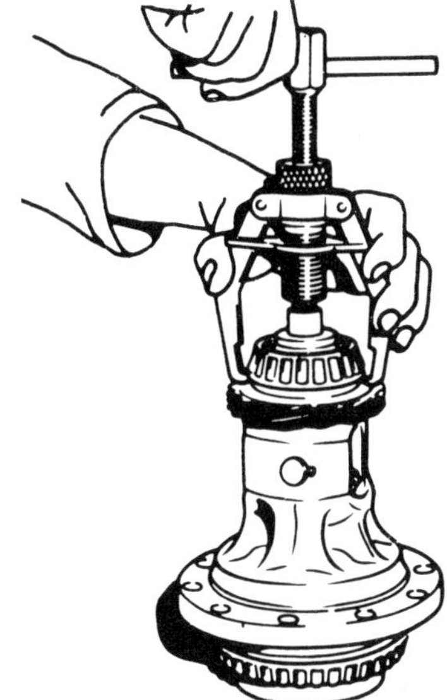

Fig. 6.17. Removing a differential roller bearing using a puller

8.6 Speedometer driven gear

8.9 Differential inner oil seal

8.10 Differential housing oil seal (small end)

9.1 Differential unit positioned in main housing

9.2 Final drive lower housing in position

9.7 Fitting the final drive bearing shims

9.12 Thrust plate 'O' ring and oil seal

10.1 Lower end of gearshift lever

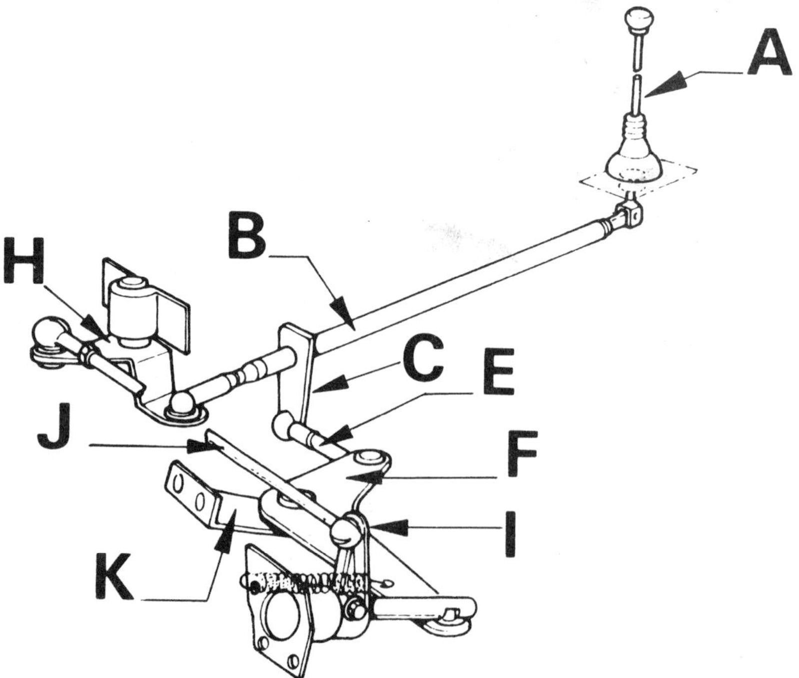

Fig. 6.18. Layout of gearshift linkage

A Gear lever
B Control tube
C Operating arm, gear selection
E Adjustable rod, gear selection
F Relay lever, gear selection
H Relay lever, gear engagement
I Relay lever
J Adjustable rod, gear engagement
K Relay support, final drive

5 The speedometer drive gear is a press fit on the outside of the differential cage. An extractor will be needed to remove it.
6 Refitting of the bearings and the speedometer drive gear will require the use of a press and it will be better to let a Chrysler dealer carry out this work if the correct tools are not available. Where the speedometer drive gear is to be renewed, then the meshing gear in the lower differential half housing must also be renewed as a matched pair (photo).
7 Dismantling of the sun and planet bevel gears is not recommended. It is better to obtain a reconditioned factory exchange differential cage complete.
8 The differential oil seals should be renewed as a matter of course. These may be renewed without removing the unit from the vehicle but the oil must first be drained and the gearbox pulled forward.
9 Extract the inner oil seal and carefully drive in a new one ensuring that its lip is towards the differential cage (photo).
10 Drive out the oil seal from the small bearing end of the housing and fit a new one squarely with its lip towards the roller bearing (photo).
11 Tap out the oil seal from the large bearing flange and fit a new one using a soft faced hammer ensuring that the lip will be towards the large bearing when it is bolted up (Fig. 6.19).
12 The differential and final drive assembly is now ready for refitting to its housing but certain adjustments are necessary. They are described in the following Section.

Fig. 6.19. Fitting a new seal into the thrust plate flange

9 Final drive (differential) unit - reassembly and adjustment

1 Lower the assembled final drive unit into the housing and at the same time locate the large roller bearing track ring (photo).
2 Fit the lower half housing into position but do not tighten the bolts more than finger tight (photo).
3 A thrust plate dummy tool should now be borrowed or hired from your Chrysler dealer (part No. 20886K) or a substitute made up. Its purpose is to align the surfaces of the upper and lower differential housings and to locate the differential bearings correctly in their seats.
4 Bolt the tool first to the main housing face and then to the lower housing (Fig. 6.20).
5 Tighten the central threaded plate of the tool until the roller bearings are seated, rotating the differential housing at the same time. Repeat this operation several times and then release the plate of the tool and tighten the half housing bolts to 16 lb ft (2.21 kg fm).
6 Remove the dummy thrust plate tool and check that the differential housing will turn easily without binding or tight spots.
7 Fit the original bearing shims (photo).
8 If a new crownwheel carrier, carrier bearing flange, carrier bearing, or casing is being fitted, the bearing pre-load must be set up using the following method.

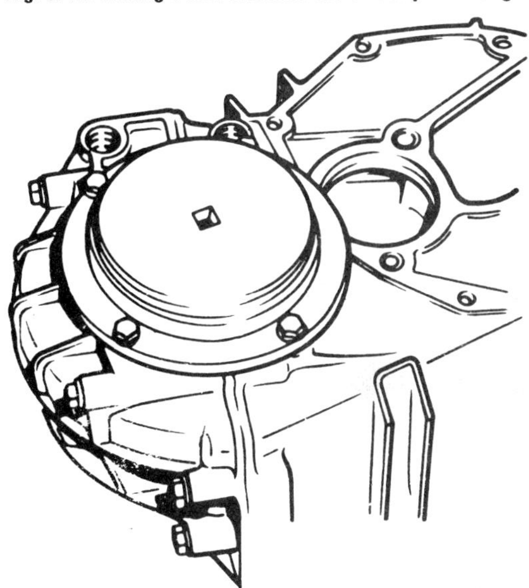

Fig. 6.20. Special tool fitted in place of the thrust plate

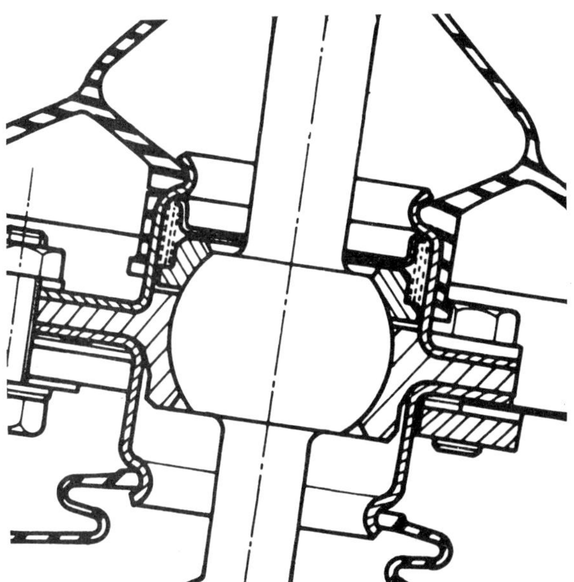

Fig. 6.22. Cross-sectional view of gear lever housing

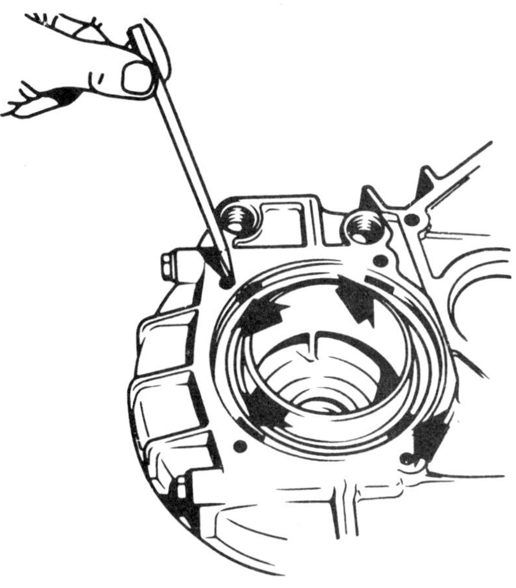

Fig. 6.21. Location of pieces of soft solder used for measuring bearing pre-load

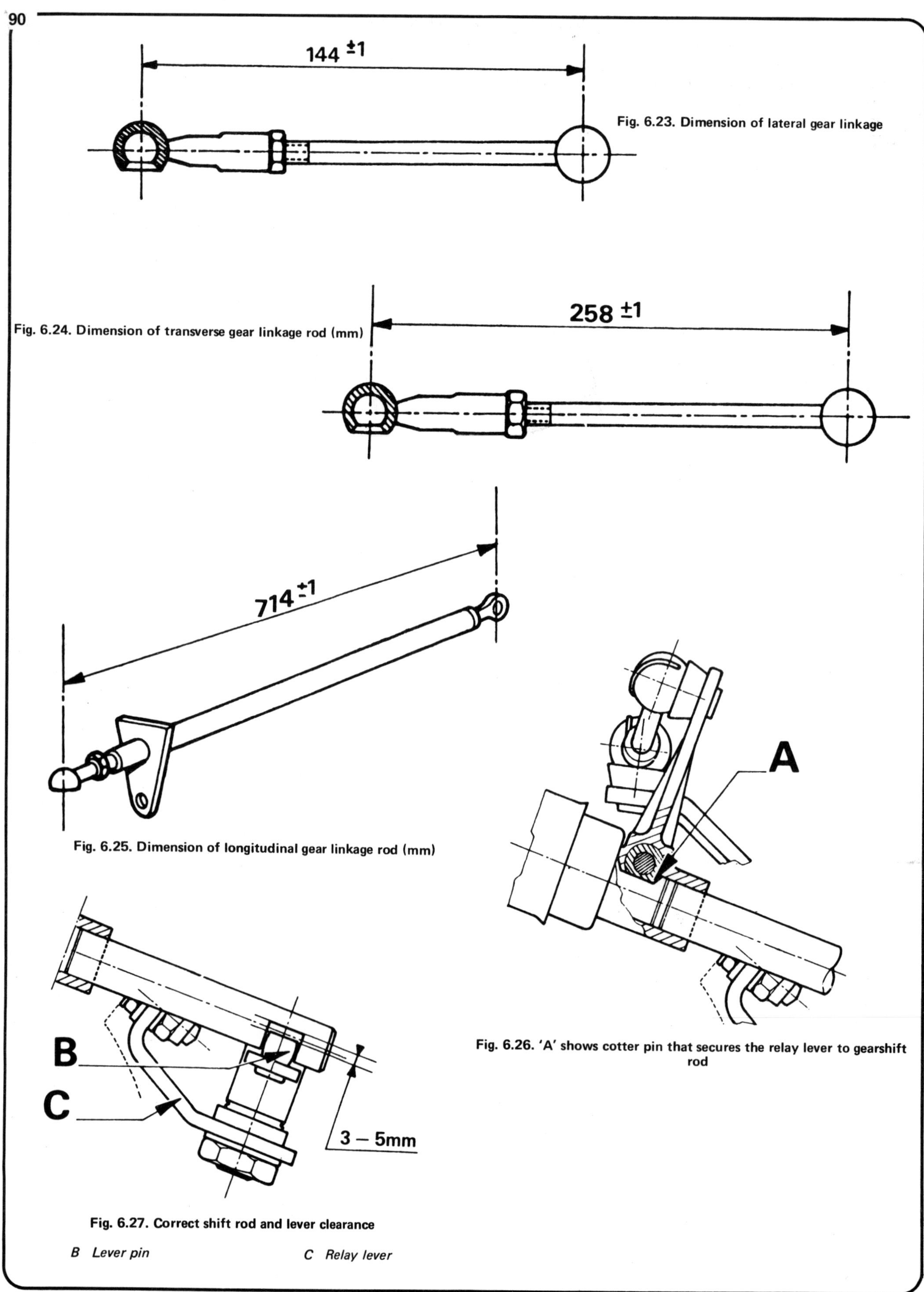

Fig. 6.23. Dimension of lateral gear linkage

Fig. 6.24. Dimension of transverse gear linkage rod (mm)

Fig. 6.25. Dimension of longitudinal gear linkage rod (mm)

Fig. 6.26. 'A' shows cotter pin that secures the relay lever to gearshift rod

Fig. 6.27. Correct shift rod and lever clearance

B Lever pin *C Relay lever*

9 Place four lengths of 1 mm diameter soft soldering wire (or Plastigage) at equal points on top of the original shims, bolt the thrust plate (without 'O' ring seal) into position, tightening the bolts to 16 lb f ft (2.21 kg fm).
10 Remove the thrust plate, measure the thickness of the crushed wire with a micrometer and this thickness plus 0.04 inch (0.1 mm) will be the required **additional** shim pack thickness to provide the necessary bearing pre-load. Shims are available in a range of thicknesses to suit most requirements. The next higher thickness should be used however where an exact tolerance cannot be matched precisely by a combination of shim thicknesses.
11 Locate the shim pack in position.
12 Fit a new 'O' ring to the thrust plate (photo).
13 Bolt the thrust plate to the housing, tightening the bolts to a torque of 16 lb f ft (2.21 kg fm).
14 The final drive (differential) unit is now ready for fitting to the vehicle as described in Section 6, followed by the gearbox, Section 2.

10 Gearshift lever and mechanism - adjustment

1 The gearshift lever is mounted in a ball housing bolted to the car floor (see Fig. 6.22 and photo).
2 Movement of the lever is transmitted to the gearbox through a longitudinal control rod and a series of levers and rods as shown in Fig. 6.18.
3 The balljoints have a nylon insert and can be prised apart after first removing the wire clip where fitted.
4 If gearchanging is difficult, and the angle of the lever appears to be incorrect or new linkage components are being fitted, check the length of the lateral rods 'E' and 'J' (Fig. 6.18).
5 If necessary remove the rod(s) and adjust the length by slackening the locknut and turning the balljoint end in the required direction. Tighten the locknut (Fig. 6.23, 6.24 and 6.25).
6 Check that the cotter pin securing the lever to the shift rod protruding from the gearbox (Fig. 6.26) is tight and there is no free movement between rod and lever.
7 Set the lever in the neutral position and check that there is a clearance of 1/8 to 3/16 in. (3 to 5 mm) between the slot in the end of the shift rod and the pin on the relay lever (Fig. 6.27).
8 If necessary obtain the correct clearance by slackening the nuts securing the relay bracket to the final drive casing and moving the bracket up or down as necessary. Tighten the nuts when the adjustment is correct.

11 Fault diagnosis - gearbox and final drive

Symptom	Reason/s	Remedy
Weak or ineffective synchromesh	Synchronising springs worn, split or damaged	Dismantle and overhaul transmission unit. Fit new gear wheels and synchronising cones.
	Synchromesh dogs worn, or damaged	Dismantle and overhaul transmission unit. Fit new synchromesh unit.
Jumps out of gear	Broken gearchange fork rod spring	Dismantle and renew spring.
	Transmission unit coupling dogs badly worn	Dismantle transmission unit. Fit new coupling dogs.
	Selector fork rod groove badly worn	Fit new selector fork rod.
	Selector fork rod securing screw and locknut loose	Tighten securing screw and locknut.
Excessive noise	Incorrect grade of oil in transmission unit or oil level too low	Drain, refill, or top up transmission unit with correct grade of oil.
	Transmission bearings worn or damaged	Dismantle and overhaul transmission unit. Renew bearings.
	Gearteeth excessively worn or damaged	Dismantle, overhaul transmission unit. Renew gear wheels.
	Mainshaft thrust washer worn allowing excessive end play	Dismantle and overhaul transmission unit. Renew thrust washers.
Excessive difficulty in engaging gear	Clutch pedal adjustment incorrect	Adjust clutch pedal correctly.
	Gearshift relay rod incorrectly adjusted	Adjust length of relay rods to the correct dimensions.

Chapter 7 Front suspension; driveshafts and hubs

Contents

Specifications

Suspension type	Torsion bar, anti-roll bar and telescopic hydraulic shock absorbers
Driveshafts	
Type	Three piece solid shaft comprising inner, intermediate and stub axle sections.
Driveshafts joints	
Inner joint	Constant velocity type
Outer joint	Universal type
Torsion bar identification	
Right-hand bar	Orange paint mark
Left-hand bar	White paint mark

Torque wrench settings	**lb f ft**	**kg f m**
Shock absorber, lower mounting	18	2.49
Shock absorber, upper mounting	11	1.52
Hub nut, driveshaft	144	19.91
Anti-roll bar to tie-rod	7	0.97
Upper suspension arm to crossmember	37	5.12
Bump stops to lower arm	11	1.52
Brake disc to hub	37	5.12
Stiffening bracket to body	37	5.12

Stiffening bracket to crossmember	15	2.07
Brake caliper to stub axle	55	7.61
Spindle nuts, lower suspension arms	55	7.61
Spindle nuts, upper suspension arms	41	5.67
Torsion bar adjusting lever to crossmember	55	7.61
Anti-roll bar bush to side member	18	2.49
Lower balljoint nut to arm	44	6.09
Lower balljoint to stub axle	250	34.58
Upper balljoint to stub axle	26	3.59
Slotted bearing nut in stub axle	214	29.59
Lower crossmember to body	8	1.11
Upper crossmember to body	4	0.55
Sub-frame to body	33	4.56
Torsion bar anchor crossmember to body	15	2.07
Torsion bar hub fork to crossmember	11	1.52

1 General description

The front suspension on the Alpine is of the independent double wishbone type with longitudinal torsion bars and telescopic dampers.

The upper suspension arms pivot on a pressed steel crossmember which is bolted to the longitudinal frame members.

The lower suspension arms pivot on spindles attached to a sub-frame comprising two tubular crossmembers and two pressed steel sidemembers.

The stub axle carriers swivel on upper and lower balljoints which are lubricated and sealed for life.

The front end of each torsion bar fits into a hexagonal socket on the inner ends of the lower suspension arms while the rear ends are located in the centre crossmember. Adjustable arms on the ends of each torsion bar sleeve enable the loading on the torsion bars to be altered to reset the vehicle ground clearance.

An anti-roll bar is attached to the frame by rubber bushes and the outer ends are connected to each lower suspension arm by tie rods.

Each driveshaft has a constant velocity joint at the inner end and a universal joint at the outer end. The joints are lubricated for life and providing the rubber gaiters are maintained in good condition the joints should last a considerable time before renewal is necessary.

2 Driveshaft - removal and refitting

1 The method of removing and refitting the driveshafts is given in Chapter 1, Sections 4 and 40 respectively.

2 It must be emphasised that care must be taken to prevent the lower suspension arm dropping right down due to the twisting effort of the pre-loaded torsion bars. Although the lower arm can be supported using a jack as described in Chapter 1, it is recommended that the telescopic damper is removed and the special restraining tool, (Chrysler Part No. CF 0004) is fitted in its place (Fig. 7.2).

3 Driveshaft joints - servicing

(a) Inner constant velocity joint

1 Secure the driveshaft in a vice and remove the circlip which retains the wider mouth of the gaiter (Fig. 7.3).

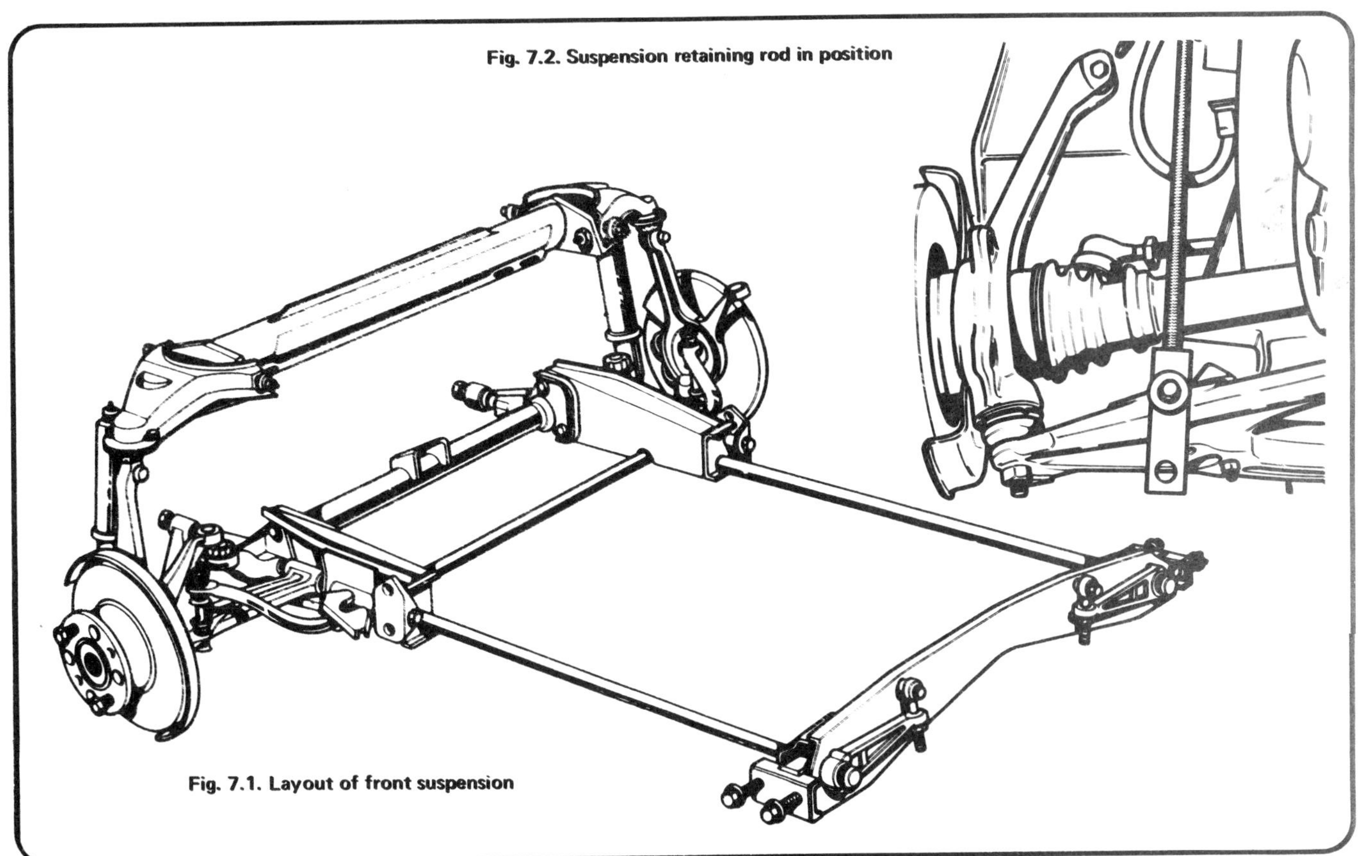

Fig. 7.2. Suspension retaining rod in position

Fig. 7.1. Layout of front suspension

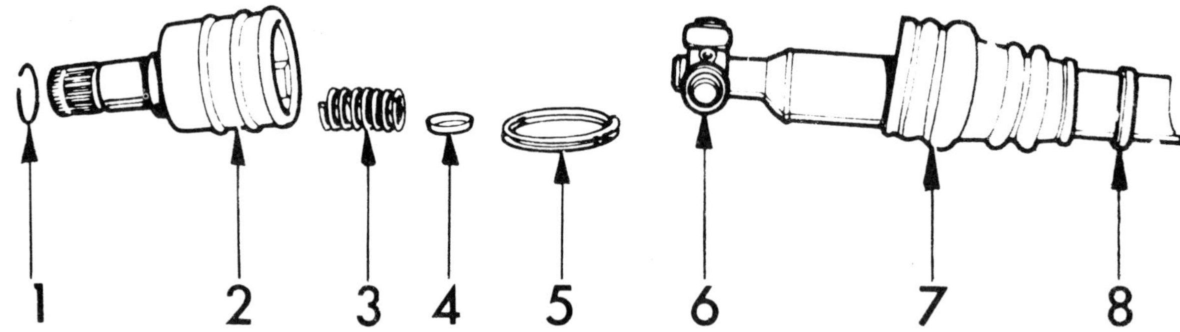

Fig. 7.3. Constant Velocity joint components

1 *Spring*
2 *Metal cap*
3 *Spring*
4 *Spring seat*
5 *Gaiter retaining ring*
6 *Spider and roller assembly*
7 *Gaiter*
8 *Gaiter retaining ring*

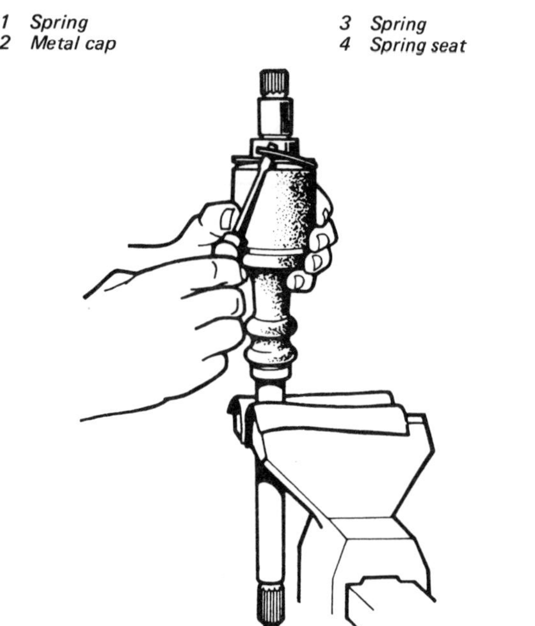

Fig. 7.4. Removing the spring ring securing the driveshaft rubber gaiter

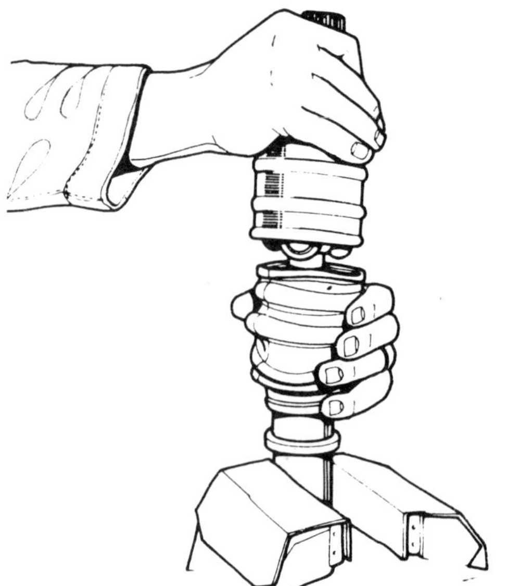

Fig. 7.5. Withdrawing the yoke from the rubber gaiter

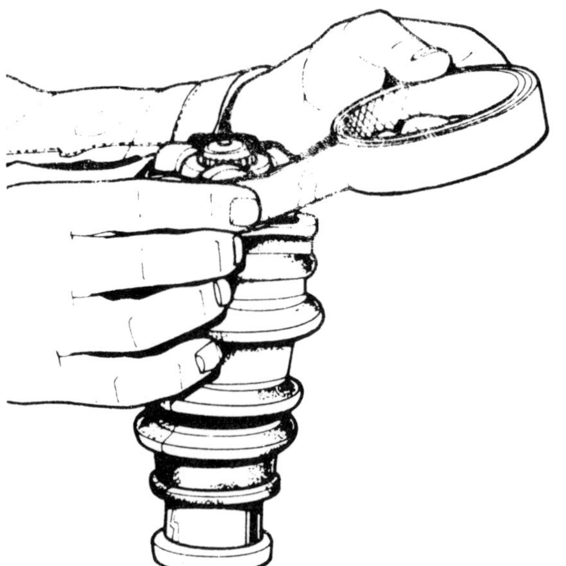

Fig. 7.6. Taping the driveshaft joint bearings

2 Draw the tulip shaped yoke upwards and remove it (Fig. 7.5).
3 Remove the spring and cap and then wipe out as much grease as possible from the joint assembly.
4 Fit masking or insulating tape round the ends of the three joint trunnions to prevent the bearings becoming dislodged (Fig. 7.6).
Note: The inner constant velocity joint spider and the outer universal joint spider must be offset from each other by $57^{\circ} \pm 3^{\circ}$ as shown in Fig. 7.7. The position of the spider in relation to the shaft should therefore be marked as shown in Fig. 7.8 before removing it.
5 Using a press and adaptor tool No. 20937M or similar, press the splined shaft through the spider assembly (Fig. 7.9).
6 Obtain a repair kit which will contain all renewable components except the tulip shaped yoke and intermediate shaft. Check all renewable parts for wear, damage, or corrosion, and renew if necessary.
7 Hold the intermediate shaft vertically in a vice. During the assembly it is necessary to make sure that every part is clinically clean.
8 Fit the new rubber retaining ring and sealing gaiter to the shaft.
9 Fill the gaiter and the tulip shaped yoke, complete with its metal cover, with grease.
10 Secure the new needle roller bearings on the new joint tripod and retain them with tape as previously described.
11 Fit the joint spider complete with bearings to the intermediate splined shaft, using a tubular drive, Fig. 7.10.
12 Peen the end of the intermediate shaft at three equidistant points to secure the joint tripod in position.
13 Remove the temporary retaining tape from the needle bearings.
14 Fit the cap and spring onto the curved end of the intermediate shaft.
15 Insert the tulip shaped yoke and metal cover into position in the bellows (Fig. 7.11).

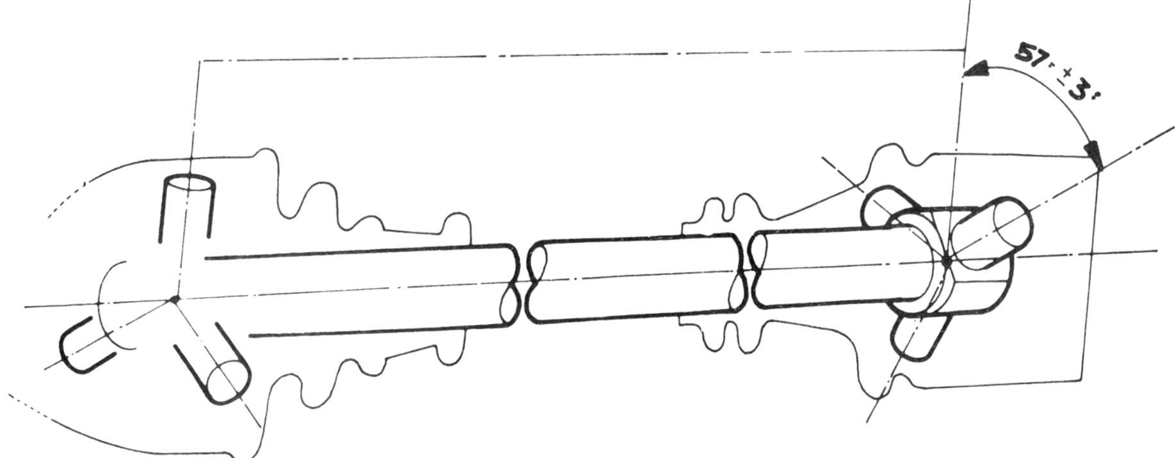

Fig. 7.7. Correct degree of offset for driveshaft inner and outer splines

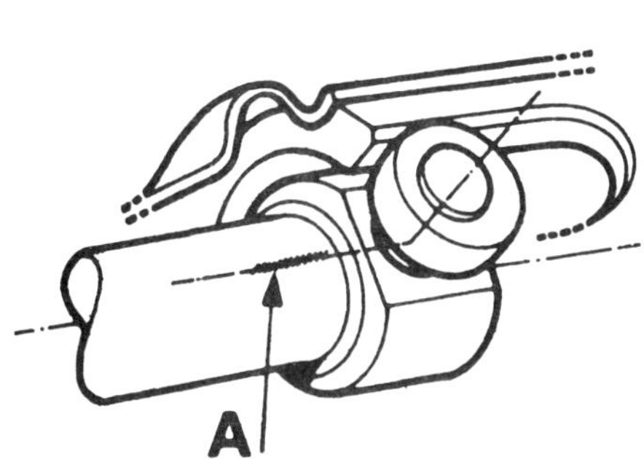

Fig. 7.8. Spider alignment mark

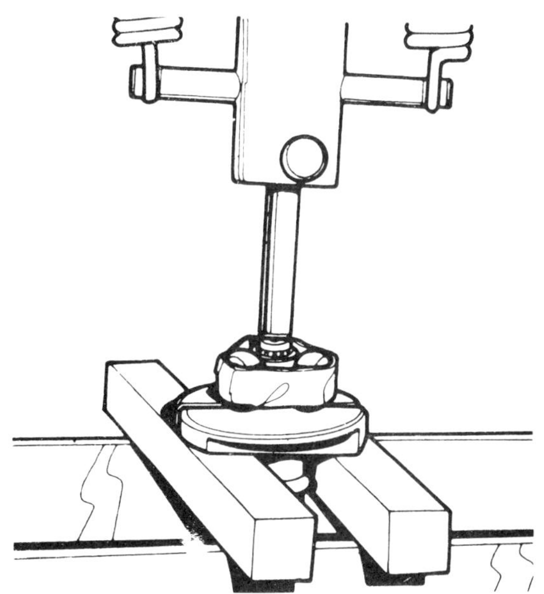

Fig. 7.9. Pressing the driveshaft from the spider

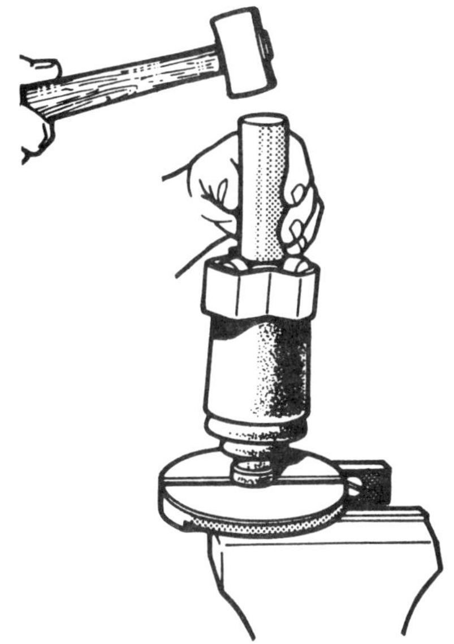

Fig. 7.10. Drifting a new spider onto the shaft

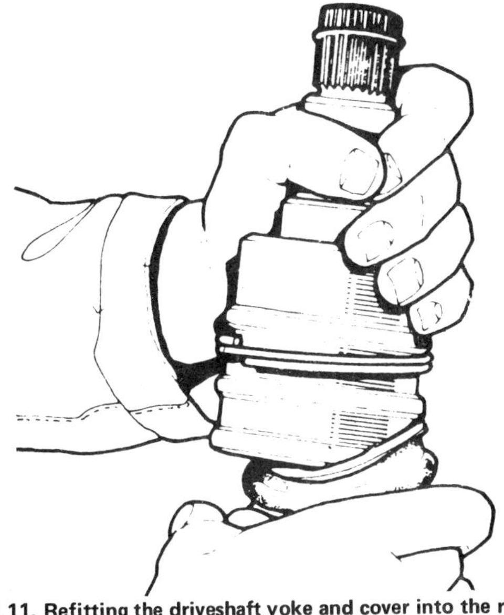

Fig. 7.11. Refitting the driveshaft yoke and cover into the rubber gaiter

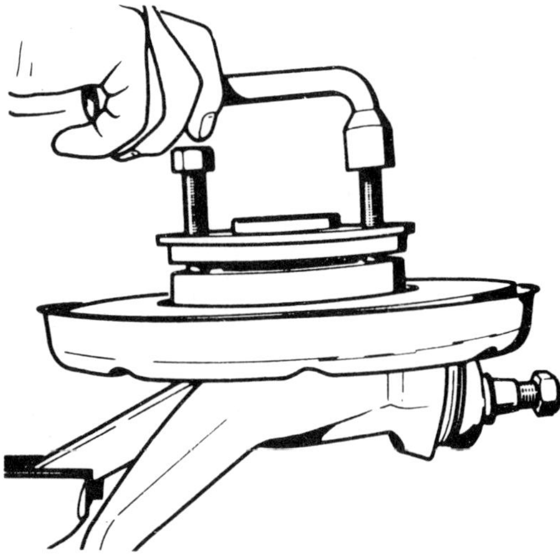

Fig. 7.12. Extracting the front wheel hub assembly

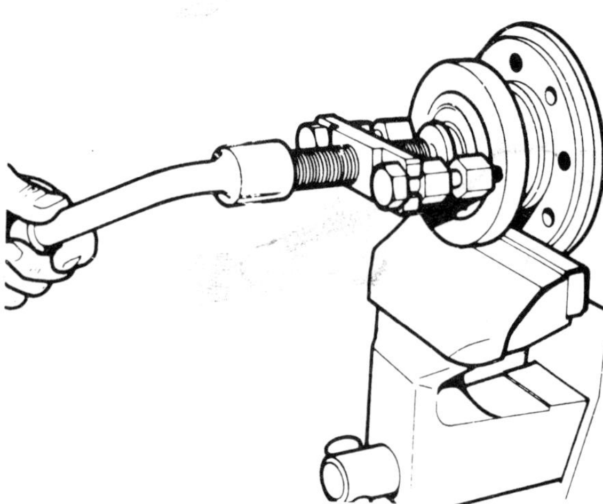

Fig. 7.13. Extracting the hub bearing ring

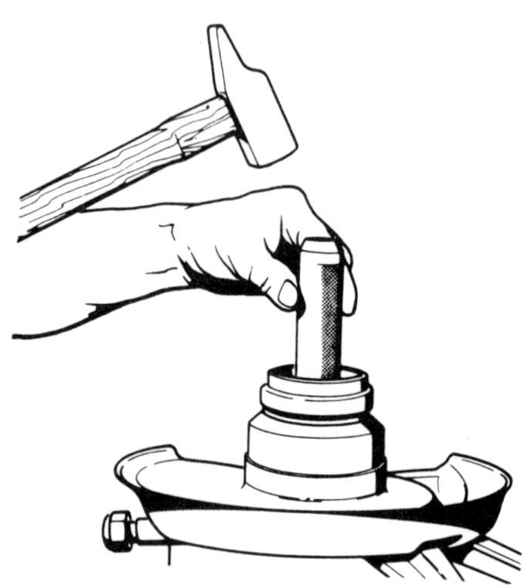

Fig. 7.14. Fitting a new oil seal to the stub axle carrier

16 Fit the smaller mouth of the bellows into the groove in the intermediate shaft and secure with the rubber retaining ring.
17 Check the movement of the assembled joint for tight spots.
18 Where the rubber bellows only are to be renewed then they and the rubber retaining ring should be cut off. Without any further dismantling, the new bellows and ring may be slid into position.

(b) Outer universal type joint

19 The outer, (roadwheel end) universal type joint is not repairable and if defective must be renewed.
20 If the driveshaft has covered a considerable mileage without any repair work being carried out on the inner constant velocity joint, the most sensible policy is to obtain a complete new driveshaft assembly from your Chrysler Dealer.
21 Alternatively, if the constant velocity joint is known to be in good condition, only the outer universal joint complete with intermediate shaft need be renewed.

4 Hubs and outer bearings - dismantling and reassembly

1 Disconnect the outer splined end of the driveshaft from the hub assembly using the method described for driveshaft removal in Chapter 1, Section 4. It is not necessary to withdraw the inner end of the shaft from the differential unit.
2 Do not forget to temporarily refit the lower balljoint securing nut.
3 Remove the disc brake caliper as described in Chapter 9.
4 Unscrew and remove the four bolts which secure the brake disc to the wheel hub.
5 Rotate the brake disc just enough so that two suitable bolts may be screwed into the hub (roadwheel fixing) bolts holes and by bearing against the brake disc with equal pressure extract the hub (Fig. 7.12).
6 Withdraw the hub together with the oil seal and bearing.
7 Remove the brake disc and then pick out the bearing balls from their plastic cage and then remove the cage.
8 Pull the bearing ring from the hub with the aid of a suitable extractor (Fig. 7.13).
9 Fit the new bearing balls and their plastic cage to the bearing ring. Pack with wheel bearing grease and then fit the assembly to the stub axle carrier.
10 Fit a new oil seal (lip upwards) into the stub axle carrier, using a suitable tubular drift (Fig. 7.14).
11 Refit the brake disc to the hub, tightening the securing bolts to the specified torque wrench setting.
12 Using a suitable bolt and plates, draw the disc/hub assembly into position on the stub axle carrier (Fig. 7.15).
13 Fit the driveshaft into the stub axle carrier and reconnect the lower balljoint and the track rod to steering arm balljoint.
14 Refit the brake caliper ensuring that a new locking plate is used.
15 Fit a new hub nut, tightening it onto the thrust washer to a torque of 145 lb f ft (20.05 kg f m). Peen the nut.
16 Refit the telescopic damper, refit the roadwheel and lower the car.

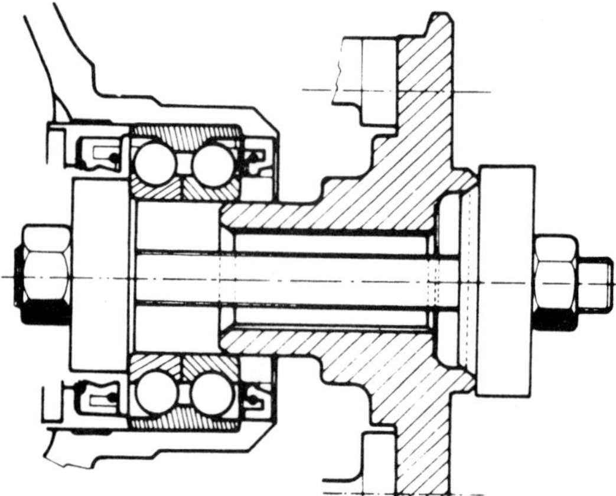

Fig. 7.15. Drawing the hub and disc assembly into the stub axle carrier

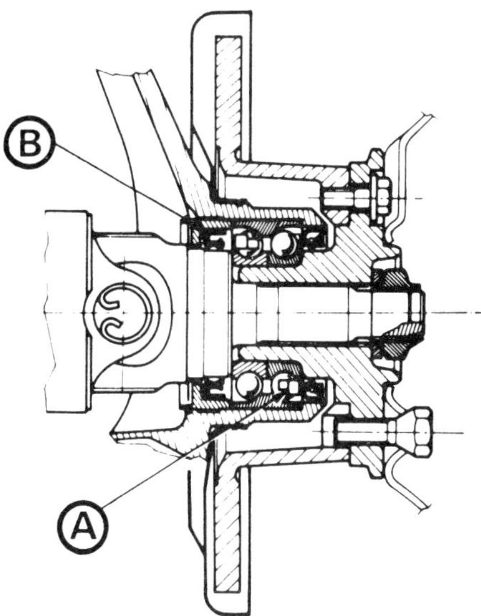

Fig. 7.16. Cross-section through front hub assembly

A Outer bearing *B Inner bearing*

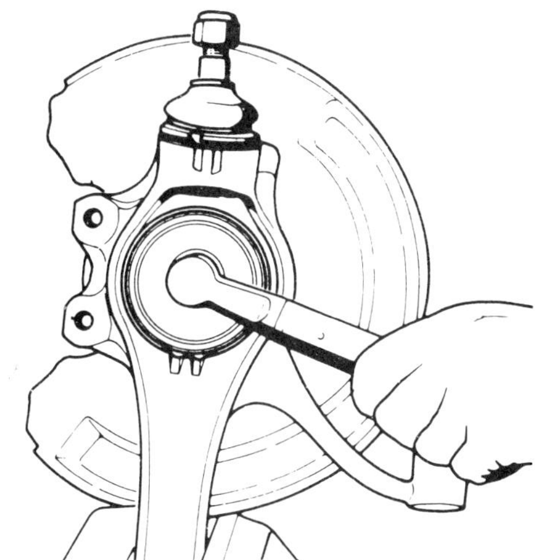

Fig. 7.18. Using special tool to remove the sleeve nut from rear of axle carrier

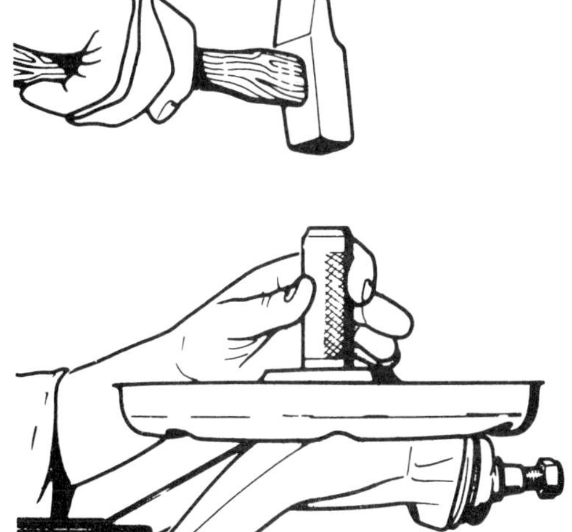

Fig. 7.19. Driving out the inner hub bearing

Fig. 7.17. Disconnecting the steering arm ball joint using an extractor

5 Inner hub bearings - dismantling and reassembly

1 These bearings are retained within the stub axle carrier by a screwed sleeve and it is recommended that the stub axle carrier be removed from the vehicle if the inner bearings are to be renewed. Location of the inner and outer hub bearings are shown in Fig. 7.16.
2 First slacken the roadwheel bolts and the large centre hub nut.
3 Jack up the car, support it on axle stands and remove the front wheel.
4 Remove the brake caliper as described in Chapter 9.
5 Remove the telescopic damper and fit the suspension restraining tool (Part No. CF 0004) in its place. Refer to Chapter 1, Section 4 if necessary.
Note: This tool **must** be used for this operation. Do not attempt to support the lower suspension arm using only a jack as described for driveshaft removal.
6 Disconnect the upper and lower stub axle carrier balljoints using a suitable extractor as described in Sections 6 and 7 of this Chapter.
7 Disconnect the steering arm balljoint using an extractor (Fig. 7.17)..
8 Remove the large centre driveshaft nut, hold the driveshaft in place to avoid stretching the rubber gaiters and withdraw the complete hub, disc and axle carrier assembly from the shaft.
9 Relieve the peening on the threaded sleeve at the rear of the stub axle carrier and unscrew the sleeve nut which will require the use of removal tool 20908H or one made up to perform the operation (Fig. 7.18).
10 Using a tubular drift, drive the inner bearing from the stub axle carrier (Fig. 7.19).
11 Before fitting the new bearing, pack it with the recommended grease. Pull it into position in the stub axle carrier by using a bolt and two plates as shown in Fig. 7.20.
12 Use a new threaded sleeve as the required peening on refitting makes the original unsuitable for re-use.
13 Fit a new oil seal into the threaded sleeve and screw it and its nut into position using the fitting tool. The lip of the oil seal will face inwards when correctly positioned, and the sleeve nut must be tightened to a torque of 214 lb f ft (29.59 kg f m).
14 Lock the sleeve in position by peening it at two points.
15 Carry out the operations described in paragraphs 9 to 14 in Section 4.
15 Reconnect the stub axle carrier upper balljoint.

6 Stub axle carrier lower balljoint - renewal

1 Remove the stub axle carrier as described in Section 5.
2 Place the carrier in a vice with the balljoint uppermost.

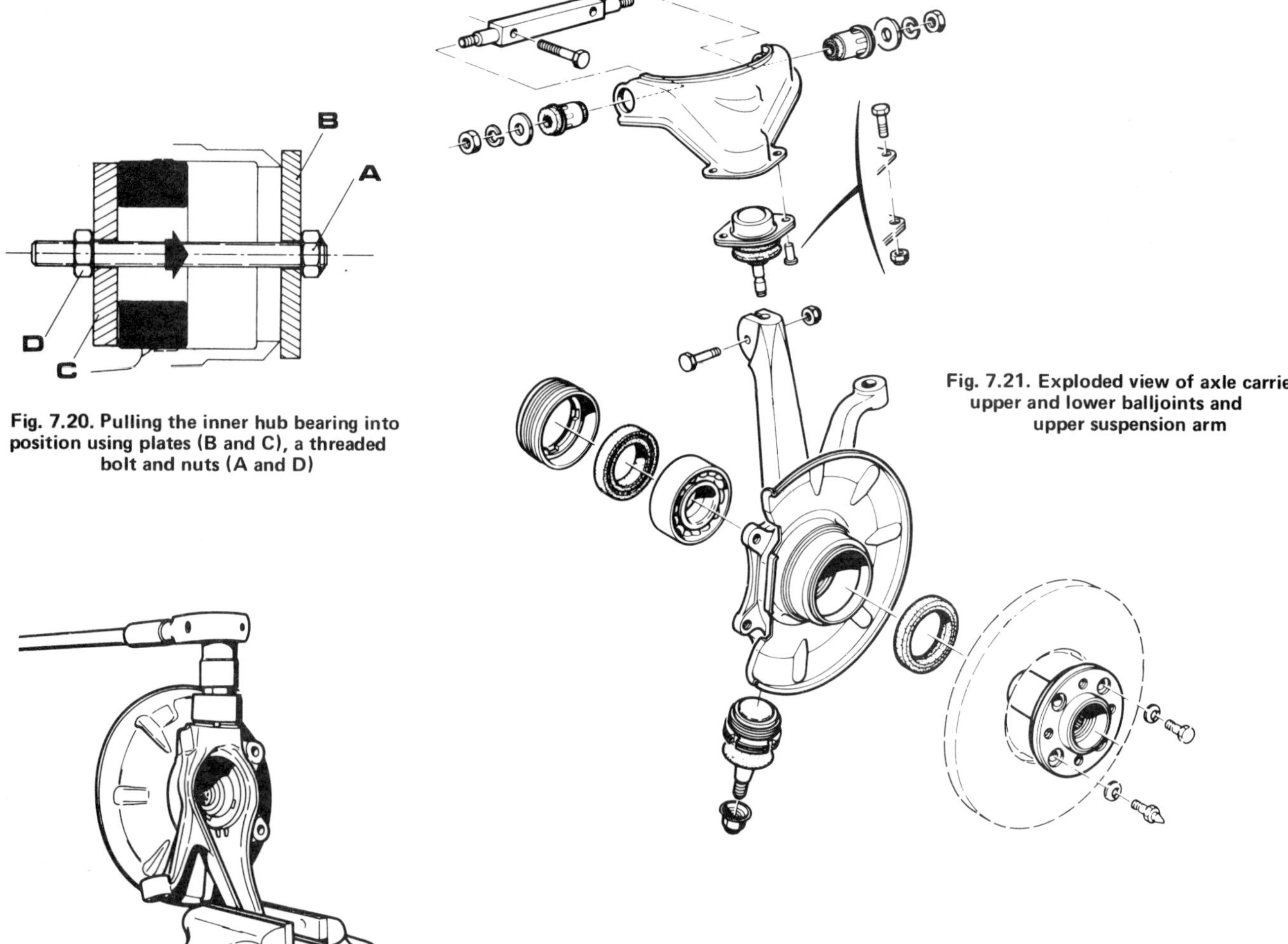

Fig. 7.20. Pulling the inner hub bearing into position using plates (B and C), a threaded bolt and nuts (A and D)

Fig. 7.21. Exploded view of axle carrier, upper and lower balljoints and upper suspension arm

Fig. 7.22. Removing the lower balljoint using special tool

3 Relieve the peening at the balljoint slotted ring.
4 A removal tool must now be employed (21811C and CJ0019) and it should be positioned and secured by the balljoint nut (Fig. 7.22).
5 Unscrew and remove the balljoint.
6 Fitting the new balljoint is a reversal of removal but take care not to pinch or tear the rubber cover. Tighten the slotted securing ring to a torque of 250 lb f ft (34.58 kg f m).
7 Remove the tool and peen the ring at one notch to lock it.
8 Refit the stub axle carrier as described in Section 5.

7 Upper suspension arm balljoint - renewal

1 Refer to Fig. 7.21. Remove the damper and fit the restraining rod to offset the torque of the torsion bar.
2 Jack up the front of the vehicle and support it on stands. Remove the roadwheel.
3 Remove the nut from the cotter pin that secures the balljoint pin to the axle carrier (Fig. 7.23) and drive out the cotter pin.
4 Drill out the rivets securing the top of the balljoint assembly to the upper suspension arm and withdraw the balljoint pin from the axle carrier.
5 The new balljoint will be supplied as a kit complete with nuts and bolts as replacement for the rivets.
6 Fitting is a reversal of dismantling but ensure that the balljoint securing nuts are located on the top surface of the upper suspension arm and are correctly locked.

8 Shock absorber - removal, testing and refitting

1 The telescopic type hydraulic shock absorber cannot be repaired and in the event of evidence occurring of bad cornering, steering wander or an unusually soft ride then the units should be removed from the car and tested.
2 Disconnect the upper and lower mountings, details of which are shown in Fig. 7.24.
3 Secure the lower damper mounting in a vice and in the vertical position. Operate the damper for the full length of its travel ten times. There should be good resistance in both directions of travel. If the action is jerky, or there is no resistance at all, renew the unit.
4 Refitting is a reversal of removal but note carefully the fitting sequence of the mountings.

9 Anti-roll bar - removal, inspection and refitting

1 The anti-roll bar is connected at each end to the lower suspension arm by a long bolt, nut and bush assembly as shown in Fig. 7.25.

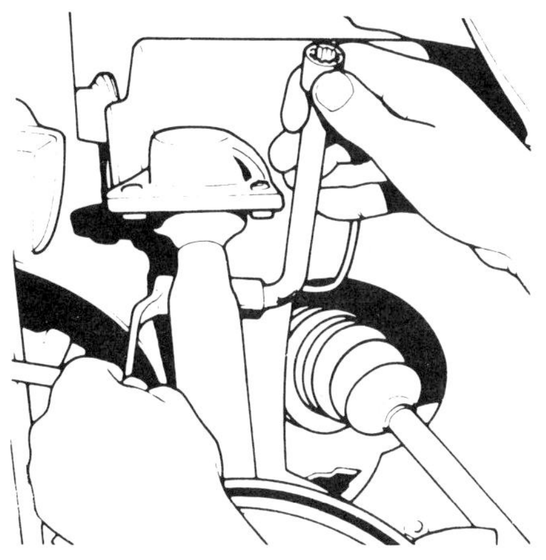
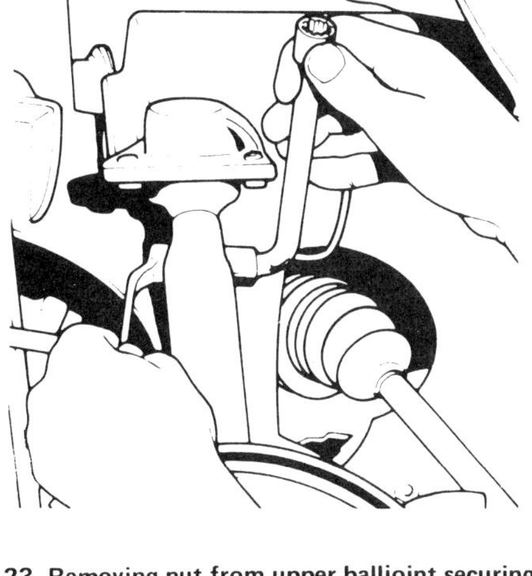

Fig. 7.23. Removing nut from upper balljoint securing pin

2 It is also supported by rubber bushes retained by semi-circular clamps.
3 Removal of the bar is carried out by withdrawing the anchor bolts and the rubber bush clamps.
4 Inspect the bar closely for cracks and also the rubber mounting components for deterioration. Renew as appropriate.
5 Refitting is a reversal of removal but do not exceed a tightening torque for the anchor or clamp nuts of 18 lb f ft (2.48 kg f m).

10 Torsion bars - removal and refitting

1 Jack up the front of the car and place axle stands beneath the crossmember or jacking points so that the suspension arms are suspended.
2 The tension of the torsion bar must now be relieved by using the special Chrysler tool No. 20916Q. As the bars are under considerable tension it is unwise to try and make do with a lever or similar.
3 Fit the special tool on the rear end of the torsion bar sleeve located in the centre crossmember and push the tool handle upwards to release the load on the adjusting rod and remove the adjusting rod pivot bolt.
4 Slowly allow the torsion bar lever to swing down and remove the tool (Fig. 7.27).
5 Remove the bolt securing the sleeve retaining fork to the rear of the crossmember and remove the fork (Fig. 7.28).
6 Pull the sleeve and lever assembly rearwards off the end of the torsion bar (Fig. 7.29).
7 Withdraw the torsion bar from the lower suspension arm by moving it to the rear and then remove it from the car by pulling it forward out of the crossmember.
8 Refitting is a reversal of removal but grease the splines of the torsion bar and the hubs into which it locates with wheel bearing type grease. The left-hand torsion bar is identified by a white paint spot, the right-hand by an orange paint spot. The torsion bars are not interchangeable. Never mark a torsion bar by scratching or filing as this may cause premature failure.
9 With the torsion bars correctly fitted in the vehicle, the tensioning arms should be fitted to the torsion bars at the angle shown in the diagram (Fig. 7.29).
10 A template should be used to obtain this initial setting and then the procedure described in the following Section must be carried out.

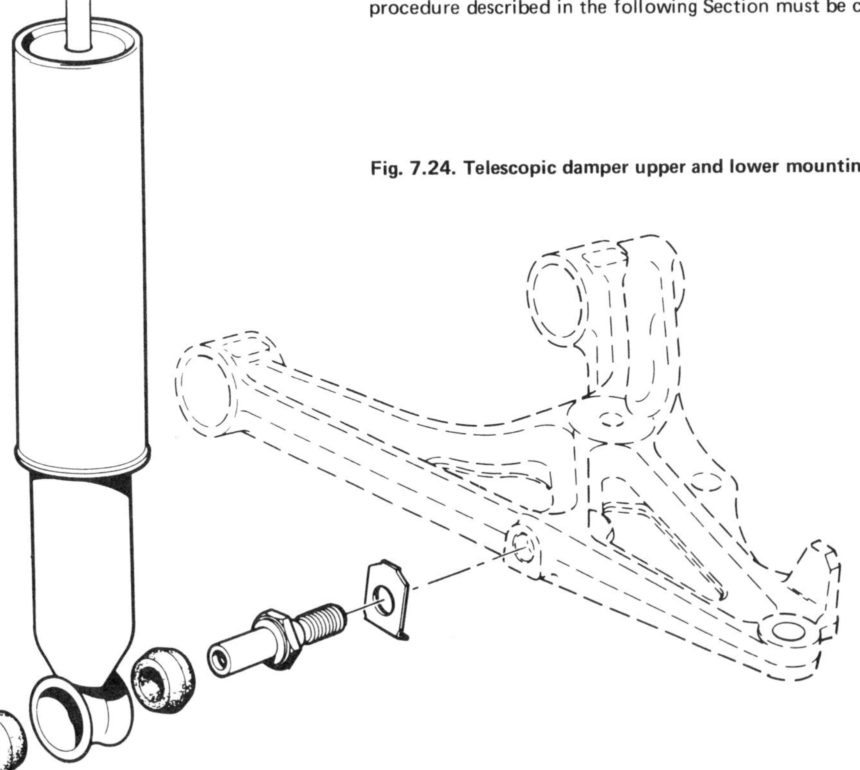

Fig. 7.24. Telescopic damper upper and lower mountings

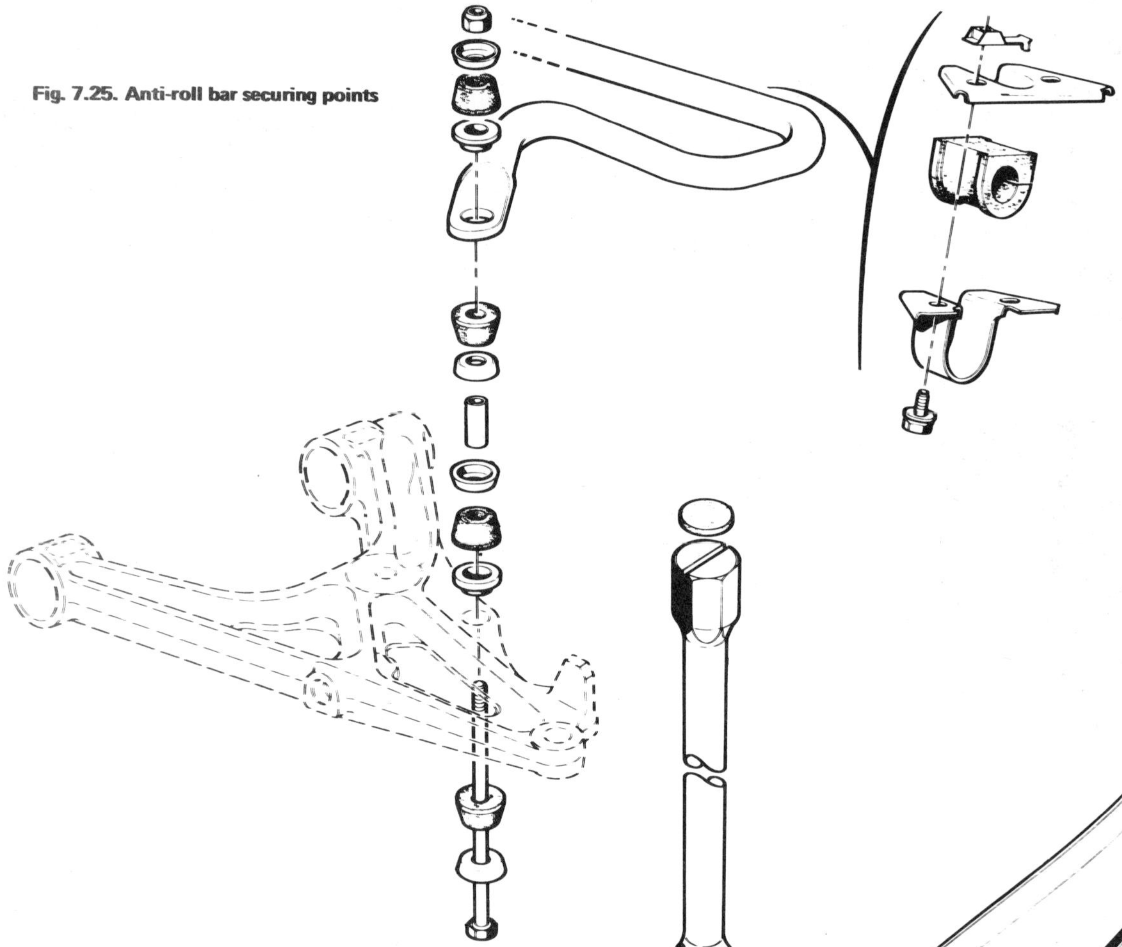

Fig. 7.25. Anti-roll bar securing points

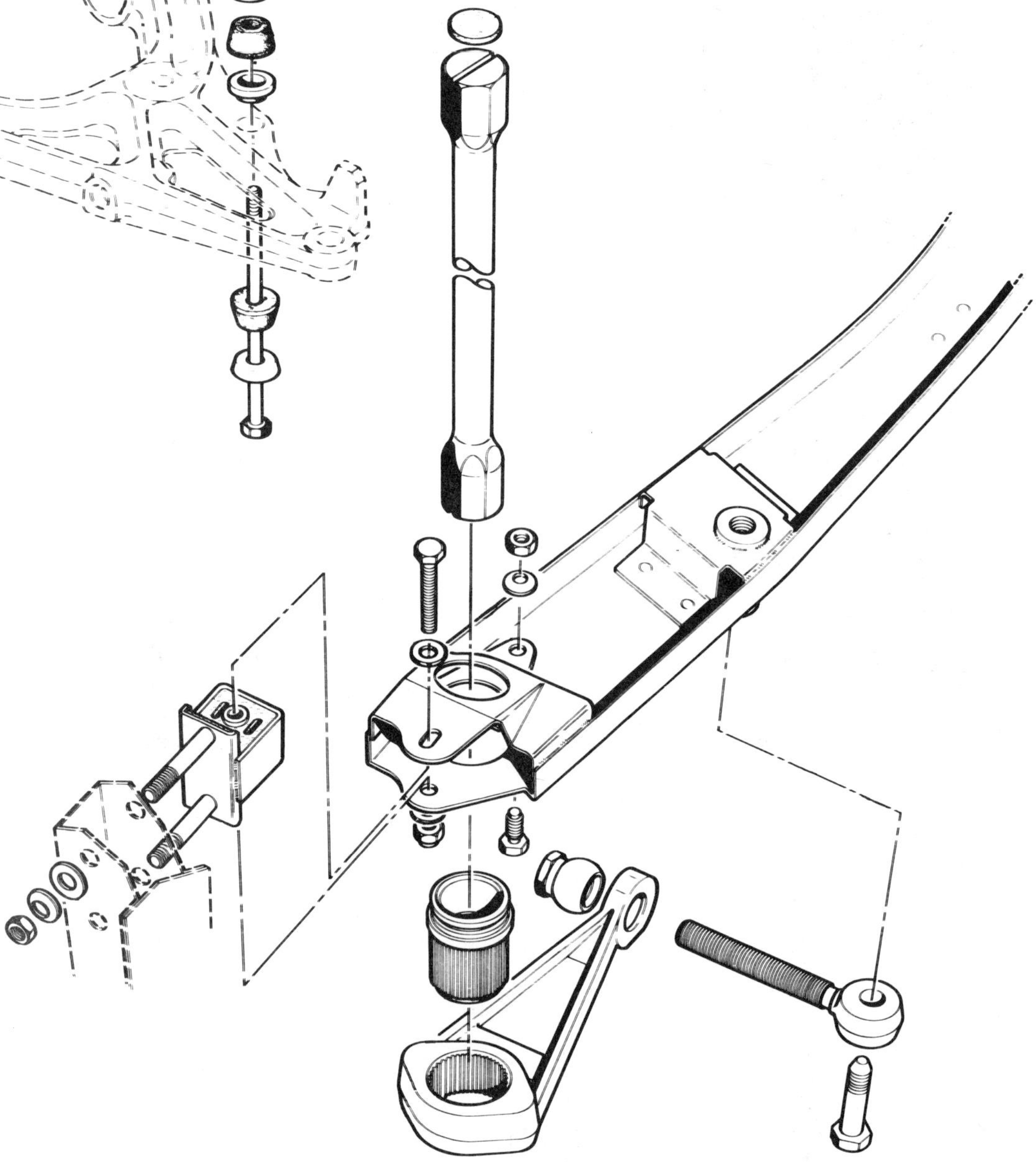

Fig. 7.26. Exploded view of torsion bar rear attachment point

11 Torsion bars - setting

1 If the torsion bars have been removed or renewed they must be set to the correct tension to ensure the safe handling characteristics of the car are maintained.
2 A special gauge bar (Part No. 21818K) and height stands, (Part No. CJ0017 for right-hand drive cars and Part No. 20917 for left-hand drive cars) are required when setting the height of the vehicle, and it is essential that after the torsion bar(s) have been fitted as described in the previous Section, the car is taken to the local Chrysler Dealer to have the car's height correctly set.
3 For the owner who is able to hire or borrow these tools, the method of setting the car's height is as follows.
4 Place the car on a level surface with the tyres correctly inflated and the fuel tank full.
5 Set the steering in the straight ahead position and disconnect both lower telescopic damper mountings.
6 Slacken the pivot bolts on the torsion bar adjusting rods.
7 Turn the adjusting nuts anticlockwise until they are flush with the ends of the adjusting rods.
8 Fit the gauge bar beneath the front of the car as far forward as possible with the brackets hooked over the torsion bars (Fig. 7.31).
9 Place the height stands on either side of the gauge bar and bounce the front of the car several times to settle it.
10 Turn each adjusting nut alternately two turns at a time to raise the car until both sides of the gauge bar are exactly level with the groove in each height stand (Fig. 7.30).
Caution: If, before commencing adjustment, the gauge bar is higher than the height stands even after bouncing the vehicle; do **not** slacken the adjusting nuts any further in an attempt to lower the car. Leave the adjustment as it is and re-check the height after the car has covered a small mileage and the suspension has settled.
11 When the height is satisfactory, tighten the adjusting rod pivot nuts, remove the height gauge bar from beneath the vehicle and reconnect the telescopic dampers.

12 Lower suspension arm - servicing

1 If wear is evident in the lower suspension arm bushes or spindle, then the assembly must be removed and the worn components renewed. Jack up the car and remove the wheel.
2 Refer to Fig. 7.30 and note the sequence of fitting of the various components **before** dismantling.
3 Remove the torsion bar as described in Section 10.
4 Disconnect the anti-roll bar at its attachment to the lower suspension arm.

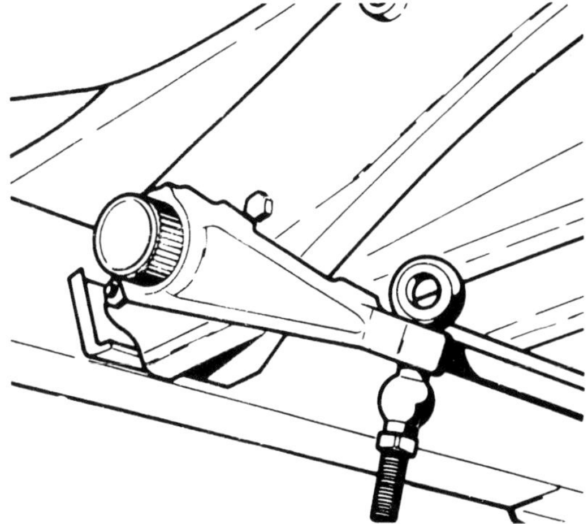

Fig. 7.27. Torsion bar adjusting rod removed

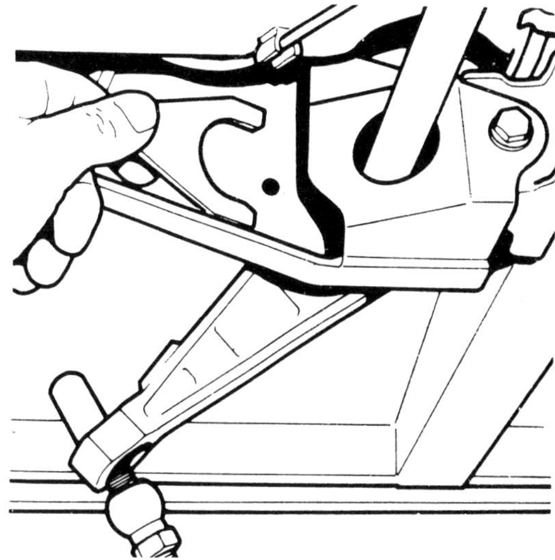

Fig. 7.28. Removing the torsion bar sleeve retaining plate from crossmember

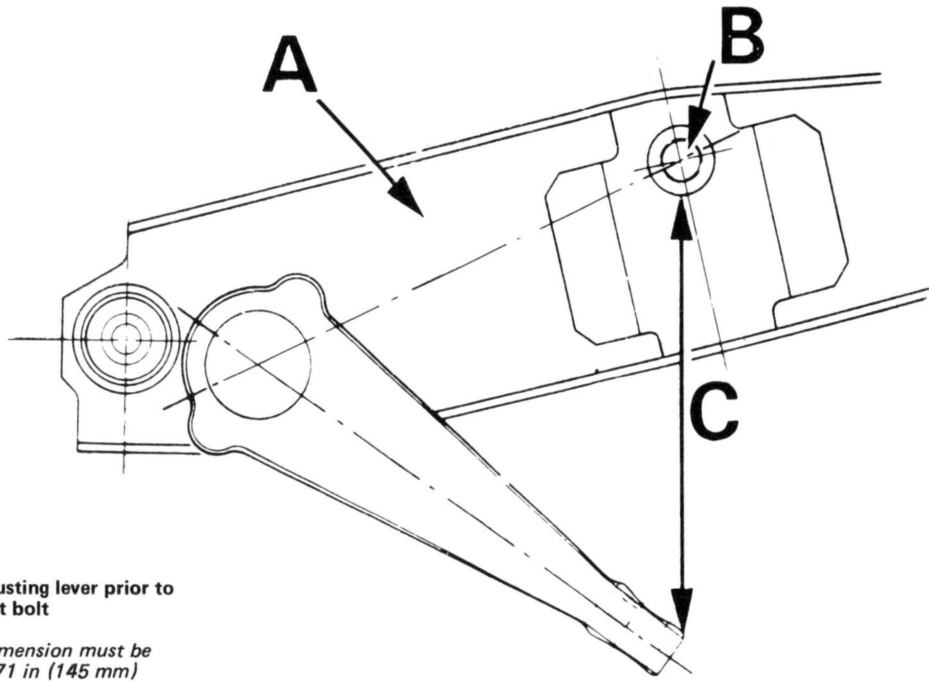

Fig. 7.29. Correct position of torsion bar adjusting lever prior to refitting the adjusting rod pivot bolt

A Crossmember
B Pivot bolt hole
C Dimension must be 5.71 in (145 mm)

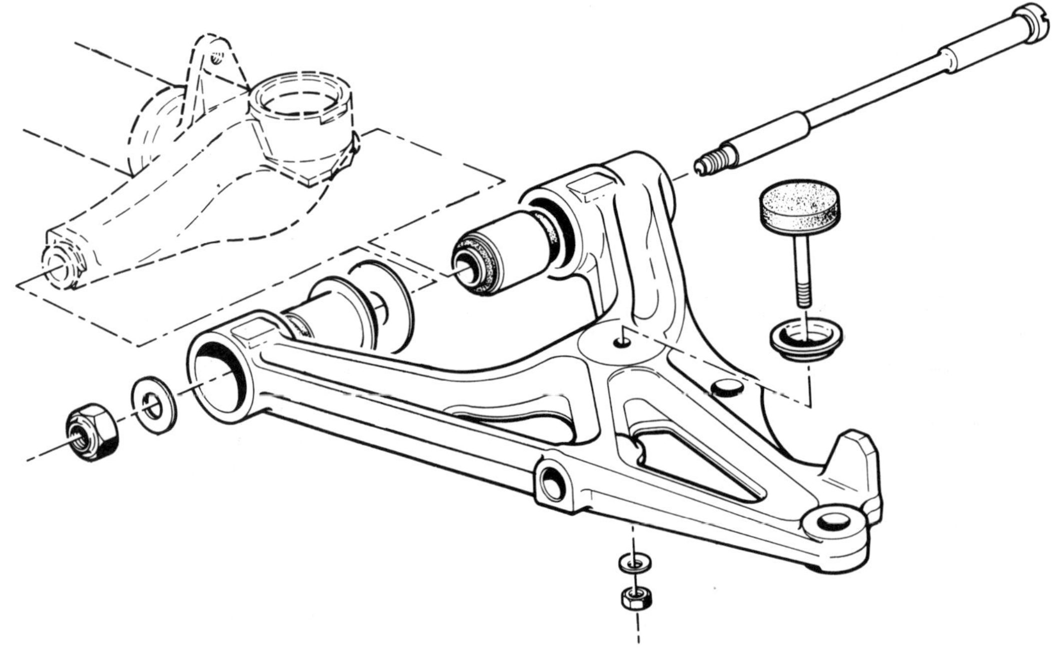

Fig. 7.30. Lower suspension arm and bushes

5 Disconnect the stub axle carrier lower balljoint as described in Section 6.
6 Unscrew and remove the nut from the spindle, withdraw the spindle, remove the bush components and lift away the suspension arm.
Note: If, while trying to remove the nut, the spindle turns with it, remove the torsion bar thrust washer from the rear end of the suspension arm and hold the spindle with a screwdriver (Fig. 7.33).
7 Refitting is a reversal of removal but tighten the spindle nut to the specified torque wrench setting.
8 Fit and set the torsion bar as described earlier in this Chapter.

13 Upper suspension arm - servicing

1 It will be necessary to remove the upper suspension arm when there is evidence of wear in the swivel bushes or pin. Its removal will also make easier the renewal of the balljoint assembly described in Section 7.
2 Remove the shock absorber and fit the restraining rod previously described.
3 Jack up the front of the vehicle and support it on stands.
4 Place a restraining strap round the stub axle carrier and secure it to the damper substitute rod.
5 Disconnect the upper suspension arm to stub axle carrier balljoint.
6 Remove the two bolts which secure the upper suspension arm to the upper crossmember (Fig. 7.34).
7 As the upper suspension arm is withdrawn, note carefully the location of the spacers and retain them for future refitting. These spacers are used to adjust the front wheel camber as described in Chapter 8.
8 Unscrew and remove the swivel pin nut and remove the various components.
9 Renew bushes and other parts as necessary.
10 Refitting is a reversal of removal. Tighten the swivel pin nut to a torque of 41 lb f ft (5.67 kg f m) and ensure that the spacers are returned to their original positions before tightening the upper suspension arm securing bolts to 37 lb f ft (5.12 kg f m).
11 Whenever the suspension has been removed and refitted, the steering geometry should be checked as described in Chapter 8.

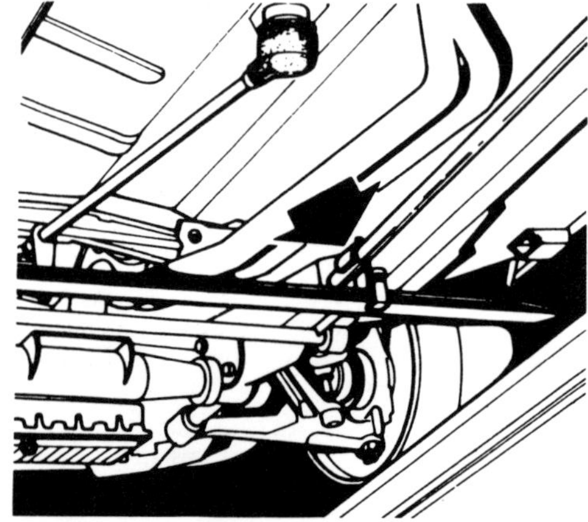

Fig. 7.31. Correct location of height gauge

Fig. 7.32. Setting the vehicle height against the special height stand

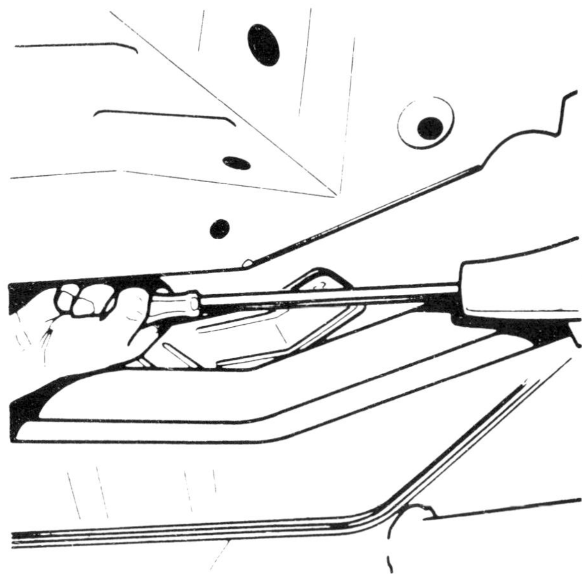

Fig. 7.33. Holding the slotted end of the lower suspension arm spindle

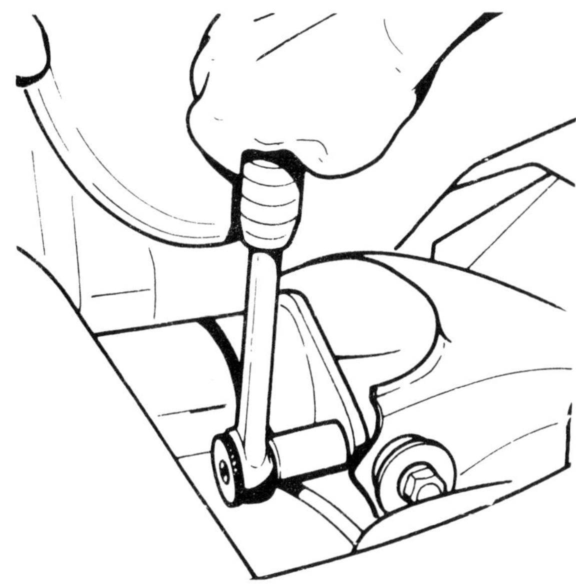

Fig. 7.34. Removing the bolts securing the upper suspension arm to the crossmember (LH side shown)

14 Upper suspension crossmember - removal and refitting

1 Substitute restraining rods for both front dampers (see Section 2).
2 Jack up the front of the vehicle and support on stands, and remove both front wheels.
3 Remove the nut from the cotter pin securing the upper balljoint to the axle carrier and drive out the cotter pin. Withdraw the balljoint from the axle carrier. Repeat the operation on the other side of the car.
4 Remove the air cleaner and hot air intake (See Chapter 3).
5 Remove the two bolts securing the right-hand side upper suspension arm to the crossmember, retain the camber adjustment shims.

Note: On left-hand drive cars, remove the left-hand side upper suspension arm retaining bolts.
6 Lift away the upper suspension arm and spindle assembly.
7 Detach any wires or pipes clipped to the crossmember.
8 Remove the bolts securing the crossmember to the two reinforcement brackets and to the longitudinal members.
9 Manoeuvre the crossmember, complete with left-hand side upper suspension arm, out under the left-hand side front wing. On left-hand drive cars the crossmember is withdrawn out under the right-hand side front wing.
10 Refit the crossmember using the reverse procedure to that of removal. If the suspension arm spindle nuts have been slackened do not retighten them until the weight of the car is on the front wheels.
11 Do not forget to refit the camber adjustment spacers.

15 Fault diagnosis - front suspension; driveshafts and hubs

Symptom	Reason/s	Remedy
General wear	Tyre pressures uneven	Check and adjust if necessary.
	Shock absorbers inoperative	Test and renew.
	Suspension balljoints worn	Disconnect and renew.
	Wheels out of balance	Balance wheels correctly.
	Hub bearings worn	Renew.
Poor road holding	Torsion bars, incorrectly set	Reset correctly.
	Incorrect steering geometry	See Chapter 8.
	Brakes binding on one side of vehicle	Dismantle and service (Chapter 10).

Chapter 8 Steering

Contents

Specifications

Type ... Rack and pinion

Turning circle ... 36 ft (11 m)

Wheel alignment

Front wheel toe-out (vehicle unladen)	1/32 to 1/8 in (1 to 3 mm)
Camber	$0^o \pm 30'$
Caster	$2^o\ 30' \pm 30'$
Steering axis inclination	$15^o\ 20' \pm 10'$

Pinion shaft endfloat ... 0.004 in (0.1 mm)

Torque wrench settings

	lb f ft	kg f m
Steering ball joint nut	22	3.04
Lock nut, track rod	33	4.56
Universal joint to upper inner column	11	1.52
Steering outer column to support	18	2.49
Lock nut, rack damper	44	6.09
Pinion self-locking nut	18	2.49
Nut, coupling pinch bolt	7	0.97
Steering rack to frame	15	2.07
Securing nut, steering hand wheel	40	5.53
Shock absorber lower mounting, front	18	2.49
Shock absorber lower mounting, rear	18	2.49
Upper suspension arm pivot to frame	37	5.12

1 General description

The Alpine is fitted with the rack and pinion type steering gear.

Turning movement from the steering wheel is transmitted through a universally jointed shaft to the steering gear pinion.

The angle of the steering shaft and the two universal joints ensure that in the event of a frontal collision the shaft will collapse sideways rather than moving rearwards, thus reducing the possibility of chest injury to the driver.

A balljoint and tie-rod (or track rod) is attached to each end of the steering rod and these terminate in a second adjustable balljoint which enables the front wheel track to be correctly set.

The track rods are connected to the steering arms which are integral with the stub axle carriers.

Shims are used between the rack and pinion steering gear mounting points and brackets and these have a direct bearing upon the track setting during movements of the front suspension.

2 Maintenance

1 No routine maintenance is required but check that the rubber bellows on the steering gear assembly and the balljoints have not deteriorated or split. Should this be evident, then renew these components.
2 Should the steering gear become stiff after a high mileage then 25 cc of recommended grease should be introduced to the steering unit through the rack damper aperture, see Section 5.
3 Keep all connecting bolts tightened to the torque wrench settings given in the Specifications.

3 Steering gear - adjustment

1 If there is play in the steering or a knocking is felt through the steering wheel when driving over bumpy surfaces, then the steering rack probably requires adjustment.
2 Jack up the front of the car, support it on axle stands and remove both front wheels.
3 Remove the nuts from both track rod balljoints and, using a suitable extractor, detach the balljoints from the steering arms.
4 Release the plunger cap lock nut.
5 Remove the nut and the used locking tab washer.
6 Now tighten the plunger cap until it bears against the plunger but do not force.
7 Mark the location of the notch in the plunger cap in relation to the steering gear housing. Loosen the plunger cap fractionally by an amount equal to half the width of the notch.
8 Jack up the front of the vehicle and turn the steering wheel slowly from lock to lock and check for tight spots. Should one be found then carry out the plunger adjustment procedure with the steering remaining in the 'tight spot' position. Again check from lock to lock.
9 Fit a new locking tab ring, fit the locknut and tighten it to the specified torque. Bend over the locking tab.
10 Reconnect the track rods and lower the jacks.

4 Steering gear - removal and refitting

1 Jack up the front of the car and support securely on stands or blocks.
2 Remove the securing nuts and using a suitable extractor, disconnect both track rod balljoints from the steering arms.
3 Disconnect the gearshift linkage balljoints from the relay levers on the steering gear and final drive casing and remove the relay lever assembly from the steering gear (refer to Chapter 6 if necessary).
4 Remove the nut from the pinchbolt on the steering gear pinion coupling and extract the pinchbolt (see Fig. 8.2).
5 Remove the four bolts securing the steering gear to the mounting brackets (Figs. 8.3 and 8.4). Make a note of the number of shims between the steering gear housing and each bracket.
6 Remove the three securing bolts from the mounting bracket on the left-hand end of the steering gear and remove the bracket.

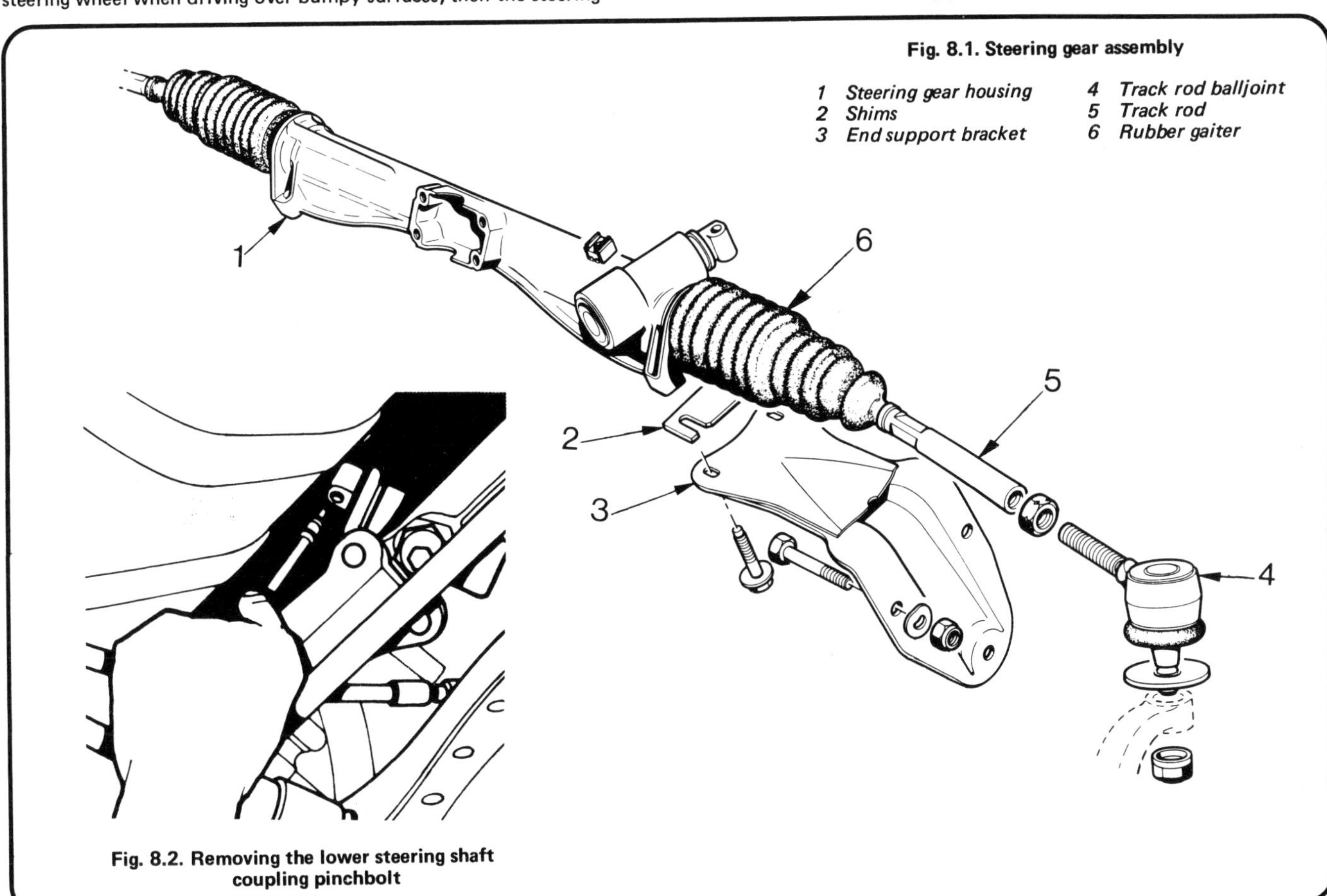

Fig. 8.1. Steering gear assembly

1 Steering gear housing
2 Shims
3 End support bracket
4 Track rod balljoint
5 Track rod
6 Rubber gaiter

Fig. 8.2. Removing the lower steering shaft coupling pinchbolt

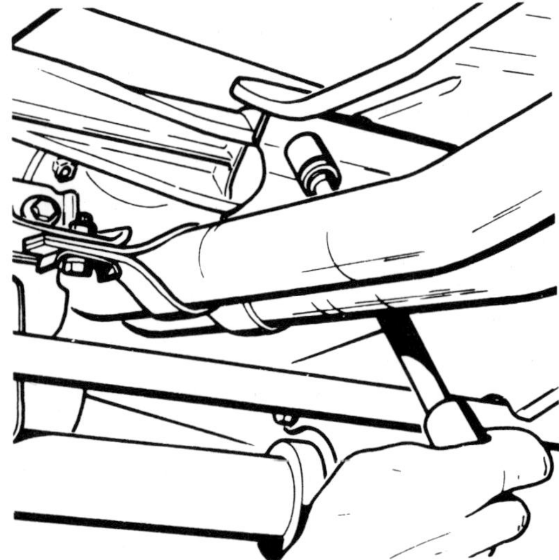

Fig. 8.3. Removing the RH side steering gear securing bolts

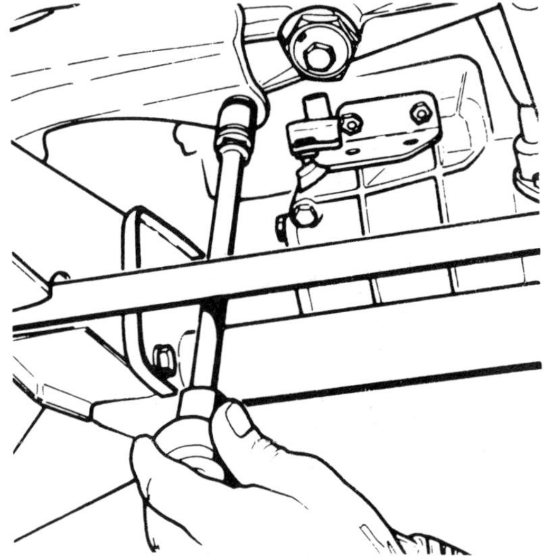

Fig. 8.4. Removing the LH side steering gear securing bolts

7 Slide the steering gear assembly through the left-hand side wing valance aperture passing the right-hand end of the steering gear over the anti-roll bar to withdraw it.

Note: On left-hand drive cars, remove the bracket from the right-hand end of the steering gear housing. Slide the steering gear to the right and rotate it so that the pinion coupling is facing downwards. Pass the left-hand end of the steering gear assembly over the anti-roll bar and withdraw it (Fig. 8.5).

8 Refitting is a reversal of removal where the original steering gear is being refitted in the vehicle. Refit the original shims in their correct location. After major steering dismantling, always check the tracking of the front wheels as described in Section 10 of this Chapter.

9 Where a new or factory reconditioned steering gear unit is fitted, the calculation of fitting shim thickness must be left to your Chrysler dealer due to the specialised nature of the equipment required and its effect upon the front wheel alignment.

5 Steering gear - dismantling, servicing and reassembly

1 Having removed the steering gear as described in the preceding Section consider whether in view of the mileage covered it would be more economical to obtain a factory exchange unit rather than recondition the existing unit. Where only minor components require renewal or the internal parts require cleaning and packing with fresh grease, then proceed as follows.

2 Remove the gearshift linkage bracket from the steering gear housing.

3 Secure the unit in a vice fitted with jaw protectors and do not overtighten.

4 Remove the spring clips and carefully pull both rubber gaiters back over the track rods.

5 With the steering rack in approximately the central position, measure the distance between the flange on the track rod coupling locknut and the end of the steering gear housing nearest the pinion shaft. Make a note of this measurement.

6 Without moving the rack, scribe a line on the pinion shaft and rack. This will enable the pinion to be refitted in the correct position relative to the rack.

7 Hold the flats on the track rods with a spanner and slacken the locknuts. Unscrew both track rods from the rack assembly.

8 Drift out the sealing cap from the pinion housing (Fig. 8.6), hold the pinion shaft and unscrew the self-locking nut from the end of the shaft (Fig. 8.7).

9 Tap back the lockwasher tab, unscrew the locknut and remove the damper plunger and spring. Retrieve any shims that are fitted.

10 Drive the pinion from its location by using a brass or copper drift.

11 Withdraw the rack from the pinion end of the housing.

12 The pinion bearing may be renewed by removing the circlips and shims (Fig. 8.9).

13 The bearing is renewable after extracting its securing circlip and then driving out the ring using a stepped drift up to the dimensions

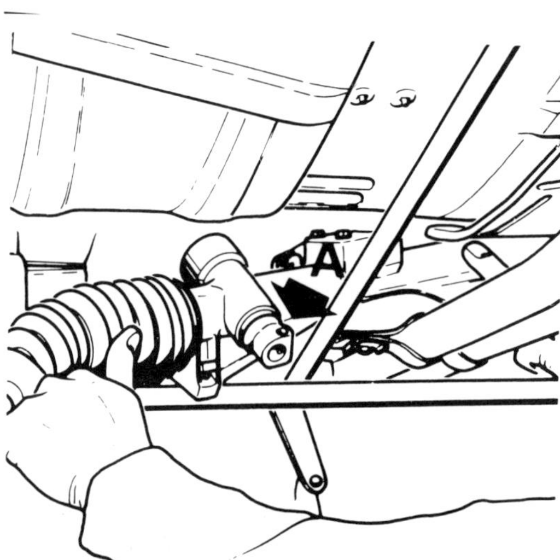

Fig. 8.5. Withdrawing the steering gear assembly (LH drive models)

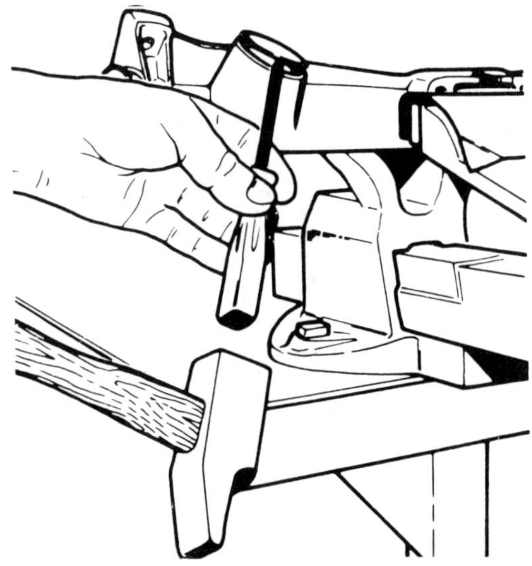

Fig. 8.6. Removing the pinion shaft sealing cap

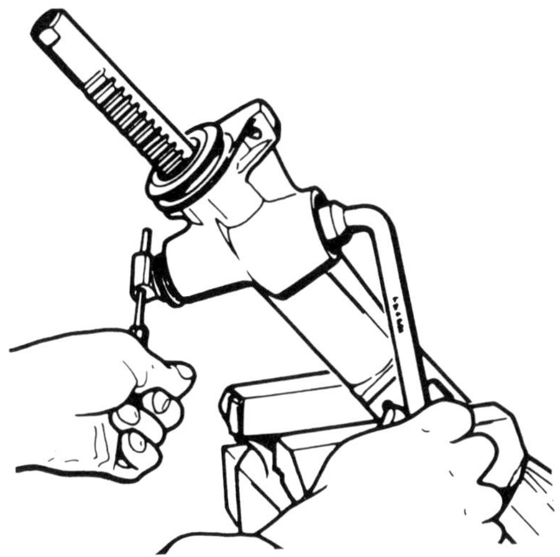

Fig. 8.7. Unscrewing the pinion shaft securing nut

135
3 x 45°
15
1 x 45°
Φ 28 − 0.1 − 0.3
Φ 25 − 0.1 − 0.3

Fig. 8.8. Dimensions of drift for removing the pinion bearing (measurements in mm)

given in the diagram, Fig. 8.8.

14 Extract the circlip, shim and the rubber guide ring. Remove the sleeve.

15 Thoroughly wash all components in paraffin and dry them with a piece of non-fluffy cloth.

16 Examine all components for wear and renew as appropriate.

17 Commence reassembly by inserting the sleeve so that its slot is opposite the lubrication groove.

18 Fit the rubber guide ring and grease it with the recommended grade of grease and then locate the shim and circlip.

19 Using the tool previously described, fit the anti-friction ring so that it is flush with the surface of the steering gear housing. Grease the anti-friction ring.

20 Fit the pinion bearing assembly by including an excessive number of shims so that the circlip will not fit into its groove. Remove one shim at a time until the circlip will just locate correctly. This will provide an endfloat of 0.1 mm (0.004 in).

21 Grease the rack assembly and slide it into the housing.

22 Measure out 80 cc of the recommended grade of grease and insert it into the steering gear by using the rack plunger as an injector. During this operation, move the rack from lock to lock over the full length of its travel. Do not exceed the stipulated quantity of grease or the bellows may burst in service.

23 Fit the rack damper plunger assembly and adjust it as described in Section 3 of this Chapter.

24 Screw both track rods, complete with rubber gaiters, into each end of the rack assembly.

25 Tighten the locknuts and check that the distance between the flange of the locknut and the inner face of the balljoint is 1/8 in (3 mm). Adjust as necessary until this dimension is achieved (Fig. 8.10).

26 Set the rack so that the end nearest the pinion is protruding from the housing by the dimension noted during dismantling.

27 Fit a new 'O' ring to the pinion shaft and with the rack held in the correct position, insert the pinion into the housing so that the scribe marks made previously are aligned.

28 Fit the washer and nut onto the end of the pinion shaft and tighten the nut to the specified torque wrench setting.

29 Fill the pinion housing with grease and tap the sealing cap back into position.

30 Refit the rubber gaiters to the steering gear housing and secure with the spring clips.

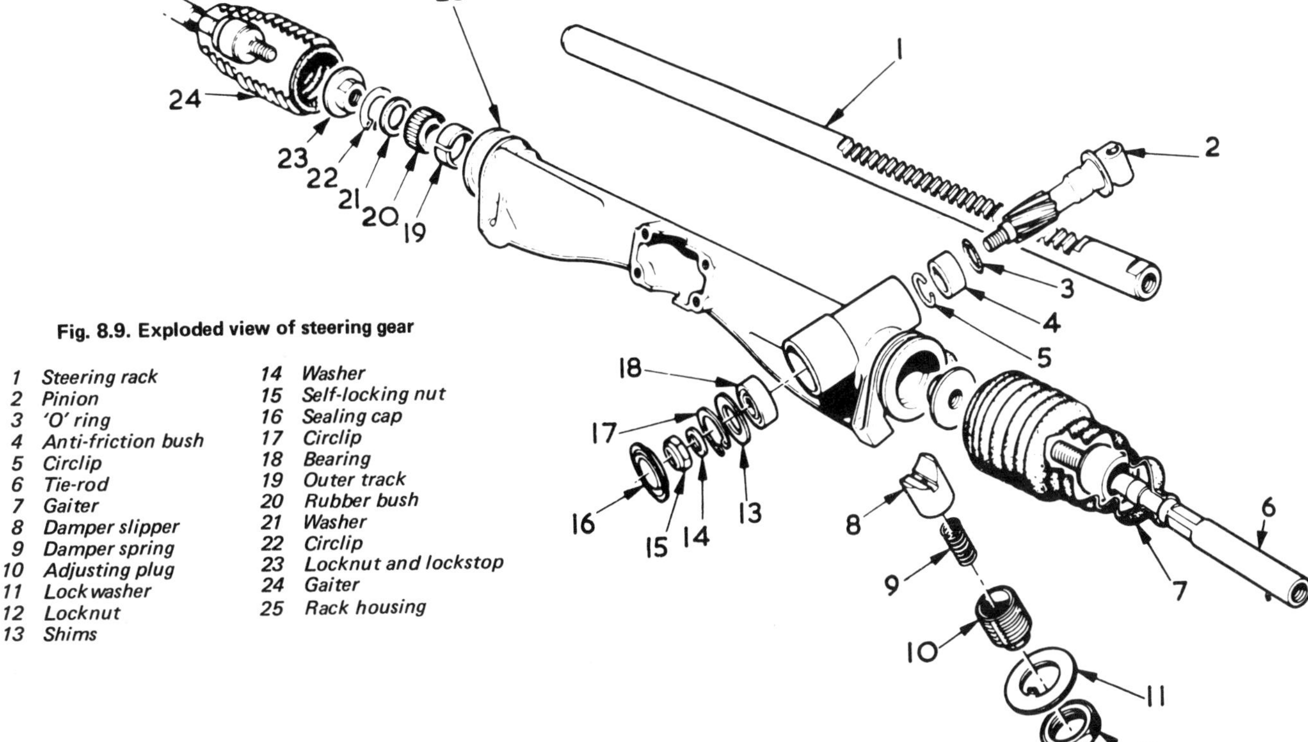

Fig. 8.9. Exploded view of steering gear

1 Steering rack
2 Pinion
3 'O' ring
4 Anti-friction bush
5 Circlip
6 Tie-rod
7 Gaiter
8 Damper slipper
9 Damper spring
10 Adjusting plug
11 Lockwasher
12 Locknut
13 Shims
14 Washer
15 Self-locking nut
16 Sealing cap
17 Circlip
18 Bearing
19 Outer track
20 Rubber bush
21 Washer
22 Circlip
23 Locknut and lockstop
24 Gaiter
25 Rack housing

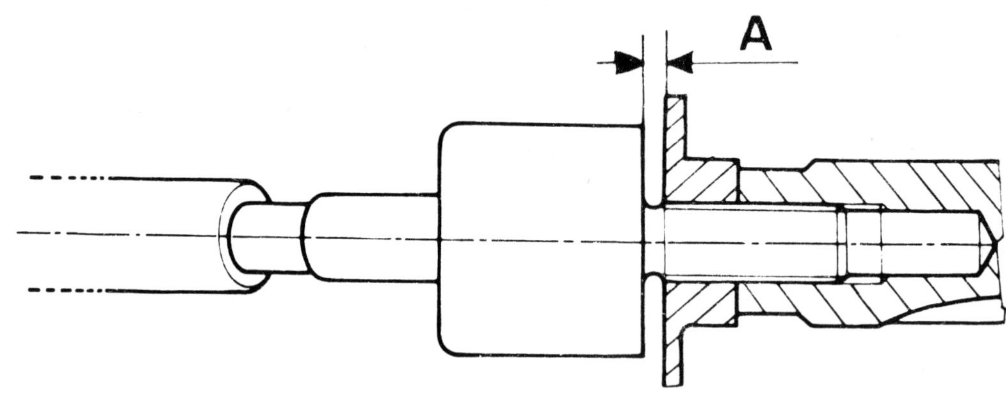

Fig. 8.10. Correct dimension between track rod inner balljoint and locknut (A = 1/8 in - 3 mm)

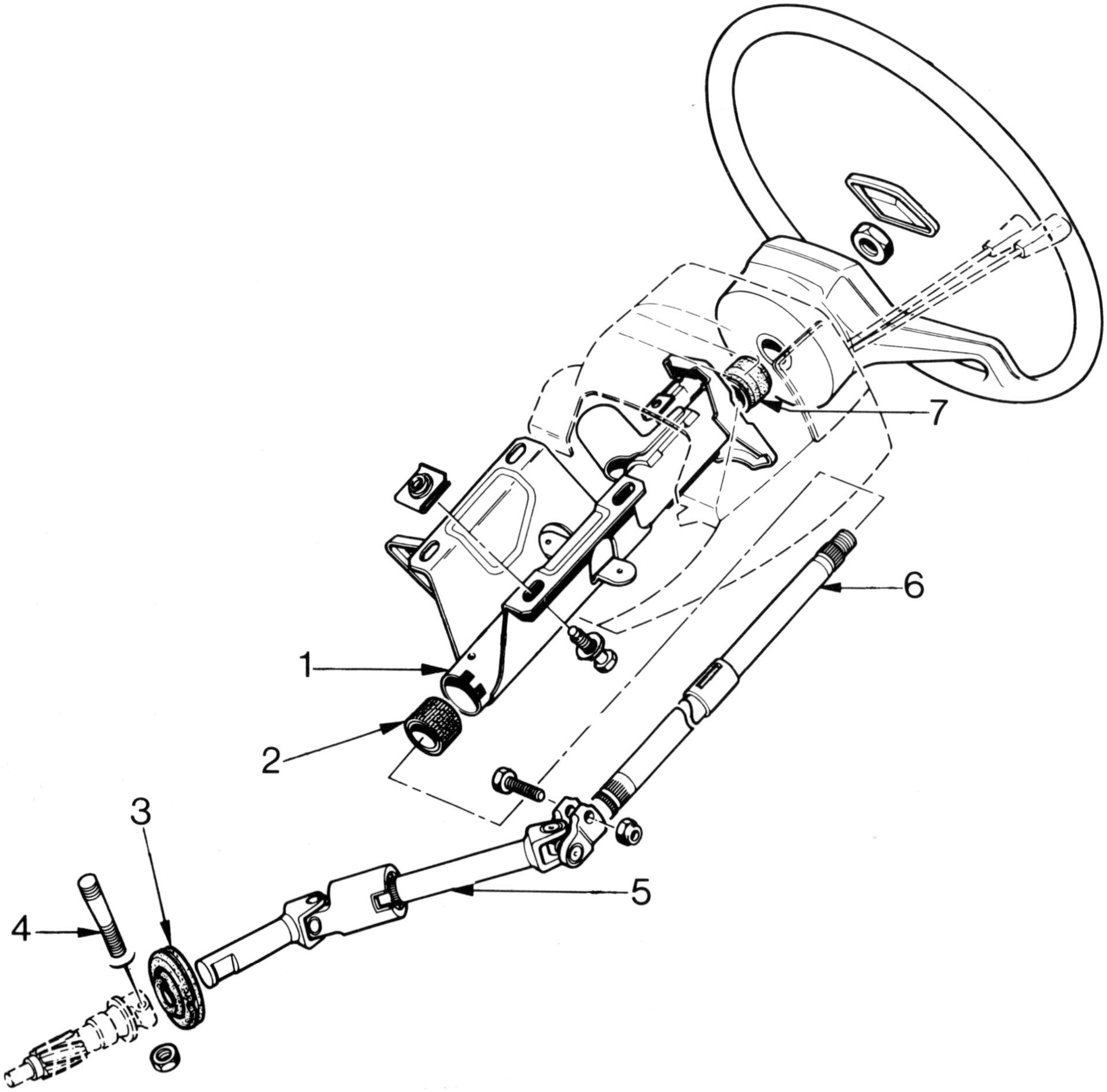

Fig. 8.11. Exploded view of steering column

1 Steering column housing
2 Lower bearing
3 Bulkhead grommet
4 Lower shaft pinchbolt
5 Lower shaft and couplings
6 Upper shaft
7 Upper bearing

6 Steering column - removal and refitting

1 With the front of the car over a pit or supported on axle stands, remove the pinchbolt securing the lower end of the steering shaft to the steering gear pinion.
2 Working inside the car, remove the lower half of the steering column coupling.
3 Disconnect the battery earth terminal.
4 Disconnect the electrical multi-plugs that connect the steering column wiring to the main harness.
5 Support the weight of the steering column assembly and remove the four bolts securing the column to the facia bracket (see Fig. 8.12).
6 Carefully pull the column rearwards until the lower end of the steering shaft is detached from the steering gear pinion, and then withdraw the complete column and shaft assembly from the car.
7 To refit the column, set the front wheels to the straight ahead position.
8 Insert the steering shaft through the rubber grommet in the lower bulkhead and guide the shaft onto the steering gear pinion.
9 Temporarily secure the column to the facia bracket with the four bolts and tighten the lower shaft pinchbolt.
10 Adjust the position of the column in the slotted holes to provide adequate clearance between the steering wheel and the cowl, and also to obtain the maximum clearance between the steering shaft and the clutch pedal. Tighten the column retaining bolts.
11 Refit the lower cowl panel.

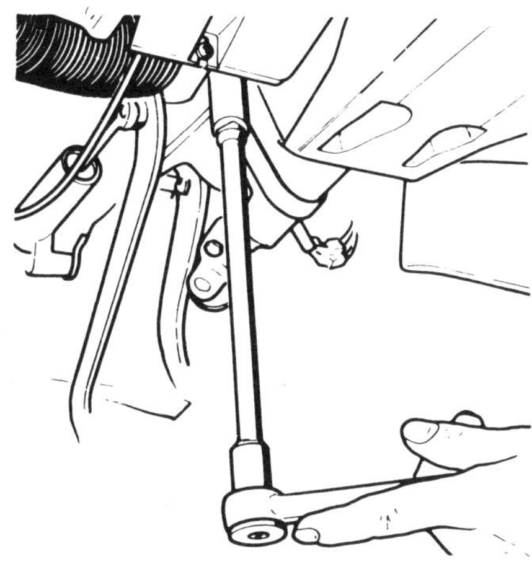

Fig. 8.12. Removing the steering column securing bolts

7 Steering column flexible couplings - renewal

1 The two flexible couplings on the steering shaft are not repairable and if they become worn they must be renewed.
2 Withdraw the lower steering shaft assembly from the steering gear pinion as described in the previous Section.
3 Remove the pinchbolt securing the upper universal joint to the steering shaft.
4 Remove the lower shaft complete with the universal joints and obtain a new shaft assembly.
5 Ensure the front wheels are in the straight ahead position and the steering wheel spokes are facing downwards, and slide the upper universal joint onto the splines of the steering shaft.
6 Refit the pinchbolt and tighten it to the specified torque.
7 Refit the steering shaft assembly to the steering gear pinion as described in the previous Section.

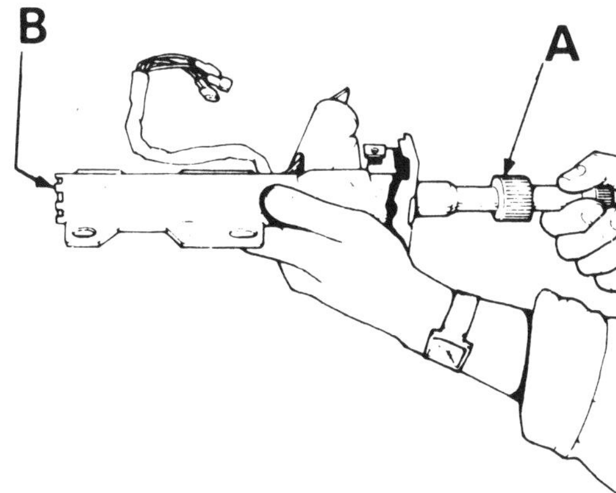

Fig. 8.13. Removing the steering shaft and upper bearing

A Upper bearing *B Lower bearing retaining tabs*

8 Steering column - dismantling and reassembly

1 The main reason for dismantling the steering column is to renew the upper and lower bearings, and to do this it is necessary to first remove the complete steering column assembly as described in Section 6.
2 Prise out the motif from the centre of the steering wheel (photo) and remove the securing nut using a socket.
3 Pull the wheel off the steering shaft splines.
4 Remove the screws retaining the steering column cowl together and lift away the two halves of the cowl.
5 Mark the position of the upper universal joint in relation to the steering shaft, remove the pinchbolt and withdraw the lower shaft complete with universal joints.
6 Tap the bottom of the shaft with a soft-faced hammer and withdraw the shaft and top bearing from the top of the steering column (Fig. 8.13).
7 Bend back the tabs securing the bottom bearing in the column and use the steering shaft to push the bearing out of the column.
8 If necessary remove the top bearing inner race using a puller.
9 Examine the bearings and shaft for wear and renew where necessary.
10 Lubricate the bearings with a molybdenum disulphide based grease before refitting them.
11 Retain the bottom bearing in position by bending in the tags on the bottom of the column. Push the top bearing into place using a thin bladed screwdriver between the shaft and column.
12 Refit the lower shaft and universal joints ensuring the marks made previously are aligned.

8.2 Steering wheel centre motif removed

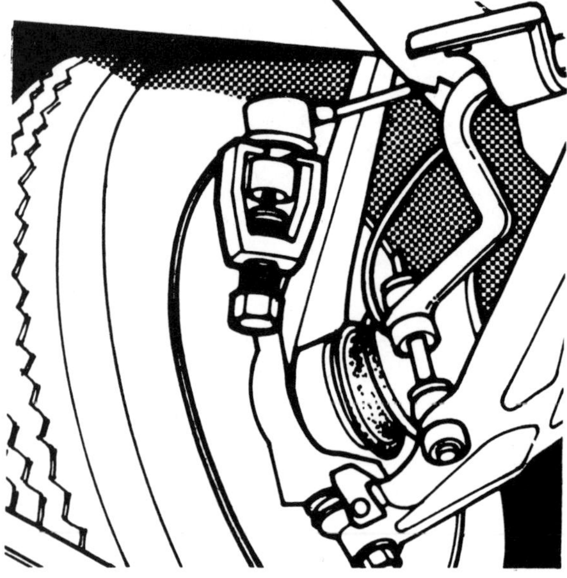

Fig. 8.14. Removing a track rod balljoint using an extractor

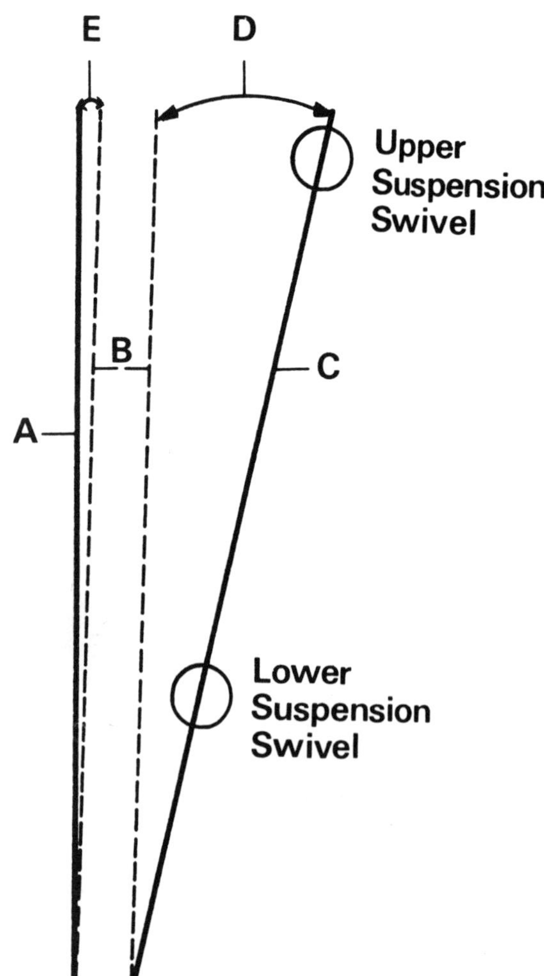

Fig. 8.16. Diagram of steering angles

A Wheel camber
B Vertical lines
C Steering axis inclination
D Angle of inclination
E Positive camber angle

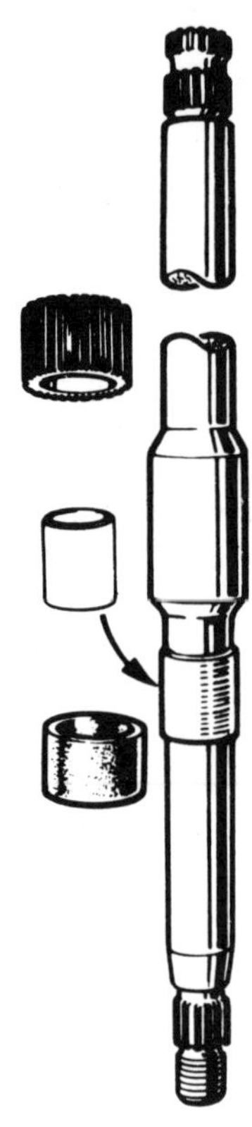

Fig. 8.15. Steering shaft and bearings

13 Refit the steering column into the car using the reverse procedure to removal.

9 Track rod ends - renewal

1 To gain easier access, first jack up the front of the car, support it on axle stands and remove the front wheels.
2 Remove the nut securing the balljoint to the steering arm and using an extractor, disconnect the balljoint tapered pin from the arm (Fig. 8.14).
3 Mark with paint the amount of thread exposed between the end of the balljoint and locknut, slacken the locknut and unscrew the balljoint from the trackrod end.
4 Screw the nut onto the new balljoint until it is in approximately the same position as the original one.
5 Lubricate the threads and screw the balljoint into the track rod until the locknut abuts the end of the rod. Hold the balljoint in the correct position and tighten the locknut.
6 Refit the balljoint to the steering arm and tighten the securing nut.
7 Repeat the procedure on the other track rod balljoint if necessary.
8 The method described will provide an approximate setting of the original front wheel tracking but before the track rod lock nuts are fully tightened, the track must be checked as described in Section 11.

10 Steering geometry

1 Accurate front wheel alignment is essential for good steering and minimum tyre wear.
2 Wheel alignment embraces four factors:

Camber which is the angle at which the front wheels are set from the vertical, when viewed from the front of the vehicle. Positive camber is the amount (in degrees) that the wheels are inclined outwards from the vertical at their tops.

Castor is the angle between the steering axis and a vertical line when viewed from each side of the vehicle. Positive castor is when the steering axis is included rearwards at the top.

Steering axis inclination is the angle, when viewed from the front of the vehicle, between the vertical and an imaginary line drawn between the upper and lower stub axle carrier swivel balljoints.

Toe-in is the amount by which the distance between the front inside edges of the roadwheels (measured at hub height) is less than the diametrically opposite distance measured between the rear inside edges of the roadwheels. Toe-out is specified for the Alpine and this is a greater measurement at the front inside edges of the wheel (photo).

Checking and adjustment of toe-out (tracking) is described in the next Section.

The steering angles just described are either set during manufacture or in the case of the Camber angle, this can be altered by varying the shims described in the preceding Chapter. Any variation of the Camber angle should be left to your Chrysler dealer who will have the necessary equipment for measuring these critical angles.

Two steering angles are shown in diagrammatic form in Fig. 8.16 and reference should be made to the Specifications Section of this Chapter for the precise angles (in degrees).

11 Front wheel track - checking and adjustment

1 Although it is preferable to leave these operations to your Chrysler dealer, an approximate setting may be made which will be useful after renewal of any of the steering or suspension components and will at least permit the car to be driven to the dealers for a more accurate check to be made, if necessary.

2 Place the vehicle on level ground with the tyres correctly inflated. Position the wheels in the 'straight ahead' position.

3 Obtain or make an alignment gauge. One may be easily made up from a piece of tubing or bar, suitably cranked to clear the engine/transmission unit with a bolt at one end to permit adjustment of its overall length.

4 With the gauge, measure the distance between the two inner wheel rims (at hub height) at the fronts of the roadwheels.

5 Mark the tyre and then roll the vehicle either forward or backwards so that the mark on the tyre rotates 180°.

6 Measure the distance between the inner edges of the wheel rims at hub height at the rear of the roadwheels. This second measurement should vary from that taken previously by being 1/32 to 1/8 in (1 to 3 mm) less to give the correct toe-out angle.

7 If the dimensions are incorrect, remove the track rod balljoints from the steering arms as described in Section 9 and slacken the locknuts.

8 Turn the balljoints by equal amounts ¼ turn at a time, refit them to the steering arms and check the toe-out measurement. The balljoints must be screwed in to decrease the toe-out and screwed out to increase it.

9 When the toe-out measurement is correct tighten the locknuts.

12 Wheels and tyres

1 The roadwheels fitted to the Alpine models are of pressed steel type, four bolt fixing.

2 To minimise tyre wear and to prevent steering wobble or vibration it is imperative to have the wheels balanced when the tyres are first fitted.

3 From time to time, check the security of the securing bolts and check that the bolt head recess in the wheel has not become enlarged or elongated. Where this is the case, the roadwheel must be renewed.

4 Any deviation from even tread wear will indicate the need for rebalancing of the wheels or checking and adjusting of the steering angles.

13 Fault diagnosis - steering

Before diagnosing faults from the following chart, check that any irregularities are not caused by:

1 *Binding brakes*
2 *Incorrect 'mix' of radial or crossply tyres*
3 *Incorrect tyre pressures*
4 *Misalignment of bodyframe.*

Symptom	Reason/s	Remedy
Steering wheel can be moved before any sign of roadwheel movement is apparent	Wear in linkage, gear or column couplings or track rod ends	Check for movement in all joints and gear and renew as required.
Car wanders and difficult to hold to a straight line	As above or wheel alignment incorrect or hub bearings loose or worn. Upper or lower suspension balljoints worn	Adjust or renew as necessary.
Steering stiff and heavy	Incorrect wheel alignment Seizure of suspension or steering balljoints	Adjust or renew.
Wheel wobble and vibration	Roadwheels out of balance Roadwheels buckled Incorrect wheel alignment Wear in steering joints Wheel nuts loose	Balance wheels. Renew wheels. Check and adjust. Renew. Tighten.

Chapter 9 Rear suspension and hubs

Contents

Specifications

Type

Independent trailing arm and coil spring with anti-roll bar and telescopic dampers

Coil spring

Free length	13.625 in (346 mm)

Torque wrench settings

	lb f ft	kg fm
Crossmember brackets to body	33	4.56
Rear crossmember pivots to brackets	44	6.08
Suspension arm pivots to crossmember	48	6.63
Damper lower mountings	15	2.07
Damper upper mountings	11	1.52
Anti-roll bar mountings	15	2.07

1 General description

The rear suspension is independent and comprises trailing arms supported on coil springs with telescopic shockabsorbers and an anti-roll bar.

The forward ends of each trailing arm pivot on rubber bushes attached to a tubular crossmember. The crossmember in turn is attached to the body underframe through rubber mountings.

The anti-roll bar is attached to a brake equaliser device which has the effect of reducing the possibility of the rear wheels locking under heavy braking conditions.

Caution: When jacking up the rear of the car using a trolley jack, ensure that the pad of the jack is positioned under the jacking points only. Attempts to raise the car by means of the rear crossmember or trailing arms may cause damage.

2 Rear hubs - removal, inspection and refitting

1 Jack up the rear of the car, support it on blocks or axle stands and remove the roadwheel.
2 Remove the retaining screws and pull off the brake drum. If difficulty is experienced, slacken the handbrake cable adjuster and automatic brake adjuster (refer to Chapter 10).
3 Prise the grease cap from the end of the hub using a screwdriver.
4 Raise the peening on the large hub nut using a small chisel and remove the nut and thrust washer.
5 Carefully withdraw the complete hub and bearings ensuring that the outer bearing does not drop out onto the floor.
6 Prise out the oil seal from the inner end of the hub and withdraw the roller bearing (Fig. 9.1).
7 If the bearings are being renewed due to wear, the inner tracks in the hub must also be renewed. Drive out the inner tracks using suitably sized pieces of tubing. Refit the new tracks ensuring the thicker end of the track faces in towards the centre of the hub (Fig. 9.3).
8 Wash out the hub in clean petrol to remove all traces of old grease.
9 Spread some of the recommended grade of grease evenly around the inside of the hub between the two bearings.
10 Grease the inner (larger) roller bearing and insert it in the hub.
11 Tap in a new oil seal ensuring that the lip faces towards the bearing.
12 Refit the hub to the axle, grease the outer (smaller) roller bearing and insert it in the hub.
13 Fit the thrust washer, engaging its tongue correctly, screw on the hub nut and tighten it to a torque of 11 lb f ft (1.52 kg fm) at the same time rotating the hub. Back off the nut until the hub turns freely without any end-float. Peen the nut collar into the stub axle groove to retain it in the predetermined position.
14 Refit the brake drum and securing screws, fill the grease cap half full with grease and tap it into position in the hub.
15 Re-adjust the handbrake cable if it was slackened off. Fit the roadwheel and lower the jack.

3 Rear springs - removal and refitting

1 Raise the rear of the car and place axle stands under the side frame members so that the suspension is suspended.
2 Place a small jack below the rear end of the suspension arm and raise it sufficiently to take the weight of the arm (Fig. 9.4).

Fig. 9.1. Removing the inner wheel bearing

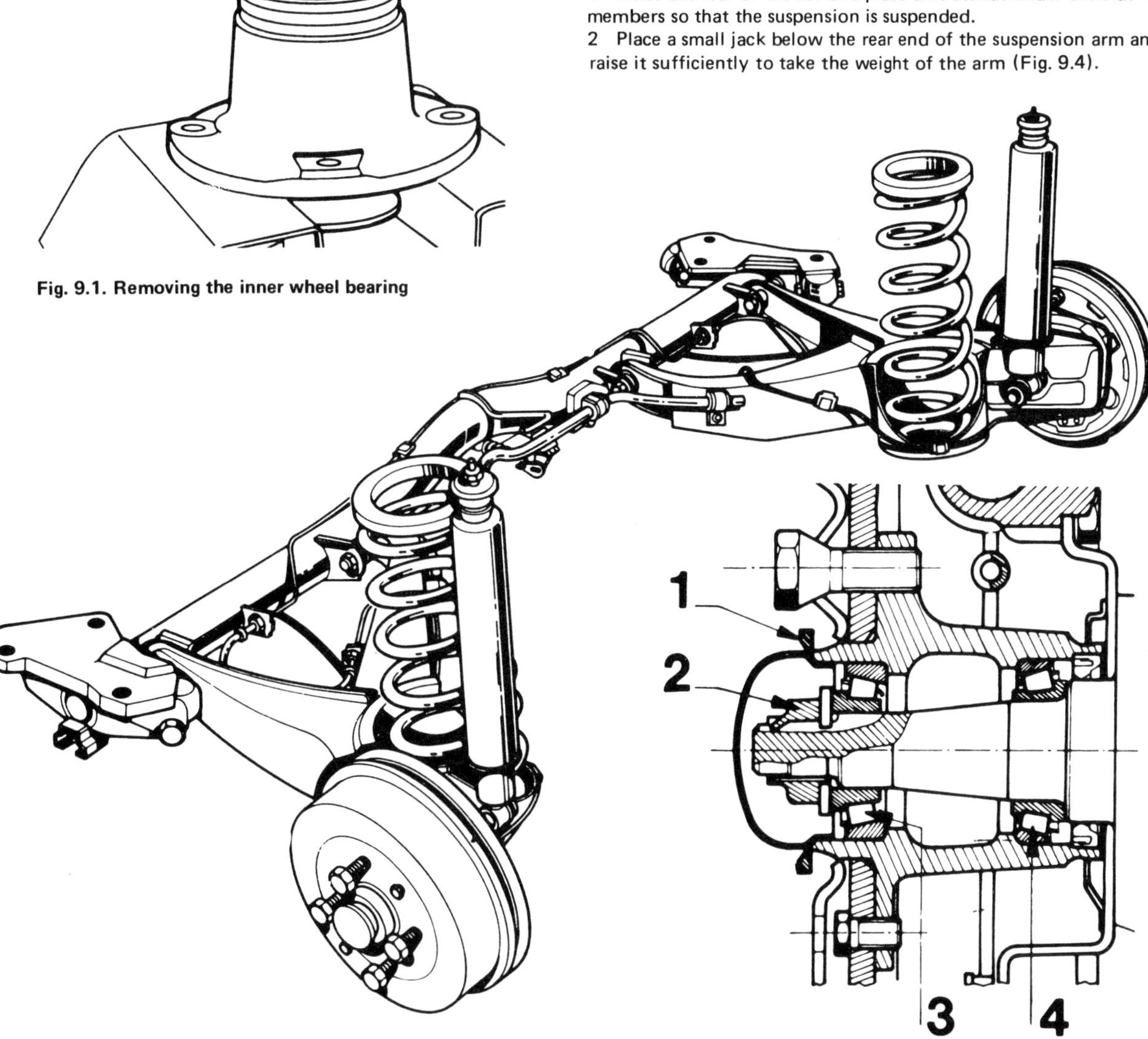

Fig. 9.2. Layout of the rear suspension system

Fig. 9.3. Cross-sectional view of rear hub assembly

1 Grease cap
2 Hub nut
3 Outer bearing
4 Inner bearing

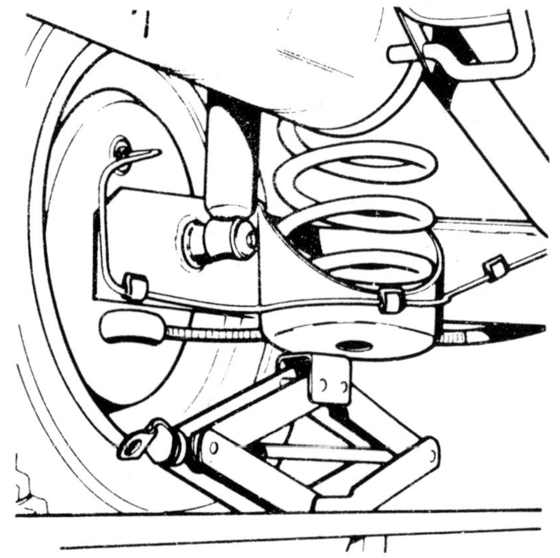

Fig. 9.4. Supporting the suspension arm prior to removing the spring

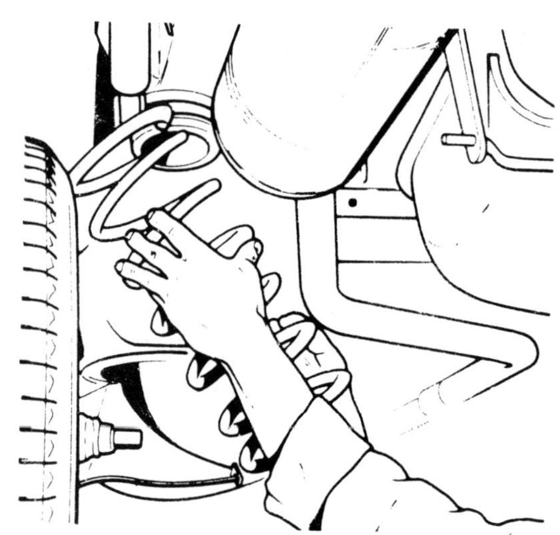

Fig. 9.5. Withdrawing the coil spring

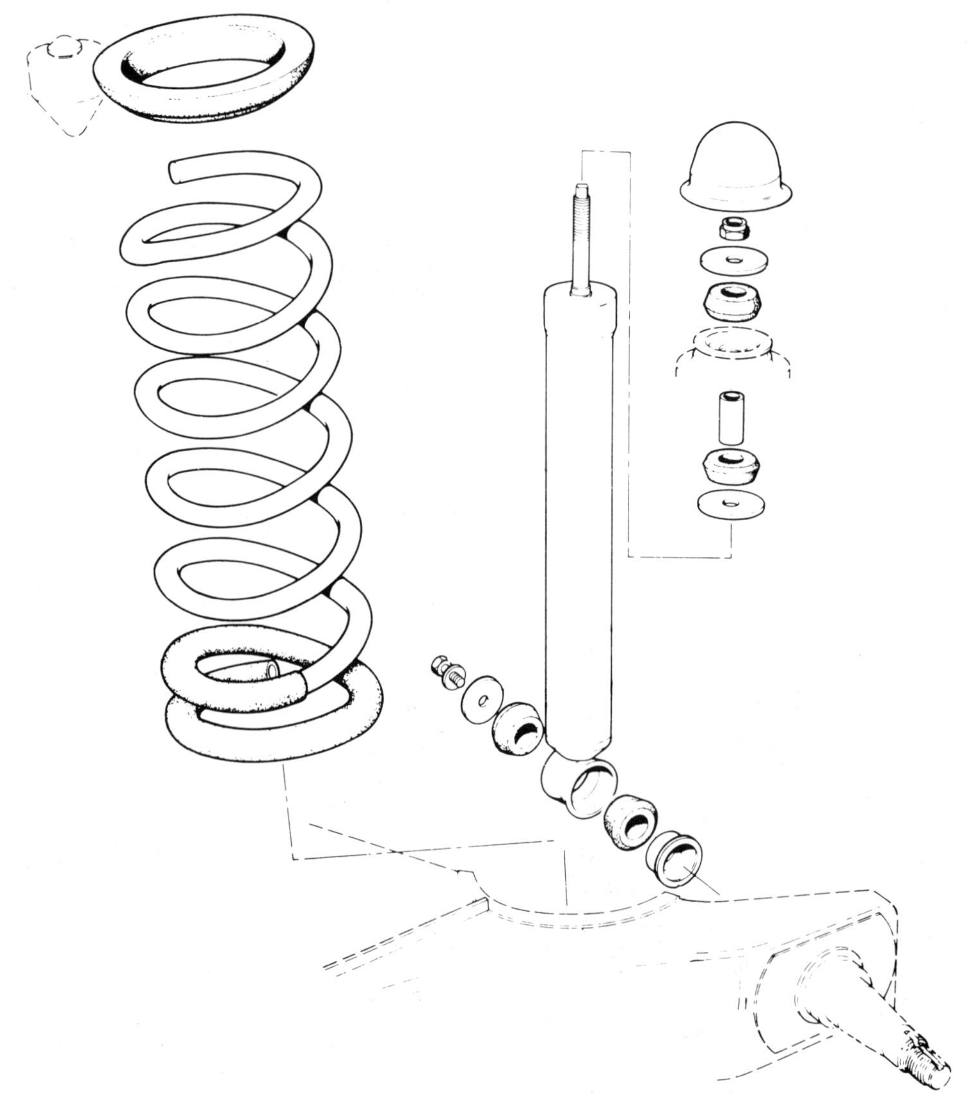

Fig. 9.6. Exploded view of damper and bushes

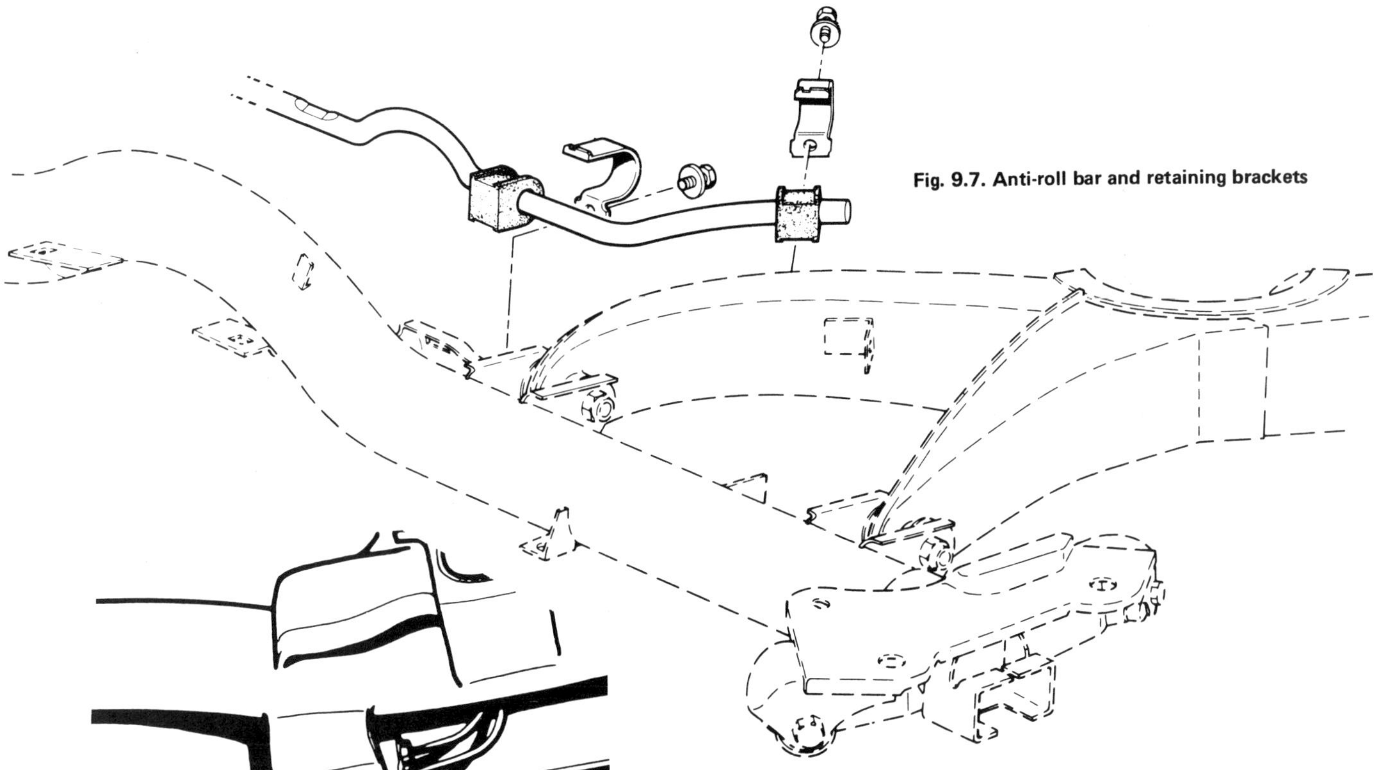

Fig. 9.7. Anti-roll bar and retaining brackets

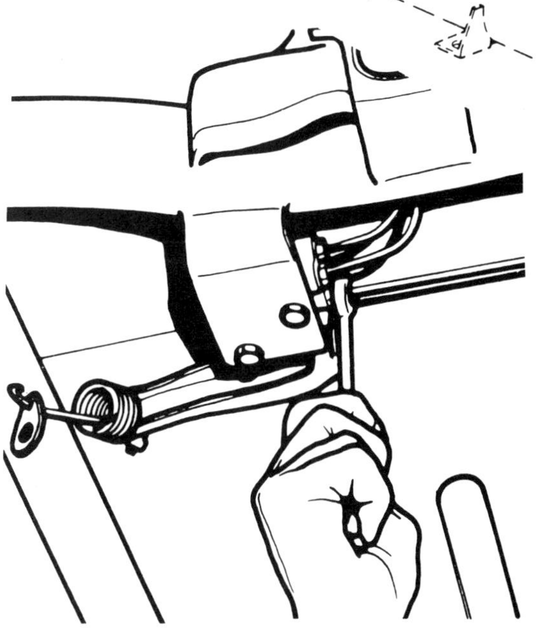

Fig. 9.8. Disconnecting the inlet pipe from the brake pressure valve

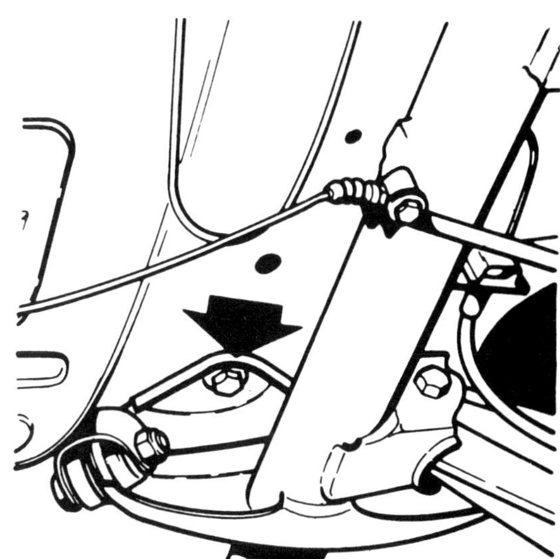

Fig. 9.9. Location of crossmember inner securing bolt (Right-hand shown)

3 Remove the damper lower mounting bolt.
4 Slowly lower the jack and remove it from beneath the suspension arm. Pull the arm downwards as far as possible and withdraw the spring (Fig. 9.5).
5 Refit the spring using the reverse procedure to that of removal.

4 Shockabsorbers - removal, testing and refitting

1 From inside the car remove the protective cap and undo the top shockabsorbers retaining nut. Retrieve the rubber bushes and spacers (Fig. 9.6).
2 Remove the lower shockabsorber retaining bolt, withdraw the shockabsorber unit and retrieve the rubber bushes and spacers.
3 Test the shockabsorbers as described in Chapter 7 for the front shockabsorbers.
4 Refit the shockabsorbers using the reverse procedure to that of removal, ensuring that the rubber bushes and spacers are refitted in the correct sequence.

5 Anti-roll bar - removal and refitting

1 Place the car over a pit or jack up the rear of the car and support it on axle stands.
2 Unhook the brake pressure valve spring from the roll bar bracket.
3 Remove the four brackets securing the roll bar to the rear suspension arms and crossmember and withdraw the bar (Fig. 9.6).
4 Renew the rubber bushes where necessary and refit the anti-roll bar using the reversal of the removal procedure.
5 Check the setting of the brake pressure valve as described in Chapter 10.

6 Rear suspension assembly - removal and refitting

1 If the rear suspension arm bushes are worn, the best policy is to remove the complete rear suspension assembly for servicing as it is quite likely that the crossmember mounting bushes will also require renewal.
2 Jack up the rear of the car and support it on firmly based axle

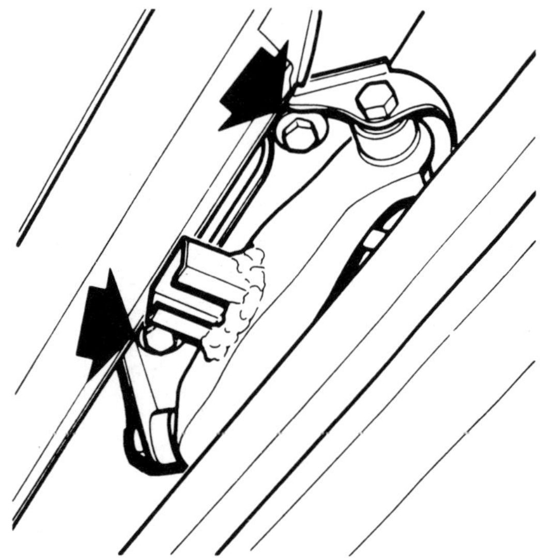

Fig. 9.10 Location of the two outer crossmember securing bolts (Right-hand shown)

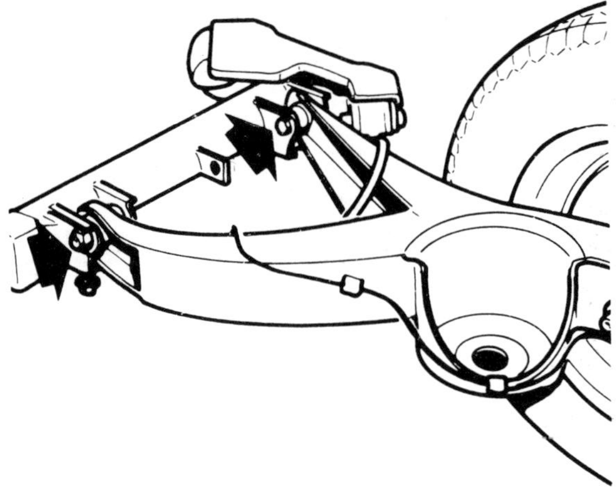

Fig. 9.11. Suspension arm pivot bolts

stands or blocks placed beneath the side frame members. Do not remove the roadwheels.
3 Disconnect the handbrake cable at the adjuster quadrant.
4 Remove the anti-roll bar as described in Section 5.
5 Remove both shockabsorber lower mounting bolts.
6 Remove both rear coil springs as described in Section 3.
7 Disconnect the brake fluid inlet pipe from the brake pressure valve (Fig. 9.8) and plug the pipe and valve aperture to prevent dirt ingress and loss of fluid.
8 Disconnect the exhaust pipe supports from the brackets on the two crossmembers and sidemember and lower the pipe and silencer carefully to the ground.
9 Support the weight of the rear suspension crossmember by placing a jack beneath the centre of it.
10 Remove the three bolts securing the suspension crossmember support brackets to each side of the car (see Figs. 9.9 and 9.10).
11 Carefully lower the jack from beneath the suspension crossmember and roll the complete suspension assembly out from under the rear of the car.
12 Refit the rear suspension assembly using the reverse procedure to that of removal.
13 Bleed the braking system and adjust the brake pressure valve setting as described in Chapter 10.

7 Rear suspension bushes - renewal

1 Remove the complete rear suspension assembly as described in the previous Section.
2 Disconnect the flexible brake hoses and plug the ends to prevent dirt ingress.
3 Remove the roadwheels from the suspension assembly.
4 Remove the pivot bolts from the suspension arm bushes and withdraw the suspension arms from the crossmember (Fig. 9.11).
5 Undo the bolts securing the support brackets to each end of the crossmember and remove the brackets (Fig. 9.13).
6 Make up an extractor tool as shown in Fig. 9.12 and withdraw the bushes from each end of the crossmember and the suspension arms. **Note:** If difficulty is experienced in removing the bushes, carefully cut through the inner steel sleeve and rubber bush with a hacksaw blade and then collapse the outer sleeve and drive it out using a suitable drift. Take great care not to cut or damage the actual crossmember or suspension arm assembly.
7 Draw the new bushes into their housing using the extractor tool made up for removal, or drive the bushes in using a piece of flat hardwood and a hammer.

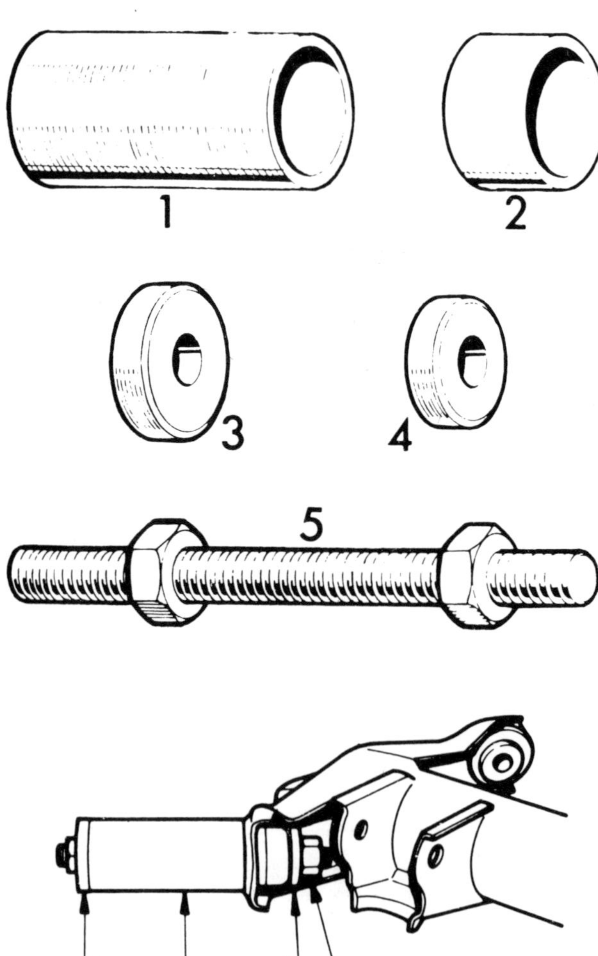

Fig. 9.12. Tool that can be made up for extracting the rear suspension bushes

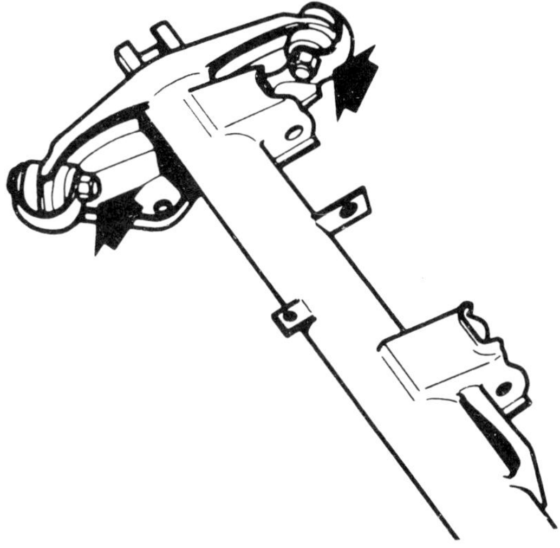

Fig. 9.13. Crossmember bracket securing bolts

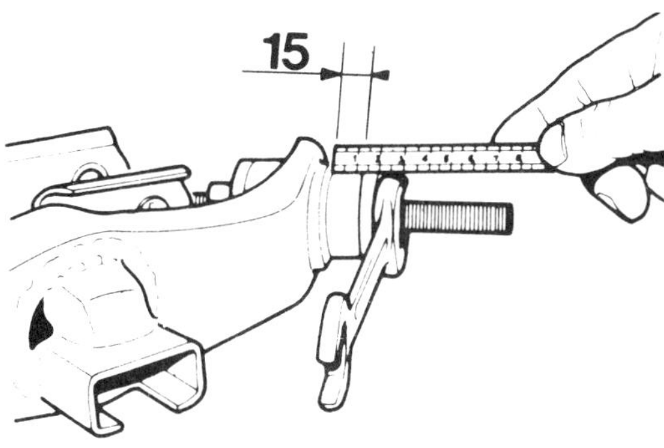

Fig. 9.14. Correct position of tear crossmember bush (dimension = 0.60 in (15 mm)

8 The crossmember bushes must be fitted so that there is 0.5 in (15 mm) protruding from the boss on the bush housing (Fig. 9.14).
9 The bushes can be lubricated with petroleum jelly (Vaseline) to assist in refitting, but never use oil or grease.
10 Refit the suspension arms and crossmember support brackets using the reverse of the removal procedure, but do **not** fully tighten the suspension arm pivot bolts at this stage.
11 Refit the complete rear suspension assembly to the car as described in Section 6.
12 Before tightening the rear suspension pivot bolts, bounce the rear of the car up and down several times to settle the coil springs. Run the car over an inspection pit; get a couple of medium weight friends to sit in the rear compartment to load the car and then tighten the suspension arm pivot bolts to the specified torque wrench setting.
13 It is recommended that the car is then taken round to your local Chrysler dealer who will have the special equipment necessary to check the height of the rear suspension.

8 Rear wheel alignment

1 The suspension angles at the rear are all set during manufacture and no adjustment is possible.
2 Should the track or other angles be suspect and be reflected in abnormal wear to the rear tyres (and there is no distortion of the suspension components due to collision damage), the hub bearings and the trailing arm bonded rubber bushes should be checked for wear and renewed if necessary.

9 Fault diagnosis - rear suspension and hubs

Symptom	Reason/s	Remedy
Excessive tyre wear	Wear in hub bearings	Renew bearings.
	Dampers inoperative	Renew.
	Wear in trailing arm bushes	Arrange renewal with Chrysler dealer.
	Tyre pressures too low	Inflate to specified pressures (cold).
Wheel wobble and vibration	Roadwheels out of balance	Re-balance on or off car.
	Roadwheels buckled	Renew.

Chapter 10 Braking system

Contents

Specifications

Type ... Front disc and rear drum operated by dual hydraulic system with servo assistance. Mechanical handbrake, rear wheels only

Front brakes

Manufacturer	Teves (Ate)
Type	Disc, with single piston floating caliper
Piston diameter	1.890 in (48 mm)
Minimum thickness of disc after resurfacing	0.34 in (10 mm)
Pad material	ABEX 336
Minimum thickness of pad and backing plate	0.28 in (7 mm)

Rear brakes

Manufacturer	Girling or DBA
Type	Drum, leading and trailing shoe, self-adjusting
Wheel cylinder inner diameter	0.81 in (2.06 mm)
Lining material	Don JM 16
Lining identification	Green paint on edge
Drum diameter (nominal)	9 in (228.6 mm)
Maximum oversize	0.040 in (1 mm)

Master cylinder

Manufacturer	Teves or Automotive Products (Lockheed)

Type	Split circuit, incorporating differential pressure warning actuator
Cylinder internal diameter	0.75 in (19 mm)
Stroke (both cylinders)	0.59 in (15 mm)

Brake servo

Manufacturer	Lockheed 'Master-Vac' or Girling FD (flexing diaphragm)

Stop light switch

Type	Mechanical

Torque wrench settings

	lb f ft	kg f m
Front brakes		
Caliper fixing bolts	54	7.47
Bleed screw	5	0.69
Brake disc to hub	37	5.12
Flexible hose to caliper	7	0.97
Brake pipe union nut	7	0.97
Driveshaft nut to hub	144	19.91
Lower suspension balljoint nut	55	7.61
Rear brakes		
Wheel cylinder to back plate	7	0.97
Back plate to suspension arm	22	3.04
Drum to hub	11	1.52
Bleed screw	4	0.55
Brake pipe to wheel cylinder	7	0.97
Brake controls		
Brake servo fixing nuts	7	0.97
Master cylinder to brake servo	7	0.97
Brake pressure reducing valve fixings	16	2.21
Brake pipe union nuts to master cylinder and brake pressure reducing valve	7	0.97
Locknut, handbrake adjuster	7	0.97
Handbrake fixings to body	13	1.8
Locknut, brake pressure reducing valve adjusting screw	7	0.97
Bracket, handbrake outer cable to suspension arm	17	2.35

1 General description

The braking system is hydraulically operated with servo assisted disc brakes on the front wheels and drum brakes on the rear.

The handbrake operates mechanically on the rear wheels only. Both front and rear brakes are self-adjusting.

The master cylinder is the dual circuit tandem type. The primary cylinder supplies the rear brakes and the secondary cylinder supplies the front brakes. Both systems are independent so that in the event of a hydraulic leak occurring in one system, the other system will remain fully operative although the brake pedal travel will increase.

A pressure differential switch is fitted to the master cylinder and if a pressure loss occurs in either the front or rear braking system, the switch will illuminate a warning light on the instrument panel. The warning light circuit has a press-to-test facility which should be checked at regular intervals.

A brake equaliser valve is mounted on the rear suspension cross-member and is actuated by the position of the anti-roll bar under varying loads. The valve automatically varies the braking effort to the rear wheels according to the vehicle load. Adjustment of the valve is critical to ensure the correct braking forces are applied under all loading and road surface conditions.

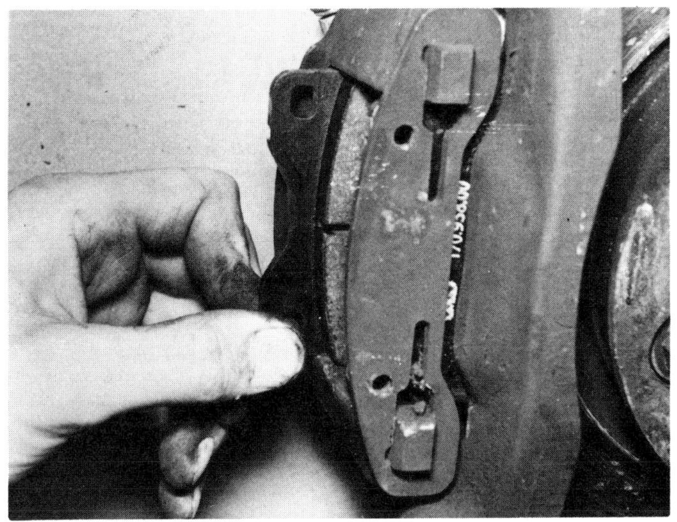

2.5 Removing the inner brake pad

2.7 Removing the outer brake pad

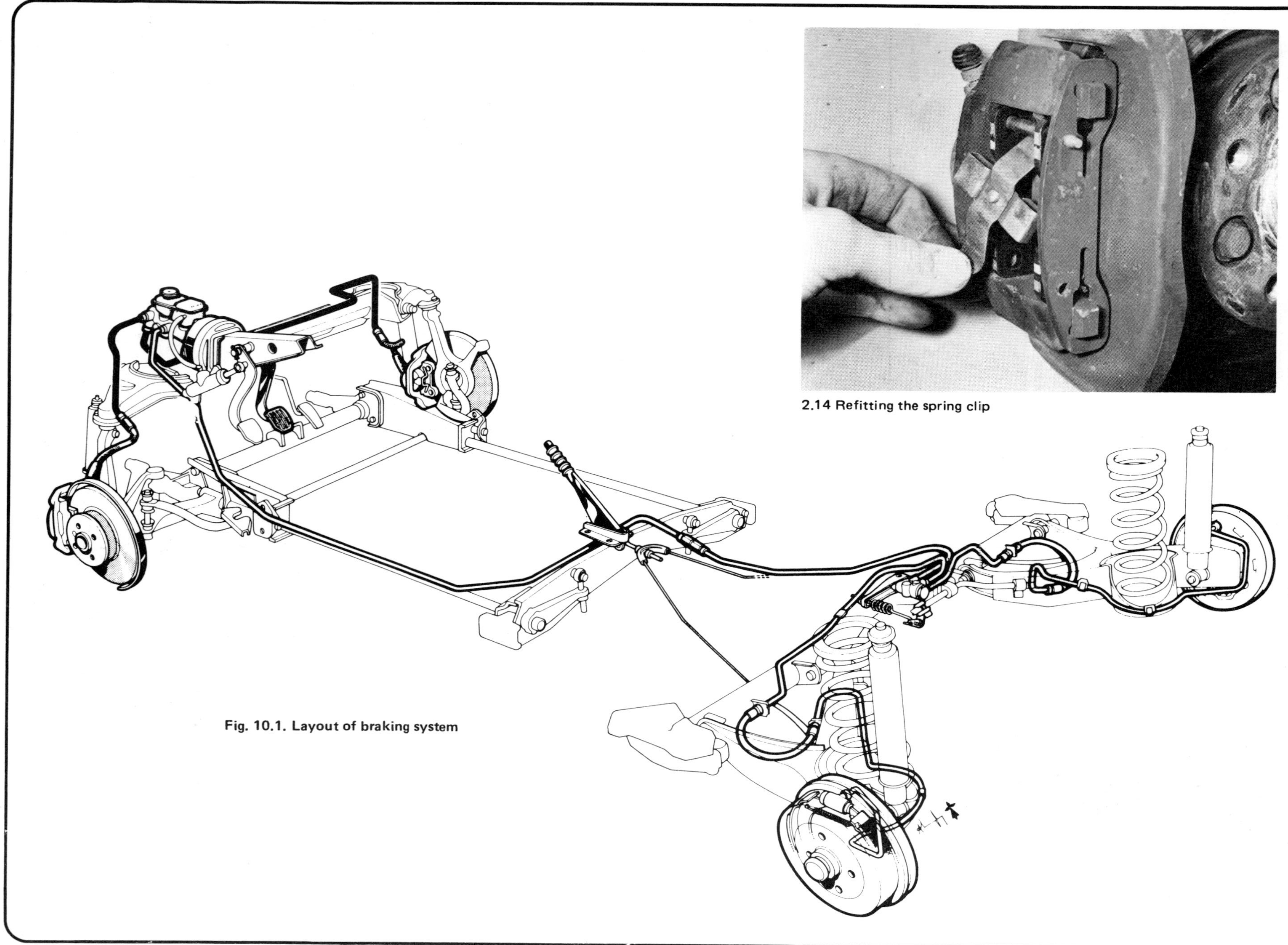

2.14 Refitting the spring clip

Fig. 10.1. Layout of braking system

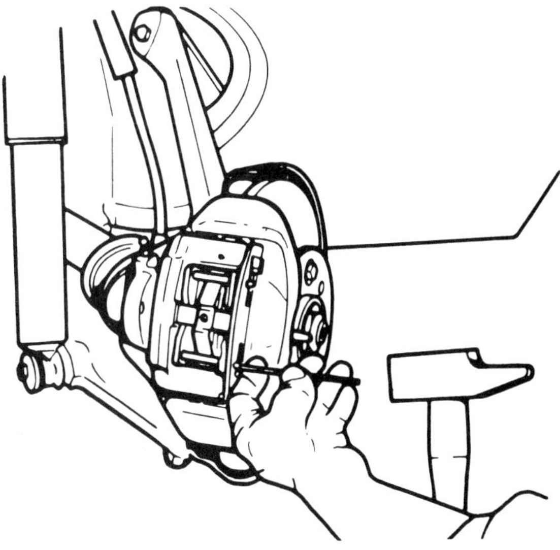

Fig. 10.2. Driving out the brake pad retaining pins

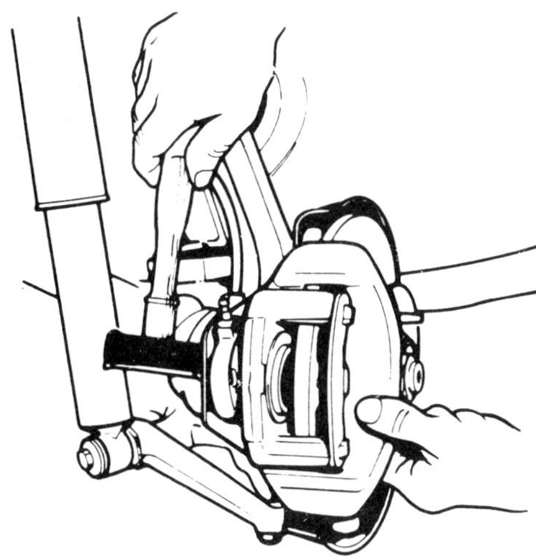

Fig. 10.3. Tapping caliper assembly across prior to removing the inner pad

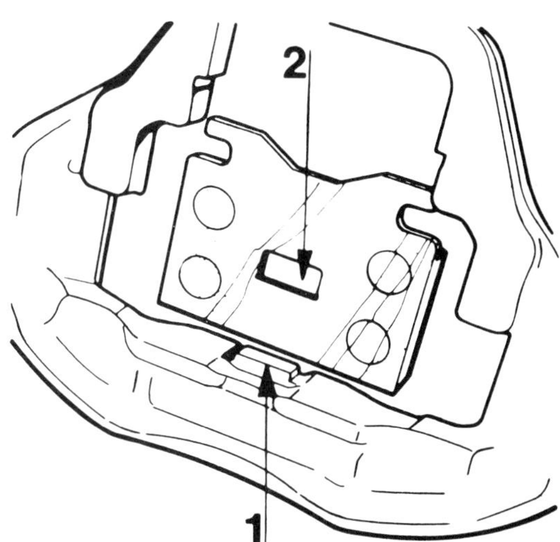

Fig. 10.4. Brake pad locating points

1 Tongue on caliper *2 Groove in pad*

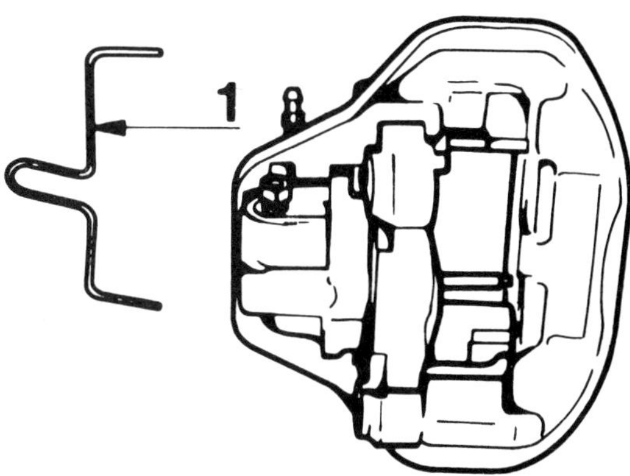

Fig. 10.5. Caliper retaining spring (1)

2 Disc brake pads - inspection, removal and refitting

1 Although the disc brakes are self-adjusting, pad wear should be checked every 3,000 miles.
2 Jack up the vehicle and remove the roadwheels.
3 Inspect the caliper unit for signs of oil or grease. Where these are evident, then the source must be found and the leak cured. Almost certain it will be due to a defective hub oil seal or leaking caliper unit piston seals.
4 Tap out the two disc pad retaining pins from the caliper (Fig. 11.2) and remove the spring.
5 Remove the inner pad first (photo).
6 Gently tap the inner side of the caliper so that it moves across approximately 3/16 in (5 mm) (Fig. 11.3).
7 The outer pad which has a locating slot in it may now be withdrawn (photo).
8 Clean the inside of the caliper assembly and check that the piston dust cover is in good condition. If there is any sign of fluid leakage around the piston, the caliper must be overhauled as described in Section 3.
9 Check the thickness of the friction pad (not including its metal backing plate). If the thickness is 3/32 in or less, renew the pads. Pads must be renewed as complete front wheel sets of four to maintain even braking.
10 If new pads are to be fitted, the caliper unit pistons must be pushed back into the cylinder to accommodate the thicker pads. Use a flat lever to do this but ensure that the piston is pressed squarely in and only sufficiently to enable the inner pad to enter the caliper unit opening. During this operation, the fluid reservoir level will rise and it may be necessary to syphon some off.
11 If difficulty is experienced in retracting the pistons, it may be necessary to open the bleed screw to release the hydraulic pressure. Take care not to let air enter the system otherwise if will be necessary to bleed the system as described in Section 10.
12 Insert the outer pad first, ensuring that the slot in the metal backing of the pad is correctly engaged with the tongue in the caliper (Fig. 10.4).
13 Insert the inner pad into the caliper assembly.
14 Slide the top retaining pin through the holes in the caliper and pads and hook the end of the spring under it (photo).
15 Push the other end of the spring down and slide in the second retaining pin.
16 Press the footbrake several times to centralise the pads and top up the reservoir if necessary.

3 Front disc brake caliper - removal, overhaul and refitting

1 Jack up the front of the car and remove the brake pads as described in the previous Section.

2 Unscrew and remove the bolts which secure the caliper to the stub axle.
3 Lift the caliper from its location and, if no further operations are to be carried out to the unit, tie it up to the suspension to prevent strain on the flexible hydraulic hoses.
4 If the caliper is to be overhauled or renewed, remove the cap from the master cylinder reservoir and place a piece of polythene sheet over the opening and then press the cap on again. This will create a vacuum and prevent loss of fluid when the hydraulic line is disconnected.
5 The flexible hose to the caliper can either be removed as described in Section 11, or a simpler method is to hold the union at the caliper end of the hose in a spanner and unscrew the caliper from the hose. Make sure when using this method that the hose is not twisted. Retain the sealing washer and plug the end of the hose to prevent loss of fluid.
6 Remove the spring clip shown in Fig. 10.5.
7 Slide the bracket out of the yoke assembly.
8 Tap the yoke assembly firmly on a wooden bench to dislodge the cylinder from the yoke. The caliper assembly is now dismantled into its three main components as shown in Fig. 10.7.
9 To dismantle the cylinder assembly, grip it in a vice with padded jaws and remove the dust cover securing clip (Fig. 10.6).
10 Remove the dust cover and tap the cylinder on a wooden bench to remove the piston and seal.
11 Inspect the piston and cylinder for signs of score marks or excessive scuffing and, if evident, obtain a new cylinder and piston assembly complete with seals.
12 If the piston and cylinder are in good condition, purchase a seal overhaul kit from your Chrysler Dealer.
13 Lubricate the new piston seal with brake fluid and fit it into the groove in the cylinder using finger pressure only.
14 Lubricate the piston and insert it into the cylinder.
15 Fit the dust cover over the end of the piston and cylinder and secure it in place with the spring clip.
16 Clean the yoke and bracket assembly and refit the cylinder into the yoke.

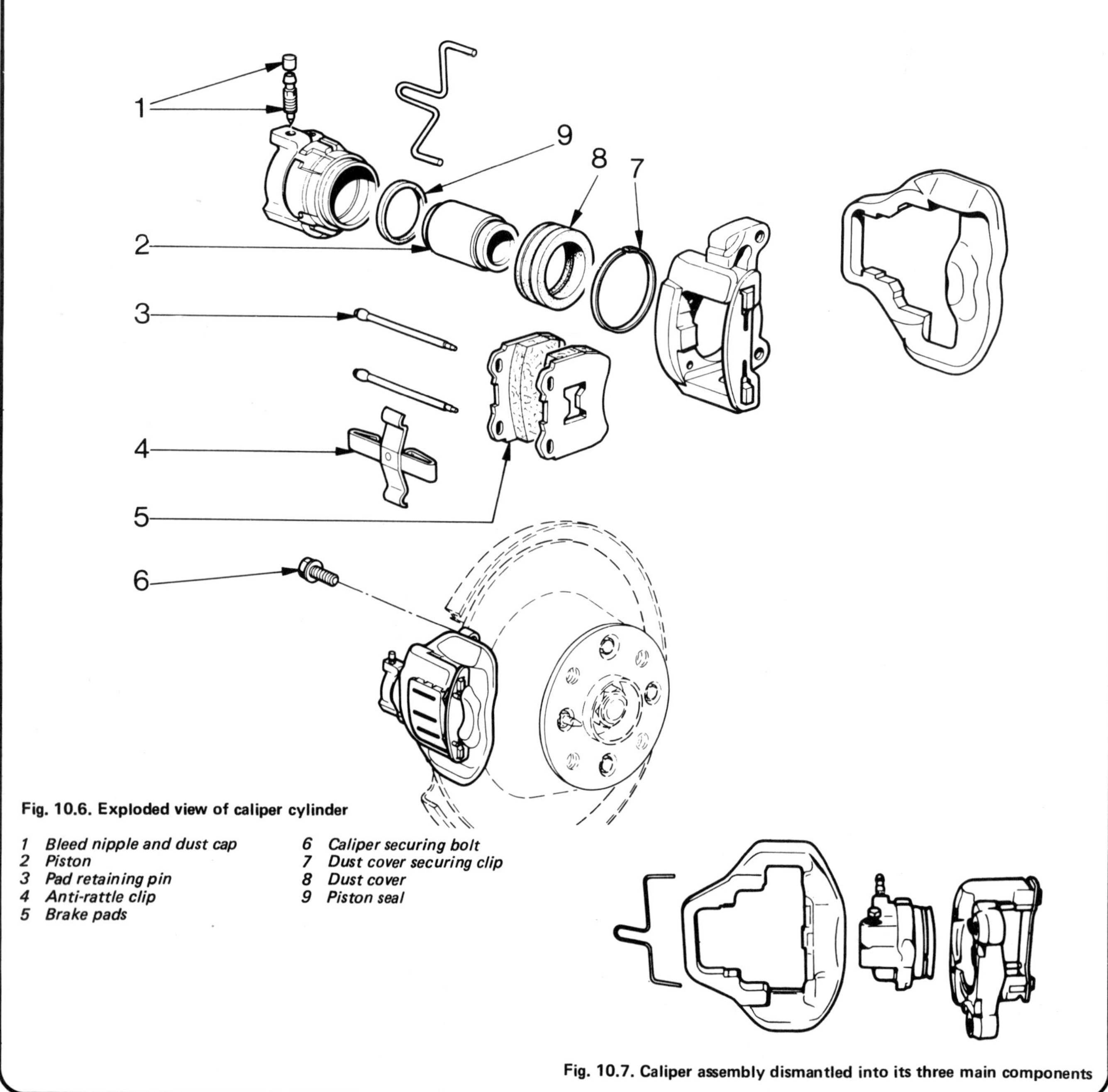

Fig. 10.6. Exploded view of caliper cylinder

1 Bleed nipple and dust cap
2 Piston
3 Pad retaining pin
4 Anti-rattle clip
5 Brake pads
6 Caliper securing bolt
7 Dust cover securing clip
8 Dust cover
9 Piston seal

Fig. 10.7. Caliper assembly dismantled into its three main components

17 Insert the bracket into the yoke, fit it over the end of the cylinder and secure it in place with the spring.
18 Reconnect the flexible brake hose to the caliper and refit the caliper to the stub axle carrier. Tighten the bolts to the specified torque wrench setting.
19 Refit the disc pads as described in Section 2.
20 Remove the polythene sheet from the reservoir and bleed the front braking circuit as described in Section 10. Refit the roadwheel and lower the car. Tighten the wheel nuts fully when the wheels are on the ground.

4 Rear brake shoes - inspection, removal and refitting

1 Every 10,000 miles the rear brake linings should be examined for wear.
2 Jack up the rear of the car, support it on axle stands and remove the roadwheels.
3 Remove the two retaining screws and pull off the drum. If the drum sticks, insert a thin screwdriver through the aperture in the rear of the back plate and release the brake adjusting pawl (Fig. 10.8)
4 Examine the linings and if they have worn down to a thickness of 1/16 in (1.5 mm) or less, or if they are contaminated with oil or grease a new set of shoes and linings should be obtained.
5 Two different types of rear brakes are fitted to the Alpine; either the Girling type (Fig. 10.10) or the DBA type (Fig. 10.11).

Shoe removal - Girling type

6 Unhook the adjuster lever spring from the forward brake shoe and remove it (photo).
7 Withdraw the adjuster lever from its pivot pin.
8 Rotate the serrated nut in the appropriate direction to reduce the adjuster pushrod to its minimum length (photo).
9 Grip the end of each spring retainer with a pair of pliers and rotate them through 90°. Remove the retainer springs and pins.
10 Push the handbrake lever forward and disengage the end of the handbrake cable (photo).
11 Unhook the ends of the lower return spring from each shoe.
12 Lift the lower end of each shoe away from the bottom retaining plate.
13 Pull the top of the shoes away from the wheel cylinder taking care not to tear the rubber boots, and remove both shoes complete with adjuster and top return spring.
14 Place a strong rubber band around the wheel cylinder to prevent the pistons being pushed out and subsequent loss of brake fluid.
15 Unhook the top spring from each shoe and remove the adjuster.
16 Remove the spring clip from the pivot pin on the trailing shoe and withdraw the handbrake lever.

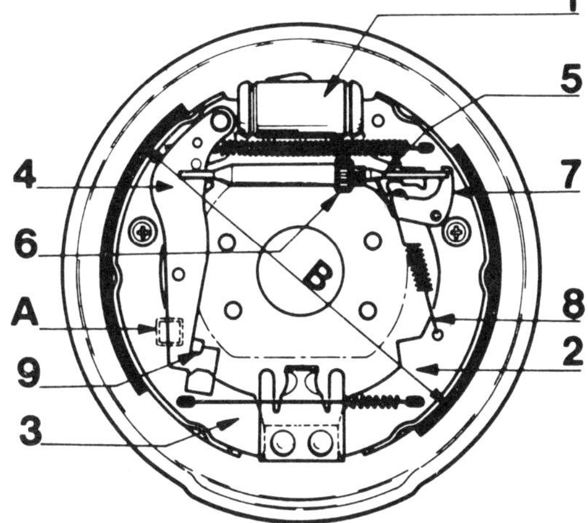

Fig. 10.10 Girling rear brake assembly

1 *Wheel cylinder*
2 *Leading (primary) shoe*
3 *Trailing (secondary) shoe*
4 *Handbrake lever*
5 *Adjuster push rod*
6 *Serrated nut*
7 *Adjuster lever*
8 *Spring, adjuster lever*
9 *Stop, handbrake lever*
A *Aperture, adjuster release*
B *Overall diameter of shoes prior to fitting drum - 227 to 227.9 mm (8 15/16 to 8 31/32 in)*

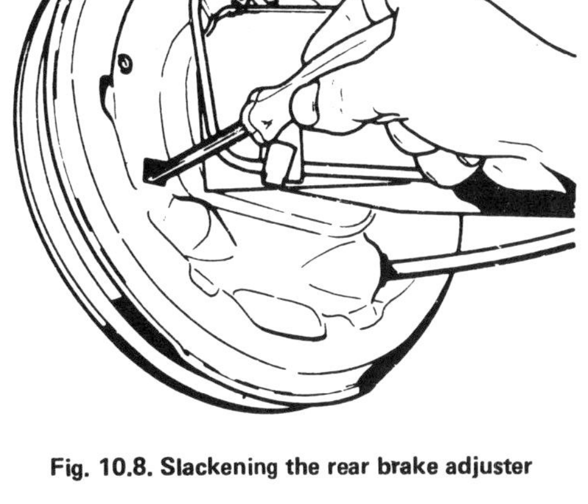

Fig. 10.8. Slackening the rear brake adjuster

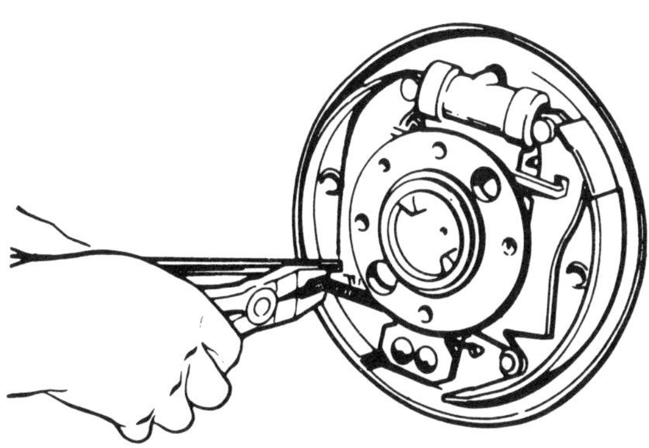

Fig. 10.9. Disconnecting the handbrake cable

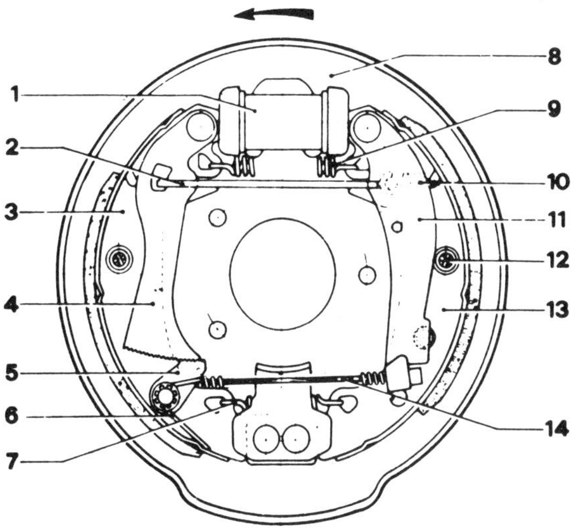

Fig. 10.11. DBA rear brake assembly

1 *Wheel cylinder*
2 *Link rod*
3 *Primary (leading) shoe*
4 *Adjuster lever*
5 *Adjuster pawl*
6 *Lower shoe return spring*
7 *Lower shoe return spring*
8 *Backplate*
9 *Upper shoe return spring*
10 *Spring, link rod and handbrake lever*
11 *Handbrake lever*
12 *Shoe steady spring*
13 *Secondary (trailing) shoe*
14 *Handbrake cable*

4.6 View of Girling type rear brake

4.8 Brake adjuster push rod and nut (Girling type brakes)

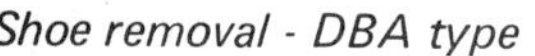

Shoe removal - DBA type

17 Remove the shoe steady springs by pressing them in with a screw-driver and turning until they disengage from the back plate.
18 Unhook the handbrake cable from the brake operating lever (Fig. 10.9).
19 Using a strong screwdriver, lever the lower ends of the shoes from behind the bottom retaining plate and pull the upper ends of both shoes from the wheel cylinder.
20 Push the shoes in towards the hub, unhook the top and bottom return springs and withdraw the shoes complete with adjuster lever and link rod (Fig. 10.12).
21 Fit an elastic band around the wheel cylinder to prevent the pistons coming out.
22 Remove the spring clip and withdraw the adjuster lever from the leading shoe.
23 Unhook the small spring and remove the link rod from the trailing shoe.
24 Remove the spring clip and withdraw the handbrake lever from the trailing shoe.
25 Thoroughly clean all traces of dust from the shoes, backplate, and drum, using a stiff brush. **Do not blow the dust clear as it is asbestos based and should not be inhaled.** Brake dust can cause judder and squeal and therefore it is important to clean away all traces.
26 Check that each piston is free in its cylinder and that the rubber dust covers are undamaged and in position. Check also that there are no hydraulic fluid leaks.
27 Prior to refitting the brake shoes, smear a trace of Castrol PM Brake Grease to the ends of the brake shoes, the rear shoe/handbrake lever pivot, the steady platform anchor posts and the adjuster surface. Do not allow any of the grease to come into contact with the brake linings or rubber boots.
28 The refitting procedure is the reversal of removal. The two pull off springs should preferably be renewed every time new shoes are fitted and and must be refitted into their original web holes.
29 On the Girling type brakes, turn the serrated nut on the pushrod to expand the shoes to the point where the brake drum will just slide over them.
30 In the case of the DBA brakes, push the adjuster lever towards the leading shoe and engage the first few teeth with the pawl.
31 Refit the brake drums and tighten the retaining screw. Push the brake pedal fully down at least ten times to enable the automatic adjusting mechanism to reset the shoes to the correct positions.
32 Check the operation of the handbrake and if necessary adjust the cable as described in Section 14.
33 Refit the roadwheels, lower the car to the ground and tighten the wheel bolts.

4.10 Handbrake cable attachment point (Girling type brakes)

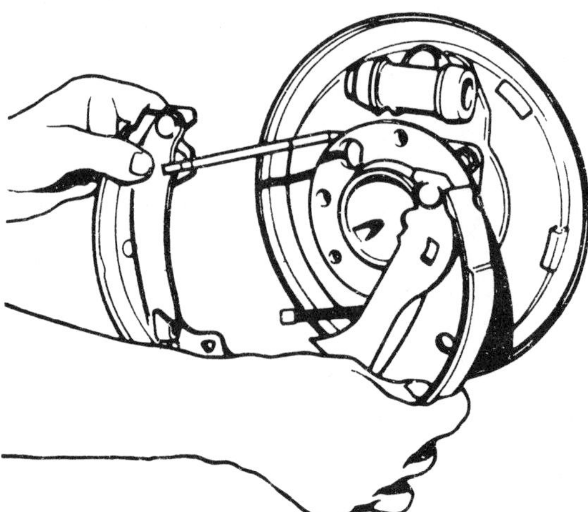

Fig. 10.12. Removing the brake shoes (DBA type)

5 Rear brake wheel cylinder - removal and overhaul

1 Two types of wheel cylinders are fitted to the Alpine (See Figs.

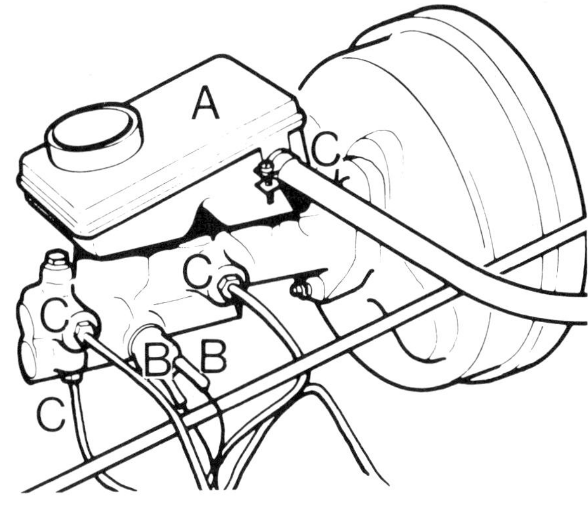

Fig. 10.13. Master cylinder assembly

A Reservoir
B Pressure switch leads
C Fluid outlet pipes

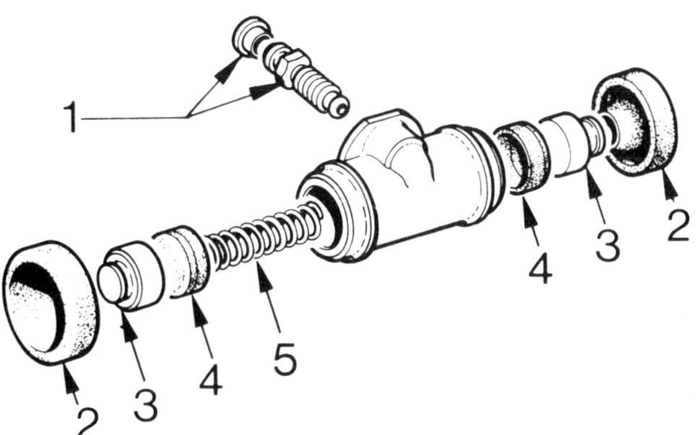

Fig. 10.14. Exploded view of Bendix type rear wheel brake cylinder

1 Bleed nipple and cap
2 Dust cover
3 Piston
4 Seal
5 Spring

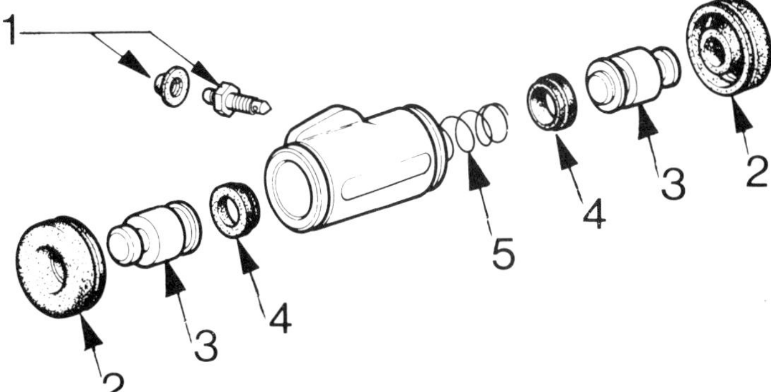

Fig. 10.15. Exploded view of Girling type rear wheel brake cylinder

1 Bleed nipple and cap
2 Dust cover
3 Piston
4 Seal
5 Spring

10.14 and 10.15) and although the method of removal and overhaul is virtually identical they are not interchangeable. When purchasing a new cylinder assembly take the old one along to your Chrysler Dealer to ensure that the correct type is obtained.

2 Jack up the rear of the car, remove the roadwheel.

3 Remove the drum and brake shoes as described in Section 4.

4 Disconnect the hydraulic fluid hose from the wheel cylinder and plug the hose.

5 Remove the two securing bolts which retain the wheel cylinder to the backplate.

6 Remove the wheel cylinder.

7 Peel off the rubber dust excluders from each end of the unit and then eject the internal components - pistons, spring and seals. This may be done by tapping the cylinder carefully on a piece of wood until the pistons emerge or by removing the bleed nipple and applying a tyre pump to the nipple orifice.

8 Wash all components in hydraulic fluid and examine the piston and cylinder internal surfaces for scratches, scoring or bright areas. Where these are evident, renew the complete wheel cylinder assembly on an exchange basis.

9 Obtain a repair kit which will contain all the necessary seals. Observe absolute cleanliness during the following operations.

10 Lubricate the bore of the cylinder with clean hydraulic fluid and insert one seal, one piston and one dust excluderat one end of the unit. Insert the spring from the opposite end, followed by the seal, piston and dust cover. Note that the lips of both seals face inwards.

11 Refit the cylinder to the backplate, refit the shoes and drum. Reconnect the fluid hose.

12 Bleed the hydraulic system as described in Section 10.

13 Refit the roadwheel, lower the car to the ground and tighten the wheel bolts.

6 Master cylinder - removal and refitting

1 Two types of master cylinder are fitted, either the Teves or Lockheed. However, the method of removal and refitting is the same for both types.

Caution: Brake fluid has the same effect as paint stripper and care must be taken to avoid dripping any on the paintwork.

2 Refer to Fig. 10.13 and disconnect the fluid outlet pipes from the reservoir and master cylinder. Plug the ends of the pipes to reduce fluid loss and prevent dirt ingress.

3 Disconnect the two wires from the pressure differential switch on the side of the master cylinder.

4 Remove the nuts and washers securing the master cylinder to the servo unit and withdraw the cylinder assembly.

5 Refit the master cylinder using the reverse procedure to that of removal and bleed the system as described in Section 10.

7 Master cylinder - servicing

1 Although the Teves and Lockheed type master cylinders differ slightly in design the method of dismantling and inspection is virtually

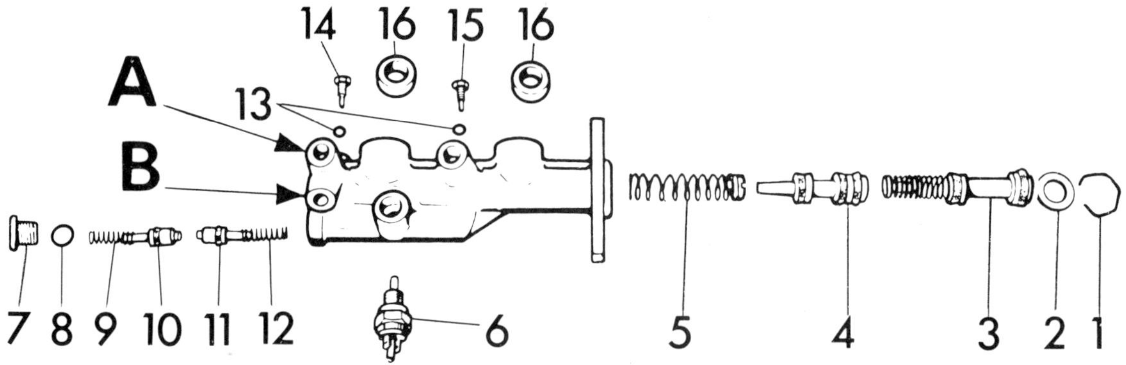

Fig. 10.16. Exploded view of Teves type master cylinder

1 Circlip	*6 Switch, warning*	*11 Piston*	*15 Rear stop screw*
2 Stop washer	*7 Plug*	*12 Spring*	*16 Sealing rings*
3 Primary piston	*8 Seal*	*13 Seal, stop screw*	*AB Outlet ports, front brakes*
4 Secondary piston	*9 Spring*	*14 Front stop screw*	
5 Piston spring	*10 Piston*		

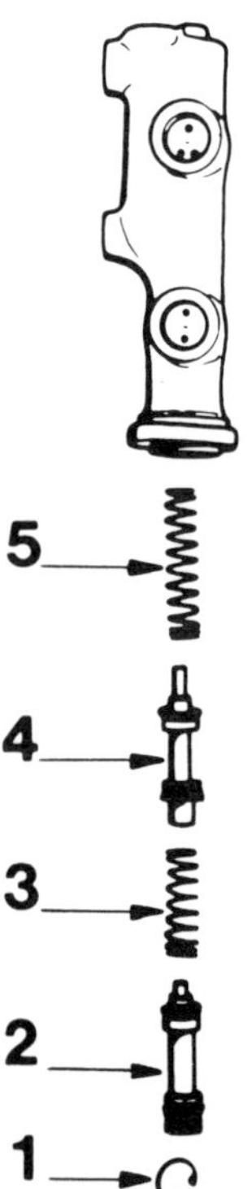

Fig. 10.17. Master cylinder pistons (Lockheed)

1 Circlip	*4 Secondary piston*
2 Primary piston	*5 Secondary spring*
3 Primary spring	

the same, and providing reference is made to the appropriate illustrations no problems should be encountered.

2 Remove the reservoir filler cap and drain the fluid into a suitable container.

3 Pull the reservoir off the master cylinder and withdraw the sealing rings from the inlet ports.

4 Push the primary piston down the cylinder bore just enough to remove the circlip and withdraw the washer (if fitted), primary piston and spring.

5 Push the secondary piston down the cylinder bore slightly and remove the stop screw(s). Withdraw the secondary piston and spring. If necessary tap the end of the cylinder on a wooden bench to dislodge the piston.

6 Unscrew the pressure differential warning switch from the cylinder assembly.

7 Unscrew the plug from the end of the cylinder and withdraw the warning switch actuating piston(s) assembly, (see Figs. 10.16 and 10.20).

8 Make a careful note of which way round all the rubber seals are fitted before removing and discarding them.

9 Note that on the Lockheed type master cylinder a washer is fitted under the piston seals.

10 Thoroughly wash all parts in either methylated spirit or clean approved hydraulic fluid and place in order ready for inspection.

11 Examine the bore of the master cylinder carefully for any signs of scoring, ridges or corrosion, and if it is found to be smooth all over, new seals can be fitted. If there is any doubt as to the condition of the bore, then a new cylinder must be fitted.

12 If examination of the seals shows them to be apparently oversize or very loose on their seats, suspect oil contamination in the system. Oil will swell these rubber seals, and if one is found to be swollen it is reasonable to assume that all seals in the braking system will require attention.

13 Before reassembly again wash all parts in methylated spirit or clean approved hydraulic fluid. Do not use any other type of oil or cleaning fluid or the seals will be damaged.

14 Commence reassembling by lubricating the bores with clean hydraulic fluid.

15 Smear the new secondary piston seals with hydraulic fluid and fit these to the secondary piston. Make sure that they are fitted the correct way round.

16 Smear the new primary piston seals with hydraulic fluid and fit these to the primary pistons. Make sure that they are fitted the correct way round.

17 Position the master cylinder between soft faces and clamp in a vice in such a manner that the main bore is inclined with the open end downwards.

18 Insert the spring and then the secondary piston assembly, second spring and the primary pistons assembly. To avoid any damage to the cup seals a flattened needle should be passed around the lip of each seal to assist entry into the cylinder bore.

19 Reposition the master cylinder so that it is now vertical with the open end upwards and place the top washer in position. Depress the primary piston slightly and fit the circlip.

20 Next fully depress the primary piston and fit the stop screw(s).

21 Fit new seals to the warning switch actuator pistons, and insert them into the cylinder housing. Refit the end plug and sealing ring.

22 Fit a new seal to the warning switch and screw it into the cylinder housing.

23 Fit new seals into the fluid inlet ports and press the reservoir into the correct position on the master cylinder.

24 The master cylinder is now ready for refitting to the car as described in Section 6.

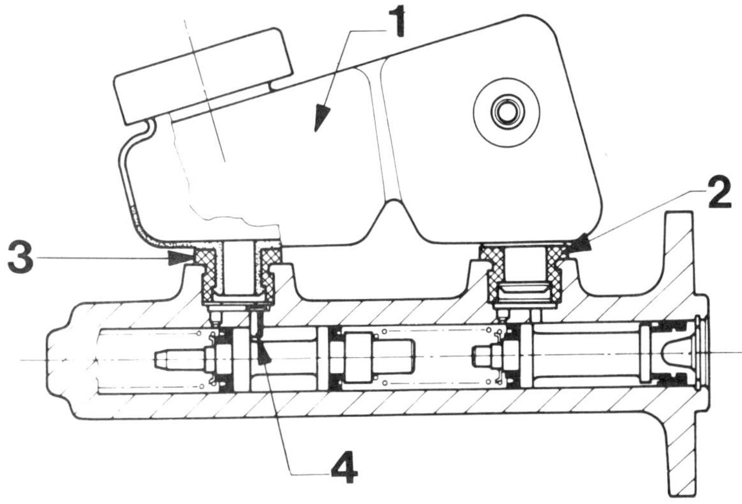

Fig. 10.18. Cross-sectional view of Lockheed type master cylinder

1 Reservoir *2 Inlet port seal (primary)* *3 Inlet port seal (secondary)* *4 Secondary piston stop pin*

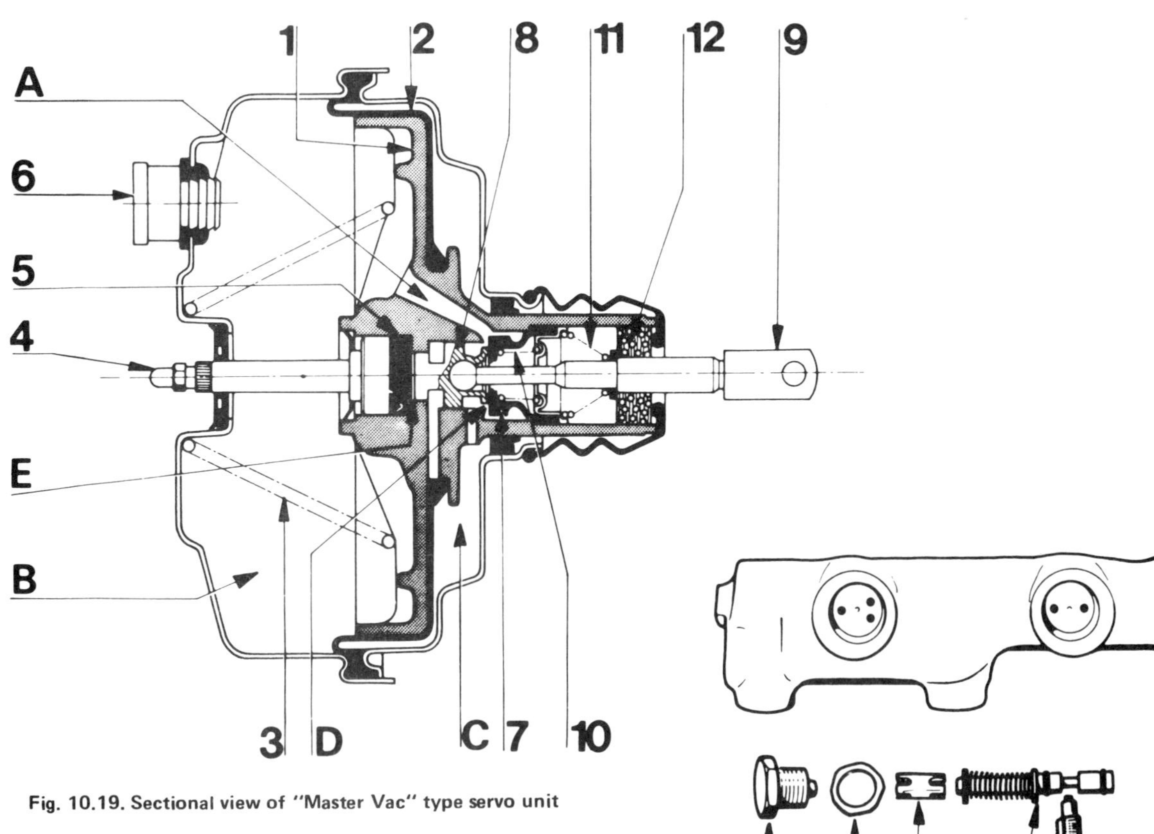

Fig. 10.19. Sectional view of "Master Vac" type servo unit

1 Valve body
2 Diaphragm
3 Return spring
4 Push rod (master cylinder)
5 Reaction disc
6 Non-return valve
7 Air valve
8 Plunger
9 Push rod (brake pedal)
10 Air valve spring
11 Valve rod spring
12 Air filter
A Vacuum passage
B Vacuum chamber
C Atmospheric chamber
D Atmospheric passage
E Valve body shoulder

Fig. 10.20. Master cylinder pressure switch actuator components (Lockheed)

1 Switch
2 Plug
3 Sealing ring
4 Distance piece
5 Piston

8 Brake servo unit - description and maintenance

Description

1 A vacuum servo unit is fitted into the brake hydraulic circuit in series with the master cylinder, to provide power assistance to the driver when the brake pedal is depressed.

The unit operates by vacuum obtained from the induction manifold and comprises, basically, a booster diaphragm and a non-return valve.

The servo unit and hydraulic master cylinder are connected together so that the servo unit piston rod acts as the master cylinder pushrod. The driver's braking effort is transmitted through another pushrod to the servo unit piston and its built-in control system. The servo unit piston does not fit tightly into the cylinder, but has a strong diaphragm to keep its edges in constant contact with the cylinder wall so assuring an air tight seal between the two parts. The forward chamber is held under vacuum conditions created in the inlet manifold of the engine and, during periods when the brake pedal is not in use, the controls open a passage to the rear chamber so placing it under vacuum. When the brake pedal is depressed, the vacuum passage to the rear chamber is cut off and the chamber opened to atmospheric pressure. The consequent rush of air pushes the servo piston forward in the vacuum chamber and operates the main pushrod to the master cylinder. The controls are designed so that assistance is given under all conditions and, when the brakes are not required, vacuum in the rear chamber is established when the brake pedal is released. Air from the atmosphere entering the rear chamber is passed through a small air filter.

Two types of servo units are fitted to the Alpine, (see Figs. 10.19 and 10.21). However the method ot operation, removal and servicing procedures are identical.

Maintenance and adjustments

2 The brake servo unit operation can be checked easily without any special tools. Proceed as follows:

3 Stop the engine and clear the servo of any vacuum by depressing the brake pedal several times.

4 Once the servo is cleared, keep the brake pedal depressed and start the engine. If the servo unit is in proper working order, the brake pedal should move further downwards, under even foot pressure, due to the effect of the inlet manifold vacuum on the servo diaphragms.

5 If the brake pedal does not move further downwards the servo system is not operating properly, and the vacuum hoses from the inlet manifold to the servo should be inspected. The vacuum control valve should also be checked. This valve is in the vacuum hose to prevent air flowing into the vacuum side of the servo from the inlet manifold when the engine stops. It is in effect a one way valve.

6 If the brake servo operates properly in the test, but still gives less effective service on the road, the air filter through which air flows into

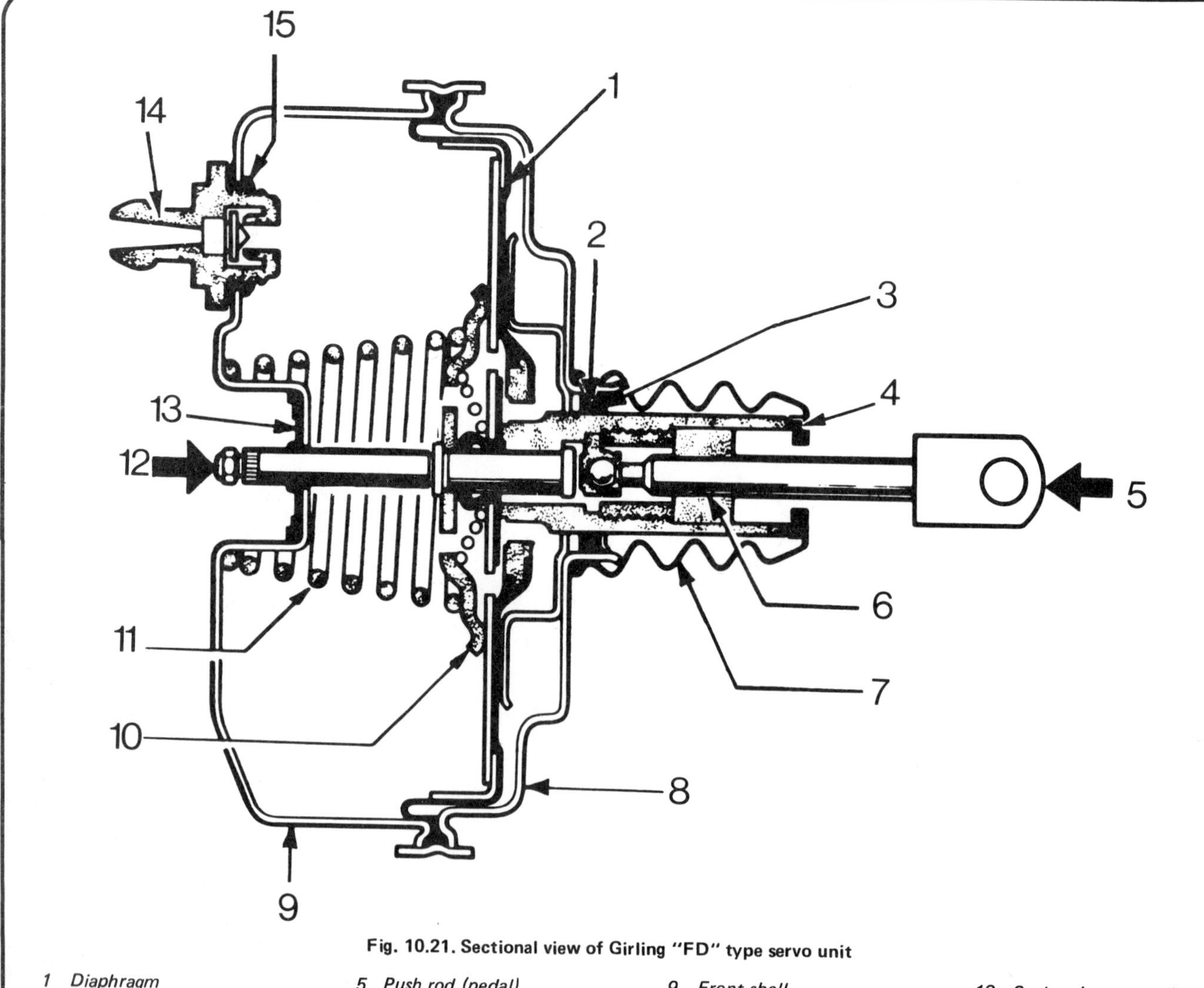

Fig. 10.21. Sectional view of Girling "FD" type servo unit

1 Diaphragm
2 Seal
3 Retainer
4 Filter retainer
5 Push rod (pedal)
6 Air filter
7 Dust cover
8 Rear shell
9 Front shell
10 Fulcrum plate
11 Return spring
12 Push rod (master cylinder)
13 Seal and support plate
14 Non-return valve
15 Grommet

the servo should be inspected. A dirty filter will limit the formation of a difference in pressure across the servo diaphragm.

7 The servo unit itself cannot be repaired and therefore a complete renewal is necessary if the measures described are not effective.

8 *Air filter replacement:* From inside the car, detach the brake pedal from the servo pushrod, then remove the rubber boot over the pushrod housing and air filter.

9 Hook out the filter and push in a new one. Refit the retainer and rubber boot.

10 *Non-return valve:* The non-return valve is fitted on the front face of the servo unit and is connected to the vacuum inlet hose.

11 It is not repairable and if faulty should be renewed.

9 Brake servo unit - removal and refitting

1 Refer to Section 6 and remove the brake master cylinder.

2 Slacken the hose clip and detach the vacuum hose from the connector on the non-return valve.

3 Remove the clip retaining the servo to the brake pedal pushrod clevis pin. Extract the clip, lift away the plain washer and withdraw the clevis pin.

4 Undo and remove the four nuts and spring washers that secure the servo unit to the mounting bracket. Lift away the servo unit.

5 Refitting the servo unit is the reverse sequence to removal. It is important that the brake hydraulic system be completely bled as described in the following Section.

10 Bleeding the hydraulic system

1 Whenever the brake hydraulic system has been dismantled to renew a pipe or hose or other major part, air will have inevitably been introduced into the pipe system. The system will therefore require 'bleeding' in order to remove this air and restore the effectiveness of the system.

2 During the 'bleeding' operation the level of the hydraulic fluid in the reservoir must be maintained at least half full, to prevent more air from being taken into the system via the reservoir and master cylinder.

3 Obtain a clean glass jar, some plastic tube (15 inches long and a suitable diameter to fit tightly over the bleed valves). A can of **new** brake fluid will also be required.

4 Clean all the brake pipes and hoses and check that all connections are tight and bleed valves closed.

5 It will be easier to gain access to the bleed valve and the rear of the assemblies if the appropriate roadwheel is removed. Chock the other wheels whilst the system is being bled. Release the handbrake.

6 Fill the master cylinder reservoir, and the bottom inch or so of the jar, with hydraulic fluid. Take extreme care that no fluid is allowed to come into contact with the paintwork, as it acts as a solvent and it will damage the finish.

7 Remove the rubber dust cap (if fitted) from the end of the bleed valve on the front disc brake caliper which is furthest away from the master cylinder. Insert the other end of the bleed tube in the jar containing 1 inch of hydraulic fluid.

8 Use a suitable open-ended spanner and unscrew the bleed valve about half a turn.

9 An assistant should now pump the brake pedal by first depressing it one full stroke, followed by three short but rapid strokes and allowing the pedal to return of its own accord. Check the fluid level in the reservoir. Carefully watch the flow of fluid into the glass jar and, when air bubbles cease to emerge with the fluid, during the next down stroke, tighten the bleed valve. Remove the plastic bleed tube and tighten the bleed valve. Refit the rubber dust cap.

10 Repeat the operations in paragraphs 4 - 6 for the second front brake.

11 The rear brake circuit should be bled in the same manner as the front, except that each brake pedal stroke should be slow with a pause of three to four seconds between each stroke.

12 Sometimes it may be found that the bleeding operation for one or more cylinders is taking a considerable time. The cause is probably due to air being drawn past the bleed valve threads when the valve is loose. To counteract this condition, it is recommended that, at the end of each downward stroke, the bleed valve be tightened to stop air being drawn past the threads.

13 If the failure indicator lamp lights up during these operations, close the nipple which is open and open one in the other brake circuit. Apply a steady pressure at the foot pedal until the lamp goes out, release the pedal and close the nipple, the leak switch pistons will have resumed their balance.

14 If, after the bleed operation has been completed, the brake pedal operation still feels spongy, this is an indication that there is still air in the system, or that the master cylinder is faulty.

15 Check and top up the reservoir fluid level with fresh hydraulic fluid. Never re-use the old brake fluid.

11 Hydraulic pipes and hoses - inspection, removal and refitting

Important: All the hydraulic pipe and flexible hose connections on the Alpine have a M10 x 1 mm metric thread as opposed to the 3/8 in UNF thread used on other Chrysler cars. The metric pipe unions, hoses etc, are identified by a black or olive paint mark and care must be taken to ensure that new items have the correct size thread.

1 Periodically, and certainly well in advance of the DoE Test, all brake pipes, connections and unions should be completely and carefully examined.

2 Examine first all the unions for signs of leaks. Then look at the flexible hoses for signs of fraying and chafing (as well as for leaks). This is only a preliminary inspection of the flexible hoses, as exterior condition does not necessarily indicate interior condition which will be considered later.

3 The steel pipes must be examined equally carefully. They must be thoroughly cleaned and examined for signs of dents or other percussive damage, rust and corrosion. Rust and corrosion should be scraped off, and, if the depth of pitting in the pipes is significant, they will require renewal. This is most likely in those areas underneath the chassis and along the rear suspension arms where the pipes are exposed to the full force of road and weather conditions.

4 If any section of pipe is to be removed, first take off the fluid reservoir cap, line it with a piece of polythene film to make it airtight and screw it back on. This will minimise the amount of fluid dripping out of the system when the pipes are removed.

5 Rigid pipe removal is usually quite straightforward. The unions at each end are undone and the pipe drawn out of the connection. The clips which may hold it to the car body are bent back and it is then removed. Underneath the car the exposed union can be particularly stubborn, defying the efforts of an open ended spanner. As few people will have the special split ring spanner required, a self-grip wrench is the only answer. If the pipe is being renewed, new unions will be provided. If not, then one will have to put up with the possibility of burring over the flats on the unions and of using a self-grip wrench for refitting.

6 Flexible hoses are always fitted to a rigid support bracket where they join a rigid pipe, the bracket being fixed to the chassis or rear suspension arm. The rigid pipe unions must first be removed from the flexible union. Then the locknut securing the flexible pipe to the bracket must be unscrewed, releasing the end of the pipe from the

12.1 Rear brake pressure equalising valve

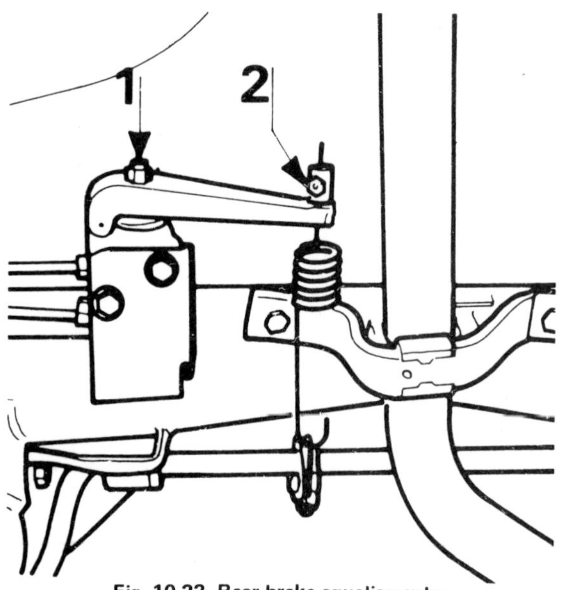

Fig. 10.22. Rear brake equaliser valve

1 Adjusting screw *2 Spring stop screw*

bracket. As these connections are usually exposed they are, more often than not, rusted up and a penetrating fluid is virtually essential to aid removal. When undoing them, both halves must be supported as the bracket is not strong enough to support the torque required to undo the nut and can be snapped off easily.

7 Once the flexible hose is removed, examine the internal bore. If clear of fluid it should be possible to see through it. Any specks of rubber that come out, or there are signs of restriction in the bore, mean that the inner lining is breaking up and the hose must be renewed.

8 Rigid pipes which need renewing can usually be purchased at your local garage where they have the pipe, unions and special tools to make them up. All that they need to know is the pipe length required and the type of flare used at the ends of the pipe. These may be different at each end of the same pipe. If possible, it is a good idea to take the old pipe along as a pattern.

9 Refitting of the pipes is a straightforward reversal of the removal procedure. It is best to get all the sets (bends) made prior to fitting. Also, any acute bends should be put in by the garage on a bending machine otherwise there is the possibility of kinking them, and restricting the bore area and thus, fluid flow.

10 With the pipes refitted, remove the polythene from the reservoir cap and bleed the system as described in Section 10.

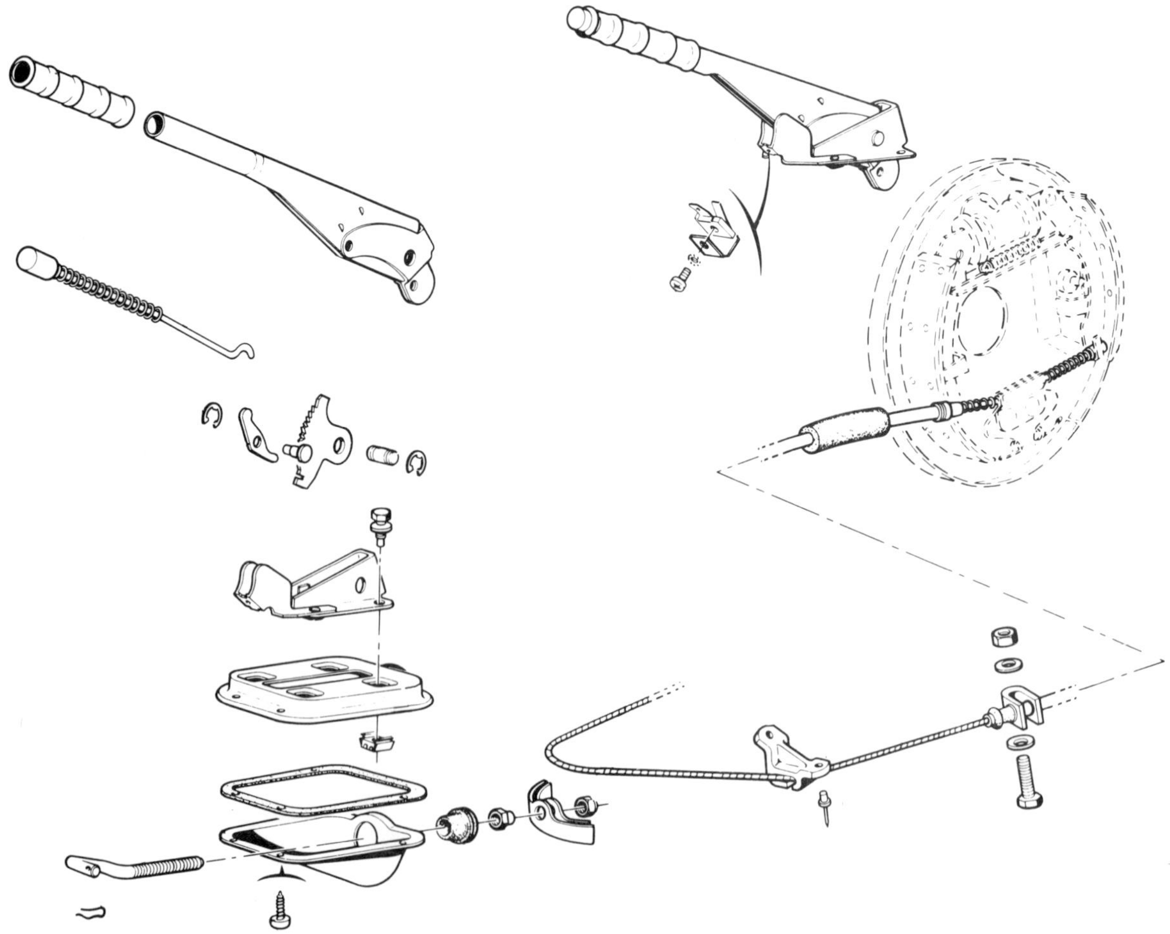

Fig. 10.23. Handbrake lever components and cable

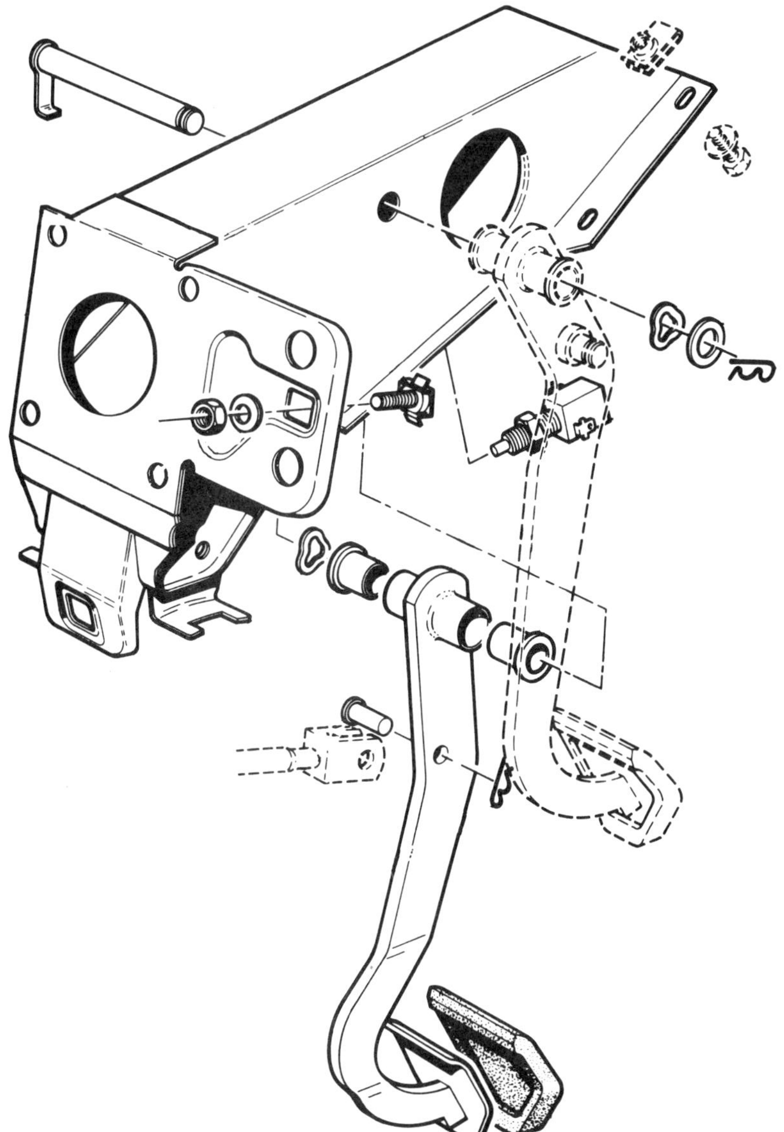

Fig. 10.24. Footbrake pedal components

12 Brake equaliser valve - checking and adjusting

1 The brake equaliser valve assembly exerts a compensating and regulating effect upon the front and rear braking effort according to the vehicle load. The equaliser valve is mounted on the rear suspension crossmember and is actuated by the pull of a spring fitted between the valve operating lever and an arm on the rear anti-roll bar (photo). It is essential for safe and effective braking that the following operations are correctly carried out.
2 First disconnect both rear shock absorber lower mountings.
3 With the car unladen check that the spring is fairly taut but that the coils are closed up and not in a stretched condition.
4 To adjust the spring tension, slacken the locknut and turn the adjusting screw in or out to reposition the spring. Do **not** make any attempt to alter the position of the spring stop screw (See Fig. 10.22).
5 The length of the spring is very important and must not be altered in any way.
6 If it is felt that the rear wheels are overbraking, slacken the locknut and turn the adjustment screw out a small amount. Tighten the locknut and retest the brakes.
7 If the rear wheel braking effort appears to be insufficient, turn the screw inwards a small amount and then recheck the brakes.
8 The valve is not repairable and if faulty must be renewed. This will necessitate bleeding the rear braking system (see Section 10).

13 Handbrake - adjustment

1 The handbrake is normally automatically adjusted when the rear drum brakes are adjusted. However, after extended service, the cable may stretch and the following procedure should be carried out. This method should also be used when a new cable or handbrake assembly has been fitted.
2 Fully release the handbrake and then pull the handbrake up five notches (clicks).
3 Release the locknut (A) on the cable equalising yoke and adjust nut (B) (Fig. 10.25).
4 Adjustment is correct when the cables are just taut and the rear wheels are fully locked when the lever is pulled up six notches (clicks).
5 When adjustment is complete, hold nut (B) quite still and tighten the locknut (A).

14 Handbrake assembly - renewal

1 The handbrake assembly comprises three sub assemblies, the lever, the operating rod and yoke and the cable.
2 A broken or overstretched cable can only be renewed as a unit as fittings and ends are not detachable.
3 To remove the cable, first detach the two ends from the rear brake

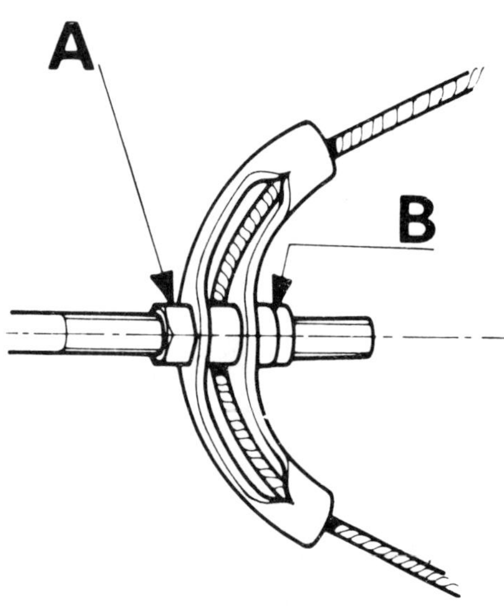

Fig. 10.25. Brake cable adjusting nuts ('A' front nut, 'B' rear nut)

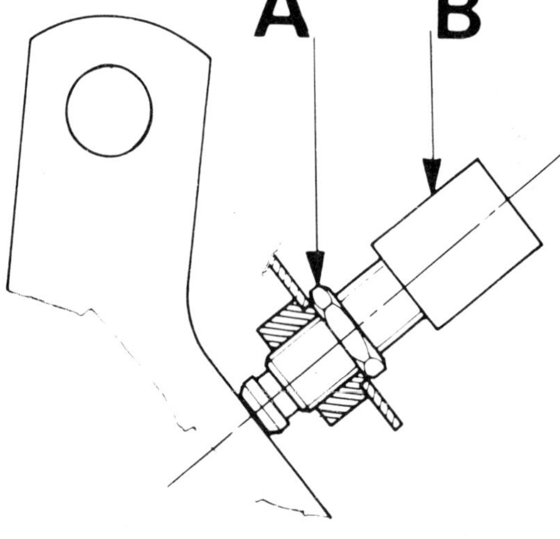

Fig. 10.26. Stop light switch

A Locknut *B Switch*

shoes as described in Section 4.

4 Pull the ends of the cable through the rear brake backplate and remove the two clips securing the cable to the underside of the car.

5 Detach the equalising yoke from the handbrake operating rod, unhook the cable from the front clips and remove it from beneath the car.

6 Refit the new cable using the reverse procedure to that of removal, and adjust it as described in the previous Section.

7 Wear or damage to the rod and yoke can be repaired by renewal of components affected.

8 It is possible to renew the lever ratchet as a separate component after dismantling by removal of the circlips and crosspins. Occasional application of grease to the ratchet and quadrant notches will help to reduce wear. Application of the handbrake with the ratchet button depressed will also increase the life of the lever components.

9 Details of the handbrake assembly are shown in Fig. 10.23.

15 Brake operating pedal - removal and refitting

1 The brake pedal operates on a common cross shaft with the clutch pedal (Fig. 10.24).

2 The method of removal and refitting is as described for the clutch pedal in Chapter 5, Section 5.

16 Brake stop light switch - adjustment

1 The brake stop light switch is located on a bracket above the brake pedal lever.

2 To adjust the function of the switch, first depress the brake pedal several times to exhaust the brake servo unit and then switch on the ignition.

3 Get a friend to watch the rear lights and then depress the pedal and check that the stop lights come on after the pedal has moved down between 1/8 - 3/4 in (4 - 20 mm).

4 Release the pedal fully and check that the stop lights extinguish.

5 Adjust the switch if necessary by slackening the locknut and screwing the switch in or out of its bracket as required. Tighten the locknut when the setting is correct (Fig. 10.26).

17 Discs and drums - reconditioning

1 After extended mileage it is possible that the brake discs and drums will become scored. Any skimming must be carried out professionally and within the tolerances specified in the Specifications.

2 Ovality in brake drums may be corrected by skimming, but excessive run-out in discs is best obviated by renewing the disc.

3 For instructions on removing the discs, refer to Chapter 7.

18 Fault diagnosis - braking system

Symptom	Reason/s
Pedal travels almost to floor before brakes operate	Brake fluid level too low. Caliper leaking. Master cylinder leaking (bubbles in master cylinder fluid) Brake flexible hose leaking. Brake line fractured. Brake system unions loose. Pad or shoe linings over 75% worn. Rear brake badly out of adjustment (automatic adjusters seized)
Brake pedal feels springy	New linings not yet bedded-in. Brake discs or drums badly worn or cracked. Master cylinder securing nuts loose.
Brake pedal feels 'spongy' and 'soggy'	Caliper or wheel cylinder leaking. Master cylinder leaking (bubbles in master cylinder fluid). Brake pipe line or flexible hose leaking. Unions in brake system loose.
Excessive effort required to brake car	Faulty vacuum servo unit. Pad or shoe linings badly worn. New pads or shoes recently fitted - not yet bedded-in. Harder linings fitted than standard causing increase in pedal pressure. Linings and brake drums contaminated with oil, grease or hydraulic fluid.
Brake uneven and pulling to one side	Linings and discs or drums contaminated with oil, grease or hydraulic fluid. Tyre pressures unequal. Brake caliper loose. Brake pads or shoes fitted incorrectly. Different type of linings fitted at each wheel. Anchorage for front suspension or rear suspension loose. Brake discs or drums badly worn, cracked or distorted.
Brakes tend to bind, drag or lock-on	Rear brakes over adjusted. Air in system. Handbrake cables over-tightened. Wheel cylinder or caliper pistons seized.
Brake warning light comes on and stays on	Leak in front or rear hydraulic circuit. Check master cylinder reservoirs.

Chapter 11 Electrical system

Contents

Specifications

System type ... 12 volt negative earth

Battery

Type ...	Lead acid
Capacity ...	40 amp/hr

Alternator

Make ...	Paris-Rhone, Ducellier or Motorola
Output	
Paris-Rhone ...	35 amps

Ducellier	35 amps
Motorola	40 amps
Field resistance	7 ohms (all types)

Alternator control unit

Make	Ducellier or Paris-Rhone
Regulating voltage	14.6 to 15.3 volts
Condenser capacity	470 mfd

Starter motor

Make	Ducellier or Paris-Rhone
Type	Pre-engaged
No. of teeth (drive pinion)	9
No. of teeth (ring gear)	112
Pinion end-float	0.020 to 0.090 in (0.51 to 2.29 mm)

Windscreen wiper motor

Make	Bosch, Marchal or Siem
Speeds	Two

Bulb ratings	**Wattage**
Headlamps	40 - 45 55 - 60 halogen
Side lamps	4
Front indicators	21
Rear indicators	21
Reverse lamps	21
Rear fog lamp	21
Stop/tail lamps	21 - 5
Rear number plate lamp	5 + 5
Interior courtesy lamps	5
Luggage compartment lamp	4
Heater illumination lamp	3

Torque wrench settings	**lb f ft**	**kg fm**
Starter motor securing bolts	15	2.07
Alternator to mounting bracket	30	4.15
Mounting bracket to crankcase	15	2.07
Strap to alternator	15	2.07

1 General description

The electrical system is of the 12 volt negative earth type. The battery is charged by a belt-driven alternator which incorporates a regulator.

The starter motor fitted as standard is of the pre-engaged type.

Although repair procedures and methods are fully described in this Chapter, in view of the long life of the major electrical components, it is recommended that when a major fault does develop, consideration should be given to exchanging the unit for a factory reconditioned assembly rather than renewing individual components of a well worn unit.

When fitting electrical accessories to cars with a negative earth system, it is important, if they contain Silicone Diodes, or Transistors, that they are connected correctly, otherwise serious damage may result to the components concerned. Items such as radios, tape recorders, electronic ignition systems, electronic tachometer, automatic dipping etc, should all be checked for correct polarity.

It is important that the battery positive lead is always disconnected if the battery is to be boost charged when an alternator is fitted. Also if body repairs are to be carried out using electronic arc welding equipment the alternator must be disconnected otherwise serious damage can be caused to the more delicate instruments. When the battery has to be disconnected it must always be reconnected with the negative terminal earthed.

2 Battery - removal and refitting

1 The battery should be removed once every three months for cleaning and testing. Disconnect the positive and negative leads from the battery terminals by slackening the clamp bolts and lifting away the clamps.

2 Undo and remove the nut and washer securing the battery clamp and lift away the clamp. Carefully lift the battery from its carrier and hold it upright to ensure that none of the electrolyte is spilled.

3 Refitting is a direct reversal of the removal procedure. Smear the terminals and clamps with petroleum jelly (vaseline) to prevent corrosion. **Never** use ordinary grease.

3 Battery - maintenance and inspection

1 Normal weekly battery maintenance consists of checking the electrolyte level of each cell to ensure that the separators are covered by 0.25 in (6.5 mm) of electrolyte. If the level has fallen, top-up the battery and check the securing bolts, the clamp plate, tray and leads for corrosion. If overfilled or any electrolyte is spilt, immediately wipe away the excess as electrolyte attacks and corrodes any metal it comes into contact with very rapidly.

2 As well as keeping the terminals clean and covered with petroleum jelly (vaseline), the top of the battery, and especially the top of the cells, should be kept clean and dry. This helps prevent corrosion and ensures that the battery does not become partially discharged by leakage through dampness and dirt.

3 Once every three months remove the battery and inspect the battery securing bolts, the clamp plate, tray and leads for corrosion. If any corrosion is found, clean off the deposit with ammonia and paint over the clean metal with an anti-rust and acid paint.

4 At the same time inspect the battery case for cracks. If a crack is found, clean and plug it with one of the proprietary compounds made for this purpose. If leakage through the cracks has been excessive then it will be necessary to refill the appropriate cell with fresh electrolyte as detailed later. Cracks are frequently caused to the top of the battery cases by pouring in distilled water in the middle of winter *after* instead of *before* a run. This gives the water no chance to mix with the electrolyte and so the former freezes and splits the battery case.

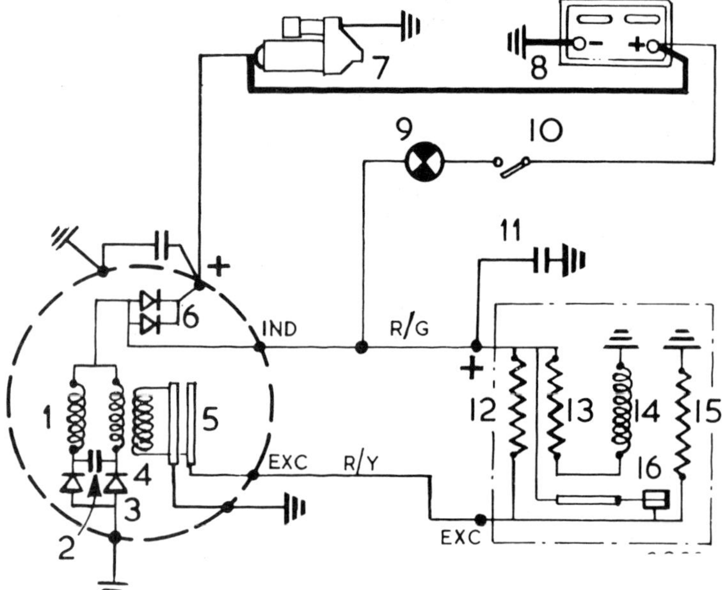

Fig. 11.1. Charging circuit diagram (single phase alternators)

1 Stator windings
2 Capacitor
3 Rectifier diodes
4 Rotor winding
5 Slip rings
6 Isolator diodes
7 Starter motor
8 Battery
9 Warning lamp
10 Ignition switch
11 Capacitor
12 Field resistor
13 Thermal resistor
14 Relay coil
15 Absorption resistor
16 VR contacts

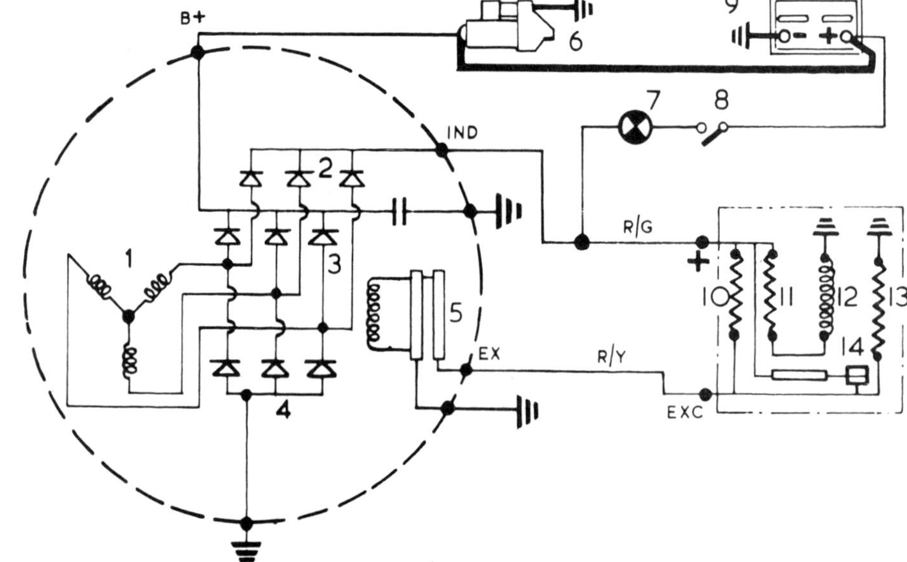

Fig. 11.2. Charging circuit diagram (three phase alternators)

1 Stator windings
2 Field diodes
3 Positive diodes
4 Negative diodes
5 Slip rings
6 Starter motor
7 Warning lamp
8 Ignition switch
9 Battery
10 Field resistor
11 Thermal resistor
12 Relay coil
13 Absorption resistor
14 VR contacts

5 If topping up the battery becomes excessive and the case has been inspected for cracks that could cause leakage, but none are found, the battery is being overcharged and the voltage regulator will have to be checked and reset, or renewed.

6 With the battery on the bench at the three monthly interval check, measure the specific gravity with a hydrometer to determine the state of charge and condition of the electrolyte. There should be very little variation between the different cells and if a variation in excess of 0.025 is present it will be due to either:

a) Loss of electrolyte from the battery at some time caused by spillage or a leak, resulting in a drop in the specific gravity of the electrolyte, when the deficiency was replaced with distilled water instead of fresh electrolyte.

b) An internal short circuit caused by buckling of the plates or a similar malady pointing to the likelihood of total battery failure in the near future.

7 The specific gravity of the electrolyte for fully charged conditions at the electrolyte temperature indicated, is listed in Table A. The specific gravity of a fully discharged battery at different temperatures of the electrolyte is given in Table B.

Table A

Specific gravity - battery fully charged

1.268 at	*100°F or 38°C*	*electrolyte*	*temperature*
1.272 at	*90°F or 32°C*	″	″
1.276 at	*80°F or 27°C*	″	″
1.280 at	*70°F or 21°C*	″	″
1.284 at	*60°F or 16°C*	″	″
1.288 at	*50°F or 10°C*	″	″
1.292 at	*40°F or 4°C*	″	″
1.296 at	*30°F or -1.5°C*	″	″

Table B

Specific gravity - battery fully discharged

1.098 at	*100°F or 38°C*	*electrolyte*	*temperature*
1.102 at	*90°F or 32°C*	″	″
1.106 at	*80°F or 27°C*	″	″
1.110 at	*70°F or 21°C*	″	″
1.114 at	*60°F or 16°C*	″	″
1.118 at	*50°F or 10°C*	″	″
1.122 at	*40°F or 4°C*	″	″
1.126 at	*30°F or -1.5°C*	″	″

4 Battery - electrolyte replenishment

1 If the battery is in a fully charged state and one of the cells maintains a specific gravity reading which is 0.025 or more lower than the others, and a check of each cell has been made with a voltage meter to check for short circuits (a four to seven second test should give a steady reading of between 1.2 and 1.8 volts), then it is likely that electrolyte has been lost from the cell at some time with the low reading.
2 Top up the cell with a solution of 1 part sulphuric acid to 2.5 parts of water. If the cell is already fully topped-up draw some electrolyte out of it with a hydrometer.
3 When mixing the sulphuric acid and water **never add water to sulphuric acid** - always pour the acid slowly onto the water in a glass container. **If water is added to sulphuric acid it will explode.**
4 Continue to top up the cell with the freshly made electrolyte and then recharge the battery and check the hydrometer readings.

5 Battery - charging

1 In winter time when heavy demand is placed upon the battery such as when starting from cold, and a lot of electrical equipment is continually in use, it is a good idea to occasionally have the battery fully charged from an external source at the rate of 3.5 to 4 amps.
2 Continue to charge the battery at this rate until no further rise in specific gravity is noted over a four hour period.
3 Alternatively, a trickle charge, charging at the rate of 1.5 amps can be safely used overnight.
4 Specially rapid 'boost' charges which are claimed to restore the power of the battery in 1 to 2 hours are not recommended as they can cause serious damage to the battery plates through overheating.
5 **While charging the battery note that the temperature of the electrolyte should never exceed 100°F (37.8°C).**

6 Alternator driving belt - checking and adjustment

1 The correct belt tension must be maintained at all times, to ensure the correct charging rate and to avoid strain on the alternator bearings.
2 Remove the drive belt protective shield and slacken the alternator mounting bolts and the bolts which secure the adjustment strap (Fig. 11.3).
3 Prise the alternator away from the engine block and tighten the adjustment strap bolts when there is a **total** free movement of ½ in (13 mm) at the centre of the longest run of the belt.
4 Make periodic inspections of the belt and renew it when any sign of fraying is evident.

7 Alternator - fault finding and repair

Due to the specialist knowledge and equipment required to test or service an alternator it is recommended that if the performance is suspect, the car be taken to an auto electrician who will have the facilities for such work. Because of this recommendation, information is limited to the inspection and renewal of the brushes. Should the alternator not charge or the system be suspect the following points may be checked before seeking further assistance.
1 Check the fan belt tension.
2 Check the battery.
3 Check all electrical cable connections for cleanliness and security.

8 Alternator - removal and refitting

1 Disconnect the leads from the battery terminals.
2 Remove the drivebelt protective shield.
3 Slacken the alternator mounting bolts and adjustment strap bolts.
4 Push the alternator in towards the engine and slip the driving belt from the crankshaft, water pump and alternator pulleys.
5 Disconnect the four leads from the rear end of the alternator.
6 On single phase type alternators (Paris-Rhone and Ducellier) remove the pivot bolt, lower the alternator sufficiently to turn it, so the pulley is uppermost, and then lift it up between the distributor and chassis frame.
7 In the case of the three phase (Motorola) alternator, first remove the pivot bolt and then the mounting bracket from the engine. Retrieve the special washer from the bracket retaining bolt nearest the timing cover end of the engine. Lower the bracket down past the engine, followed by the alternator.
8 Refit the alternator using the reversal of the removal procedure.
9 Adjust the drivebelt tension as described in Section 6 and ensure that the leads are reconnected to the alternator as follows:

Black lead to earth (–)
Red lead to positive (+)
Red/yellow lead to 'EXC'
Red/green lead to 'IND'

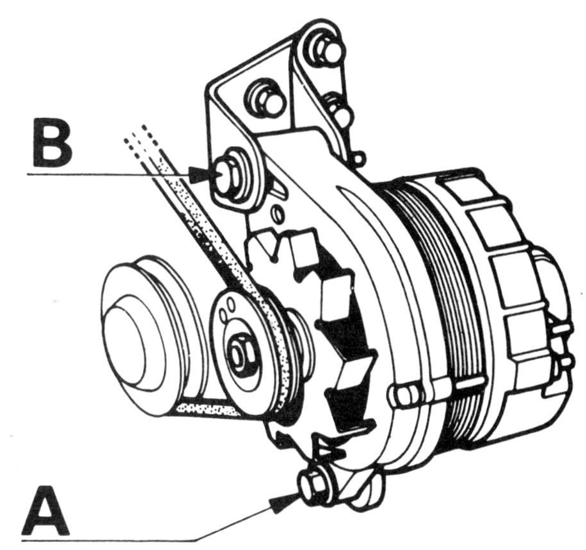

Fig. 11.3. Alternator securing bolts

A Adjusting bolt *B Pivot bolt*

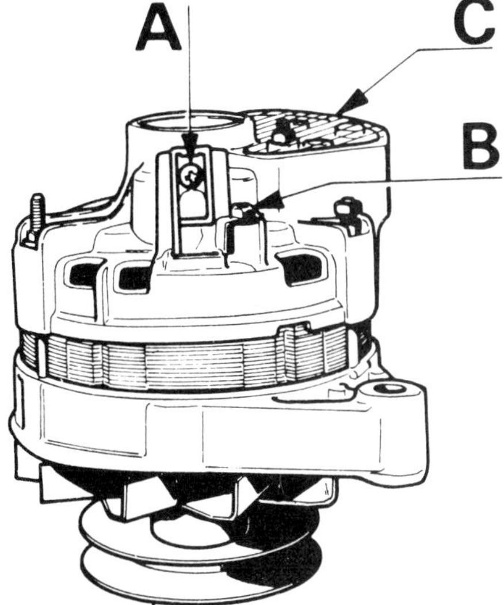

Fig. 11.4. Rear casing of Ducellier alternator

A Brush holder securing screws
B Brush holder securing screws
C Rear cover

Fig. 11.5. Exploded view of Ducellier alternator

1	*Pulley nut and washer*	*17*	*Bearing retainer*
2	*Spacer*	*18*	*Spacers*
3	*Pulley*	*19*	*Terminal nut*
4	*Spacers*	*20*	*Plain washer*
5	*Fan*	*21*	*Locknut*
6	*Through bolt*	*22*	*Plain washer*
7	*Drive end bracket*	*23*	*Insulating washer*
8	*Bearing drive end*	*24*	*Diode heat sink*
9	*Stator laminations*	*25*	*Crimped washer*
10	*Rotor assembly*	*26*	*Insulating washer*
11	*Bearing, slip ring end*	*27*	*Insulator*
12	*'O' ring*	*28*	*Insulating block*
13	*Diode cover*	*29*	*Terminal screw*
14	*Slip ring end bracket*	*30*	*Brush terminal*
15	*Earth connection, stator*	*31*	*Slip ring brush*
16	*Diode connections, stator*	*32*	*Brush holder*

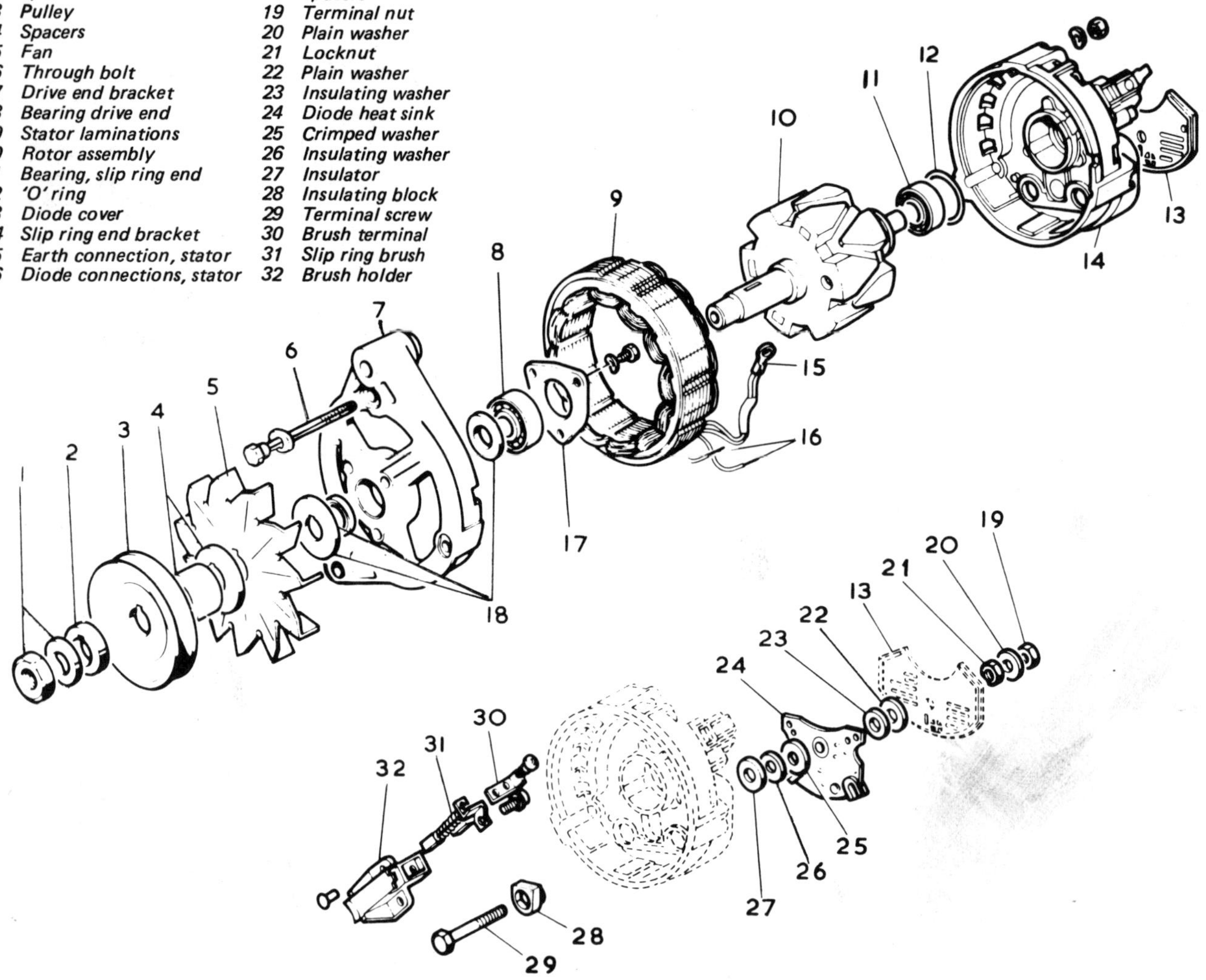

9 Alternator (Ducellier) - servicing

1 Unscrew and remove the two screws which secure the brush holder to the alternator rear casing and extract the brush holder (Fig. 11.4).
2 Withdraw the earth brush from its holder.
3 Withdraw the second brush after removal of the securing screw.
4 Clean the brushes and brush holder with a rag soaked in clean fuel and check that they slide easily in their holders.
5 If the brushes are well worn, they should be renewed.
6 This should be the limit of servicing. If the rotor or stator are damaged or the front or rear bearings are worn then it is quite uneconomical to consider a repair even if the individual components were obtainable and it is recommended that a factory reconditioned unit is obtained.
7 Refitting of the brushes and brush holder is a reversal of removal.

10 Alternator (Paris-Rhone) - servicing

1 The procedure for brush removal is similar to that described in the preceding Section. An exploded view of the alternator is shown in Fig. 11.8.
2 The screws which secure the brush holder are shown in Fig. 11.6.
3 Pull the brushes from their spring holders.
4 Refer to paragraphs 4, 5, 6 and 7 of the preceding Section.

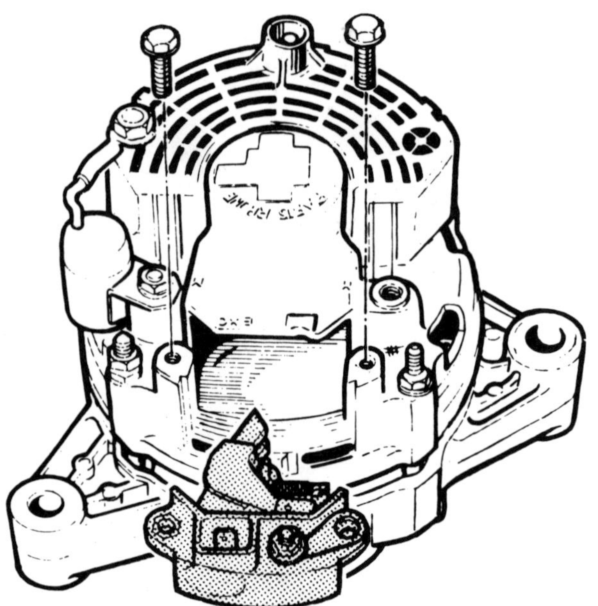

Fig. 11.6. Brush holder and retaining screws on Paris - Rhone alternator

11 Alternator (Motorola) - servicing

1 The heavy duty, three phase Motorola alternator is fitted for operation in cold climates.
2 To renew the brushes undo the two screws securing the cover plate to the rear end of the alternator and lift away the plate taking care not to strain the connecting wire (Fig. 11.7).
3 Remove the securing screws and withdraw the brushholder, taking care not to damage the brushes.
4 Clean or renew the brushes as described in Section 9. An exploded view of the Motorola alternator is shown in Fig. 11.9.

12 Alternator voltage regulator - description

1 The voltage regulator comprises a vibrating contact that controls the alternator output by limiting the current in the field windings.
2 The regulator, which is located inside the engine compartment on the left-hand wing valance is a sealed unit and if it is suspected of being faulty must be renewed.

13 Starter motor - general description

1 The starter motor is of the pre-engaged type which is designed to ensure that the pinion is engaged with the ring gear on the flywheel (torque converter-automatic) before the starter motor is energised.
2 Conversely, the drive does not disengage, until the starter motor is de-energised.
3 The starter motor may be of Ducellier make, Fig. 11.10 or Paris-Rhone Fig. 11.11.

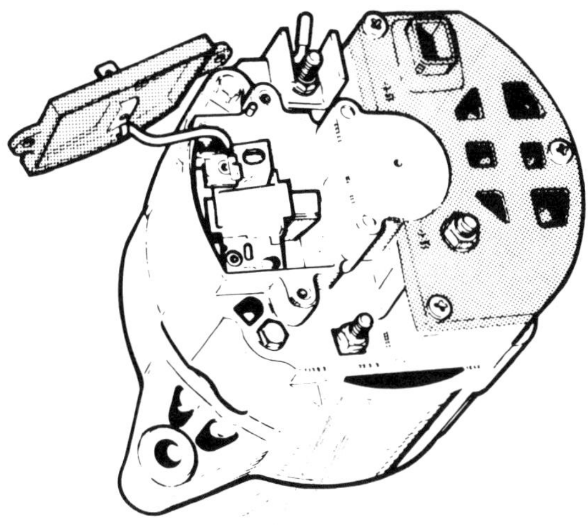

Fig. 11.7. Brush holder cover plate on the Motorola alternator

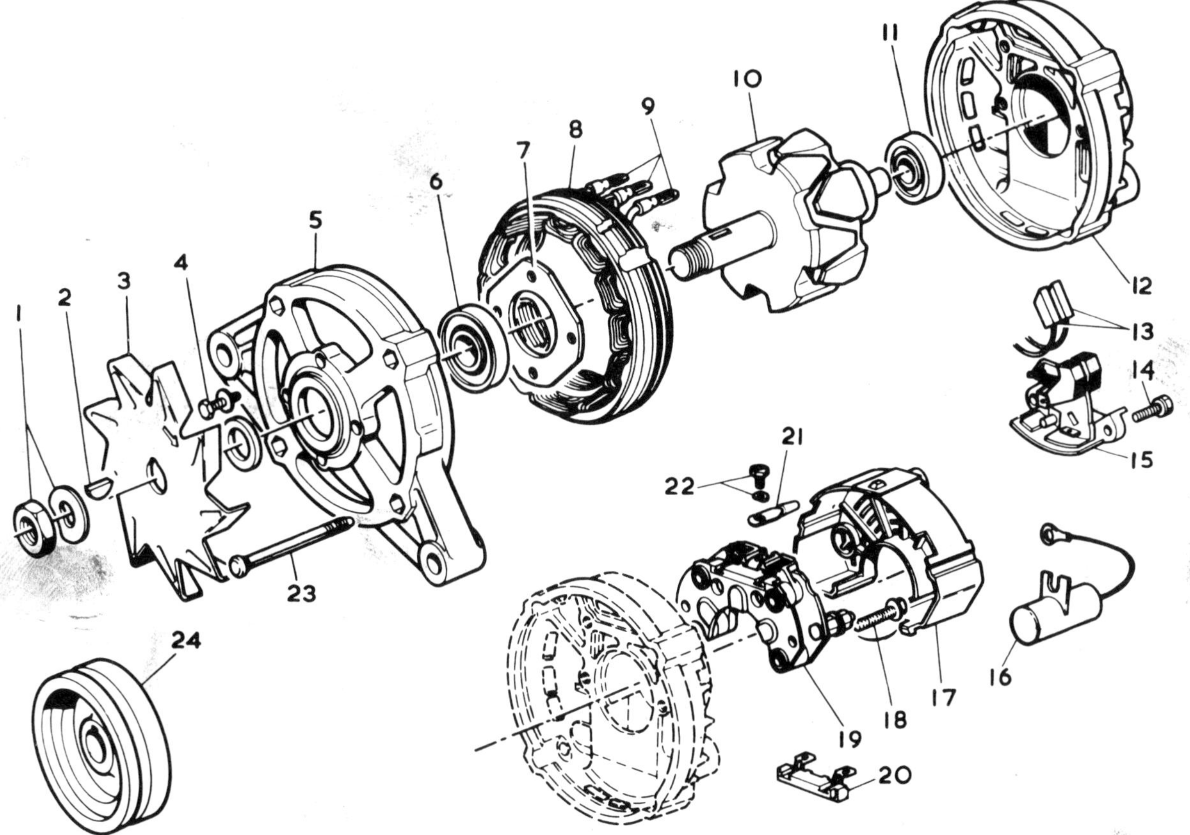

Fig. 11.8. Exploded view of Paris - Rhone alternator

1 Nut and washer
2 Driving key
3 Fan
4 Screw, bearing retainer
5 Drive end bracket
6 Bearing, drive end
7 Bearing retainer
8 Stator laminations
9 Stator leads
10 Rotor assembly
11 Bearing, slip ring end
12 Slip ring end bracket
13 Brushes
14 Screw, brush holder
15 Brush holder
16 Capacitor (when fitted)
17 Diode cover
18 Screw, diode heat sink
19 Diode heat sink assembly
20 Capacitor
21 Terminal, warning lamp
22 Terminal screw
23 Through bolt
24 Pulley

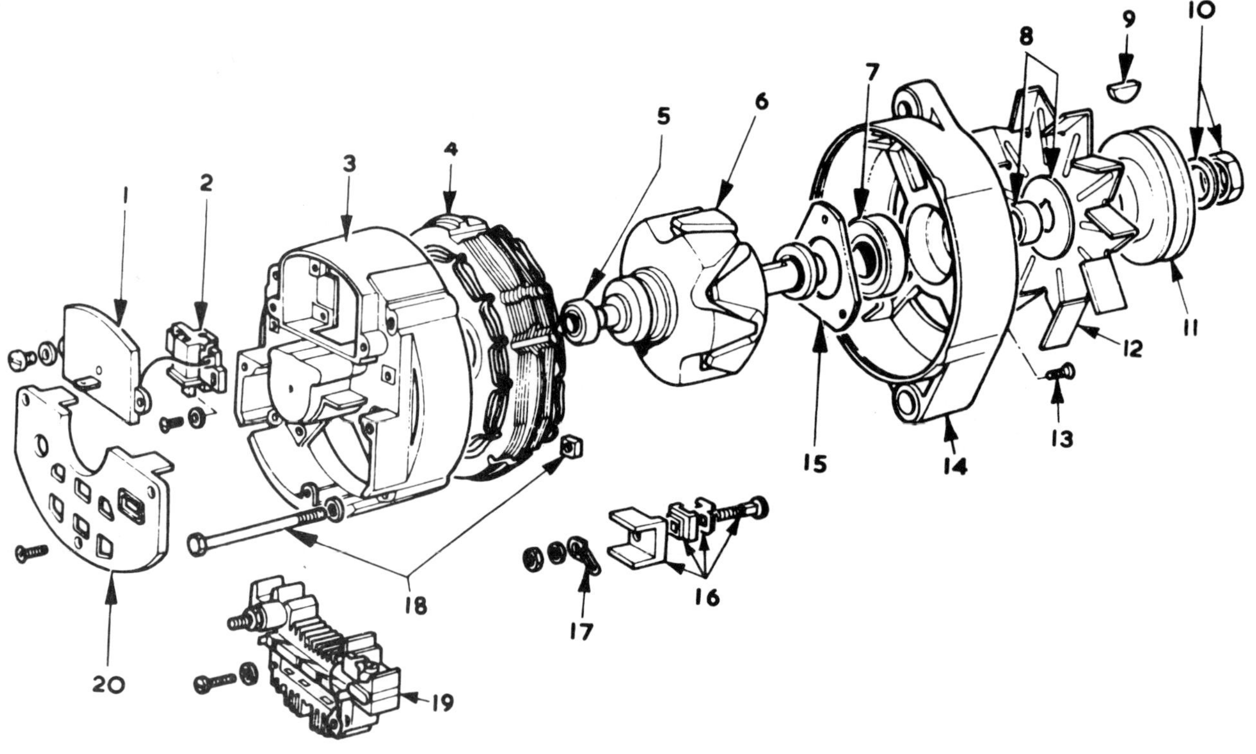

Fig. 11.9. Exploded view of Motorola alternator

1 Brush holder plate
2 Brush holder
3 Bracket, slip ring end
4 Stator
5 Bearing, slip ring end
6 Rotor assembly
7 Bearing, drive end
8 Spacer and washer
9 Driving key
10 Pulley nut and washer
11 Pulley
12 Fan
13 Retainer screw
14 Bracket, drive end
15 Bearing retainer
16 Terminal screw
17 Terminal, warning light
18 Through bolt and nut
19 Diode and heat sink assembly
20 Rear cover

14 Starter motor - testing in vehicle

1 If unsatisfactory operation of the starter motor is experienced, check that the battery connections are tight and that the battery is charged.
2 Check the security of cable terminals at the starter motor solenoid and the leads at the combined ignition starter switch.
3 Do not confuse a jammed starter drive with an inoperative motor. If a distinct click is heard when the starter switch is operated but the motor will not turn then it is certain to be due to a jammed starter drive and the vehicle should be rocked in gear to release it.
4 Where the foregoing possibilities have been eliminated, proceed to test the starter but first disconnect the LT lead from the distributor to prevent the engine from firing.
5 Connect a 0-20 voltmeter between the starter terminal and earth, operate the starter switch and with the engine cranking, note the reading. A minimum voltage (indicated) of 4.5 volts proves satisfactory cable and switch connections. Slow cranking speed of the starter motor at this voltage indicates a fault in the motor.
6 Connect the voltmeter between the battery and the starter motor terminal and with the starter motor actuated, the voltage drop should not exceed more than half the indicated battery voltage (12 volts). Where this is exceeded it indicates excessive resistance in the starter circuit.

15 Starter motor - removal and refitting

1 Disconnect the battery leads.
2 Disconnect the leads from the starter motor terminals.
3 Unscrew the securing bolts which hold the starter motor to the clutch bellhousing and remove the sump bracket bolt.
4 Withdraw the starter motor from beneath the vehicle.
5 Refitting is a reversal of removal.

16 Starter (Ducellier) - dismantling, servicing and reassembly

1 Remove the end cover (2) (Fig. 11.10).
2 Unscrew and remove the armature end bolt (2) and withdraw the various armature shaft end components and the brush holders and plate.
3 Unscrew the nuts from the two tie bolts (7) and pull off the body (9). Remove the circlips from the fork bearing pin (location arrowed) and drift out the pin.
4 Withdraw the armature and lift the solenoid connecting fork out of engagement with the pinion drive assembly (5).
5 The pinion drive assembly may be dismantled by compressing the end collar (13) and detaching the circlip (14).
6 Dismantling beyond this stage should not be undertaken as if bearings or field coils require attention it will be more economical to exchange the unit for a factory reconditioned one, apart from the fact that special tools are needed to release the pole screws and to remove and fit new bearings.
7 Check for wear in the starter brushes and renew them if their overall length is less than 9/16 in (14 mm). The brushes must be unsoldered and the new ones soldered into position. Take care to localise the heat during the operation and do not damage the insulation of the field coils.
8 Clean the commutator on the armature with a fuel soaked cloth. Any pitting or burning may be removed with fine glass paper, not emery. If the commutator is so badly pitted that it would require skimming on a lathe to remove it, renew the complete starter.
9 Checking of suspect field coils for continuity should be carried out by connecting a battery and bulb between the starter terminal and each brush in turn.
10 Reassembly is largely a reversal of dismantling but use a new collar (13) and circlip (14) and stake the collar rim in several places to retain the circlip.
11 Ensure that all starter drive components are clean and lightly oil them with thin oil when assembled.
12 Check the starter drive pinion end-float as described in Section 18.

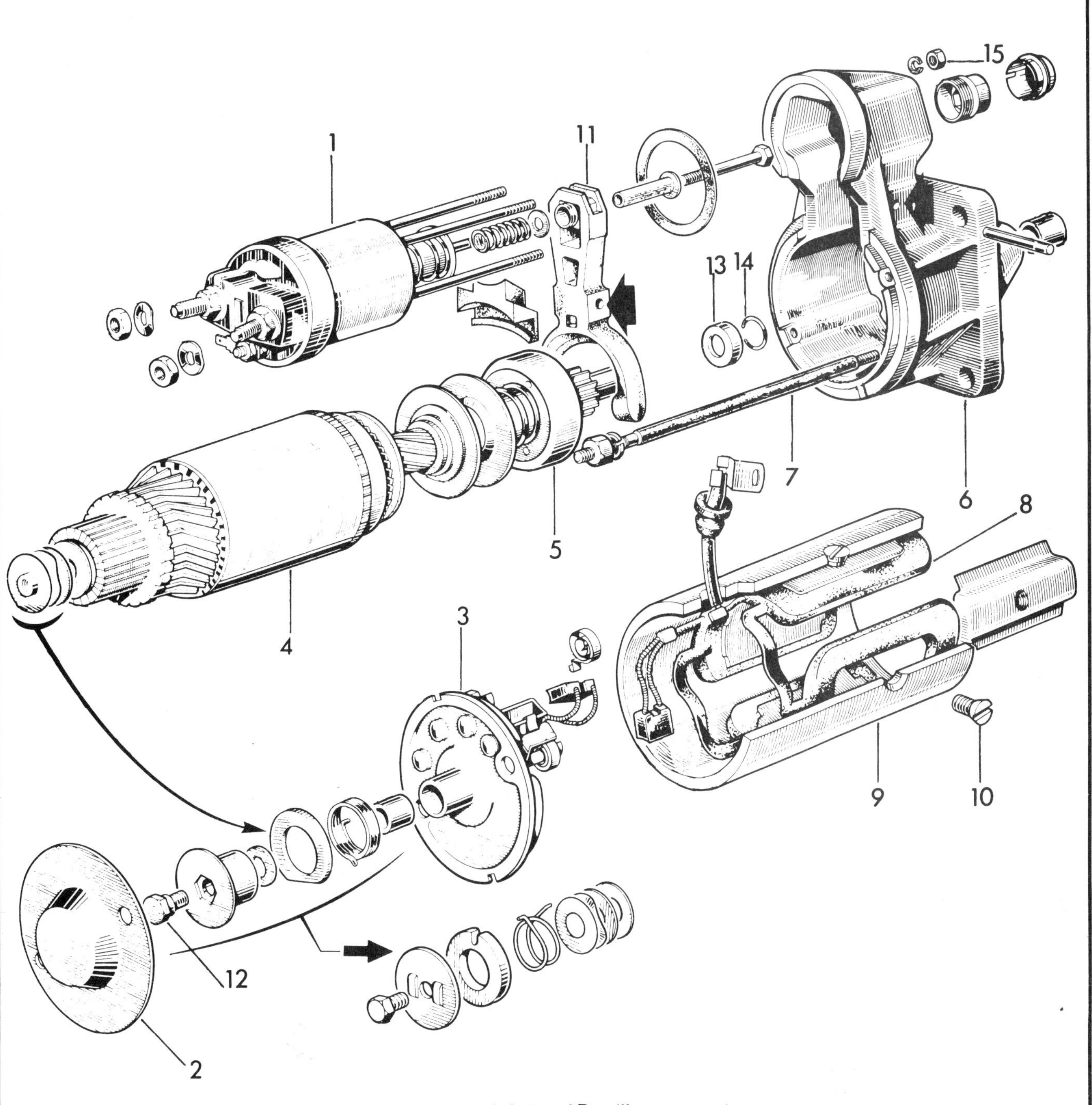

Fig. 11.10. Exploded view of Ducellier starter motor

1 Solenoid body	*5 Pinion drive*	*9 Body*	*13 Collar*
2 End cover	*6 Bearing cover*	*10 Pole screw*	*14 Circlip*
3 Brush holders	*7 Tie bolt*	*11 Engagement fork*	*15 Adjuster nut*
4 Armature	*8 Field coil*	*12 Bolt*	

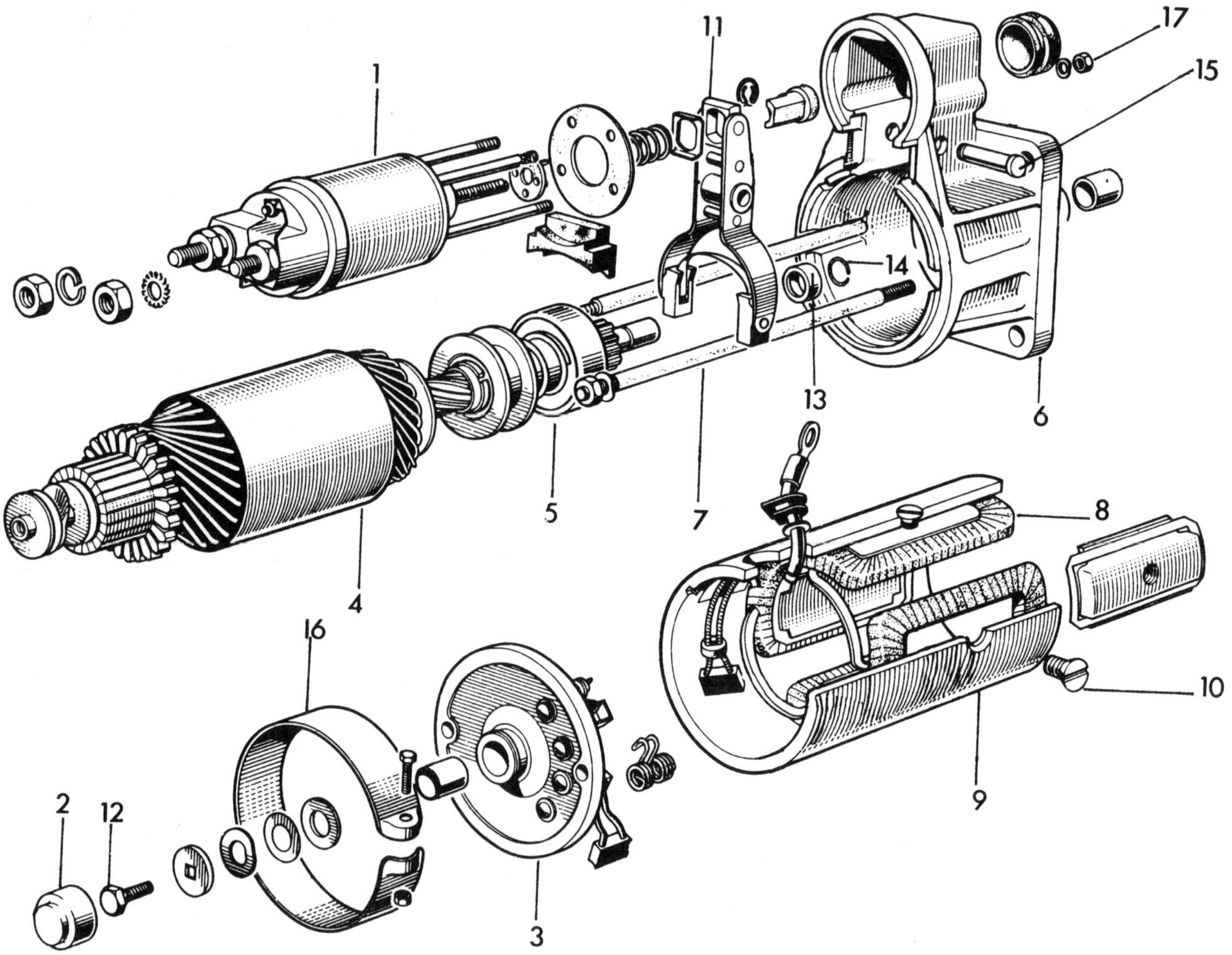

Fig. 11.11. Exploded view of Paris - Rhone starter motor

1 *Solenoid body*
2 *End cover*
3 *Brush holder*
4 *Armature*
5 *Pinion drive*
6 *Bearing cover*
7 *Tie bolt*
8 *Field coil*
9 *Body*
10 *Pole screw*
11 *Engagement fork*
12 *Bolt*
13 *Collar*
14 *Circlip*
15 *Selector fork pin*
16 *Inspection slip band*
17 *Adjuster nut*

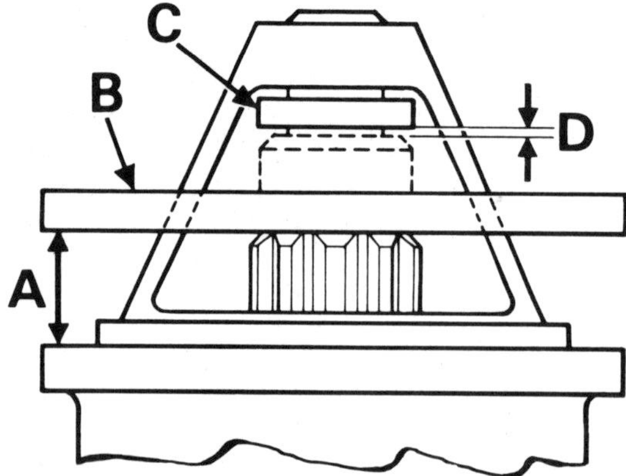

Fig. 11.12. Checking the starter motor pinion clearances

A Dimension with solenoid at rest 14 mm (9/16 in)
B Straight edge
C Pinion stop
D Clearance with solenoid energised 0.5 to 1.5 mm (0.019 to 0.058 in)

17 Starter (Paris-Rhone) - dismantling, servicing and reassembly

1 Refer to the previous Section and carry out the operations described but in conjunction with Fig. 11.11.

18 Starter motor drive pinion end-float - checking and adjusting

1 Disconnect the field coil wire from the solenoid terminal.
2 Using a 6 volt dry battery, energise the solenoid which will cause the pinion drive assembly to move forward into its engaged position. Press the pinion towards the motor to take up any end-float and using feeler gauges, check the clearance between the end of the pinion and the face of the thrust collar. The clearance should be 0.019 to 0.058 in (0.5 to 1.5 mm).
3 With the solenoid de-energised, check that the dimension between the outer edge of the pinion and the motor flange is 0.56 in (14 mm). See Fig. 11.12.
4 If adjustment is necessary, screw the nut in or out as required.

19 Flasher circuit - fault tracing and rectification

1 A flasher unit is located beneath the instrument panel next to the steering column. It plugs into a multiconnector and is retained by a

single screw.
2 If the flasher unit works twice as fast as usual when indicating either right or left turns, this is an indication that there is a broken filament in the front or rear indicator bulb on the side operating quickly.
3 If the external flashers are working but the internal flasher warning light has ceased to function, check the filament of the warning bulb and renew as necessary.
4 With the aid of the wiring diagram check all the flasher circuit connections if a flasher bulb is sound but does not work.
5 With the ignition switched on check that the current is reaching the flasher unit by connecting a voltmeter between the 'plus' terminal and earth. If it is found that current is reaching the unit, connect the two flasher unit terminals together and operate the direction indicator switch. If one of the flasher warning lights comes on this proves that the flasher unit itself is at fault and must be renewed as it is not possible to dismantle and repair it.

20 Windscreen wiper arms and blades - removal and refitting

1 Before removing a wiper arm, turn the windscreen wiper switch on and off to ensure the arms are in their normal parked position parallel with the bottom of the windscreen.
2 To remove the arm, pivot the cap back to expose the retaining nut (photo).
3 Unscrew the nut using a 13 mm spanner and pull the wiper arm off the splined drive spindle.
4 When refitting an arm, position it so it is in the correct relative parked position and then press the arm head onto the splined drive until it is fully home on the splines.
5 Renew the windscreen wiper blades at intervals of 12000 miles or annually or whenever they cease to wipe the screen effectively.

21 Windscreen wiper mechanism - fault diagnosis and rectification

1 Should the windscreen wipers fail, or work very slowly, then check the terminals on the motor for loose connections and make sure the insulation of all wiring has not been damaged thus causing a short circuit. If this is in order then check the current the motor is taking by connecting an ammeter in the circuit and turning on the wiper switch. Consumption should be between 2.3 and 3.1 amps.
2 If no current is passing through the motor, check that the switch is operating correctly.
3 If the wiper motor takes a very high current check the wiper blades for freedom of movement. If this is satisfactory check the gearbox cover and gear assembly for damage.
4 If the motor takes a very low current ensure that the battery is fully charged. Check the brush gear and ensure the brushes are bearing on the commutator. If not, check the brushes for freedom of movement and, if necessary, renew the tension springs. If the brushes are very worn they should be replaced with new ones. Check the armature by substitution if this part is suspect.

20.2 Wiper arm retaining nut

22 Windscreen wiper motor - removal and refitting

1 The wiper motor is attached to the rear bulkhead in the engine compartment..
2 Disconnect the battery leads.
3 Disconnect the multi-pin electrical plug from the motor.
4 Remove the three bolts securing the motor to the rear bulkhead panel.
5 Withdraw the motor slightly and hook a piece of wire round the wiper linkage arm to prevent it falling down behind the panel.
6 Prise off the linkage balljoint from the arm on the motor and withdraw the motor.
7 To remove the linkage first remove the wiper arms as described in Section 20. Undo the securing screws and lift away the scuttle panel below the windscreen.
8 Remove the nuts, washers and rubber seals securing the spindles to

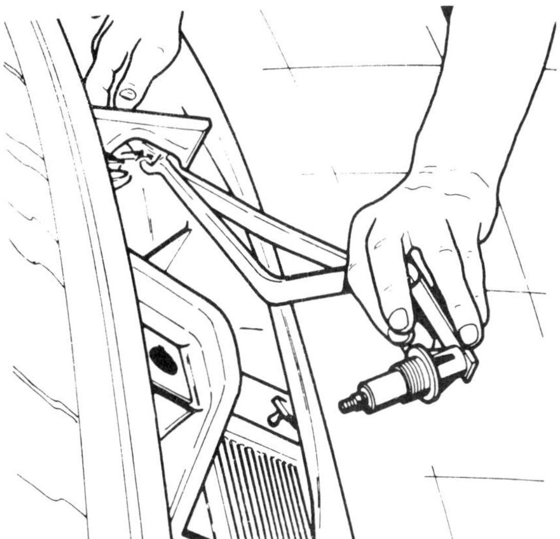

Fig. 11.13. Removing the wiper linkage

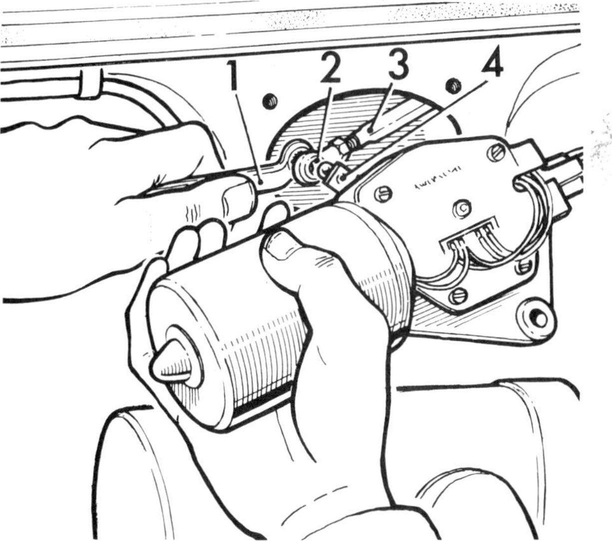

Fig. 11.14. Refitting the wiper linkage balljoint to the motor

1 Ring spanner
2 Balljoint
3 Linkage arm
4 Motor arm

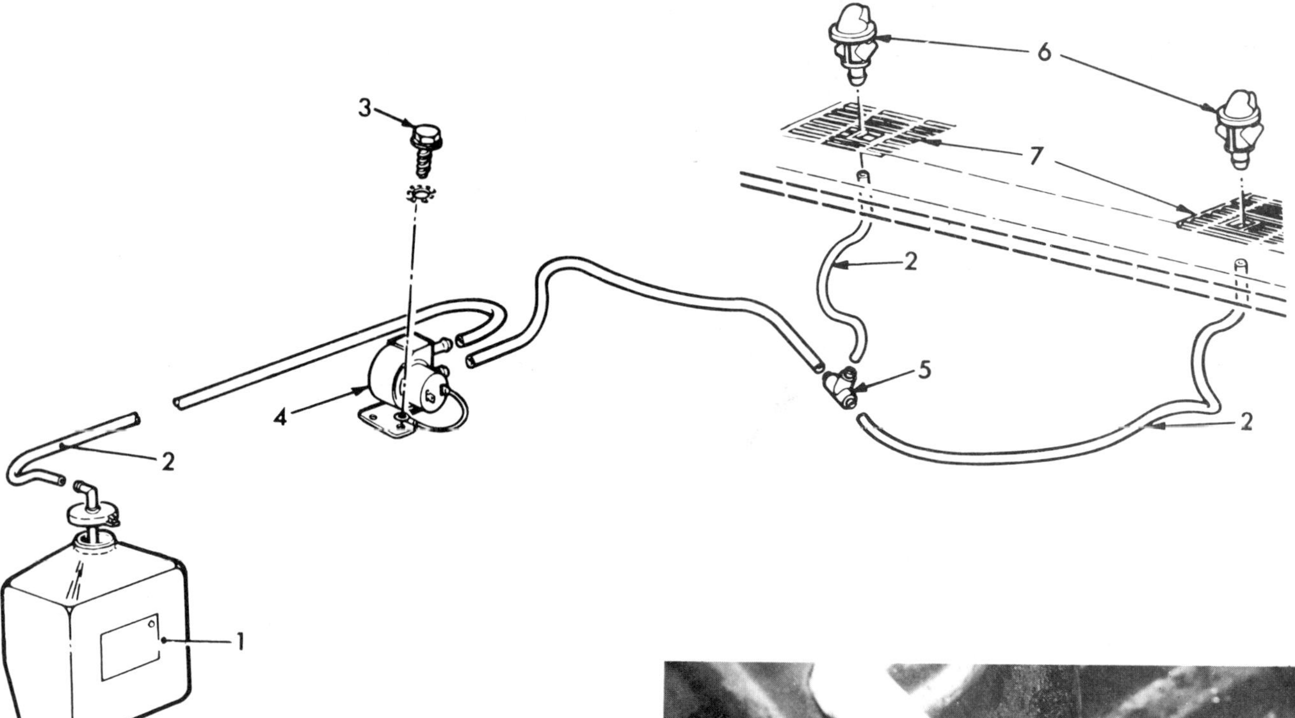

Fig. 11.15. Layout of windscreen washer system

1 *Reservoir*
2 *Flexible tubes*
3 *Pump fixing screw*
4 *Pump*
5 *"T" piece*
6 *Jet nozzles*
7 *Grilles*

the body brackets and lift out the linkage assembly (Fig. 11.13).
9 Any servicing of the motor should be limited to the operations described in Section 21 otherwise the motor should be exchanged for a factory reconditioned unit. Any wear in the linkage should be rectified by renewal of the components concerned.
10 Refit the motor and linkage using the reverse procedure to that of removal. Use a ring spanner to press the linkage balljoint back onto the wiper motor arm (see Fig. 11.14).

23 Windscreen washer - description and servicing

1 The layout of the windscreen washer system is shown in Fig. 11.15.
2 The washer motor is attached to the right-hand valance inside the engine compartment. It cannot be repaired and if faulty must be renewed.
3 Servicing should be limited to occasionally checking the security of the tubes and connectors and the security of the electrical leads to the switch and pump motor. Keep the washer fluid container topped up as described in the Routine Maintenance Section at the front of this manual.
4 The spray pattern can be adjusted by inserting a pin in the jet orifice and swivelling the jet(s) in the required direction.

24 Horns - description, fault tracing and rectification

1 Twin horns are located in the engine compartment adjacent to the radiator. The horns are operated by the multi-purpose switch on the steering column.
2 If the horns fail to operate, disconnect the terminal from each horn and connect a test light between the horn feed wire and earth. Switch on the ignition and get an assistant to operate the horn stalk and check that the test lamp illuminates.
3 If the lamp lights but the horns do not operate, the horns are faulty. They are not repairable and must be renewed.

25.1 Headlight bulb electrical plug

25.2 Removing the headlight bulb

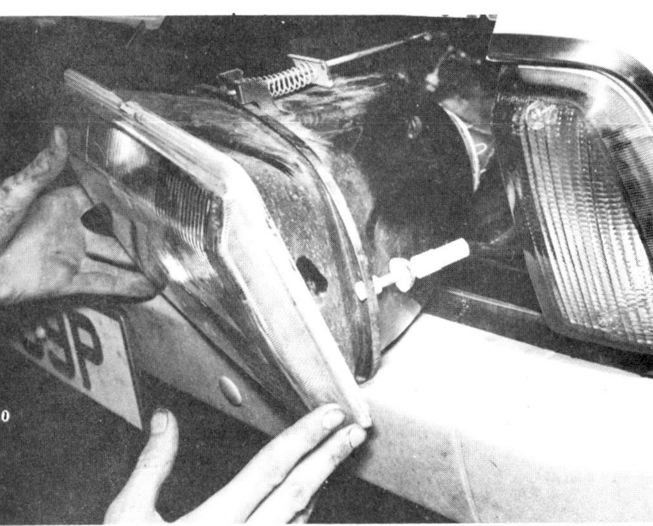
26.5 Withdrawing the headlight assembly

28.1 Removing the front side lamp bulb holder

4 If the test lamp fails to light, check that the wiring is not loose or disconnected. Clean the horn terminals and re-test.

25 Headlights - bulb renewal

1 Open the bonnet and pull the electrical plug off the rear of the headlight unit (photo).
2 Release the spring clips and withdraw the bulb (photo).
Note: On some Halogen type bulbs it is necessary to turn the bulb outer ring so that the tags are aligned with the notches.
3 Refit the bulb using the reverse procedure to that of removal.

26 Headlight unit - removal and refitting

1 Open the bonnet and disconnect the battery leads.
2 Disconnect the headlight plug and sidelamp from the rear of the headlight unit.
3 Press the upper front of the headlight unit inwards and disengage the nylon adjusting knob from its slot.
4 Push the two spring clips upwards to release them from the side adjusting knobs.
5 Withdraw the headlight unit from the front of the car (photo).
Note: If the car is fitted with headlight washer/wipers the front grille must be removed prior to removing the headlight unit (refer to Chapter 12).
6 Refit the headlight unit using the reversal of the removal procedure and adjust the alignment as described in the following Section.

27 Headlights - alignment

1 To compensate for the different height of the vehicle when it is either loaded or unloaded, there is a two position nylon control knob at the rear of the headlight unit (see Fig. 11.16). When resetting the control knob press the headlight lens inwards slightly to relieve the tension on the spring.
2 Completely resetting the headlight alignment is achieved by rotating the three nylon knobs on the rear of the light unit as shown in Fig. 11.17.
3 It is always advisable to have the headlamps aligned on proper optical beam setting equipment but if this is not available the following procedures may be used.
4 Position the car on level ground 30 feet in front of a dark wall or board. The wall or board must be at right angles to the centre line of the car.

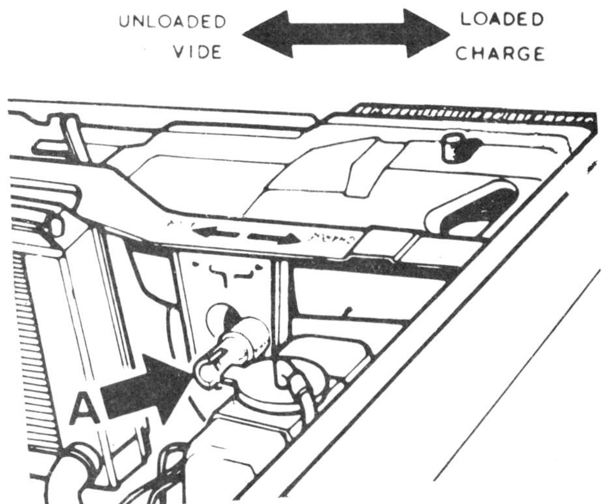

Fig. 11.16. Headlight adjusting knob "A"

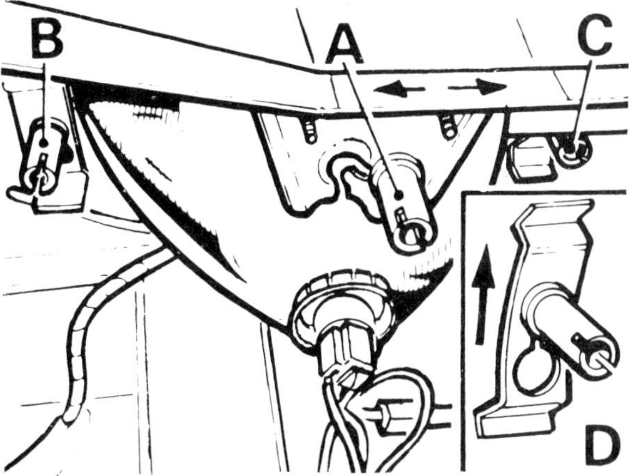

Fig. 11.17. Headlight beam resetting knobs

A Vertical adjuster
B Lateral adjusters
C Lateral adjuster
D Headlight securing clip

5 Draw a vertical line on the board in line with the centre line of the car.
6 Bounce the car on its suspension to ensure correct settlement and then measure the height between the ground and the centre of the headlamps.
7 Draw a horizontal line across the board at this measured height. On this horizontal line mark a cross at a point equal to half the distance between the headlamp centres either side of the vertical centre line.
8 Adjust the headlight position by rotating the lower nylon knobs in the required direction for lateral alignment, and the top knob for vertical alignment. The knobs have slotted ends and can be turned using a coin.
9 If a beamsetter is used the top knob must be in the unloaded position prior to adjustment.

28 Front sidelamp - bulb renewal

1 Access to the bulb is gained by pulling the bulb holder from the lower rear end of the headlight unit (photo).
2 Renew the bulb with one of the same wattage and push the holder back into place.

29 Front indicator - bulb renewal

1 Access is obtained simply by removing the two lens securing screws (photo).
2 Renew the bulbs with ones of the same type and wattage. Do not overtighten the lens securing screws.

30 Rear lamp cluster - bulb renewal

1 Remove the three retaining screws and withdraw the rear lens (photo).
2 Renew any defective bulbs with ones of the same wattage, do not overtighten the lens retaining screws.
3 The complete bulb holder assembly can be removed if required by pressing down four of the six retaining clips and withdrawing the unit from the car body aperture (photo).

31 Number plate lamp - bulb renewal

1 Remove the two screws and withdraw the light unit just enough to disconnect the two leads.
2 Remove the rubber seal and renew the defective bulb with one of the same wattage (photo).

32 Interior lamp - bulb renewal

1 Carefully lever out the lens using a small screwdriver.
2 After renewing the bulb ensure that the wire is tucked inside before pushing the lens back into place.

33 Luggage compartment lamp - bulb renewal

1 Remove the lens by squeezing the ends together between thumb and forefinger.
2 Renew the bulb and push the lens back into place.

34 Push switches - renewal

1 First pull off the knobs from the air control levers and the temperature control knob.
2 Remove the retaining screws and carefully withdraw the centre panel just enough to provide access to the rear of the push switches (photo).
3 Disconnect the leads from the rear of the switch. Press in the two retainers on the switch body and withdraw it from the front of the

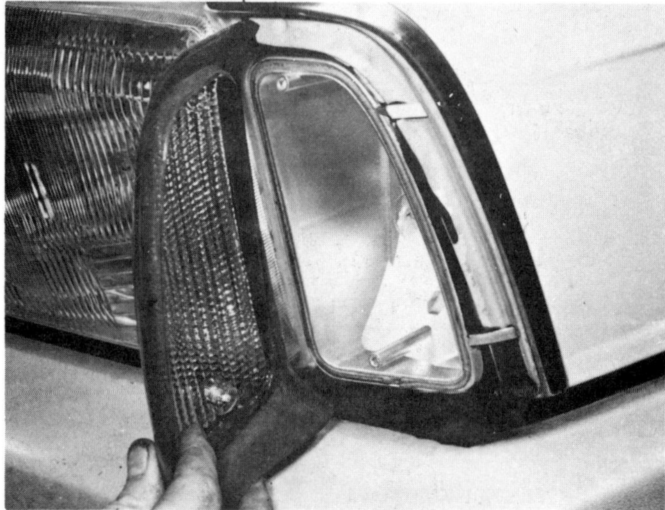

29.1 Removing a front indicator lens

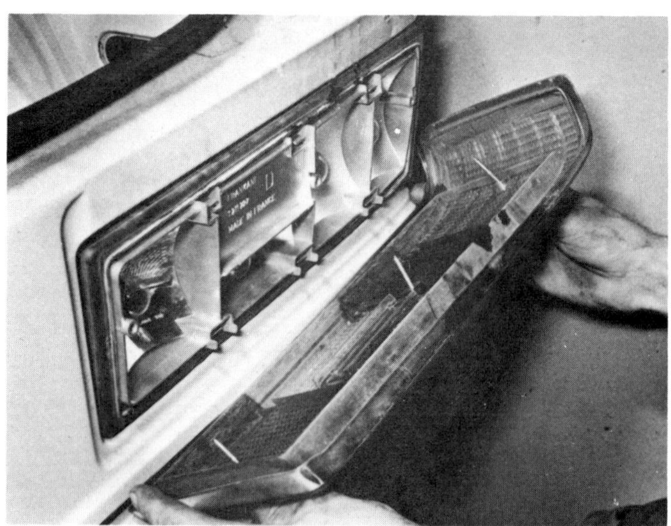

30.1 Removing a rear light cluster lens

30.3 Withdrawing the complete rear light cluster assembly

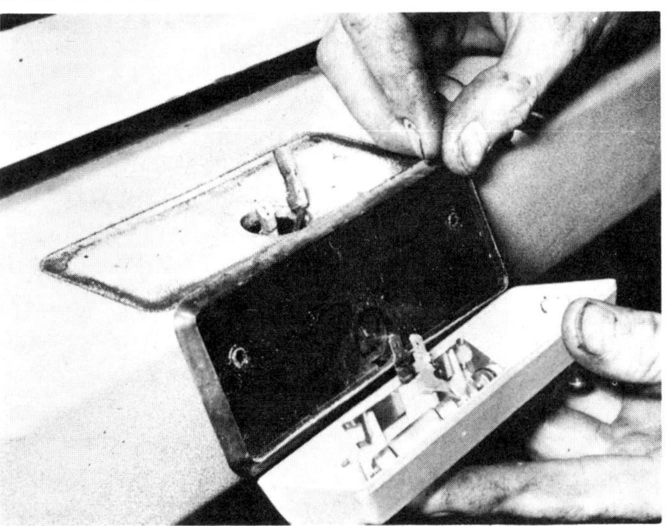
31.2 Replacing the number plate bulbs

34.2 Withdrawing the centre switch panel

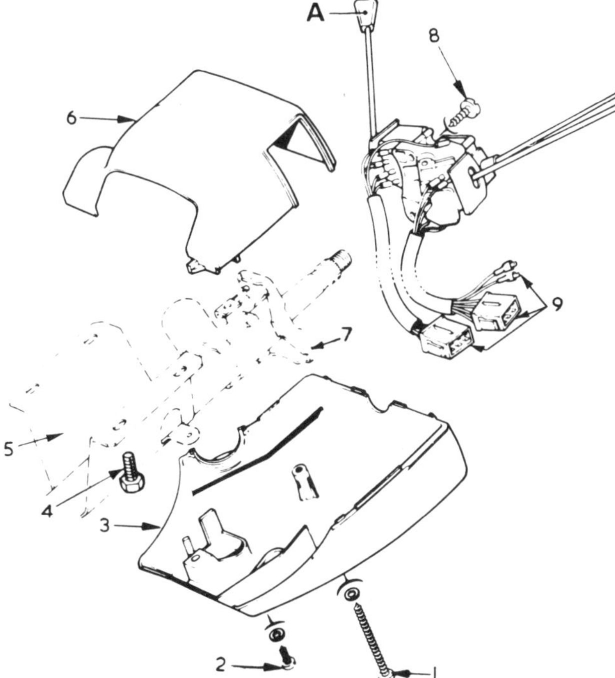

Fig. 11.18. Steering column combination switch

1 *Securing screw, (long)*
2 *Securing screw, (short)*
3 *Lower shroud*
4 *Set screw*
5 *Column bracket*
6 *Upper shroud*
7 *Switch mounting bracket*
8 *Switch securing screw*
9 *Switch connectors*

A = Wipers, washer B = Indicators C = Lights and horns

panel.

4 The switches are not repairable and if faulty must be renewed. Refit the switches and centre panel using the reversal of the removal procedure.

35 Steering column combination switch - removal and refitting

1 Disconnect the battery leads.

2 Prise off the centre motif from the steering wheel and remove the securing nut.

3 Mark the position of the steering wheel in relation to the splined shaft and then withdraw the wheel from the shaft.

4 Undo the retaining screws and remove the lower half of the steering column shroud (photo).

5 Remove the four bolts from the column securing bracket and lower the column sufficiently to withdraw the top half of the shroud (refer to Chapter 8 if necessary).

6 Remove the three retaining screws, disconnect the two multi-pin plugs and the two line connectors and withdraw the switch (Fig. 11.18).

7 The combination switch is not repairable and if any part of it is faulty the complete switch assembly must be renewed.

8 Refit the switch using the reverse procedure to that of removal.

35.4 Lower half of the steering column shroud removed

37.1 Location of the fuse holder unit

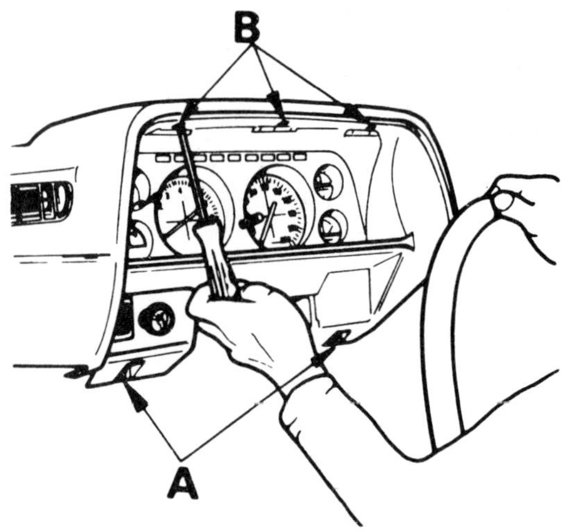

Fig. 11.19. Instrument panel securing screws

A Two lower screws *B Three upper screws*

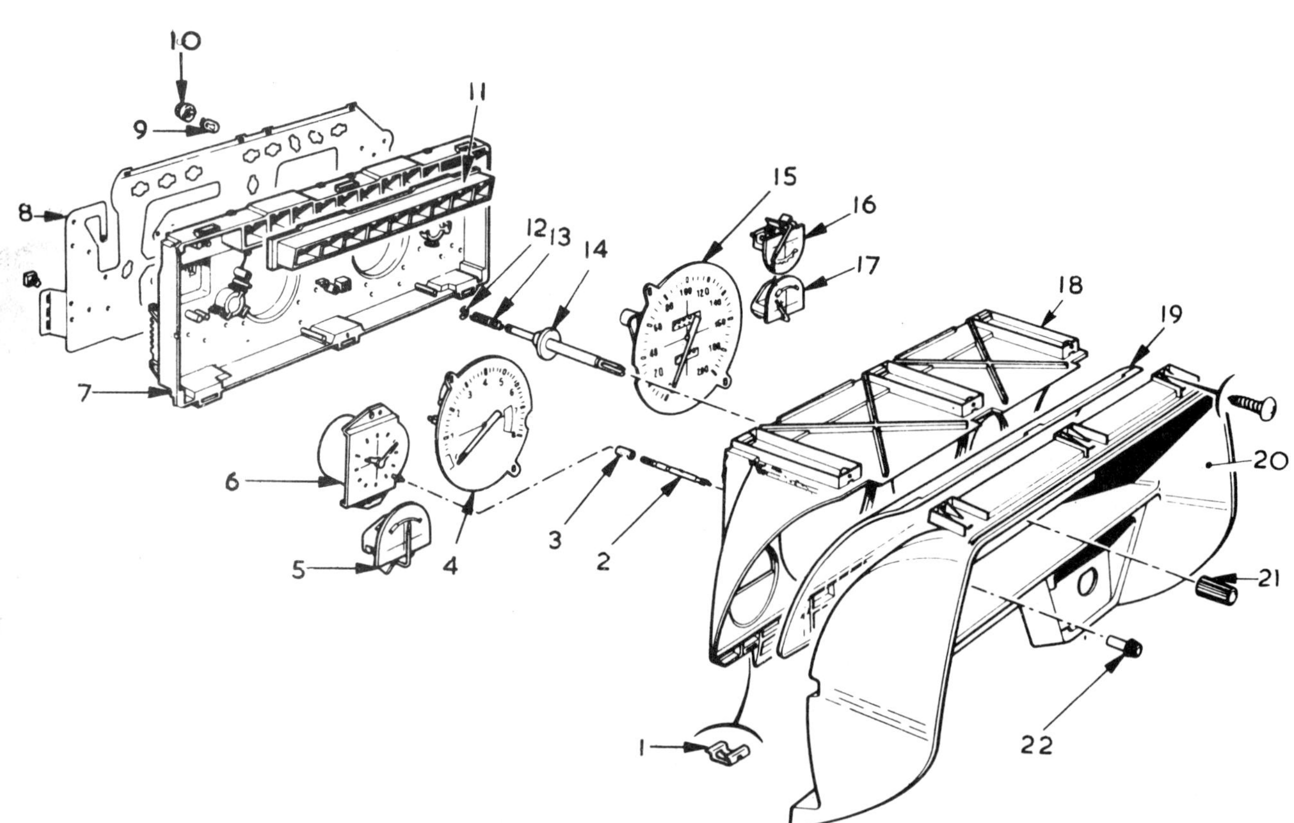

Fig. 11.20. Exploded view of six-dial instrument panel

1 Spring clip, (cowl to case)
2 Clock reset spindle
3 Bush
4 Tachometer
5 Water temperature gauge
6 Electric clock
7 Instrument case
8 Printed circuit
9 Bulb
10 Bulb holder
11 Warning light lenses
12 Circlip
13 Spring
14 Trip reset spindle
15 Speedometer
16 Fuel gauge
17 Oil pressure
18 Inner cowl
19 Curved window
20 Outer cowl
21 Trip reset knob
22 Clock reset knob

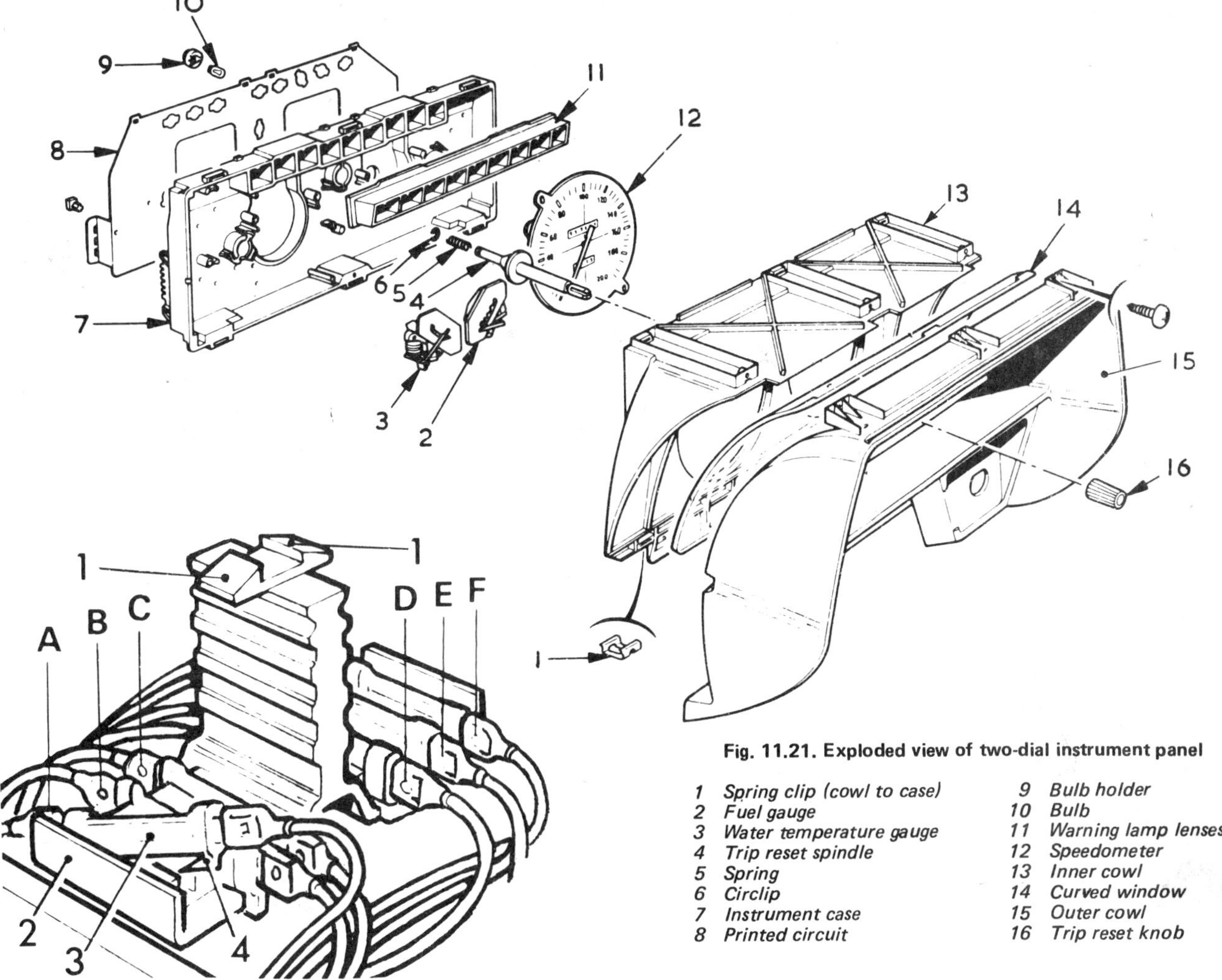

Fig. 11.21. Exploded view of two-dial instrument panel

1 Spring clip (cowl to case)
2 Fuel gauge
3 Water temperature gauge
4 Trip reset spindle
5 Spring
6 Circlip
7 Instrument case
8 Printed circuit
9 Bulb holder
10 Bulb
11 Warning lamp lenses
12 Speedometer
13 Inner cowl
14 Curved window
15 Outer cowl
16 Trip reset knob

Fig. 11.22. Fuse holder assembly

1 Retaining clips
2 Fuse holder
3 Fuse
4 Fuse locating claw

(A, B, C, D, E and F = Fuse identification)

36 Instrument panel - removal and refitting

1 The Alpine is fitted with either a two dial or six dial instrument panel depending on the model. However, the method of removal and dismantling is similar for both types of panel.

2 First disconnect both battery terminals.

3 Disconnect the choke cable from the carburettor, remove the cable grommet from the rear bulkhead and pull the cable through from the inside of the car.

4 Remove the trim panel below the instrument panel (if fitted).

5 Remove the four bolts securing the steering column bracket and lower the complete column assembly.

6 Refer to Fig. 11.19 and remove the upper and lower retaining screws from the front of the instrument panel.

7 Detach the speedometer drive cable from the rear of the panel.

8 Partially withdraw the panel and disconnect the two multi-pin plugs from the printed circuit board.

9 Disconnect the two terminals from the panel light dimmer switch (if fitted).

10 Carefully lift the instrument panel assembly away from the car.

11 To dismantle the instrument panel assembly refer to Figs. 11.20 or 11.21 as appropriate and proceed as follows.

12 If a clock is fitted, pull off the hand reset knob.

13 Remove the outer cowl retaining screws and remove the cowl and curved lens from the main instrument panel assembly.

14 Remove the six spring clips and withdraw the inner cowl.

15 Remove the warning lights lens carrier.

16 The instruments and gauges can be removed by undoing the nuts or bolts from the rear of the panel and withdrawing them from the front. The clock (if fitted) has a single retaining nut at the rear and two screws on the front of the panel.

17 To remove the printed circuit board, unplug all the warning light and panel lighting bulb holders. Unclip the flexible board from the locating pegs in the casing, detach the clock connecting tab and carefully withdraw the board.

18 To clean the board use methylated spirits and a piece of clean cloth. Examine the metallic connecting strips for breaks or fractures.

19 Reassemble and refit the instrument panel using the reverse procedure to that of removal. **Note:** It is possible to refit the warning and lighting bulbs without removing the instrument panel, by reaching up from beneath the dash panel.

37 Fuses

1 The fuse block is located in the engine compartment on the right-hand side wing valance (see photo).

2 The fuses can be removed by unclipping the holder from the wing and pressing the two projections inwards to open the holder (Fig. 11.22).

3 Each fuse is lettered and protects the following circuits:

Fuse A — Side lamps, rear lamps, number plate lamp, instrument panel lamps, heater controls, ashtray and centre panel illumination.
Fuse B — Rear fog lamp
Fuse C — Heater blower motor.
Fuse D — Wiper and washer motors, stop lights, and reverse lights.
Fuse E — Rear window heater and cigar lighter (if fitted).
Fuse F — Electric clock, interior lights, flasher unit, glove box light and luggage compartment light.

4 All the fuses are 10 amp with the exception of the cigar lighter and rear window heater fuse which is 16 amp.
5 Always renew fuses with ones of the same rating and establish the reason for the fuse blowing as quickly as possible.

38 Electric window lift - description

An electric motor and window lift linkage is fitted to each left and right-hand front door. Two rocker switches on the facia panel control the window mechanism, which is operative only when the ignition switch is in the 'M' (ignition on) position. A thermal overload cutout is fitted to the electric motors. The wiring harness is protected by a flexible rubber sheath at the point where it is routed into the door casings.

When a window reaches either extremity of travel, the rocker switch must be released. Failure to do this will cause the lift motor overload cutout to operate, putting the system temporarily out of action.

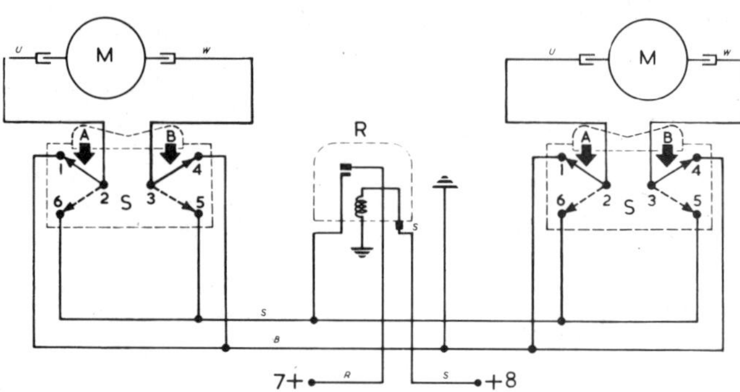

Fig. 11.23. Circuit diagram for electric windows

M Lift motors
S Rocker switches
7+ Power supply to motors
+8 To ignition switch

Colour code U = Blue, W = White, S = Slate, B = Black, R = Red

39 Fault diagnosis - electrical system

Symptom	Reason/s	Remedy
No current at starter motor	Battery discharged	Charge battery.
	Battery defective internally	Fit new battery.
	Battery terminal leads loose or earth lead not securely attached to body	Check and tighten leads.
	Loose or broken connections in starter motor circuit	Check all connections and tighten any that are loose.
	Starter motor switch or solenoid faulty	Test and replace faulty components with new.
Current at starter motor: faulty motor	Starter motor pinion jammed in mesh with flywheel gear ring	Disengage pinion by turning squared end of armature shaft.
	Starter brushes badly worn, sticking, or brush wires loose	Examine brushes, renew as necessary, tighten down brush wires.
	Commutator dirty, worn or burnt	Clean commutator, recut if badly burnt.
	Starter motor armature faulty	Overhaul starter motor, fit new armature.
	Field coils earthed	Overhaul starter motor.
Electrical defects	Battery in discharged condition	Charge battery.
	Starter brushes badly worn, sticking, or brush wires loose	Examine brushes, renew as necessary, tighten down brush wires.
	Loose wires in starter motor circuit	Check wiring and tighten as necessary.
Dirt or oil on drive gear	Starter motor pinion sticking on the screwed sleeve	Remove starter motor, clean starter motor drive.
Mechanical damage	Pinion or flywheel gear teeth broken or worn	Fit new gear ring to flywheel, and new pinion to starter motor drive.
Lack of attention or mechanical damage	Pinion or flywheel gear teeth broken or worn	Fit new gear teeth to flywheel, or new pinion to starter motor drive.
	Starter drive main spring broken	Dismantle and fit new main spring.
	Starter motor retaining bolts loose	Tighten starter motor securing bolts. Fit new spring washer if necessary.
Wear or damage	Battery defective internally	Remove and fit new battery.
	Electrolyte level too low or electrolyte too weak due to leakage	Top up electrolyte level to just above plates.

Symptom	Reason/s	Remedy
	Plate separators no longer fully effective	Remove and fit new battery.
	Battery plates severely sulphated	Remove and fit new battery.
Insufficient current flow to keep battery charged	Alternator belt slipping	Check belt for wear, replace if necessary, and tighten.
	Battery terminal connections loose or corroded	Check terminals for tightness, and remove all corrosion.
	Alternator not charging properly	Remove and overhaul alternator.
	Short in lighting circuit causing continual battery drain	Trace and rectify.
	Alternator control unit not working correctly	Renew control unit.
Alternator not charging	Drivebelt loose and slipping, or broken.	Check, renew and tighten as necessary.
	Brushes worn, sticking, broken or dirty	Examine, clean or renew brushes as necessary.
	Brush springs weak or broken	Examine and test. Renew as necessary.
	Commutator dirty, greasy, worn, or burnt	Clean commutator and undercut segment separators.
	Armature badly worn or armature shaft bent	Fit new or reconditioned armature.
	Commutator bars shorting	Undercut segment separations.
	Alternator bearings badly worn	Fit exchange unit.
	Alternator field coils burnt, open, or shorted	Remove and fit rebuilt unit.
	Commutator no longer circular	Recut commutator and undercut segment separators.
	Open circuit in wiring of cut-out and regulator unit	Remove, examine and renew as necessary. Take car to specialist Auto-Electrician.
Fuel gauge		
Fuel gauge gives no reading	Fuel tank empty!	Fill fuel tank.
	Electric cable between tank sender unit and gauge earthed or loose	Check cable for earthing and joints for tightness.
	Fuel gauge case not earthed	Ensure case is well earthed.
	Fuel gauge supply cable interrupted	Check and renew cable if necessary.
	Fuel gauge unit broken	Renew fuel gauge.
Fuel gauge registers full all the time	Electric cable between tank unit and gauge broken or disconnected	Check over cable and repair as necessary.
Horn		
Horn operates all the time	Horn push either earthed or stuck down	Disconnect battery earth. Check and rectify source of trouble.
	Horn cable to horn push earthed	Disconnect battery earth. Check and rectify source of trouble.
Horn fails to operate	Blown fuse	Check and renew if broken. Ascertain cause.
	Cable or cable connections loose, broken or disconnected	Check all connections for tightness and cables for breaks.
	Horn has an internal fault	Remove and overhaul horn.
Horn emits intermittent or unsatisfactory noise	Faulty or loose wiring	Check wiring.
Lights		
Lights do not come on	If engine not running, battery discharged.	Push-start car, charge battery.
	Light bulb filament burnt out or bulbs broken	Test bulbs in live bulb holder.
	Wire connections loose, disconnected or broken	Check all connections for tightness and wire cable for breaks.
	Light switch shorting or otherwise faulty	By-pass light switch to ascertain if fault is in switch and fit new switch as appropriate.
Lights come on but fade out	If engine not running battery discharged	Push-start car, and charge battery.
Lights give very poor illumination	Lamp glasses dirty	Clean glasses.
	Reflector tarnished or dirty	Fit new reflectors.
	Lamps badly out of adjustment	Adjust lamps correctly.
	Incorrect bulb with too low wattage fitted	Remove bulb and replace with correct grade.
	Existing bulbs old and badly discoloured	Renew bulb units.
	Electrical wiring too thin not allowing full current to pass	Re-wire lighting system.
Lights work erratically - flashing on and off, especially over bumps	Battery terminals or earth connection loose	Tighten battery terminals and earth connection.
	Lights not earthing properly	Examine and rectify.

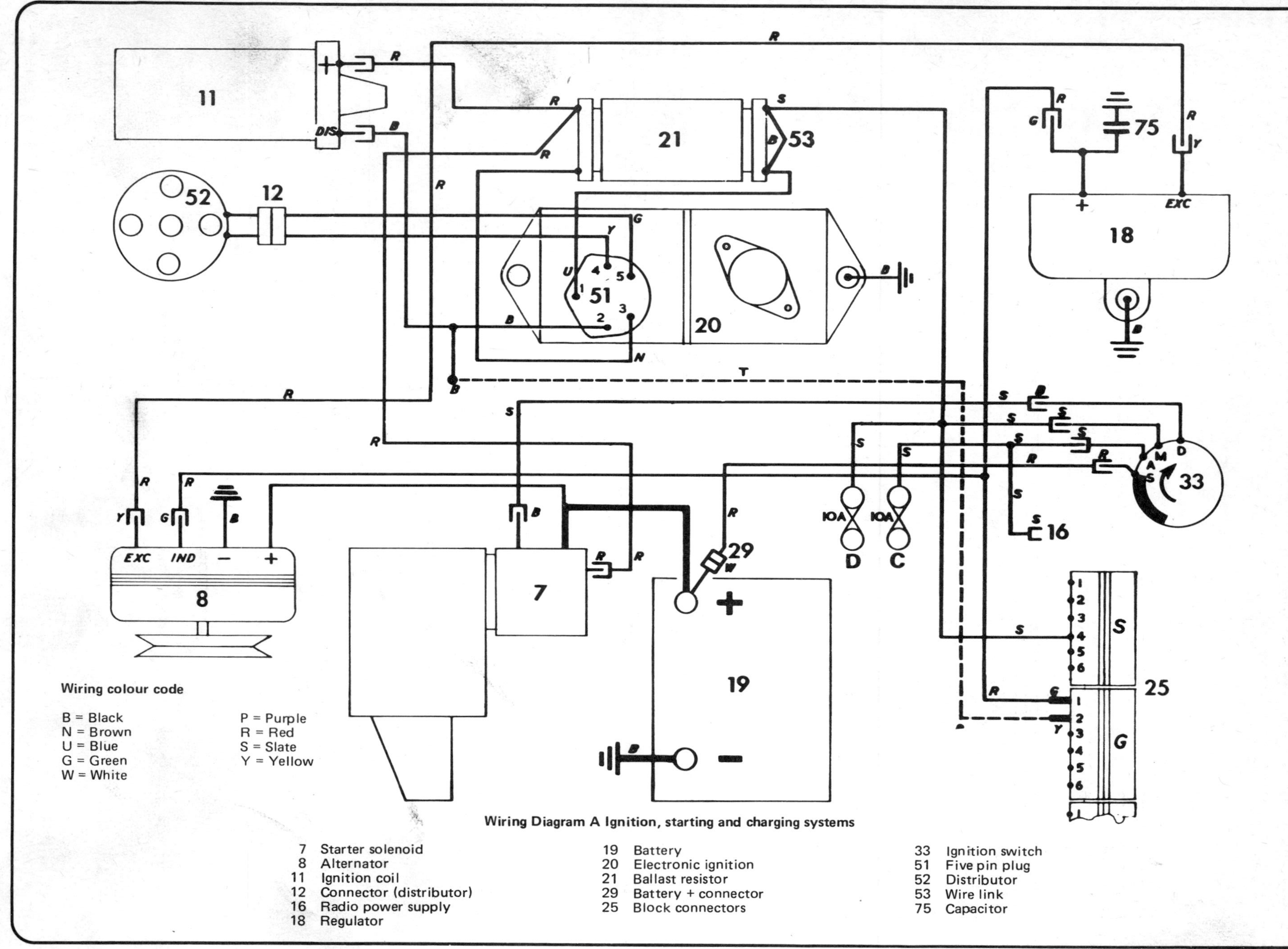

Wiring Diagram A Ignition, starting and charging systems

7 Starter solenoid
8 Alternator
11 Ignition coil
12 Connector (distributor)
16 Radio power supply
18 Regulator
19 Battery
20 Electronic ignition
21 Ballast resistor
29 Battery + connector
25 Block connectors
33 Ignition switch
51 Five pin plug
52 Distributor
53 Wire link
75 Capacitor

Wiring colour code

B = Black
N = Brown
U = Blue
G = Green
W = White
P = Purple
R = Red
S = Slate
Y = Yellow

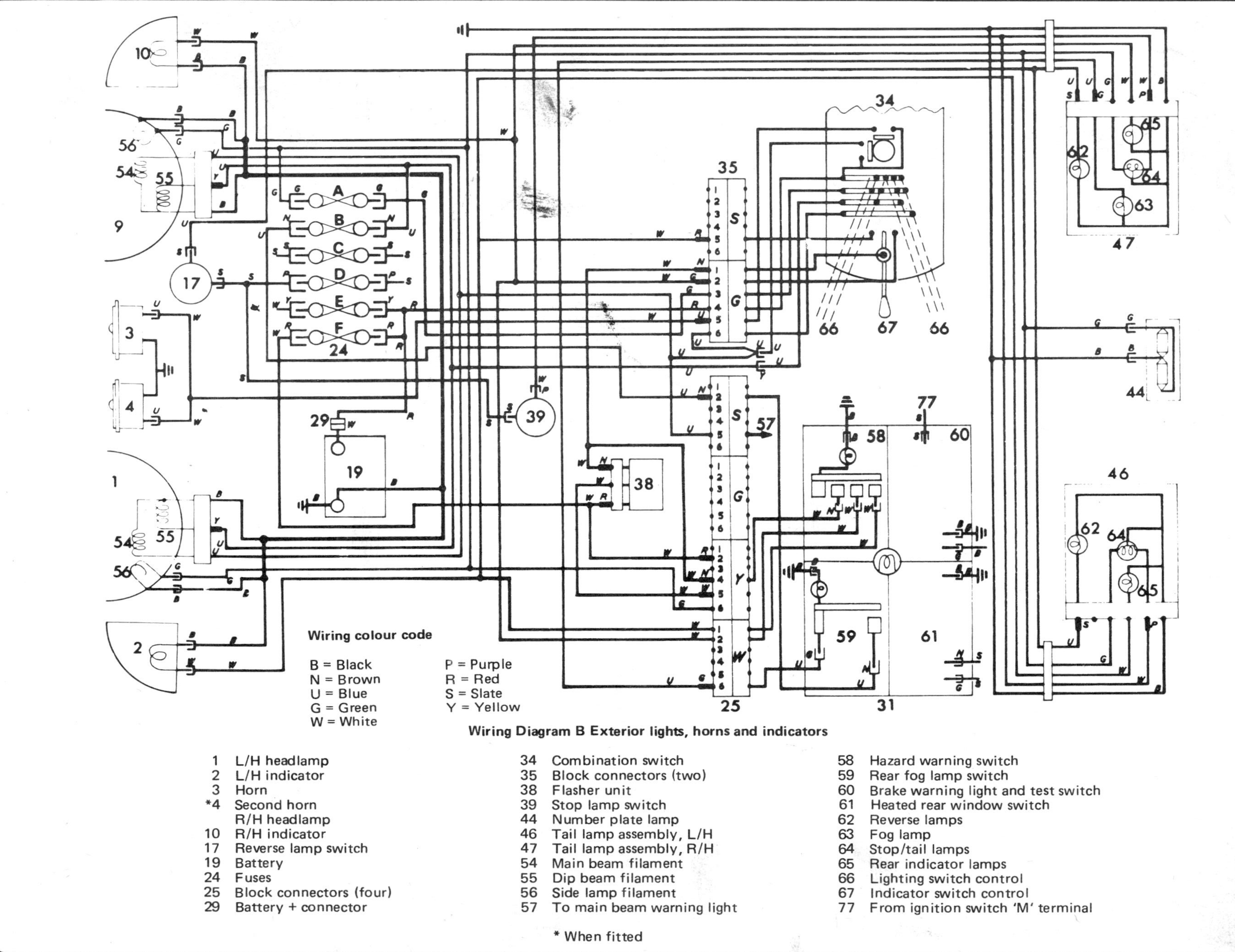

Wiring colour code

B = Black
N = Brown
U = Blue
G = Green
W = White
P = Purple
R = Red
S = Slate
Y = Yellow

Wiring Diagram B Exterior lights, horns and indicators

1	L/H headlamp	34	Combination switch	58	Hazard warning switch
2	L/H indicator	35	Block connectors (two)	59	Rear fog lamp switch
3	Horn	38	Flasher unit	60	Brake warning light and test switch
*4	Second horn	39	Stop lamp switch	61	Heated rear window switch
	R/H headlamp	44	Number plate lamp	62	Reverse lamps
10	R/H indicator	46	Tail lamp assembly, L/H	63	Fog lamp
17	Reverse lamp switch	47	Tail lamp assembly, R/H	64	Stop/tail lamps
19	Battery	54	Main beam filament	65	Rear indicator lamps
24	Fuses	55	Dip beam filament	66	Lighting switch control
25	Block connectors (four)	56	Side lamp filament	67	Indicator switch control
29	Battery + connector	57	To main beam warning light	77	From ignition switch 'M' terminal

* When fitted

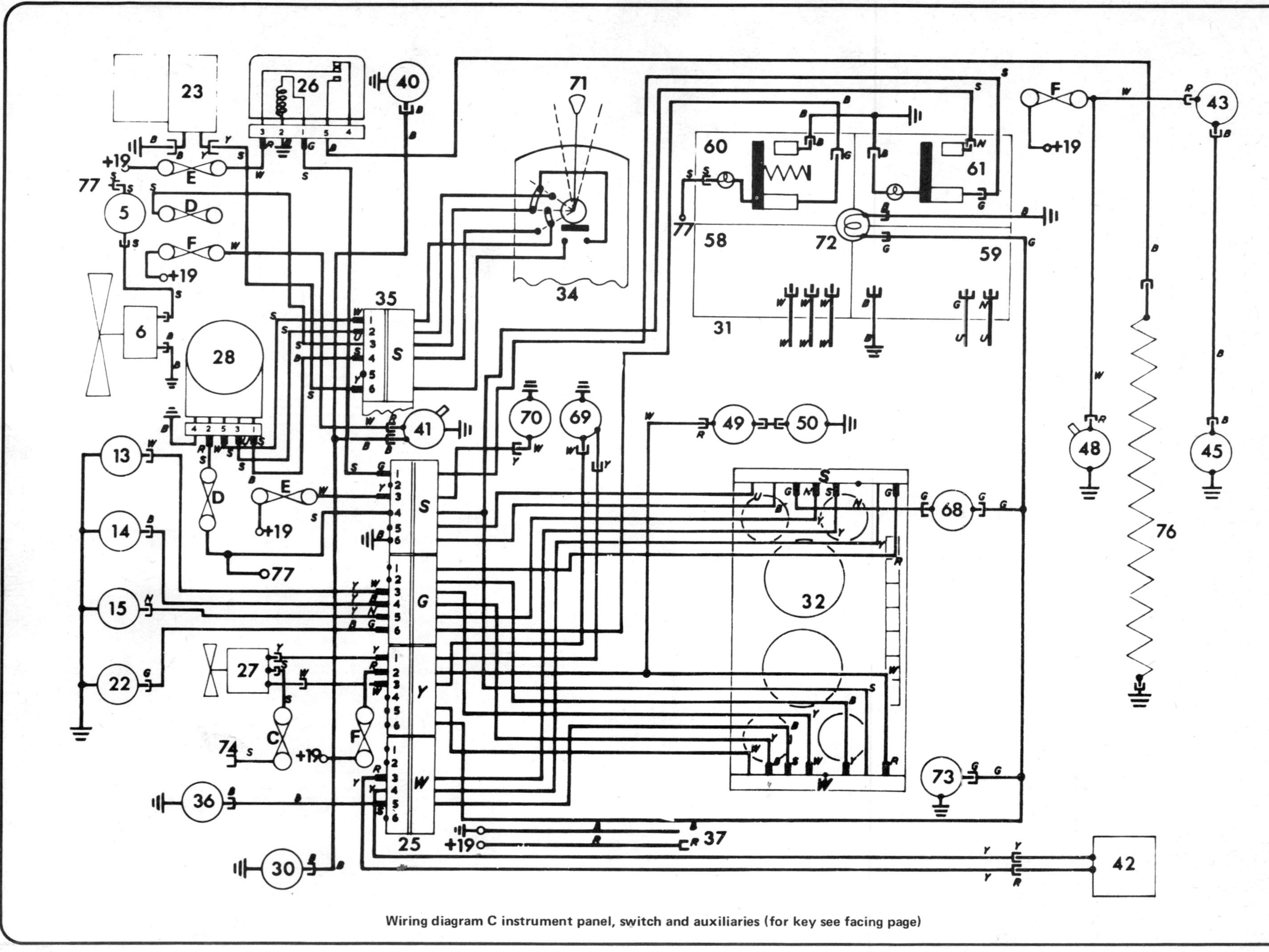

Wiring diagram C instrument panel, switch and auxiliaries (for key see facing page)

Wiring Diagram C Instrument panel, switches and auxiliaries

5 Radiator
6 Radiator fan
13 Water temperature sender
14 Oil warning switch
*15 Oil pressure sender
19 Battery positive supply
22 Braking pressure differential warning actuator
23 Screenwash pump
25 Four block connectors
26 Heated rear window relay
27 Heater blower fan
28 Screen wiper motor
30 Courtesy switch
32 Instrument panel printed circuit
34 Combination switch
*36 Handbrake warning switch
*37 Accessory connectors
40 Courtesy switch
41 Front interior lamp
42 Fuel gauge tank unit
*43 Luggage compartment lamp
*45 Luggage compartment lamp switch
*48 Rear interior lamp
*49 Glove box lamp
*50 Glove box lamp switch
58 Hazard warning switch
59 Rear fog lamp switch
60 Brake warning check switch
61 Heated rear window switch
*68 Instrument panel rheostat
69 Heater blower switch
70 Cigar lighter
71 Wash/wipe control
72 Centre panel lamp
73 Switch illumination lamp
74 From ignition switch 'A' terminal
76 Heated rear window
77 From ignition switch 'M' terminal

* When fitted

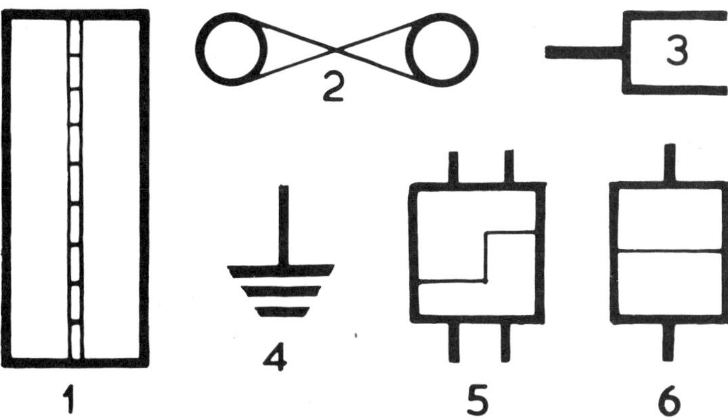

Symbol identification

1 Block connector
2 Fuse
3 Connector
4 Earth
5 Two pin connector
6 Single pin connector

Chapter 12 Bodywork and fittings

Contents

1 General description

The vehicle body structure is a welded fabrication of many individual shaped panels to form a 'monocoque' bodyshell. Certain areas are strengthened locally to provide for suspension system, steering system, engine support anchorages and transmission. The resultant structure is very strong and rigid (Fig. 12.1).

It is as well to remember that monocoque structures have no load paths and all metal is stressed to an extent. It is essential therefore to maintain the whole bodyshell both top and underside, inside and outside, clean and corrosion free. Every effort should be made to keep the underside of the car as clear of mud and dirt accumulations as possible. If you were fortunate enough to acquire a new car then it is advisable to have it rust proofed and undersealed at one of the specialist workshops who guarantee their work.

2 Maintenance - exterior

The general condition of a car's bodywork is the one thing that significantly affects its value. Maintenance is easy but needs to be regular and particular. Neglect - particularly after minor damage - can quickly lead to further deterioration and costly repair bills. It is important to keep watch on those parts of the bodywork not immediately visible, for example the underside, inside all the wheel arches and the lower part of the engine compartment.

The basic maintenance routine for the bodywork is washing, preferably with a lot of water from a hose. This will remove all the loose solids which may have stuck to the car. It is important to flush these off in such a way as to prevent grit from scratching the finish. The wheel arches and underbody need washing in the same way to remove any accumulated mud which will retain moisture and tend to encourage rust. Paradoxically enough, the best time to clean the underbody and wheel arches is in the wet weather when the mud is thoroughly wet and soft. In very wet weather the underbody is usually cleaned of large accumulations automatically and this is a good time for inspection.

Periodically it is a good idea to have the whole of the underside of the car steam cleaned, engine compartment included, for removal of accumulation of oily grime which sometimes collects thickly in areas near the engine and gearbox, so that a thorough inspection can be carried out to see what minor repairs and renovations are necessary.

If steam facilities are not available there are one or two excellent grease solvents available which can be brush applied. The dirt can then be simply hosed off. Any signs of rust on the underside panels and chassis members must be attended to immediately. Thorough wire brushing followed by treatment with an anti-rust compound, primer and underbody sealer will prevent continued deterioration. If not dealt with the car could eventually become structurally unsound, and therefore, unsafe.

After washing the paintwork wipe it off with a chamois leather to give a clear unspotted finish. A coat of clear wax polish will give added protection against chemical pollutants in the air and will survive several subsequent washings. If the paintwork sheen has dulled or oxidised use a cleaner/polisher combination to restore the brilliance of the shine. This requires a little more effort but it usually is because regular washing has been neglected. Always check that door and drain holes and pipes are completely clear so that water can drain out. Brightwork should be treated the same way as paintwork. Windscreens and windows can be kept clear of smeary film which often appears, if a little ammonia is added to the water. If glass work is scratched, a good rub with a proprietary metal polish will often clean it. Never use any form of wax or other paint/chromium polish on glass.

3 Maintenance - interior

The flooring cover, usually carpet, should be brushed or vacuum cleaned regularly to keep it free from grit. If badly stained, remove it from the car for scrubbing and sponging and make quite sure that it is dry before refitting. Seats and interior trim panels can be kept clean with a wipe over with a damp cloth. If they do become stained (which can be more apparent on light coloured upholstery) use a little liquid detergent and soft nailbrush to scour the grime out of the grain of the material. Do not forget to keep the headlining clean in the same way as the upholstery. When using liquid cleaners inside the car do not over-wet the surfaces being cleaned. Excessive damp could get into the upholstery seams and padded interior, causing stains, offensive odours or even rot. If the inside of the car gets wet accidently it is worthwhile taking some trouble to dry it out properly. **Do not** use oil or electric heaters inside the car for this purpose. If, when removing mats for cleaning, there are signs of damp underneath, all the interior of the car floor should be uncovered and the point of water entry found. It may be only a missing grommet, but it could be a rusted through floor panel and this demands immediate attention as described in the previous Section. More often than not both sides on the panel will require treatment.

4 Minor body damage - repair

See photo sequences on pages 158 and 159

Repair of minor scratches in the car's bodywork

If the scratch is very superficial, and does not penetrate to the metal of the bodywork - repair is very simple. Lightly rub the area of the scratch with a paintwork renovator, or a very fine cutting paste, to remove loose paint from the scratch and to clear the surrounding bodywork of wax polish. Rinse the area with clean water.

Apply touch-up paint to the scratch using a thin paint brush; continue to apply thin layers of paint until the surface of the paint in the scratch is level with the surrounding paintwork. Allow the new paint at least two weeks to harden, then, blend it into the surrounding paintwork by rubbing the paintwork in the scratch area with a paintwork renovator, or a very fine cutting paste. Finally apply wax polish.

An alternative to painting over the scratch is to use adhesive paint patches. Use the same preparation for the affected area; then simply, pick a patch of a suitable size to cover the scratch completely. Hold the patch against the scratch and burnish its backing paper; the patch will adhere to the paintwork, freeing itself from the backing paper at the same time. Polish the affected area to blend the patch into the surrounding paintwork.

Where a scratch has penetrated right through to the metal of the bodywork, causing the metal to rust, a different repair technique is required. Remove any loose rust from the bottom of the scratch with a penknife; then apply rust inhibiting paint to prevent the formation of rust in the future. Using a rubber or nylon applicator fill the scratch with body-stopper paste. If required, this paste can be mixed with cellulose thinners to provide a very thin paste which is ideal for filling narrow scratches. Before the stopper paste in the scratch hardens, wrap a piece of smooth cotton rag around the tip of a finger. Dip the finger in cellulose thinners and then quickly sweep it across the surface of the stopper-paste, this will ensure that it is slightly hollowed. The scratch can now be painted over as described earlier in this Section.

Repair of dents in the car's bodywork

When deep denting of the car's bodywork has taken place, the

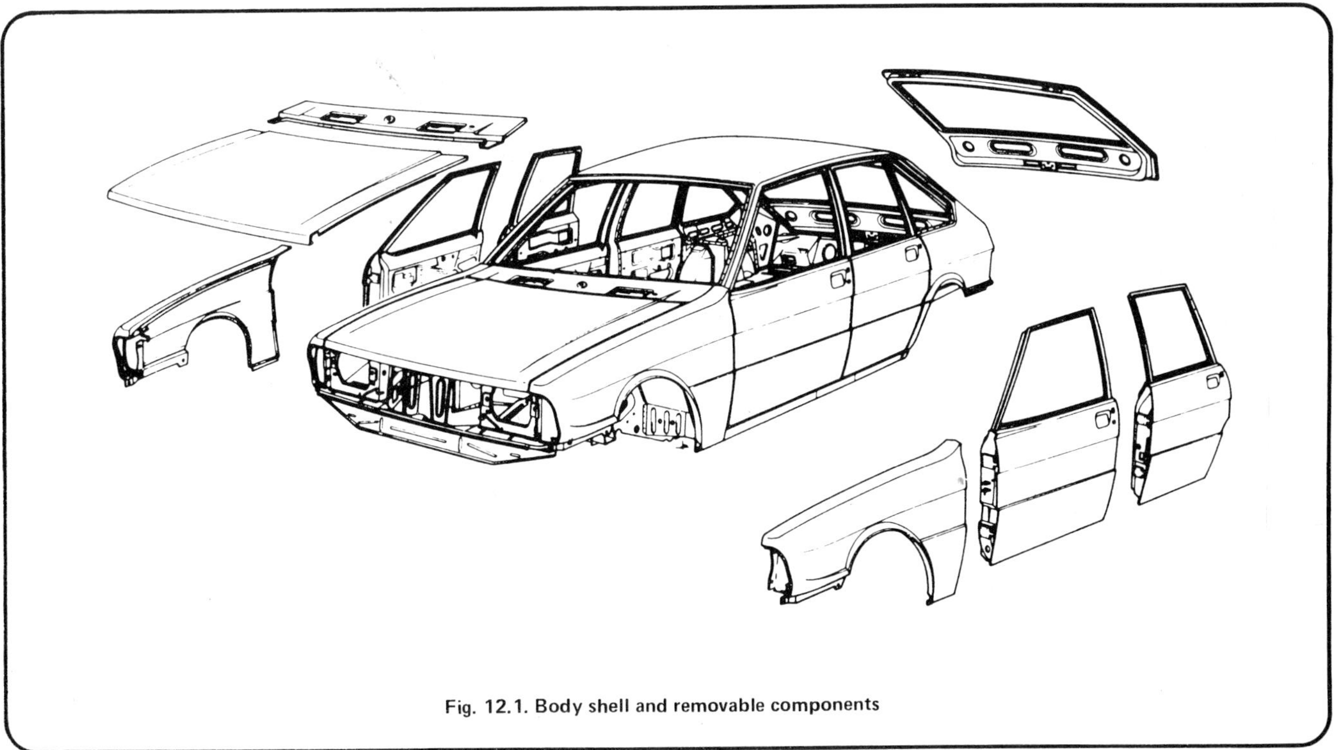

Fig. 12.1. Body shell and removable components

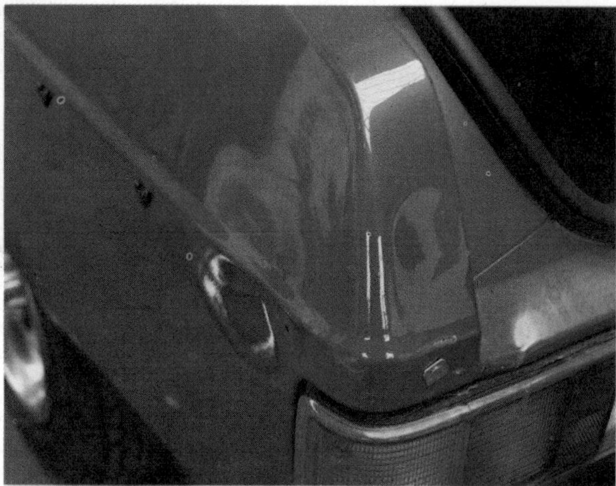

This sequence of photographs deals with the repair of the dent and scratch (above rear lamp) shown in this photo. The procedure will be similar for the repair of a hole. It should be noted that the procedures given here are simplified - more explicit instructions will be found in the text

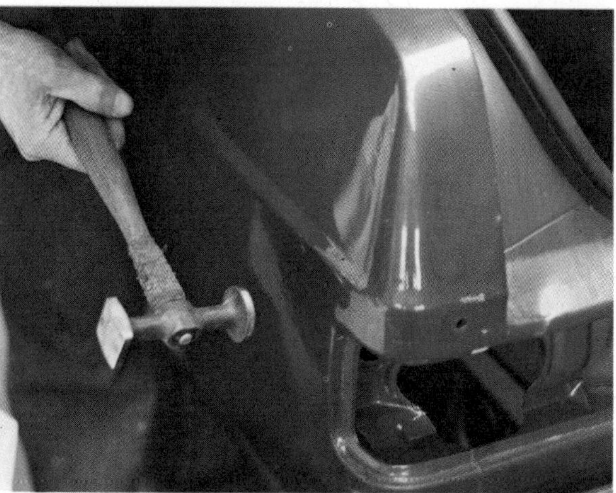

In the case of a dent the first job - after removing surrounding trim - is to hammer out the dent where access is possible. This will minimise filling. Here, the large dent having been hammered out, the damaged area is being made slightly concave

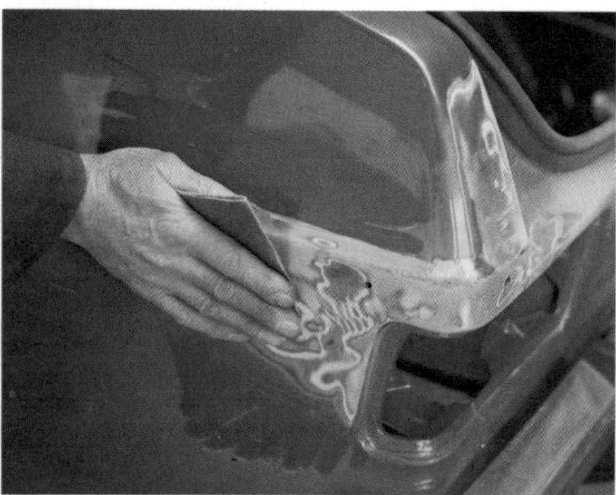

Now all paint must be removed from the damaged area, by rubbing with coarse abrasive paper. Alternatively, a wire brush or abrasive pad can be used in a power drill. Where the repair area meets good paintwork, the edge pf the paintwork should be 'feathered', using a finer grade of abrasive paper

In the case of a hole caused by rusting, all damaged sheet-metal should be cut away before proceeding to this stage. Here, the damaged area is being treated with rust remover and inhibitor before being filled

Mix the body filler according to its manufacturer's instructions. In the case of corrosion damage, it will be necessary to block off any large holes before filling - this can be done with zinc gauze or aluminium tape. Make sure the area is absolutely clean before ...

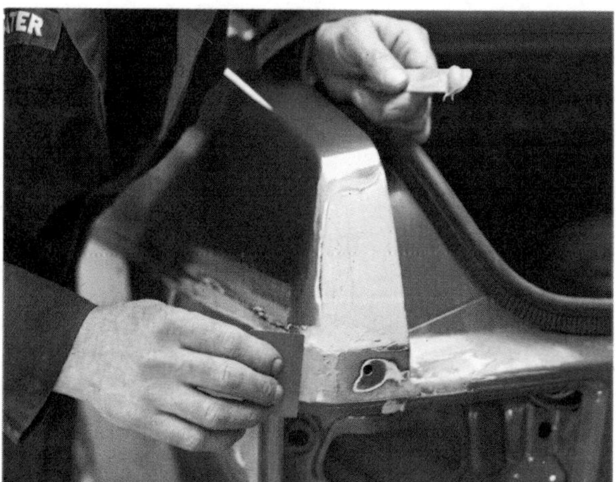

... applying the filler. Filler should be applied with a flexible applicator, as shown, for best results: the wooden spatula being used for confined areas. Apply thin layers of filler at 20-minute intervals, until the surface of the filler is slightly proud of the surrounding bodywork

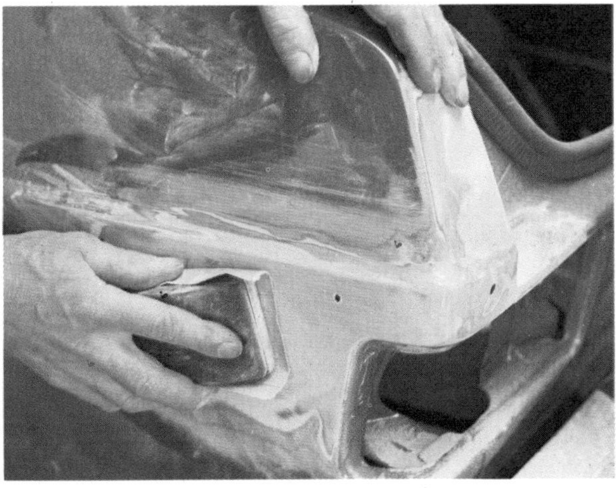

Initial shaping can be done with a Surform plane or Dreadnought file. Then, using progressively finer grades of wet-and-dry paper, wrapped around a sanding block, and copious amounts of clean water, rub-down the filler until really smooth and flat. Again, feather the edges of adjoining paintwork

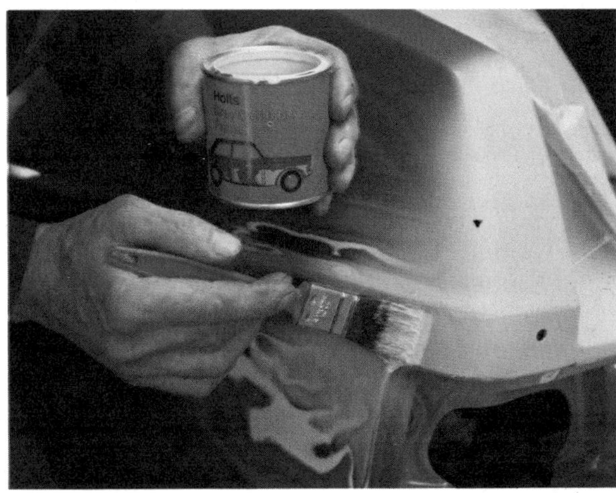

The whole repair area can now be sprayed or brush-painted with primer. If spraying, ensure adjoining areas are protected from over-spray. Note that at least one-inch of the surrounding sound paintwork should be coated with primer. Primer has a 'thick' consistency, so will fill small imperfections

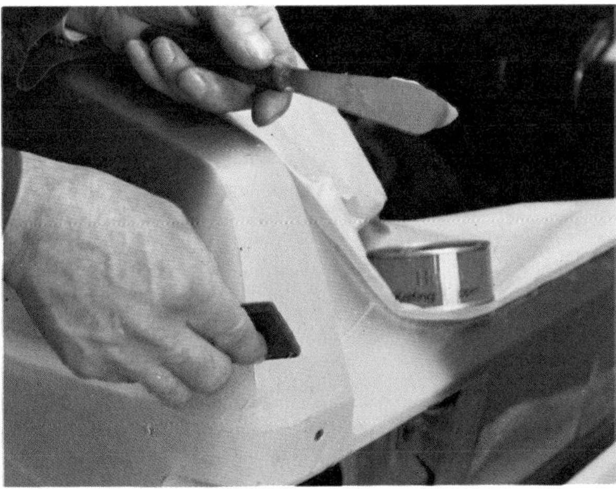

Again, using plenty of water, rub down the primer with a fine grade of wet-and-dry paper (400 grade is probably best) until it is really smooth and well blended into the surrounding paintwork. Any remaining imperfections can now be filled by carefully applied knifing stopper paste

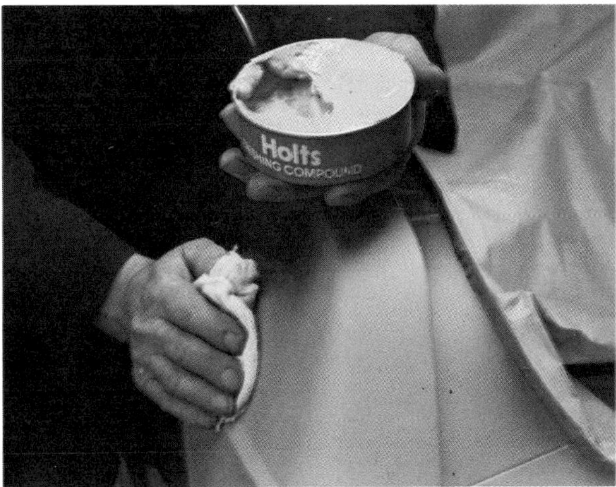

When the stopper has hardened, rub-down the repair area again before applying the final coat of primer. Before rubbing-down this last coat of primer, ensure the repair area is blemish-free - use more stopper if necessary. To ensure that the surface of the primer is really smooth use some finishing compound

The top coat can now be applied. When working out of doors, pick a dry, warm and wind-free day. Ensure surrounding areas are protected from over-spray. Agitate the aerosol thoroughly, then spray the centre of the repair area, working outwards with a circular motion. Apply the paint as several thin coats.

After a period of about two-weeks, which the paint needs to harden fully, the surface of the repaired area can be 'cut' with a mild cutting compound prior to wax polishing. When carrying out bodywork repairs, remember that the quality of the finished job is proportional to the time and effort expended first task is to pull the dent out, until the affected bodywork almost attains its original shape. There is little point in trying to restore the original shape completely, as the metal in the damaged area will have stretched on impact and cannot be reshaped fully to its original contour. It is better to bring the level of the dent up to a point which is about 1/8 inch (3 mm) below the level of the surrounding bodywork. In cases where the dent is very shallow anyway, it is not worth trying to pull it out at all.

If the underside of the dent is accessible, it can be hammered out gently from behind, using a mallet with a wooden or plastic head. Whilst doing this, hold a suitable block of wood firmly against the outside of the dent. This block will absorb the impact from the hammer blows and thus prevent a large area of bodywork from being 'belled-out'.

Should the dent be in a section of the bodywork which has double skin or some other factor making it inaccessible from behind, a different technique is called for. Drill several small holes through the metal inside the dent area - particularly in the deeper sections. Then screw long self-tapping screws into the holes just sufficiently for them to gain a good purchase in the metal. Now the dent can be pulled out by pulling on the protruding heads of the screws with a pair of pliers.

The next stage of the repair is the removal of the paint from the damaged area, and from an inch or so of the surrounding 'sound' bodywork. This is accomplished most easily by using a wire brush or abrasive pad on a power drill, although it can be done just as effectively by hand using sheets of abrasive paper. To complete the preparations for filling, score the surface of the bare metal with a screwdriver or the tang of a file, or alternatively, drill small holes in the affected area. This will provide a really good 'key' for the filler paste.

To complete the repair see the Section on filling and respraying.

Repair of rust holes or gashes in the car's bodywork

Remove all paint from the affected area and from an inch or so of the surrounding 'sound' bodywork, using an abrasive pad or a wire brush on a power drill. If these are not available a few sheets of abrasive paper will do the job just as effectively. With the paint removed you will be able to gauge the severity of the corrosion and therefore decide whether to renew the whole panel (if possible) or to repair the affected area. New body panels are not as expensive as most people think and it is often quicker and more satisfactory to fit a new panel than to attempt to repair large areas of corrosion.

Remove all fittings from the affected area except those which will act as a guide to the original shape of the damaged bodywork (eg, headlamp shells etc). Then, using tin snips or a hacksaw blade, remove all loose metal and any other metal badly affected by corrosion. Hammer the edges of the hole inwards in order to create a slight depression for the filler paste.

Wire brush the affected area to remove the powdery rust from the surface of the remaining metal. Paint the affected area with rust inhibiting paint; if the back of the rusted area is accessible treat this also.

Before filling can take place it will be necessary to block the hole in some way. This can be achieved by the use of one of the following materials: Zinc gauze, Aluminium tape or Polyurethane foam.

Zinc gauze is probably the best material to use for a large hole. Cut a piece to the approximate size and shape of the hole to be filled, then position it in the hole so that its edges are below the level of the surrounding bodywork. It can be retained in position by several blobs of filler paste around its periphery.

Aluminium tape should be used for small or very narrow holes. Pull a piece off the roll and trim it to the approximate size and shape required, then pull off the backing paper (if used) and stick the tape over the hole; it can be overlapped if the thickness of one piece is insufficient. Burnish down the edges of the tape with the handle of a screwdriver or similar, to ensure that the tape is securely attached to the metal underneath.

Polyurethane foam is best used where the hole is situated in a section of bodywork of complex shape, backed by a small box section (eg, where the sill panel meets the rear wheel arch - most cars). The usual mixing procedure for this foam is as follows: Put equal amounts of fluid from each of the two cans provided in the kits, into one container. Stir until the mixture begins to thicken, then quickly pour this mixture into the hole, and hold a piece of cardboard over the larger apertures. Almost immediately the polyurethane will begin to expand, gushing frantically out of any small holes left unblocked. When the foam hardens it can be cut back to just below the level of the surrounding bodywork with a hacksaw blade.

Having blocked off the hole the affected area must now be filled and sprayed - see Section on bodywork filling and re-spraying.

Bodywork repairs - filling and re-spraying

Before using this Section, see Sections on dent, deep scratch, rust hole, and gash repairs.

Many types of bodyfiller are available, but generally speaking those proprietary kits which contain a tin of filler paste and a tube of resin hardener are best for this type of repair. A wide, flexible plastic or nylon applicator will be found invaluable for imparting a smooth and well contoured finish to the surface of the filler.

Mix up a little filler on a clean piece of card or board - use the hardener sparingly (follow the maker's instructions on the pack), otherwise the filler will set very rapidly.

Using the applicator, apply the filler paste to the prepared area; draw the applicator across the surface of the filler to achieve the correct contour and to level the filler surface. As soon as a contour that approximates the correct one is achieved, stop working the paste - if you carry on too long the paste will become sticky and begin to 'pick-up' on the applicator.

Continue to add thin layers of filler paste at twenty-minute intervals until the level of the filler is just 'proud' of the surrounding bodywork.

Once the filler has hardened, the excess can be removed using a plane or file. From then on, progressively finer grades of abrasive paper should be used, starting with a 40 grade 'wet-and-dry' paper. Always wrap the abrasive paper around a flat rubber, cork, or wooden block - otherwise the surface of the filler will not be completely flat. During the smoothing of the filler surface the 'wet-and-dry' paper should be periodically rinsed in water - this will ensure that a very smooth finish is imparted to the filler at the final stage.

At this stage the 'dent' should be surrounded by a ring of bare metal, which in turn should be encircled by the finely 'feathered' edge of the good paintwork. Rinse the repair area with clean water, until all of the dust produced by the rubbing down operation is gone.

Spray the whole repair area with a light coat of grey primer - this will show up any imperfections in the surface of the filler. Repair these imperfections with fresh filler paste or bodystopper, and once more smooth the surface with abrasive paper. If bodystopper is used, it can be mixed with cellulose thinners to form a really thin paste which is ideal for filling small holes. Repeat this spray and repair procedure until you are satisfied that the surface of the filler, and the feathered edge of the paintwork are perfect. Clean the repair area with clean water and allow to dry fully.

The repair area is now ready for spraying. Paint spraying must be carried out in a warm, dry, windless and dust free atmosphere. This condition can be created artificially if you have access to a large indoor working area, but if you are forced to work in the open, you will have to pick your day very carefully. If you are working indoors, dousing the floor in the work area with water will 'lay' the dust which would otherwise be in the atmosphere. If the repair area is confined to one body panel, mask off the surrounding panels; this will help to minimise the effects of a slight mis-match in paint colours. Bodywork fittings (eg, chrome strips, door handles etc) will also need to be masked off. Use genuine masking tape and several thicknesses of newspaper for the masking operation.

Before commencing to spray, agitate the aerosol can thoroughly, then spray a test area (an old tin, or similar) until the technique is mastered. Cover the repair area with a thick coat of primer; the thickness should be built up using several thin layers of paint rather than one thick one. Using 400 grade 'wet-and-dry' paper, rub down the surface of the primer until it is really smooth. While doing this, the work area should be thoroughly doused with water, and the wet-and-dry paper periodically rinsed in water. Allow to dry before spraying on more paint.

Spray on the top coat, again building up the thickness by using several thin layers of paint. Start spraying in the centre of the repair area and then using a circular motion, work outwards until the whole area and about 2 inches of the surrounding original paintwork is covered. Remove all masking material 10 to 15 minutes after spraying on the final coat of paint. Allow the new paint at least 2 weeks to harden fully, then, using a paintwork renovator or a very fine cutting paste, blend the edges of the new paint into the existing paintwork. Finally, apply wax polish.

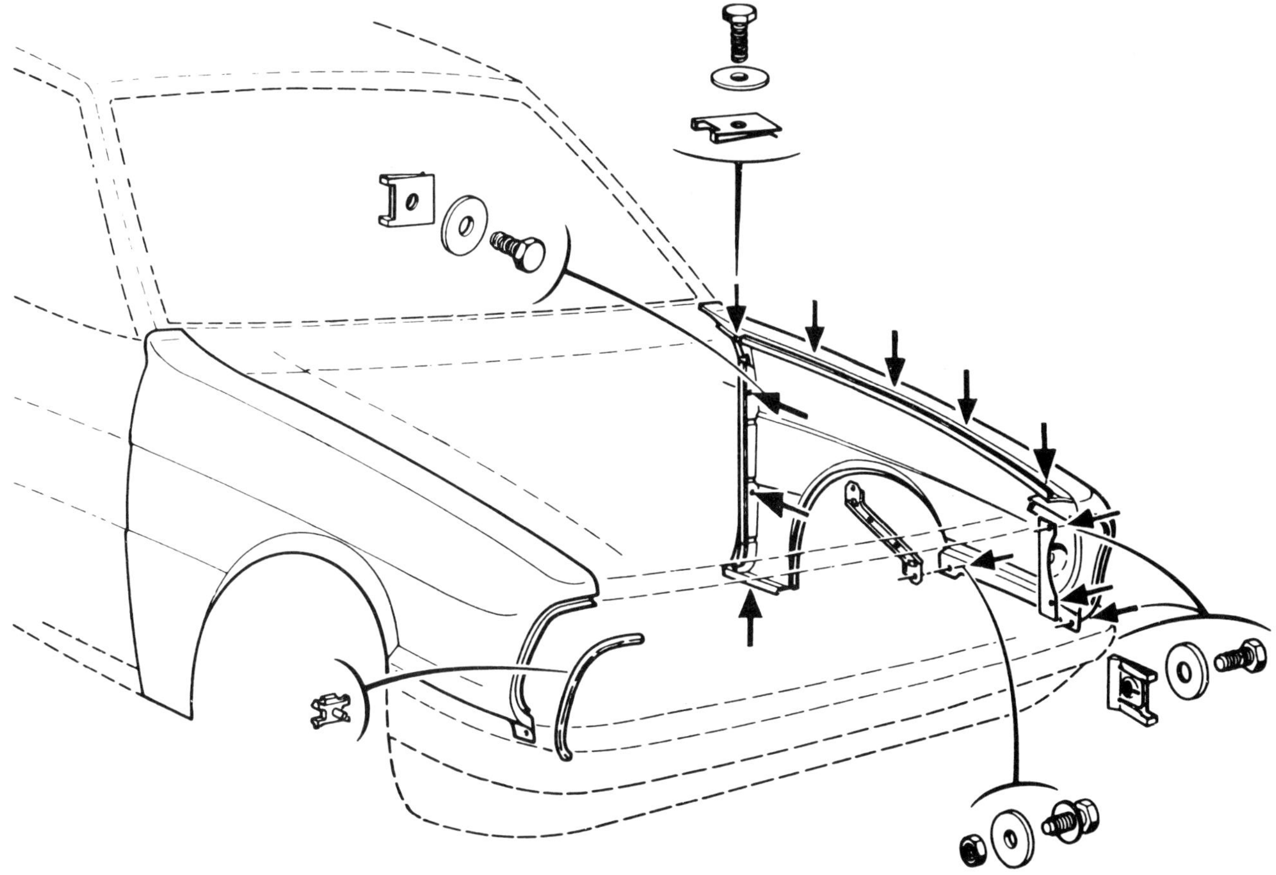

Fig. 12.2. Location of front wing securing bolts

5 Major body repairs

Where serious damage has occurred or large areas need renewal due to neglect, it means certainly that completely new sections or panels will need welding in and this is best left to professionals. If the damage is due to impact it will also be necessary to completely check the alignment of the body shell structure. Due to the principle of construction the strength and shape of the whole can be affected by damage to a part. In such instances the services of a Chrysler agent with specialist checking jigs are essential. If a body is left misaligned it is first of all dangerous as the car will not handle properly and secondly uneven stresses will be imposed on the steering, engine and transmission, causing abnormal wear or complete failure. Tyre wear may also be excessive.

6 Maintenance - hinges and locks

1 Oil the hinges of the bonnet, tailgate and doors with a drop or two of light oil periodically. A good time is after the car has been washed.
2 Oil the bonnet release catch pivot pin and the safety catch pivot pin periodically.
3 Do not over lubricate door latches and strikers. Normally a little oil on the rotary cam spindle alone is sufficient.

7 Doors - tracing rattles and their rectification

1 Check first that the door is not loose at the hinges and that the latch is holding the door firmly in position. Check also that the door lines up with the aperture in the body.
2 If the hinges are loose or the door is out of alignment it will be necessary to reset the hinge positions.
3 If the latch is holding the door properly it should hold the door tightly when fully latched and the door should line up with the body. If it is out of alignment it needs adjustment. If loose, some part of the lock mechanism must be worn out and requiring renewal.
4 Other rattles from the door would be caused by wear or looseness in the window winder, the glass channels and sill strips or the door buttons and interior latch release mechanism.

8 Wings - removal and refitting

1 The front wings are bolted in position and are fairly easy to remove and refit.
2 First disconnect the battery.
3 Remove the wiper arms and the heater panel at the rear of the bonnet (refer to Section 22).
4 Remove the headlight and the front direction indicator assembly (see Chapter 11).
5 Remove the front bumper as described in Section 17.
6 Jack up the front of the car, support it on axle stands and remove the front wheel.
7 Refer to Fig. 12.2 and remove the bolts and support stay securing the front wing to the bodyshell.
8 It may be necessary to cut through the wing-to-body sealing compound before the wing can be removed.
9 Clean all trace of sealing mastic from the body mating flanges.
10 Place a bead of sealing compound on the whole length of the body to wing mating flange and then locate the front wing in position. Screw in the securing bolts, with their threads well greased, finger tight.
11 Move the wing slightly as required to obtain an exact and flush fit with adjacent body panels and then tighten the securing bolts.
12 As new wings are supplied in primer, the external surface will now have to be sprayed in cellulose to match the body. If the vehicle is reasonably new this can be carried out using a colour matched aerosol spray but if the body paint is badly faded it is advisable to leave the refinishing to a professional bodyshop.
13 The procedure for a rear wing is similar but before the damaged wing can be removed, the rear lamp cluster, the rear bumper and the fuel filler cap cover must be removed.

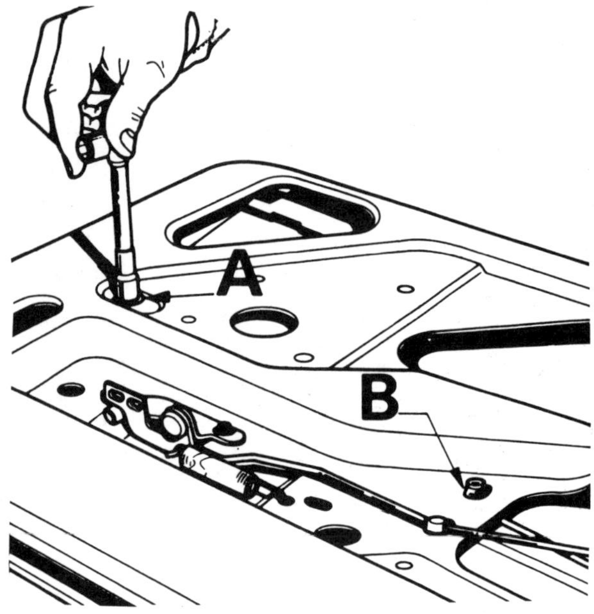

Fig. 12.3. Removing a rear door lock

A Inner retaining bolt *B Anti-rattle bush*

9 Windscreen glass - removal and refitting

1 Where a windscreen is to be renewed due to shattering, the facia air vents should be covered before attempting removal. Adhesive sheeting is useful to stick to the outside of the glass to enable large areas of crystallised glass to be removed.

2 Remove both wiper arms as described in Chapter 11.

3 Remove the interior mirror by pushing it upwards out of the bracket.

4 Where the screen is to be removed intact then an assistant will be required. First release the rubber surround from the bodywork by running a blunt, small screwdriver around and under the rubber weatherstrip both inside and outside the car. This operation will break the adhesion of the sealer originally used. Take care not to damage the paintwork or cut the rubber surround with the screw-driver.

5 Have your assistant push the inner lip of the rubber surround off the flange of the windscreen body aperture. Once the rubber surround starts to peel off the flange, the screen may be forced gently outwards by careful hand pressure. The second person should support and remove the screen complete with rubber surround and metal beading as it comes out.

6 If you are having to renew your windscreen due to a shattered screen, remove all traces of sealing compound and broken glass from the weatherstrip and body flange.

7 Now is the time to remove all pieces of glass if the screen has shattered. Use a vacuum cleaner to extract as much as possible. Switch on the heater boost motor and adjust the screen controls to screen defrost but watch out for flying pieces of glass which might blow out of the ducting.

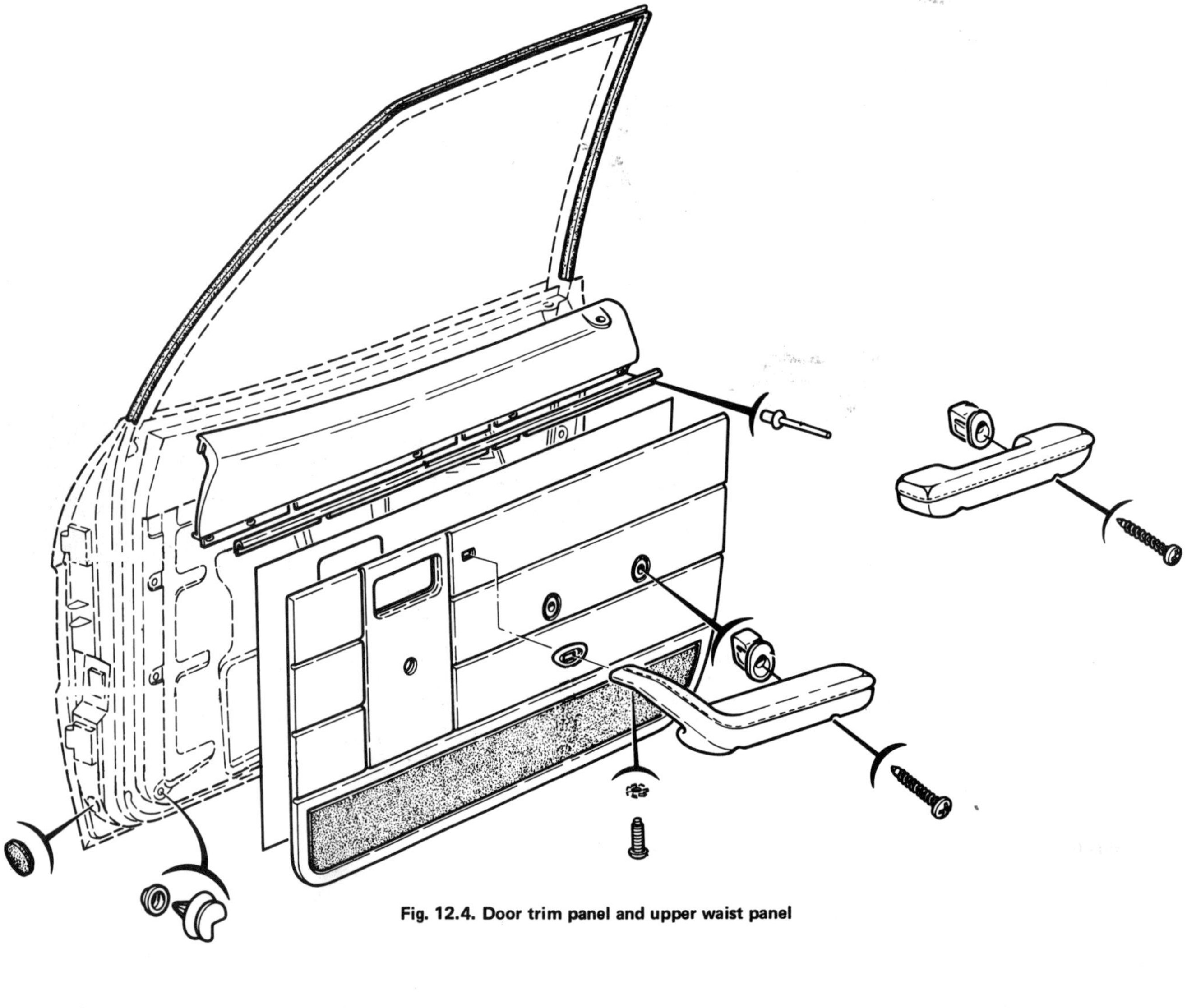

Fig. 12.4. Door trim panel and upper waist panel

10.2 Inside door handle retaining screw

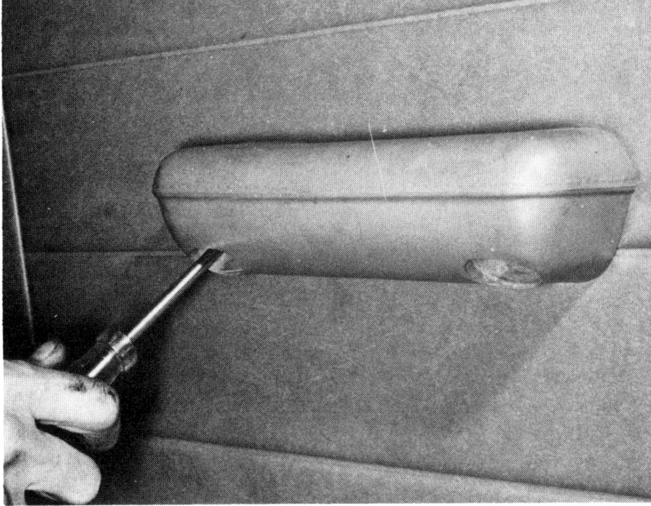
10.3 Removing the arm rest

8 Carefully inspect the rubber moulding for signs of splitting or deterioration.
9 To refit the glass, first fit the weatherstrip onto the glass with the joint at the lower edge.
10 Insert a piece of thick cord into the channel of the weatherstrip with the two ends protruding by at least 12 in (305 mm) at the top centre of the weatherstrip.
11 Mix a concentrated soap and water solution and apply to the flange of the windscreen aperture.
12 Offer the screen up to the aperture and with an assistant to press the rubber surround hard against one end of the cord, move round the windscreen, so drawing the lip over the windscreen flange of the body. Keep the draw cord parallel to the windscreen. Using the palms of the hands, thump on the glass from the outside to assist the lip in passing over the flange and to seat the screen correctly onto the aperture.
13 To ensure a good watertight joint apply some Seelastik SR51 between the weatherstrip and the body and press the weatherstrip against the body to give a good seal.
14 Any excess Seelastik may be removed with a petrol moistened cloth.

10 Door locks - removal, refitting and adjustment

1 First wind the window up to the closed position.
2 Pull the inside door latch open and remove the screw retaining it to the lever (photo).
3 Remove the arm rests which are secured to the interior panels of the doors by self-tapping screws (photo).
4 Press the window winder handle escutcheon plate inwards and remove the spring clip which retains the handle to the winder mechanism shaft (photo).
5 Insert a screwdriver between the door interior panel and the door and lever the panel clips from their locations. Once the first securing clip has been displaced, use the fingers instead of the screwdriver and by giving the panel a sharp jerk, the remaining clips can be removed in succession.
6 Carefully remove the polythene sheet water barrier now exposed.
7 Unscrew the locking pushbutton from the top of the door.
8 Disconnect the three control rods from the lock mechanism, remove the retaining screws and withdraw the lock through the door aperture.
9 The inside (remote control) door latch can be removed by releasing the return spring and retaining screws and withdrawing the handle assembly complete with control rod (photo).
10 The procedure for removing the rear door locks is the same, with the addition that the anti-rattle bush and retaining bolt must also be

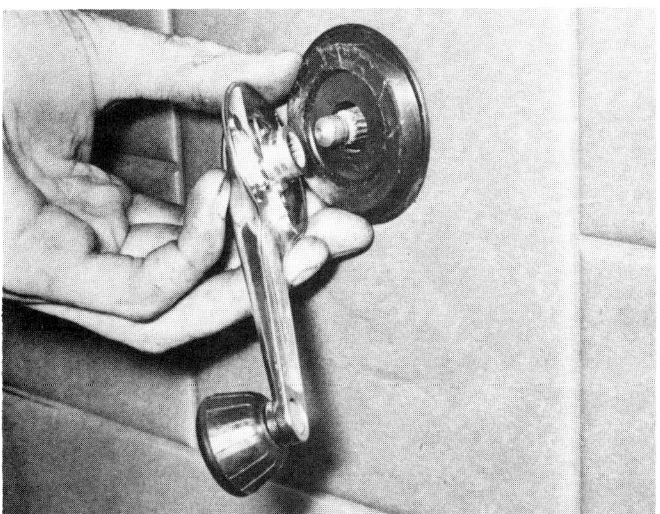
10.4 Removing the window winder handle

10.9 Inside door latch retaining screws and return spring

removed (see Fig. 12.3).

11 The exterior door handle, push button and cylinder lock are retained by a nut, screw and clip, all accessible through one of the door interior apertures.

12 It is seldom worthwhile to attempt to repair a door lock or remote control mechanism, renew as an assembly.

13 Refitting is a reversal of removal but take care to adjust the stroke of the external push button in relation to the lock operating plate. Ensure that the polythene sheet beneath the interior trim panel is refitted.

14 Check the door closure. Adjust the position of the striker plate on the door pillar if necessary, so that the door closure is firm and rattle free and the edge of the door is flush with the surrounding body panel surfaces when fully closed.

11 Window winder mechanism and glass - removal and refitting

1 Carry out operations as described in the preceding Section, paragraphs 1 to 6 and 9.

2 Remove the bolts securing the lower glass channel to the carrier (Fig. 12.5).

3 Secure the glass in the closed position with wooden wedges to prevent it dropping down when the guides are removed.

4 Remove the upper and lower bolts retaining the regulator guide (See Figs. 12.8 and 12.9).

5 Remove the bolts securing the winder (regulator) mechanism to the door.

6 Carefully withdraw the winder mechanism through the door aperture.

7 To remove the glass it is necessary to drill out the 'pop' rivets from the waist trim finisher and remove the waist trim panel. Withdraw the inner seal.

8 To remove the glass rotate it through 90° so that the front is towards the bottom of the door and carefully withdraw it (Fig. 12.10).

9 Renew the winder mechanism if the return spring or if the cable is frayed or broken.

10 Refit the glass and winder mechanism using the reverse procedure to that of removal.

11 Adjust the position of the upper and lower guide rail retaining bolts so that the glass can be raised and lowered smoothly and squarely.

12 Adjust the cable tension by means of the adjustable stop on the outer cable to obtain the correct movement of the glass (Fig. 12.11).

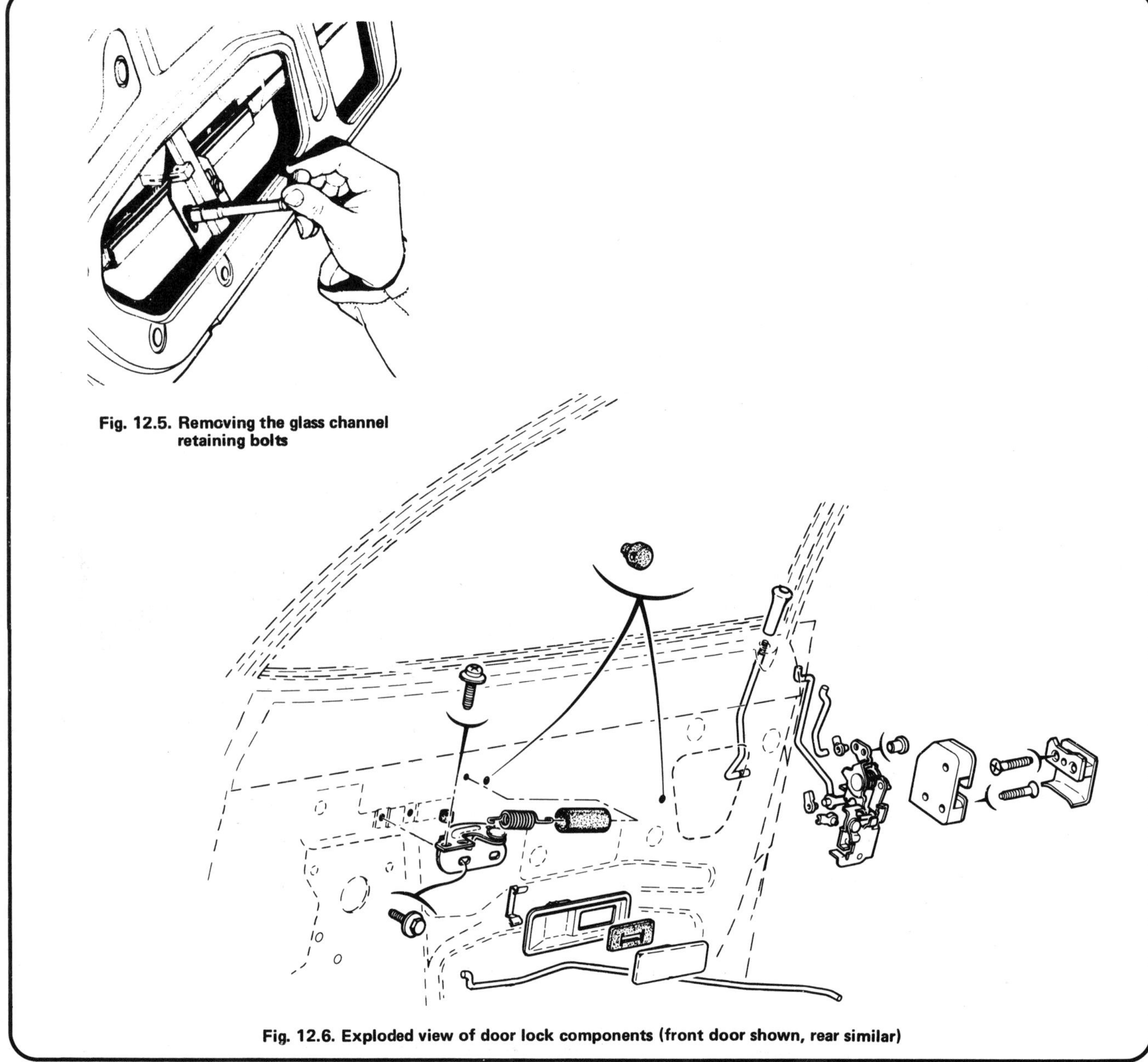

Fig. 12.5. Removing the glass channel retaining bolts

Fig. 12.6. Exploded view of door lock components (front door shown, rear similar)

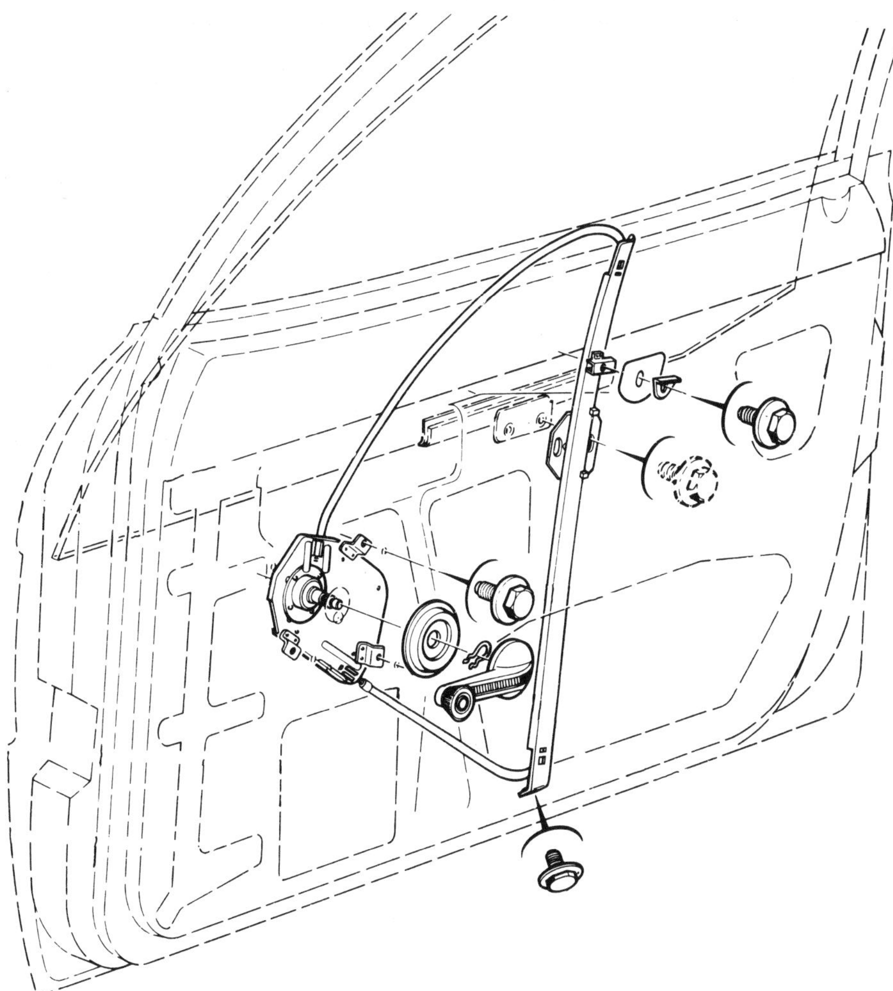

Fig. 12.7. Exploded view of window winder components

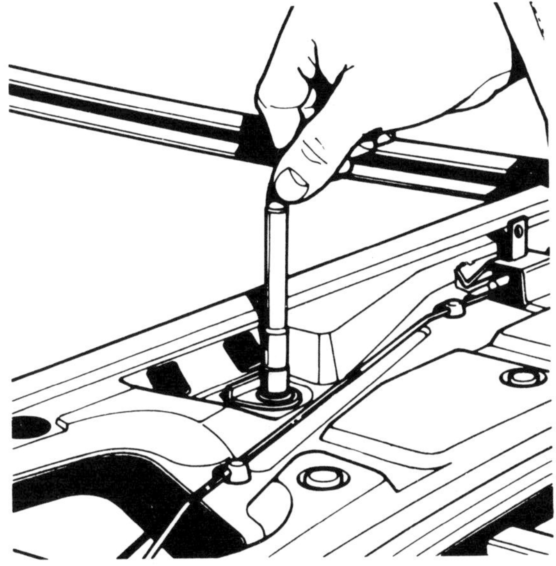

Fig. 12.8. Removing the regulator guide rail upper retaining bolt

Fig. 12.9. Removing the regulator guide rail lower retaining bolt

12 Doors - removal and refitting

1 First it is necessary to carefully grind off the riveted end of the check strap pin and remove the pin.
2 Get a friend to support the weight of the door and using a pin punch, drive out the roll pins from each hinge.
3 The position of the door can only be adjusted by bending the hinges in the required direction using the special Chrysler tool no. CO.0016.
4 Refit the door using the reverse procedure to that of removal. Fit the check strap using a new pin and rivet it in position.

13 Bonnet - removal and refitting

1 Open the bonnet and place pieces of cloth below each rear corner of the bonnet to protect the paintwork.
2 Lightly pencil a line around each hinge to ensure the bonnet is refitted in the correct position.
3 With the help of a friend, support the weight of the bonnet, remove the hinge bolts and carefully lift away the bonnet.
4 Refit the bonnet using the reverse procedure to that of removal. If necessary adjust the position of the hinges so that the bonnet fits correctly when closed.

14 Bonnet lock and cable - removal and refitting

Note: If the bonnet release cable has broken the bonnet can be opened by inserting a long screwdriver through the radiator grille and operating the release catch.
1 Remove the radiator grille as described in Section 15.
2 Disconnect the release cable from the lock.
3 Remove the screw securing the interior bonnet release handle to the bracket and withdraw the handle complete with cable.
4 The lock assembly can be removed by unscrewing the four retaining bolts and lifting out the lock assembly and stiffener plates.
5 Refit the cable and lock assembly using the reverse procedure to that of removal.
IMPORTANT: When fully closed there should be 3/16 in (5 mm) clearance between the underside of the bonnet and the top of the headlights. This clearance can be obtained by slackening the locknut and screwing the striker rod on the bonnet either in or out as required.

15 Radiator grille - removal and refitting

1 The grille is constructed of moulded plastic and is retained in

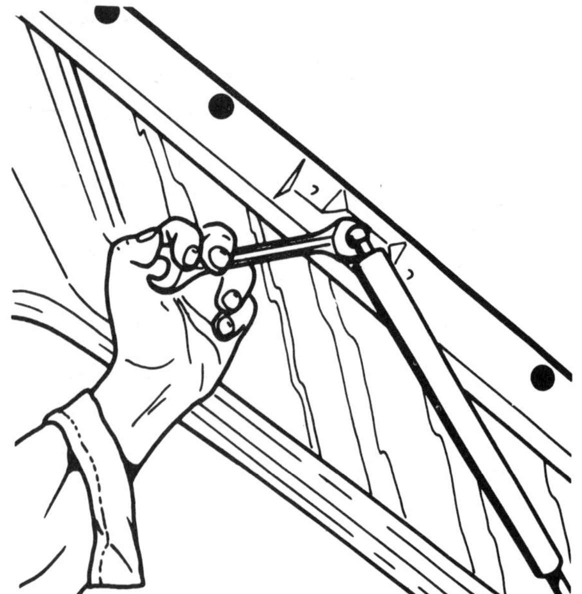
Fig. 12.12. Removing the tailgate support struts

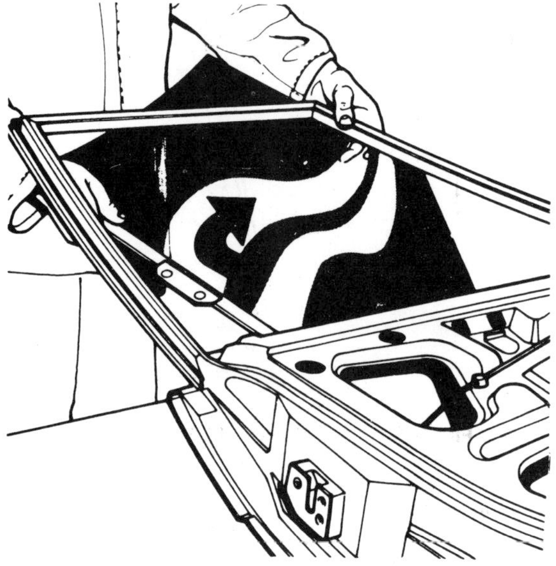
Fig. 12.10. Withdrawing the door glass

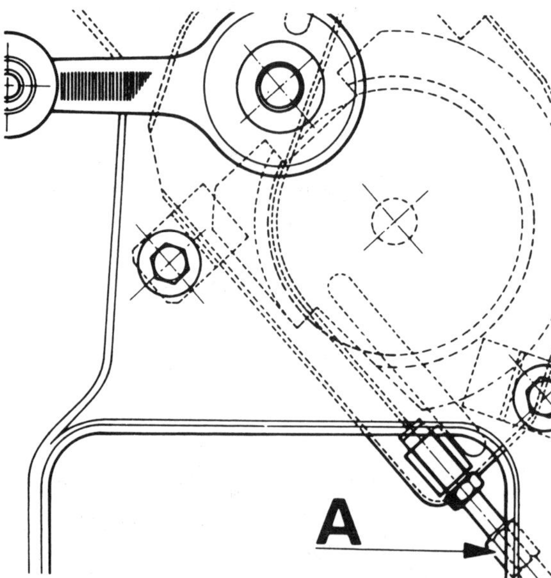

Fig. 12.11. Window winder cable adjustable stop 'A'

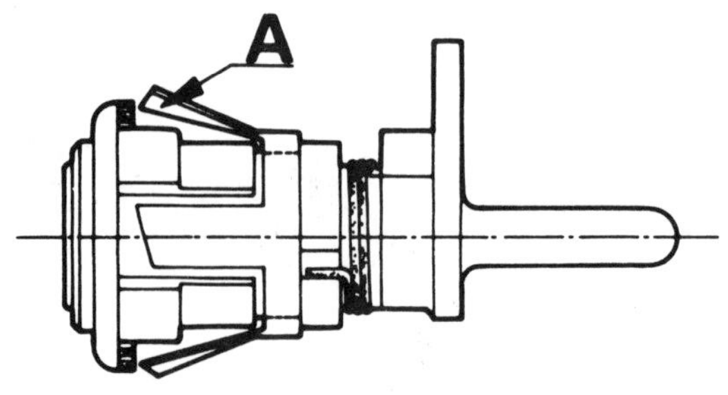

Fig. 12.13. Tailgate lock barrel assembly showing spring retaining catches 'A'

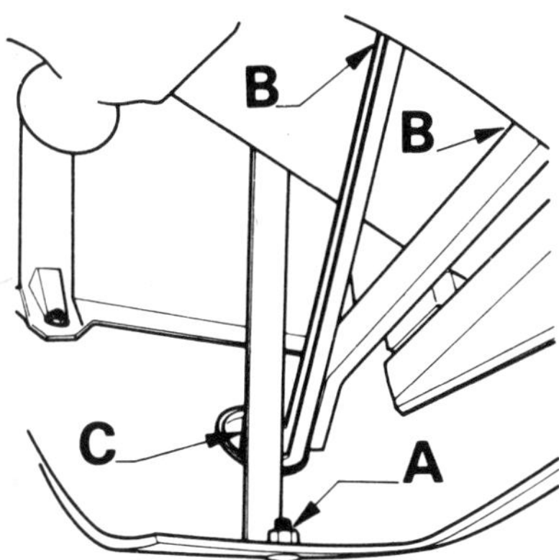

Fig. 12.14. Front bumper side support struts

A Bottom retaining bolt
B Support struts
C Side retaining bolt

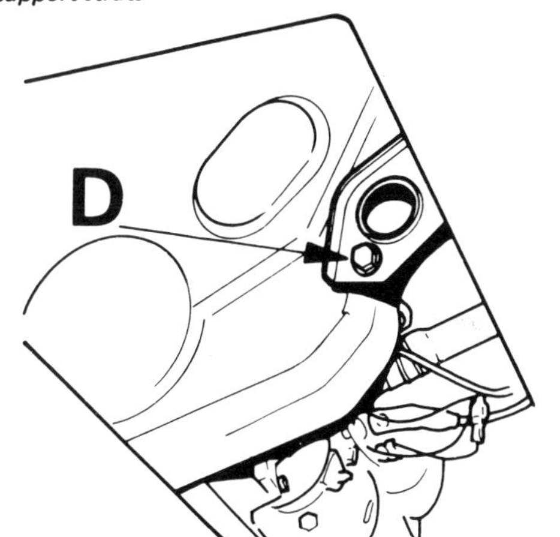

Fig. 12.15. Front bumper centre support bracket and retaining bolt 'D'

position by three pegs at the lower end which are located in rubber bushes and a single retaining screw at the top.

2 Open the bonnet and remove the retaining screw from the bonnet lock mounting panel.

3 Push the retaining clips down and lift out the grille.

4 Refit the grille using the reversal of the removal procedure.

16 Tailgate - removal and refitting

1 Disconnect the battery and detach the two wires to the rear window heating elements.

2 Support the tailgate in the open position and detach the upper mountings of the two gas-filled support struts (Fig. 12.12).

3 Carefully peel back the aperture seal adjacent to the tailgate hinges.

4 Get a friend to support the weight of the tailgate and drive out the roll pin from each hinge using a pin punch.

5 If required the lock barrel can be removed from the tailgate by pressing the spring catches and withdrawing the lock (Fig. 12.13).

6 Refit the tailgate using the reverse procedure to that of removal. Adjust the position of the tailgate in the body aperture by slackening the bolts securing the hinges to the body. Tighten the bolts when the tailgate is correctly positioned.

17 Front bumper - removal and refitting

1 Remove the two bolts on each side of the bumper, securing the support struts (Fig. 12.14).

2 Remove the two bolts on each side securing the side struts to the body frame. Remove the side struts complete with stiffener plates.

3 Remove the bolt on the right-hand side securing the drivebelt cover to the centre bracket (Fig. 12.15).

4 Withdraw the front bumper from the car.

5 Refit the bumper using the reverse procedure to that of removal.

18 Rear bumper - removal and refitting

1 Disconnect the battery and detach the two wires to the number plate (refer to Chapter 11 if necessary).

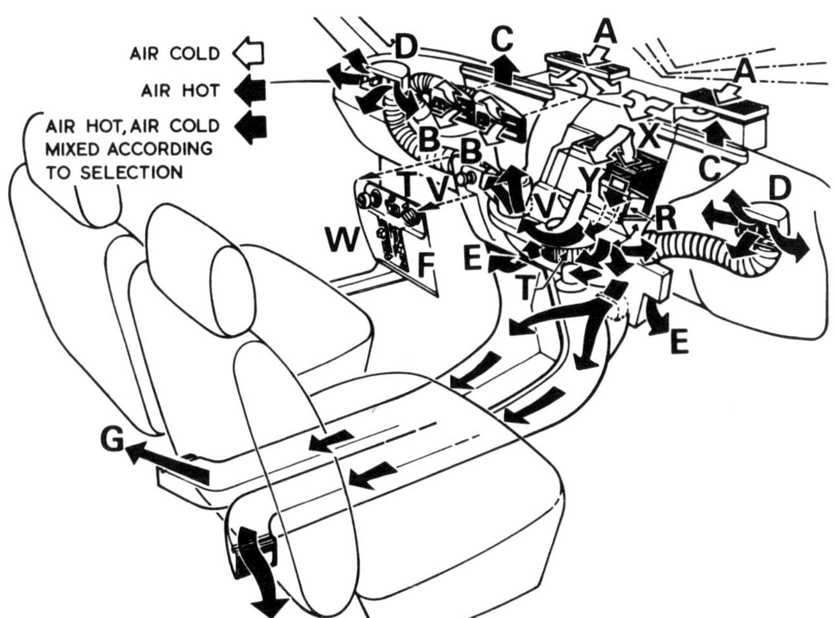

Fig. 12.16. Diagram showing heated air flow

A Fresh air inlets
B Fresh air outlets, not connected to blower
C Heated air outlets, windscreen demisting
D Heated air outlets, front door glass (adjusted by diffusers)
E Heated air outlets to front compartment
F Air flap and control of heated air to front and rear compartments
G Heated air outlets to rear compartment (on models with centre console)
R Heater matrix
T Two speed blower motor and control switch
V Air mixing flaps and control
W Demisting flaps and ducts control lever
X Air inlet to matrix
Y Fresh air vent (unheated

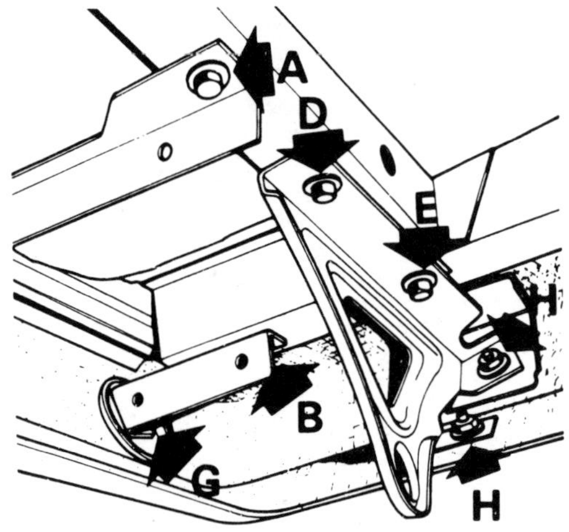

Fig. 12.17. Rear bumper brackets and retaining bolts (see text for key)

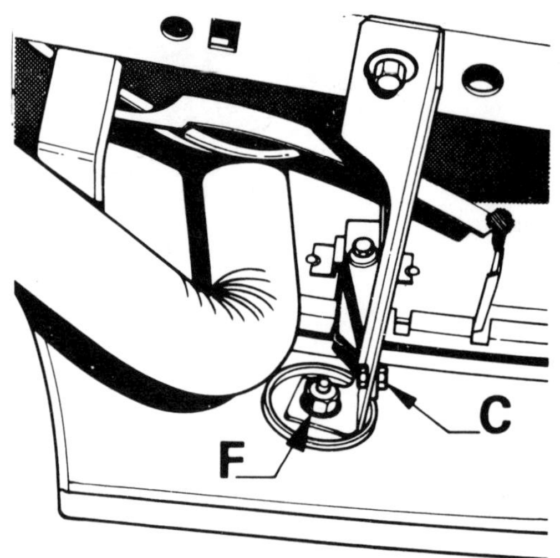

Fig. 12.18. Forward bumper to bracket securing bolts (see text for key)

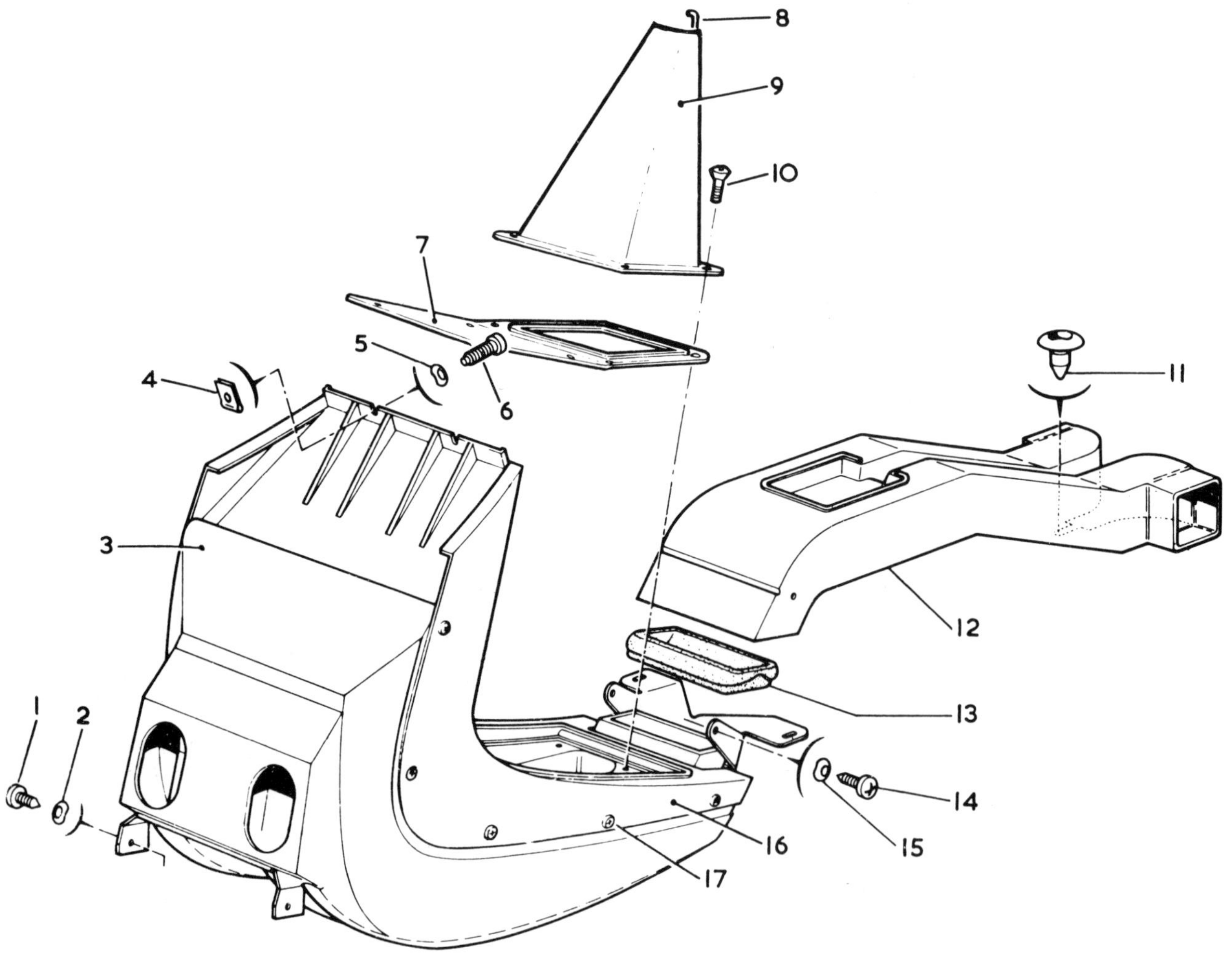

Fig. 12.19. Centre console and rear compartment heater ducts (when fitted)

1 Screw
2 Washer
3 Console - lower portion
4 Spire nut
5 Washer
6 Screw
7 Console floor
8 Gaiter grip pin
9 Gaiter
10 Screw
11 Nylon pin
12 Rear duct
13 Rubber seal
14 Screw
15 Washer
16 Console - upper portion
17 Screw

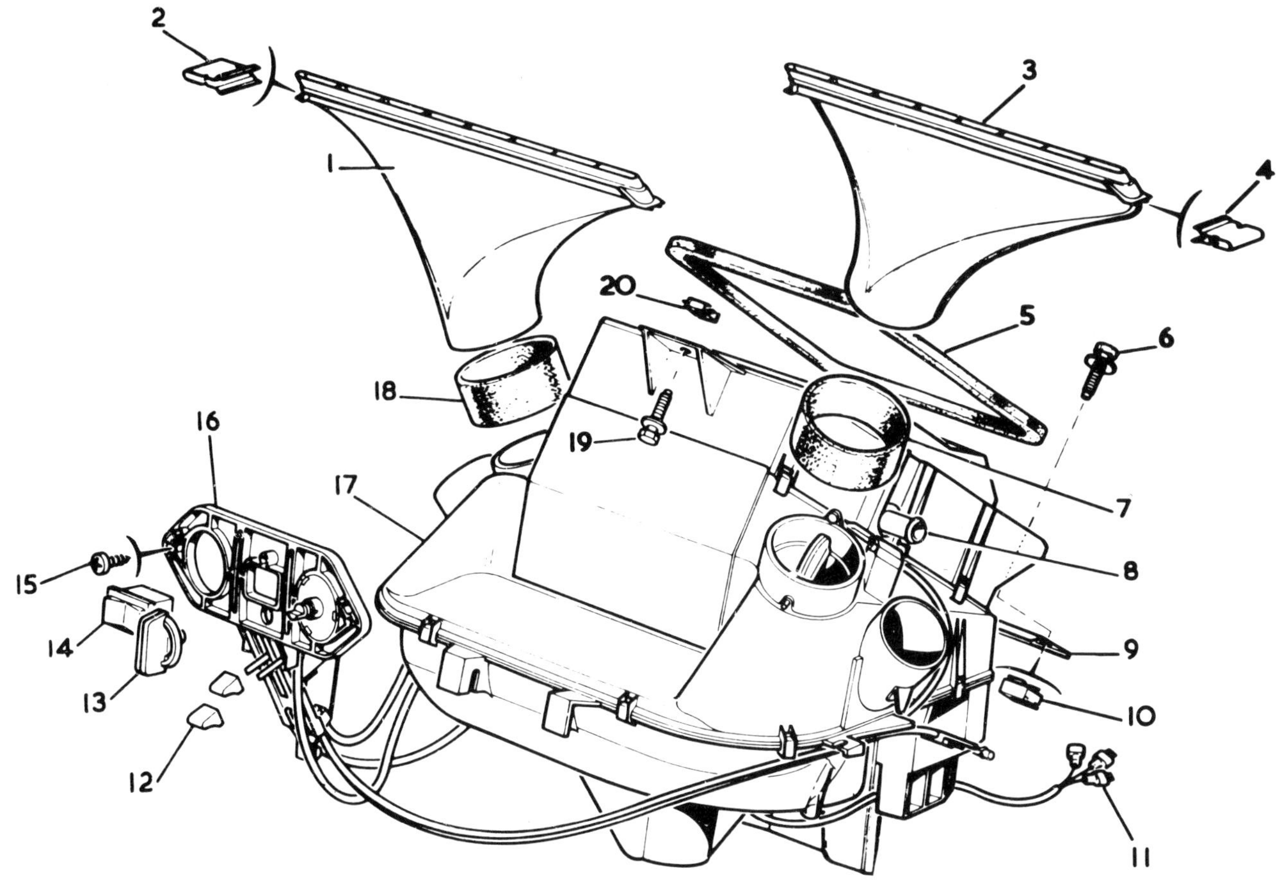

Fig. 12.20. Heater unit and controls

1 Demister duct
2 Spring clip
3 Demister duct
4 Spring clip
5 Seal
6 Bolt
7 Sleeve connection
8 Heater hose connection
9 Clamp plate
10 Cage nut
11 Blower motor connections
12 Control knobs
13 Temperature control
14 Blower switch
15 Screw
16 Heater panel
17 Heater unit
18 Sleeve connection
19 Screw
20 Cage nut

2 Place wooden blocks beneath each side of the bumper to support the weight and, referring to Figs. 12.17 and 12.18, remove bolts A, B, C, D and E securing the support bracket to the frame members.
3 Withdraw the bumper complete with bracket from the car.
4 To remove the support brackets from the bumper, detach bolts F, G and H.
5 Refit the bumper and support brackets using the reverse procedure to that of removal. Check the bumper alignment before fully tightening the securing bolts.

19 Heater unit - general description

The heater unit is mounted below the instrument panel. Air is drawn in through the intake grilles on the panel below the windscreen and, depending on the position of the heater control levers, either passes through the water heated matrix to provide hot air to the car interior, or bypasses the matrix to provide cold air.

The temperature of the air entering the car can be set to any intermediate heat range by means of the temperature control knob on the centre switch panel.

A slide lever also on the centre panel enables the air flow into the car to be completely shut off if required and a second slide lever provides selection of windscreen or car interior heating.

A three speed blower motor provides a boosted air flow if required.

A diagram of the heater unit air flow is shown in Fig. 12.16.

20 Heater unit - removal and refitting

1 Disconnect the battery terminals and drain the cooling system as described in Chapter 2.
2 If a centre console is fitted refer to Fig. 12.19 and undo the retaining screws. Ease the console forward to clear the rear heater ducts and then lift it over the handbrake and gear lever.
3 Remove the instrument panel assembly as described in Chapter 11.
4 Remove the securing screws and lift out the parcel shelf.
5 Disconnect the rubber sleeves from the windscreen heating ducts.
6 Disconnect all electrical leads, water hoses and control cables from the heater unit (Fig. 12.20). If necessary remove the centre switch panel as described in Chapter 11.
7 From inside the engine compartment, slacken the two screws that secure the front heater retaining bracket to the rear bulkhead.
8 Remove the screw securing the rear of the heater unit to the car interior.
9 Unhook the front of the heater from the bulkhead bracket and lift out the complete heater assembly.
10 Refit the heater unit using the reverse procedure to that of removal. Do not forget to refill the cooling system before starting the engine.

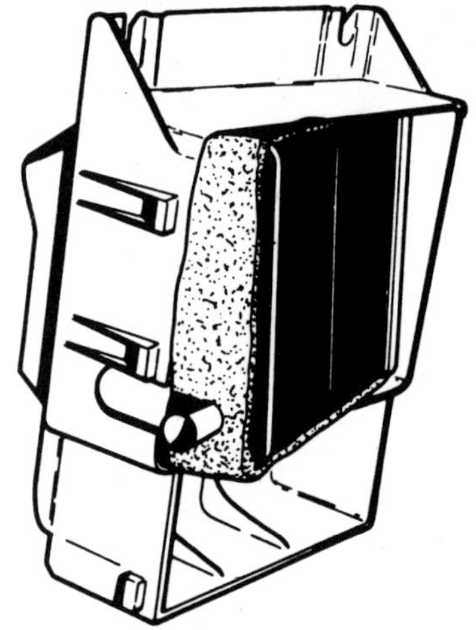

Fig. 12.21. Removing the heater matrix

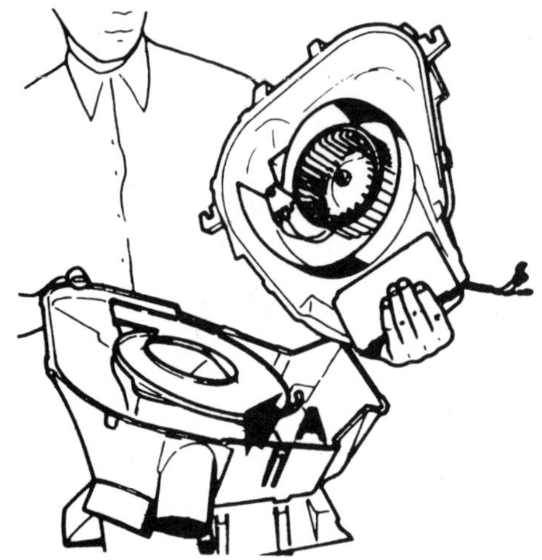

Fig. 12.22. Separating the two halves of the heater unit casing

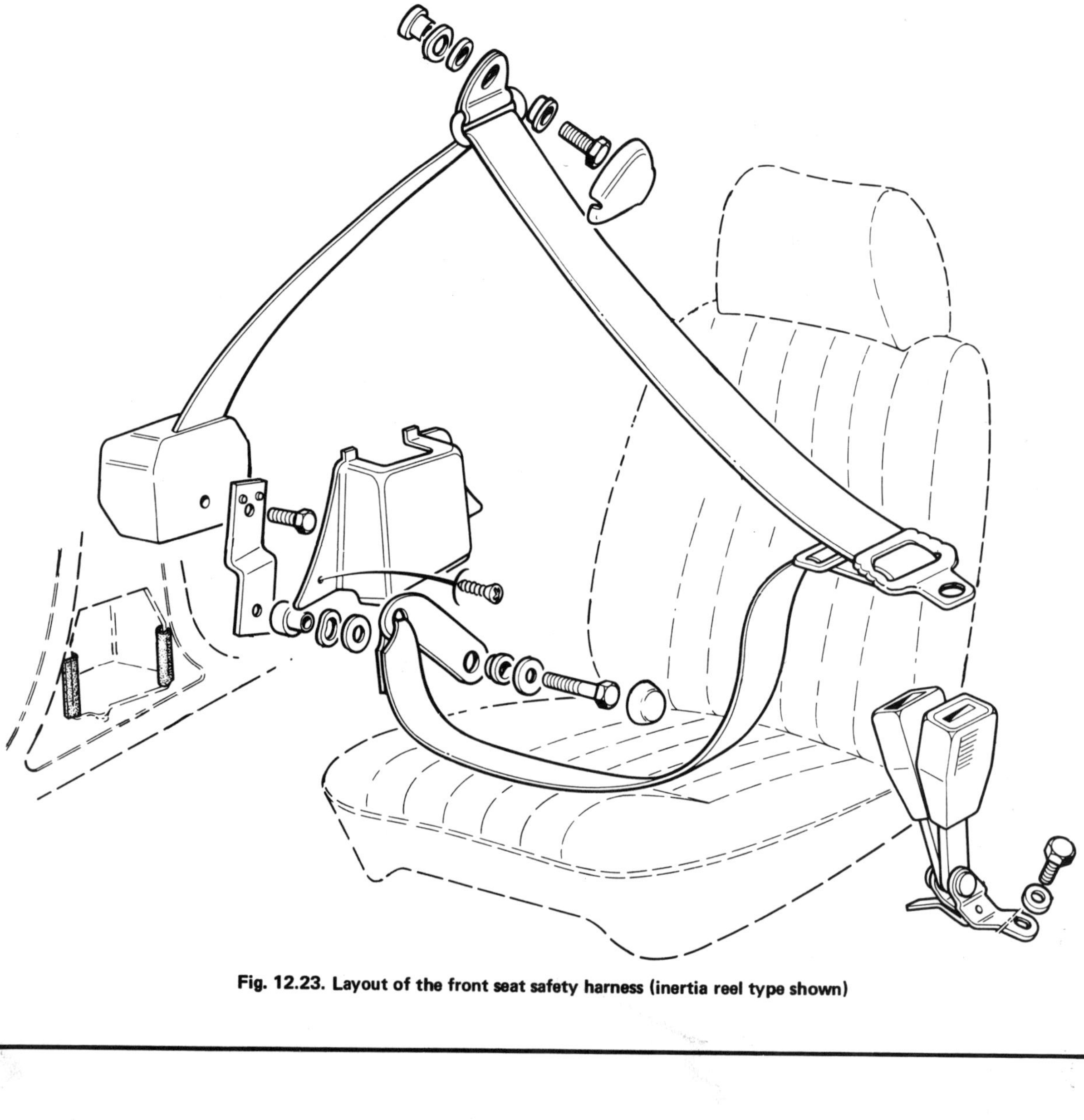

Fig. 12.23. Layout of the front seat safety harness (inertia reel type shown)

Fig. 12.24. Removing the rear air intake panel retaining screws

21 Heater unit - dismantling and reassembly

1 Release the six retaining clips securing the upper casing, remove the casing and lift out the heater matrix (Fig. 12.21).
2 Release the eight clips securing the casing and separate the two halves of the casing (Fig. 12.22).
3 Lift out the fan deflector plate.
4 Mark the position of the fan on the motor spindle, remove the securing nut and withdraw the fan from the motor.
5 Remove the two motor securing nuts, detach the two supply wires and lift out the motor.
6 Release the two spring clips and remove the support bracket from the motor.
7 The motor is not repairable and if faulty should be renewed.
8 Check the matrix. Where there is evidence of water leakage from this component, renew it, attempts to solder it are seldom satisfactory. It is possible to unblock the matrix by reverse flushing with a cold water hose but the use of descaling or cleansing compounds is not recommended as the water tubes are so narrow that any sediment resulting from such treatment will probably only clog the matrix in another position.
9 Refitting is a reversal of dismantling but check that the controls are correctly connected and adjusted.

22 Air intake panel - removal and refitting

1 Remove the bonnet as described in Section 13.
2 Remove both windscreen arms and blades as described in Chapter 11.
3 Carefully ease the front of each intake grille up out of the panel. Prise the adhesive pads at the rear of each grille away from the panel, disconnect the plastic washer pipes and remove the grilles.
4 Remove the four retaining screws from the grille apertures (Fig. 12.24).
5 Remove the six retaining screws from the forward edge of the panel and carefully lift out the panel.
6 Refit the intake panel and grilles using the reverse procedure to that of removal. Do not forget to refit the washer pipes before pushing the grilles back into the panel.

23 Seat belts

1 Seat belts of the three point fixing type are fitted.
2 Components of the belts and anchorages are shown in Fig. 12.23.
3 On no account must the sequence of fitting of the anchorage plates, distance pieces or washers be changed nor the location of the fixing points be moved.
4 Periodically, inspect the straps for fraying or general deterioration and renew if necessary with ones of identical type.

Metric conversion tables

			Millimetres to Inches		Inches to Millimetres	
Inches	Decimals	Millimetres	mm	Inches	Inches	mm
1/64	0.015625	0.3969	0.01	0.00039	0.001	0.0254
1/32	0.03125	0.7937	0.02	0.00079	0.002	0.0508
3/64	0.046875	1.1906	0.03	0.00118	0.003	0.0762
1/16	0.0625	1.5875	0.04	0.00157	0.004	0.1016
5/64	0.078125	1.9844	0.05	0.00197	0.005	0.1270
3/32	0.09375	2.3812	0.06	0.00236	0.006	0.1524
7/64	0.109375	2.7781	0.07	0.00276	0.007	0.1778
1/8	0.125	3.1750	0.08	0.00315	0.008	0.2032
9/64	0.140625	3.5719	0.09	0.00354	0.009	0.2286
5/32	0.15625	3.9687	0.1	0.00394	0.01	0.254
11/64	0.171875	4.3656	0.2	0.00787	0.02	0.508
3/16	0.1875	4.7625	0.3	0.1181	0.03	0.762
13/64	0.203125	5.1594	0.4	0.01575	0.04	1.016
7/32	0.21875	5.5562	0.5	0.01969	0.05	1.270
15/64	0.234275	5.9531	0.6	0.02362	0.06	1.524
1/4	0.25	6.3500	0.7	0.02756	0.07	1.778
17/64	0.265625	6.7469	0.8	0.3150	0.08	2.032
9/32	0.28125	7.1437	0.9	0.03543	0.09	2.286
19/64	0.296875	7.5406	1	0.03937	0.1	2.54
5/16	0.3125	7.9375	2	0.07874	0.2	5.08
21/64	0.328125	8.3344	3	0.11811	0.3	7.62
11/32	0.34375	8.7312	4	0.15748	0.4	10.16
23/64	0.359375	9.1281	5	0.19685	0.5	12.70
3/8	0.375	9.5250	6	0.23622	0.6	15.24
25/64	0.390625	9.9219	7	0.27559	0.7	17.78
13/32	0.40625	10.3187	8	0.31496	0.8	20.32
27/64	0.421875	10.7156	9	0.35433	0.9	22.86
7/16	0.4375	11.1125	10	0.39270	1	25.4
29/64	0.453125	11.5094	11	0.43307	2	50.8
15/32	0.46875	11.9062	12	0.47244	3	76.2
31/64	0.484375	12.3031	13	0.51181	4	101.6
1/2	0.5	12.7000	14	0.55118	5	127.0
33/64	0.515625	13.0969	15	0.59055	6	152.4
17/32	0.53125	13.4937	16	0.62992	7	177.8
35/64	0.546875	13.8906	17	0.66929	8	203.2
9/16	0.5625	14.2875	18	0.70866	9	228.6
37/64	0.578125	14.6844	19	0.74803	10	254.0
19/32	0.59375	15.0812	20	0.78740	11	279.4
39/64	0.609375	15.4781	21	0.82677	12	304.8
5/8	0.625	15.8750	22	0.86614	13	330.2
41/64	0.640625	16.2719	23	0.90551	14	355.6
21/32	0.65625	16.6687	24	0.94488	15	381.0
43/64	0.671875	17.0656	25	0.98425	16	406.4
11/16	0.6875	17.4625	26	1.02362	17	431.8
45/64	0.703125	17.8594	27	1.06299	18	457.2
23/32	0.71875	18.2562	28	1.10236	19	482.6
47/64	0.734375	18.6531	29	1.14173	20	508.0
3/4	0.75	19.0500	30	1.18110	21	533.4
49/64	0.765625	19.4469	31	1.22047	22	558.8
25/32	0.78125	19.8437	32	1.25984	23	584.2
51/64	0.796875	20.2406	33	1.29921	24	609.6
13/16	0.8125	20.6375	34	1.33858	25	635.0
53/64	0.828125	21.0344	35	1.37795	26	660.4
27/32	0.84375	21.4312	36	1.41732	27	685.8
55/64	0.859375	21.8281	37	1.4567	28	711.2
7/8	0.875	22.2250	38	1.4961	29	736.6
57/64	0.890625	22.6219	39	1.5354	30	762.0
29/32	0.90625	23.0187	40	1.5748	31	787.4
59/64	0.921875	23.4156	41	1.6142	32	812.8
15/16	0.9375	23.8125	42	1.6535	33	838.2
61/64	0.953125	24.2094	43	1.6929	34	863.6
31/32	0.96875	24.6062	44	1.7323	35	889.0
63/64	0.984375	25.0031	45	1.7717	46	914.4

Index

Printed by
Haynes Publishing Group
Sparkford Yeovil Somerset
England